The Representative

Who are we, anyway, that we should dare to criticize the highest spiritual authority of the century? Nothing but simple defenders of the spirit, but ones who make an unlimited claim on those whose task it is to represent the spirit.

Albert Camus

The Representative

ROLF HOCHHUTH

Translated with a preface by

ROBERT DAVID MACDONALD

LONDON

METHUEN & CO LTD

11 NEW FETTER LANE · EC4

First published as 'Der Stellvertreter'
© 1963 Rowohlt Verlag GmbH, Reinbek bei Hamburg
First published in Great Britain 1963
Reprinted 1963
Reprinted 1964
This translation © 1963 Methuen & Co Ltd
Printed in Great Britain by
W. & J. Mackay & Co Ltd, Chatham
Catalogue No. 02/6504/24 (hardbound)
02/6308/24 (paperback)
1.3

Contents

CARDINAL TARDINI

Pius XII could say, with the Apostle: I have been nailed with Christ to the Cross. . . . He took upon himself the suffering . . . that gave his heroic will the strength to sacrifice himself for his brothers and his children. . . . This extraordinarily noble spirit . . . tasted the cup of suffering drop by drop.

PRAYER from the photographic album PIO XII IL GRANDE

'O Jesus. . . . Thou hast deigned to raise Thy faithful servant Pius XII to the most high office of Thy Representative, and vouchsafed to him the grace fearlessly to defend the faith, courageously to represent Justice and Peace . . ., so that we may one day see him . . . participating in the honour of Thy altars. Amen.'

SØREN KIERKEGAARD

Take an emetic . . . you, you who are reading this, you know well enough what a Christian understands by a martyr: a man who is scourged, maltreated, dragged from one prison to another and who is finally crucified, beheaded or burned.

If, therefore . . . the late Bishop . . . is to be styled a martyr and canonized as such, then a protest must be made. Now he is dead – God be praised, it could not have happened while he was alive. He was buried with full pomp: a memorial will be erected over him; but that will be enough, and in no way must he be allowed to go down in History as a martyr.

FRANÇOIS MAURIAC

We have not yet had the consolation of hearing Simon Peter's successor clearly and sharply condemning, without a trace of tactful circumlocution, the crucifixion of these countless 'brothers of Christ'. One day during the occupation I asked Cardinal Suhard, who worked so hard for them behind the scenes, to 'order us to pray for the Jews'; and he threw up his arms. No doubt the occupying forces were able to bring irresistible pressure to bear, no doubt the silence of the Pope and his cardinals was a most terrible duty; the important thing being to avoid even worse misfortunes. Nevertheless a crime of such magnitude falls in no small measure to the responsibility of those witnesses who never cried out against it—whatever the reason for their silence.

viii

Preface

by Robert David MacDonald

In our century the human imagination, hitherto considered the faculty without limits, has had some heavy burdens put upon it. Two wars have, between them, disposed of more lives than all the wars of the nineteenth century put together. A single explosion can now bring in its train more deaths than all the wars of history. Half a century after Jules Verne a man can go around the world in eighty minutes. Man can no longer grasp what he can achieve, and he therefore accepts the facts as he is told them, rather as, in former times, he would have made an Act of Faith with regard to an ecclesiastical dogma.

The position of the artist in dealing with material of this nature is particularly difficult. As the one man whose imagination should be capable of mastering such material, he is necessarily compelled to try to do so. Yet it is the nature of an artistic experience that, if it cannot be directly absorbed as being immediately relevant to its audience, it will inevitably degenerate more or less into a purely aesthetic stimulus, exciting or depressing as the case may be. The aesthetes of the 'nineties used as their rallying-cry 'Art-for-Art's-sake', because they wished to oppose the view of 'Art-for-a-purpose'. The danger inherent in their view is that it is all too easy to begin to appreciate the play of colour, light and form in the mushroom cloud, as it hangs over the stricken city, because the enormities that are taking place below it are no longer possible to grasp. The concept of race-murder, though not an invention of our century, is one which surfeits even the ghoulish appetite that waits for each air disaster to be the worst in history. The idea that the fate of a whole people, and perhaps of the world, lay at one time not so far removed from our own in the hands of a bunch of men who in other circumstances might have lived out pathetic, slightly dotty but relatively harmless lives as amiable cranks or shifty perverts in some South Coast resort, is one that we reject as unimaginable – and this makes it all the easier to forget.

While assembling documentary material in preparation for the stage production of *The Representative*, the director, the designer and myself were all struck by the similarity of our experience, namely, that after examining a certain number of photographs of the atrocious and obscene harvest of the concentration camps, we all found ourselves tempted to select material on grounds of aesthetic rather than documentary value – the tortured twisting of a hand so like the Grünewald altarpiece was preferred to the plain fact of a human death reduced to the level of the crushing of a louse on one's thumb-nail, a snail under the wheels of a car. The mind is first sickened, then numbed, as the body by pain, and finally stages a withdrawal from the experience. The fate of the European Jews has become something which people often resent discussing, like Hiroshima and thalidomide, and it is significant and not a little frightening that it is possible to find a copy of the report of the notorious 'Doctor's Trial' in bookshops of doubtful character flanked, as by lictors, by popular treatises on flagellation.

What is a dramatist to do with material which has made the statuesque horrors of the Jacobean drama both more real and more ridiculous, but which, after a lapse of barely twenty years, has been politely rejected, to become the stuff of vicarious erotic fantasy? Clearly a newsreel documentary presentation can no longer be effective; Hitler is as remote as Tamburlaine. A recital of statistics can be impressive by its detachment, but soon grows wearisome. The pattern familiar to us from countless screenplays, the particularized attack on our emotions, the hit below the emotional belt as the crippled child is tripped by the guffawing storm-trooper, the intense young student machine-gunned as he helps the pregnant woman to escape across the field, all this is as well-intentioned and as useless as those heavily loaded plays on historical subjects which gather dust on the shelves of so many theatrical managers' offices.

All history is the history of our own times – every event must be reinterpreted by each generation. The work of the historian is as transitory as the history about which he writes; it is the instrument by which each generation comes to terms with the past. Hochhuth's play, *The Representative*, is just such an instrument. It is not a play about the problem of collective guilt and the finding of scapegoats – the stock accusation levelled at every German play concerned with anti-Semitism – it is a play about the problem of choice. While there is no doubt in the author's mind where much of the guilt lies, the whole content of the play is concerned with the proposition that for every man there is a choice, and even by avoiding making that choice, he is in fact choosing.

The theatre nowadays cannot afford to console itself with being a home for escapism or art-for-art's sake; if it is to survive at all it must fulfil its function as a platform of prophecy, a place in which to judge, to proclaim, to confess and to shock. The reality of our time is not to be conveyed any longer in specifically 'private' situations. In an age where a concept of the individual's role in society has arisen which permits him to live out his entire life without even feeling the necessity to reflect on the choice of good or evil, there must be a broadening of the dramatic objective. We must be shown the battlefield on which the conflict is to be decided, and the forces that will decide the conflict.

In the light of the play's notoriety we must remember that this is by no means the first time its subject has been raised. In 1953 Gerald Reitlinger wrote: 'In the view of the present author, this failure [of Pope Pius] to notice that the Jews were being herded to their death from the very shadow of St Peter's proceeded not from subtle benevolence, nor from pro-German sympathies, but from plain fear.' In a work of scholarship this statement went unremarked. While expressly rejecting Reitlinger's view, Hochhuth has given the theatre the privilege of bringing the question into a prominence it deserves.

It was, of course, only to be expected that the play would on its first appearance stir up a formidable dust of controversy around its central thesis, but it would be unfortunate if the dust were to blind one to the quality of the play itself, to its wider implications, and lead an audience to believe that it was simply a nine-days'-wonder, a somewhat disconcerting, even shocking polemic. Where a nine-teenth-century realist would have created a 'private' situation out of the same material, and a later Expressionist, recognizing the need to widen his field, might perhaps have created a situation so 'general' as to have little real application (*The* priest, *The* prelate, *The* hangman . . .), Hochhuth takes one of the most momentous and agonizing crises of history, and by fixing it firmly in time and space, brings home to us its most profound and lasting implications. It is not, as has been widely construed and rumoured, mainly by people acting on an assumption unsupported by actually having read the play, a gratuitous and vicious attack on the Catholic Church – almost any page proves this accusation to be absurd. I feel that the same chance that made Hochhuth be born a German also made him write this play, and not perhaps a play about the decision to bomb Hiroshima – unless the State Department is even more chary of opening its archives than the Vatican or the Kremlin. He has simply taken a crisis of our immediate past and shown us its relevance to our present and our future.

For it is the tragedy of the present day that the choice is so limited as to be almost no choice at all. There is choice or absence of choice – it is act or resign. In this particular case the closest parallel we have nearer home is the political scene during the English Reformation. Here, too, the Catholic Church incurred the reproach that its fidelity to Rome made it treasonous to the secular State. The attitude of the Nazis to the Catholic Church – the only Christian denomination for which Hitler had even a passing respect, mainly for its organization – was clear from the moment the Concordat of 1933 was signed, if not before. Perhaps it is true to say that no blame can attach itself to those who did not see the direction in which Hitler was going. Many politicians were caught by the change in the wind – Papen, Schleicher, Hugenberg, all astute men in the best possible position for observation. But with the ink of the signatures hardly dry on the first document to give Hitler international recognition, the Nazis began to show their hand. The unholy trinity of the Marxists, the Jews and the Catholics was subjected to all possible forms of execration. On the day of Cardinal Pacelli's election to the throne of St Peter the *Berliner Morgenpost* wrote: 'The election of Cardinal Pacelli will not be received with much satisfaction in Berlin, because he has always stood in opposition to National Socialism', and there are reports of the numerous and detailed sources of information which reached the Vatican in which it is shown all too clearly exactly how full his knowledge of the facts of the persecutions was. Yet to the world nothing was said. François Mauriac has written: 'No doubt the occupying forces were able to bring irresistible pressure to bear, no doubt the silence of the Pope and his cardinals was a most terrible duty, the important thing being to avoid even worse misfortunes'. It is true to say that it is almost entirely due to Pius XII that the Catholic Church came through the storm of the second world war almost undamaged. Nevertheless, the choice is to be made in the spirit of the Christian whom Kierkegaard called a 'witness for truth'. There was a duty still more terrible than the maintaining of silence – the duty of breaking it. Even at the risk of sending the whole organized Church back to the catacombs of Rome, the silence had to be broken. The reasons for the Pope's silence are carefully weighed in Act IV of the play: Pius saw with more clarity than some of the Allied politicians the danger of making Stalin into Hitler's heir. Yet this cannot do more than explain Pius's action or lack of action, it cannot excuse it. The decision to be made was outside politics, the *scène à faire*, the obligatory choice, irrelevant whether it was right or wrong.

This is such a dark chapter in history, a tragedy of such dimension, that we are all of us tempted to try to forget it, since it is, or seems, too enormous and atrocious to be treated as an inexhaustible well, full of moral lessons to be drawn up from it. It is too easy to reflect superficially on the fact that there are men today prosecuting boys for stealing penknives who twenty years ago were conscientiously checking off lists of plundered property ('20,000 pocket-watches, 4,000 wristwatches, 5,000 fountain-pens, 24 braille watches', etc.).

It is a choice which we in England were spared the need of making – this time. But it was still *our* humanity, the humanity of the men whose eyes we catch in our streets, and our shaving-mirrors, that was capable of doing these things under certain historical conditions and pressures. To kill a man a tyrant may need the concurrence or connivance of a few; but to kill a whole race of men, demands the acquiescence of all. In this play we stand at *anus mundi*, and see what we have done, can still do. We are the Christian inheritors of the tradition that the Jews are the murderers of God, and it is not only in the silence of His Representative but in our own inaction that He is crucified again.

Characters

POPE PIUS XII
BARON RUTTA, *Reichs Munitions Union*

FATHER RICCARDO FONTANA, *S.J.*

KURT GERSTEIN, *Obersturmführer SS.*

THE DOCTOR

A CARDINAL
PROFESSOR HIRT, *Reichs University, Strassburg*

THE APOSTOLIC NUNCIO *in Berlin*
LUCCANI, *a converted Jew*
SERVANT, *in the house of Count Fontana*

COUNT FONTANA, *legal adviser to the Holy See*
COLONEL SERGE, *attached to Army High Command*

THE FATHER-GENERAL *of a religious order*
MÜLLER-SAALE, *of the Krupp works at Essen*

EICHMANN, *Obersturmbannführer*
A MANUFACTURER, *prisoner of the Gestapo*

DR LOTHAR LUCCANI
DR FRITSCHE, *Sturmbannführer*

SALZER, *Head of the German Police in Rome*
OFFICER OF THE SWISS GUARD

JULIA LUCCANI

Her children, A BOY *of nine*
A GIRL *of five*

REGIERUNGSRAT DR PRYZILLA
A ROMAN COBBLER
A PHOTOGRAPHER
BROTHER IRENÄUS

HELGA

CARLOTTA

SIMONETTA

A PRIEST *in the Nuncio's residence*
WITZEL, *Sergeant of the SS*
A JEWISH KAPO

JACOBSON

THE 'SMART' ITALIAN MILITIAMAN
GUARD-DUTY OFFICER *at Auschwitz*

LEUTNANT VON RUTTA, *Luftwaffe*
KATITSKY, *SS soldier*
A WRITER *in the Vatican*

DR LITTKE, *staff doctor with the Army*
THE 'DELINQUENT' ITALIAN MILITIAMAN
SWISS GUARD *in the Papal palace*

THE SPEAKERS *of the monologues*

*The characters grouped together by twos, threes, and sometimes fours
may be played by the same actor – since, in an age of general conscription it is not necessarily a question of merit or blame, or even a
question of character, whether a man puts on this or that uniform or is
on the side of hangman or victim.*

    *Apart from the Pope, the Nuncio, Gerstein, Hirt, and Eichmann, all
names and characters are imaginary.*

Act One · The Mission

Beware of the man whose God is in Heaven.
BERNARD SHAW

SCENE ONE

Berlin, late one afternoon in August 1942.
The reception room in the Nuncio's residence in the Rauchstrasse. A few pieces of Empire furniture. The severity of the room is only interrupted by a large, colourful and almost friendly reproduction of Rubens' 'Deposition from the Cross'. Two double doors, one in the left background leading to the workroom of the Nuncio; the other to the right, leading to the antechambers and the stairwell.
The Apostolic Nuncio, His Excellency Cesare Orsenigo, was, in 1942, a man of 69. Press photographs show us an extremely vigorous man of middle height. The narrow, bony face exhibits no empty surfaces, but is completely dominated by the mouth and nose, which, like the chin, are exceptionally large. The open gaze shows a readiness to sympathize. The face seems to be marked not by spirit, but rather by will and the effort of self-discipline. Freiherr Ernst von Weizsäcker, Secretary of State at the Foreign Office till early in 1943, then Hitler's Ambassador to the Holy See, called the Nuncio a realistically-minded Milanese, who willingly avoided 'intensifying irreconcilable differences between the Curia and the Third Reich into fundamental disagreements'. He also attests that Orsenigo managed to present his complaints to the German Government – it was a question of Polish priests in Hitler's concentration camps – 'with a calm amiability, in the most friendly fashion'.
However that may be, the Nuncio's sympathetic face does not provide any answer to the question of how this priest, who lived in Berlin during the whole of the Hitler era and who had been, by 8 November 1938 at the latest, an eyewitness of the reign of terror against the Jewish citizens, could still reconcile with his conscience the preservation of the Concordat between the Vatican and the German Government even when the deportations began of Jews converted to Catholicism. It is obvious

that a man who bears responsibility for extended periods under an auto-crat – whether Hitler or Pius XII – is bound to lose his individuality, since he can hardly express his personal feelings, and since in his official capacity he is reduced to the level of carrier-out of orders; the use of the arrogant uncommitted jargon of diplomacy perhaps makes this easier.

The representation of historical characters is no longer a question of exact portraiture. Even in the case of such of the Nuncio's partners in conversation as Adolf Hitler and Hermann Göring, one cannot, in the photographs available, even under the most uncompromising scrutiny, and after the event, find the remotest trace of the actions of which they were capable. This fact seems to prove the almost total inefficacy of photographs for the purpose of character delineation. All that is necessary here is that the elderly actor who plays the Nuncio should wear the usual dress of a titular Archbishop, namely, pectoral cross, black soutane, purple skull-cap, dog-collar and scapular.

Riccardo Fontana's intervention for the persecuted and his martyrdom for the Church are free adaptations of the deeds and aims of Provost Bernhard Lichtenberg of the Cathedral in Berlin, who prayed publicly for the Jews, was sentenced to imprisonment and who asked Hitler's myrmidons that he be allowed to share the fate of the Jews in the East. This request was granted. Lichtenberg was, moreover, concerned with the question of the Pope's reaction to this idea. However, Lichtenberg was not sent to a ghetto in the East, but transferred to Dachau. He died on the way there in 1943, probably a natural death. The respect of the executioners for the public image of this priest made it seem advisable to hand over his body and to allow several thousand Berliners to attend the funeral.

Kurt Gerstein, Obersturmführer of the S.S., whose name was placed by the Jewish community in Paris on the memorial tablet for the victims of Fascism, had perhaps, according to the English historian Reitlinger, the most astonishing mission of the Second World War; a figure so uncanny, so divided and profound that he is easier to invent than describe. His own curriculum vitae, which he gave to the Allies in 1945 before his trail disappeared in a Paris prison, can be no more included here than the unequivocally positive statements of reputable ministers of both confessions and of the Secretary of the Swedish Embassy, Baron von Otter.

*Gerstein appears – one can see it already in a photograph of 1931 – to
have been a marked man, a Christian of a type so 'modern' that to
understand him completely one needs to read Kierkegaard. In 1942,
when he appeared in the Nuncio's palace and was thrown out, he was 37.
He is wearing the field-grey uniform of an officer of the Waffen-S.S.
The priest, who serves the tea, is wearing a monk's habit.*

*The Nuncio is holding a street-map of Berlin in his hand and speaking
to Riccardo:*

NUNCIO: You see, and here – the Hedwigskirche.
>Ten years ago we had only forty-four churches
>in Berlin . . . apart from the convent chapels, of course.
>The Jews had the same number of synagogues.
>But while the number of our churches
>has continued to grow,
>there is now not one single synagogue left.

RICCARDO (*casually*):
>Could not Your Excellency intervene in this matter?

NUNCIO (*raising his hand warningly, that he is not to be brought out of
patience*):
>As Nuncio I have no authority for that.
>I am, exempli causa, intervening
>against injustice in divided Poland.
>Even limiting myself to complaints about misconduct
>towards priests,
>I am shown the door by Herr von Weizsäcker,
>politely but firmly: no authority.
>We have first to recognize the new frontiers.
>I could only speak for Jews
>if they have been converted.
>But Herr Hitler takes good care not to deport
>these, too. Ah, the good father himself
>is bringing tea. Splendid . . . thank you.
>Is there some cake coming?
>(*A priest has entered, set up the tea-table, and answers with
>a heavy Bavarian accent.*)

PRIEST: Right away, Excellency. And if it's
>too strong again, there's some hot water.

NUNCIO (*folding up street-map . . . with smiling pedantry*):
>Thank you, thank you – there. I present you with
>the map; each of my colleagues

3

who does not yet know Berlin
gets the plan of the capital before his first meal even . . .
so that you don't lose your way.
(*The priest goes out.*)

RICCARDO (*bows, puts map away*):
Many thanks, Excellency. That is very good of you.

NUNCIO (*at the tea-table, more intimately*):
Were you not afraid to come to Berlin at this time?
In Rome you were safe from bombing.
Here we have warnings every night.

RICCARDO: At my age, Excellency, the life of a priest
has not enough danger. My cousin was killed in Africa.
I am delighted to get away from Rome.

NUNCIO (*cheered*): How young you are; twenty-seven –
and already a minutant. You'll go far, my young friend.
It is considered extraordinary that His Holiness
was a minutant at twenty-six.

RICCARDO: Your Excellency must remember
I have the right father for it.

NUNCIO (*heartily*): Don't be so modest: had you been nothing
but the protégé of your estimable father,
the Cardinal would never
have taken you into the Secretariat.
(*confidentially*)
Is the Chief still
as ill disposed to me as ever?

RICCARDO (*embarrassed*): But, Excellency, nobody is ill disposed . . .

NUNCIO (*a hand on his arm, rises with his teacup*):
Now, now, you know quite well, I have
been persona non grata in Rome for some time now.

RICCARDO (*hesitant, defensively*):
Possibly the Vatican imagines it to be easier
than it is, to represent the Holy
See here in Berlin . . .

NUNCIO (*in violent self-justification, walking up and down*):
The Pope must know what he wants:
peace with Hitler à tout prix – or the
authority for me to intervene decisively
against crimes, like my brother Nuncio in
Slovakia. He protested a fortnight ago,
extremely strongly, against the murder

4

of the Pressburg Jews in the district of Lublin . . .
What, my dear friend, does Rome expect?
I'd have handed in my resignation long ago,
but I'm afraid my job
would then go to some nonvaleur.

RICCARDO: Your Excellency does not consider
that the Concordat with Hitler should
be revoked?

NUNCIO: Oh no, on the contrary! His late Holiness Pius XI
was certainly ready to do so. But since
the old Pope's death, Herr Hitler has checked
several measures that his sometimes very stupid retainers
have wanted to take against us. He himself
is outwardly neutral towards the Church:
correct, like Marshal Göring.
In Poland, to be sure, he is trying to blackmail us.
Herr Goebbels, his propaganda man,
is very tractable, even co-operative.
It is amazing that they did not dare to lay hands
on Bishop Galen, even though he accused them
in public, from the pulpit, of the murder
of the insane. Hitler has, in fact,
complied with Galen's demands.

RICCARDO (*with energy*): But surely the Church *can* demand this,
Excellency! – Certainly now, when the bishops
of half Europe are recruiting for Hitler's crusade
against Moscow? I was reading in the train
what a bishop with the troops on the Eastern Front . . .

NUNCIO (*lively, annoyed*): There now, Count, it is precisely *that*
which I do *not* like: we should not recruit
for Hitler as long as these murders are being so recklessly
committed behind his lines . . . London talks
of seven hundred thousand Jews, in Poland alone.
Of course, we know about that sort of thing from history books:
a crusade always begins with a pogrom.
But these figures – appalling.
And doubtless not much exaggerated;
you know how they are murdering even priests in Poland.
We must adopt an attitude of considerable reserve.
I ask you, was it necessary for
The Bishop of Bohemia and Moravia,

5

now – or only a short while back – to ask
Herr Hitler for permission so that Heydrich,
the Chief of Police of Berlin and Prague . . .

RICCARDO: But wasn't he shot? Assassinated?

NUNCIO: Yes, in the open street – a whole village
paid for it, women and children . . .
Must the See of Bohemia come cap in hand
to Herr Hitler for permission to ring
the bells and say a requiem for the dear departed?
(*indignantly*)
A requiem for Heydrich shows a want of taste.
It goes too far . . .
Well – and here's something to eat,
thank you, my friend . . . thank you.
(*The priest brings the cake. He leaves the door open so we can hear
the pompous build-up to a special announcement from Hitler's
headquarters: heroic motifs, trumpets, trombones, drumrolls from
Liszt's 'Preludes'.*)

PRIEST: There, Excellency – a bit of cake
and there's another special announcement coming over in a
minute . . .

NUNCIO: Help yourself, Herr Minutant . . . there:
now let's hear what they've got to say.
(*he smiles, explaining to Riccardo*)
The incidental music! . . . ha! . . . ritual! . . .
The Nazi ideology
gives us nothing to be afraid of, but their ritual
is severe competition for us,
and suits the vast majority very nicely.
(*The priest withdraws towards the door, but stays in the room. The
fanfares die away, a voice announces from the radio.*)

RADIO: Attention, please. Attention, please. This is the radio of
Greater Germany. Here is a special announcement from the
Führer's headquarters: 25th of August 1942. The High Command of the Armed Forces announced at midday today that,
after bitter resistance by the Soviet forces, German troops
reached the summit of Mount Elbrus, a height of 5,600 metres,
and hoisted the German flag. With this victory, the Caucasus is
now firmly in German hands.
(*The heroic motif again, then the tune of the song 'Von Finnland
bis zum Schwarzen Meer'.*)

PRIEST (*proudly*): Five and a half thousand: higher than Mont Blanc.
My nephew is with the mountaineers, in the East.
He was with them at Narvik too – got promoted.

NUNCIO (*politely, without interest*): Ah, yes – your nephew, God protect him.

PRIEST: Thank you, Excellency, yes, let's hope so.
(*He goes out, closing the door. The music gets quieter, then finally
stops.*)

RICCARDO: Does Your Excellency feel there are grounds to fear
that Herr Hitler will only respect
the Church for the duration of the war?

NUNCIO: It did, at one time, look like that, my dear Count –
since conquerors will always act immorally.
But since Herr Hitler has allowed himself
to be provoked, albeit most unwillingly,
by Japan, and by Mr Roosevelt,
into declaring war on America –
since this stupidity,
(or was it a *dira necessitas*?)
the Church of Christ, at any rate,
need have no further cause for alarm
on his account. He won't be able to bring
both England *and* America to their knees,
not even if he *is* in the Kremlin.

RICCARDO (*sceptically*): But when he has beaten Russia, Excellency,
he will be economically unassailable.
Who would be left to overthrow him then?
His tanks are in Egypt and almost in Stalingrad;
and, in the Atlantic, the U-boat fleet . . .

NUNCIO (*interrupts again, kindly, ironic, superior*):
Easy, my young friend, not so fast.
In one of the many excellent books
(*he goes to the shelf, takes out a book and leafs through it*)
which we put on the Index,
Ranke's *History of the Popes*,
I found recently a passage of great consolation. –
Here's the book.
'The moment', says Ranke, '*any* principle,
whatever it is, aims at absolute rule in the West,
a strong resistance will oppose itself to it, every time,
rising out of the deepest well-springs of life.

That is the genius of Europe.'
Philip II met his match in England,
Napoleon in Britain *and* in Russia.
Why not Hitler ? Baron von Weizsäcker tells
me in confidence, Russia is not beaten yet.
And now America – ? However he comes off,
it will be a Pyrrhic victory.

RICCARDO : Your Excellency thinks that Herr Hitler
will *have* to listen to reason ?

NUNCIO : Oh yes, he will *want* to in fact.
One saw it at Dunkirk quite clearly.
He let the English escape; his principle
was obviously 'modération dans la force.'
Mark you, Mr Churchill did not show much gratitude –
have some more cake, Minutant. Even Hitler
cannot expose the Spaniards, the French,
the Balkan countries, the Italians,
the Belgians, and above all, his own Catholics
here in Germany – all of whom,
whether willingly or not, are supporting his crusade
against Moscow – even he cannot expose
half Europe to the risk of interdict.
If he declares us enemies of the State –
the Rome–Tokyo–Berlin axis will snap.
It is a good thing that Japan is so eager
at the moment for the signing of a Concordat.
The fact that the White House wants
to prevent it only goes to show
how sought-after we are becoming on both sides.
In St Hedwig's on Sunday, at the consecration
of a priest by the bishop, I noticed
a lieutenant of the S.S. He made
his confession, went to communion. – Oh, no,
as far as the Church is concerned,
Herr Hitler is a realist. The countries
that have been helping him in Russia
will have to stand by him when he is dealing
with England and America. Just think how the power
of the Catholics in America grows day by day.
Herr Hitler must reckon with that, too.
He will learn what his friends

8

Franco and Mussolini learnt a long while back;
that only *with* us, *with* the Church, not against it,
is Fascism unbeatable. Mr Molotov grasped the point
some time ago. In 1934
he confessed that if the Church in Germany
were to ally itself to Hitler's people –
and at the time it looked very much as if it would,
it was an auspicious beginning –
it would be the end of Communism in Europe . . . What's that?
What's the matter? What's going on out there?
(*The Nuncio has risen, stands for a moment, listens, then goes muttering over to the door leading to the antechamber. Offstage there is an agitated exchange of words, rising to shouts. We hear the voice of the priest, whose Bavarian accent gets stronger, the louder his voice. Between his phrases, which are only half understandable, are heard the urgent, imploring words of a man whose voice betrays that he is making a powerful effort to remain polite.*)

VOICES (*offstage*): You're in uniform!

But you must announce me!

The Nuncio's residence is foreign territory – take yourself off or I'll fetch the police . . .

Please, five minutes. The Nuncio . . .

He's got a visitor from Rome.

He *must* listen to me!

We're not interested in what you want here, I tell you.
(*Riccardo, silently amused, has gone to stand against the wall as the Nuncio opens the door to the antechamber. The S.S. officer Kurt Gerstein, cap in hand, enters immediately. The priest continues to try and restrain him or drag him out again. Gerstein and the priest simultaneously:*)
Excellency, this is unheard of.

I must talk to you, Excellency.
Just two minutes, please, I beg you.

Shall I get the police . . . ?
What a way to behave in here, I must say.

NUNCIO: What is this? What do you think you're doing?

9

GERSTEIN: My name is Gerstein, Excellency – please
　　listen to me. I have a report
　　for the Vatican which . . .
NUNCIO: Sir, I am extremely displeased
　　that you should invade my house in this fashion . . .
　　your place of work is presumably
　　in the Prinz-Albrechtstrasse . . .
　　(*The priest has crossed the room quickly towards the telephone, and
　　lifts the receiver. Gerstein hurries over to him and says:*)
GERSTEIN: Excellency – please don't call.
　　If my office found out about my visit . . .
NUNCIO (*gesturing the priest to leave the telephone alone*):
　　You call this invasion a visit?
PRIEST (*quickly*): Once and for all, leave this house now.
GERSTEIN: Excellency, a message for the Vatican.
　　It cannot wait a day,
　　not an hour: I have just come
　　from Poland, from Belzec and
　　Treblinka – north-east of Warsaw.
　　There every day, Excellency,
　　every day
　　ten thousand Jews, *more* than
　　ten thousand, Excellency,
　　are being murdered, gassed . . .
NUNCIO: For God's sake, be quiet!
　　Go and tell that to Herr Hitler. Go on.
　　According to the interpretation of the German Government
　　I have no authority to proceed
　　against these . . . against anything that is happening in Poland.
GERSTEIN (*a shout*): Excellency!
NUNCIO: Who are you anyway? I have no authority,
　　I tell you, to deal personally
　　with members of the German armed forces . . .
　　Are you a Catholic? Anyway, I must ask you
　　to leave at once . . . Go now, go along.
　　(*His Excellency does not want confirmation of these monstrous
　　happenings, for he is a good man, and the official acknowledge-
　　ment of these reports would make it harder for him to settle his
　　demands, with Herr von Weizsäcker as before, 'conscientiously,
　　as well as possible, with a calm amiability in the most friendly
　　fashion'.*)

PRIEST (*he has gone to the door, holds it, and says very gently*):
Right, come along now.

GERSTEIN (*beside himself, slams the door loudly and says with energy, tormented, close to the Nuncio*):
Excellency, every hour I see the trains
coming from all over Europe
to those factories of death . . . No, I am not
a Catholic. But Chaplain Buchholz, who
looks after the condemned in Plötzensee,
is a friend of mine. You can also refer
to Superintendent Otto Dibelius and
Consistory Councillor Hermann Ehlers. Before his arrest,
Pastor Niemöller of Dahlem . . .

NUNCIO (*politely but firmly*): Very well, I believe you, but I must,
alas, put a stop to this conversation –
I'm sorry, you must go.

GERSTEIN: Speak to Herr von Otter
of the Swedish Embassy, Excellency!
I met him in the sleeping car
Warsaw–Berlin. He knows everything.
The *Vatican* must help, Excellency.
It alone
can still help here; you must help us!

NUNCIO (*angry, because he is at a loss*):
Why do you come to *me*? You wear
yourself the uniform of the murderers.
I tell you again, I have not the authority . . .

GERSTEIN (*shouting*): Authority! You represent in Berlin the –
the Representative of Christ on earth –
and you shut your eyes to the most horrible thing –
that man has ever done to man.
You keep silent, while every hour . . .

NUNCIO: Control yourself, lower your voice . . . not in here,
I must end this conversation now . . .

GERSTEIN (*almost entreating*): Oh, please – no – excuse me.
I know, Excellency – it is not you,
it is the Holy Father who *must* help here;
the conscience of the world must be . . .
(*The Nuncio withdraws. He has only failed quite to enter the door
to his study because Riccardo is not following him, but listening
fascinated to Gerstein.*

11

Gerstein continues:)
. . . Exccllency, please listen to me.
(*with great meaning*)
I can't go on. I have seen it –
I see it all the time – it follows me
right into this room.
Listen – the – I must
tell you . . .
(*Gerstein, a hand before his eyes, has sunk into a chair. He stands
up straight away. Looking at no one, his glance is turned in upon
himself, and his eyes have an unquiet flickering madness in them as
has been described by Frau Bälz of the Institute of Current Affairs
in Munich, among other witnesses. The conversation he held one
night with Frau Bälz took place round about the same time as
Gerstein's unproductive visit to the Nuncio. The Secretary at the
Swedish Embassy, Baron von Otter, writes that Gerstein spoke to
him in the corridor of the wagon-lit 'in tears and with a breaking
voice'. The factual tone of what he now says is not kept up. His
sentences often lose themselves in muttered inarticulate words, then
he speaks once more out loud and as if hunted, or lets out short ex-
clamations like someone crying out in a dream.*
*After the first sentences the Nuncio returns a few steps towards him.
The priest closes the door quietly without leaving the room, while
Riccardo stares at the Nuncio with such insistent reproach as to
constitute a direct insult.*)
(*without a pause*)
Up to now the gas chambers have been
working on carbon monoxide, exhaust gas,
but the motors are very often hard to start.
At Belzec I had to see how the victims once –
it was on the 20th of August –
had to wait two hours and forty-nine minutes
before the gas came.
Four times seven hundred and fifty human beings
in four rooms forty-five cubic metres in size.
Some pray, some cry, some scream,
but the majority are silent.
The gassing lasted twenty-five minutes.
But it has to go quicker now,
that was why they sent me there . . .
I am an engineer and a doctor.

(*shouts*)
I won't do it. I won't do it . .
the naked corpses stand there like pillars of salt;
you can still distinguish families in death
because they have clasped and clung on to each other.
They have to be forced apart with meat hooks –
Jews have to do that.
Ukrainians drive them to it with whips.
(*no more in a condition to concentrate, he loses himself in detail; his
eyes are hollow*)
There was a former manager from one of the big stores here
and a violinist, decorated in the
Great War . . . served at the front for Germany.
And the bodies of the children. A young girl
at the head of the procession, naked like all of them:
mothers all stark naked, with babies at the breast.
Most of them know quite well, the smell of gas . . .

NUNCIO (*trying to leave*): Please, I can't listen to any more.
Why? You Germans! Why? . . .
My dear man, my heart goes out to the victims.

GERSTEIN: Excellency, the Vatican has come to terms with Hitler!
But you can see it here in the streets, here in Berlin,
in Oslo, in Paris, in Kiev . . . for more than
a year you can see, every priest can see
how the Jews are being carted off. The Allied
Radio announces that countless Jews are being murdered.
When, Excellency, will you finally decide
to tear up the Concordat?

RICCARDO (*overwhelmed*): Excellency . . . all this agrees exactly
with the reports received by my Order
but which no one could believe.

NUNCIO (*full of genuine sympathy, moved, but helpless*):
Count, please . . . be silent, do not
try to interfere here . . . Why does this man
not go to Herr Hitler?
(*Gerstein laughs terribly.*)

RICCARDO (*imploringly*): He is not an agent provocateur,
Excellency . . . Count Ledochowski has
sent very similar reports from Poland . . .

NUNCIO (*losing his temper under excessive pressure*):
Why does he come to *me*? The Curia

is not there, after all, to multiply
the disorder in the world, it is ordained
by God, for peace . . .

GERSTEIN: Peace even with murderers? Excellency!
(*he points to the picture of 'The Deposition'*)
Cursed are the peacemakers.
He felt responsible, Excellency –
doesn't His Representative?

NUNCIO (*very moved and fatherly*):
Herr Ger – stensteiner, control yourself.
I share your sorrow for the murdered victims.

GERSTEIN (*a shout*): Every *hour*, Excellency, *every* hour,
new victims – these are murder factories. Factories.
Can't you understand at all?

NUNCIO: Herr Leutnant – please, whatever my own feelings
in this matter, I quite simply cannot take them
into account. By 1939
I had already intervened in a private capacity,
but I was ordered in the exercise
of my office, assiduously to avoid
any subject that could lead to conflict
between your government and Rome.
I should not even be talking to you now.
Please, you must go. Please go.
God bless you: God help you. I will pray for the victims.
(*The Nuncio gestures Riccardo to follow him, while he goes to the
door at the back and opens it.*)
Count – please, this is an order: come along!

RICCARDO: Gerstein was the name – I will find you.
(*Gerstein does not take these words in; he can only see that he
has achieved nothing. Riccardo is grasped by the shoulder by the
Nuncio, who has returned, and almost dragged through the door
into the study. Before the Nuncio can shut the door, Gerstein
follows him once more, passionately, beside himself.*)

GERSTEIN: Excellency, listen, listen
to the dying words of an old Jewess –
she cried out before she was driven into
the gas, with a whip – she cried down the blood
that was spilt there
on the heads of the murderers, Excellency!
And we are also guilty of this blood,

if we keep silence.

NUNCIO (*turning round once more, quietly*):
Control yourself, and pray.
(*He goes out. The priest shuts the door after him and says mildly :*)

PRIEST: Take a grip on yourself, man, what do you
think you're at, talking to His Excellency like that – what
can *he* do about it ? Now please, run along.
We can't do anything about it either.
(*Gerstein has realized that he has lost. Just one more senseless try :
he digs into his jacket pocket, pulls out papers and tries hard to
arouse the priest's interest in them.*)

GERSTEIN: Look – here is proof. Look at it !
Orders from the Camp Commandants
of Belzec and Treblinka
for the provision of hydro-cyanic acid.
I have to provide prussic acid. I am a member
of the S.S. Health Department . . . look . . .
(*He is alone in the room. He turns right round once more, the
papers in his hand. The priest, who had gone out, now comes in with
a tray to clear away the tea things, and says at once, threateningly
and helpfully . . .*)

PRIEST: Don't you know . . .
that the Nuncio's residence is watched
by the police ? Man,
if they have seen you come in here
in uniform . . . Now, run along, please.
My, what terrible stories, Mary and Joseph,
even if they are Jews. . . .
(*Gerstein has left before the last sentence has been spoken.*)

Curtain

Since they have feet, one does not see that they are automata.
OTTO FLAKE

The Crown of creation
Mankind, the Brute.
GOTTFRIED BENN

SCENE TWO

The same day. Nine o'clock in the evening.

The 'Jägerkeller' at Falkensee outside Berlin: a small hotel, 'requisitioned' as a guesthouse by the German police and the Reichsführung S.S. a few weeks back, since the beginning of the regular Allied bombardments.

The roomy cellar, which gave the house its name. The room is split in two by an ample open staircase, beneath which a man can walk upright, which comes fairly far down to the foreground of the cellar. The chairs for the drinkers, some eight people, in the background on the right of the staircase, are out of sight. To the left, by the staircase and also in the background well in sight, are the starting-place and run-up of the bowlers, who roll their bowls to the left through a 'Gothic' arch into the wings – the bowling alley. Near to this is the large blackboard, on which every throw is noted. We can hear the muffled sound of the rolling balls and the falling pins. Left on the back wall the track, in which the bowls roll back to the starting-place from the bowling alley. Right, about half-way between the front of the stage and the sitting-corner out of sight in the background, is a cold buffet, looked after by Helga, very young, very blonde, half waitress, half housekeeper.

An imposing portrait of Hitler, Riedinger hunting prints, two crossed rapiers with student-corps caps from the old days, and the latest addition: a large photograph of the death-mask, taken in Prague two months ago, of the assassinated Reichsprotektor Heydrich.

Without, of course, being bound to follow this procedure, the bowlers usually play like this: as the scorer calls out their names – which doesn't invariably happen – they come from upstage right, going through and under the staircase, bowl, go to the scorer at the foot of the staircase where the results are written up on the board, cross the stage in the foreground, get to the buffet, then back to their seats in the background. They often watch their colleagues bowling, shouting and laughing. More often still they disappear, seldom on their own, into a door down right marked 'H', to reappear, with a typical checking movement of the hand, evidently strengthened in their feelings of comradeliness, and make their way back to the buffet.

During these circular trips conversations develop – people either talk to the scorer at the blackboard, or sit a moment with others on the stairs, or flirt with Helga, or even discuss official business which the whole circle does not need to hear, in the foreground, while enjoying a ham roll.

The host is Adolf Eichmann, amicable and pedantic, whose frightening effectiveness has so little of the gruesome splendour of a Grand Inquisitor that in 1945 he was not even looked for – it was the study of the documents that first unmasked him as the most industrious retailer ever to serve the cause of wholesale death : here he remains as colourless as any of his contemporaries who enjoy studying railway timetables and want to get on in their jobs at any price.

Also present, Director Freiherr von Rutta, an extremely distinguished civilian from the Ruhr aristocracy : cold to the point of inhibition. He is now making an effort to be 'one of the boys', and with the growing merriment his Rhineland accent is growing stronger. A representative of those circles about which von Hassell wrote in 1941, after a trip through the Ruhr districts : 'Morale not bad. Lots of "Heil Hitlers" . . . typical leaders of industry, always politically incapable and recognizing the acquisition of money as the only real thermometer.'

His son, a Luftwaffe Lieutenant, hardly more than 20, a nice boy with good manners, has just been awarded the Iron Cross. Alarmed at thus suddenly becoming the centre of attraction, he obediently takes on the tone of the coarse cellar jargon, although the front has not yet made him cynical. A good soldier, he is more courtly and timid towards someone like Helga, with her engagement ring, than she would wish.

The life and soul of the party is the 56-year-old Professor August Hirt, a fat senior doctor in the field-grey uniform of the Waffen-S.S., anatomist and skull-collector of the 'Reichs University, Strassburg' – a gargantuan, room-filling soak with a chest like a barrel, who cultivates his cynical-genial Swabian German on drinking evenings, correctly estimating its humorous effect. He was never caught, probably never even sought, although the idiocy and cruelty he committed in the name of science exceeded even the normal limits of many prominent S.S. doctors. As he is today still practising his medical art under another name, let us give him here the one he was born with. (The historical Hirt was a repulsive cynic, with the head of a vulture and a shot-away lower jaw.)

His associate, Dr Littke, at the time still a young staff doctor with a military unit, is a pallid careerist, one-sidedly specializing in his professional interests, to the complete atrophy of all other aspects of life and knowledge; he will be a professor in no time at all.

Another Army officer is Colonel Serge, of the High Command of the Army, prisoner-of-war section. In World War One Serge was a Captain of the Royal and Imperial Cavalry. Now stuck away in the Bendlerstrasse in Berlin, he tries vainly to practise his humanity on the tormented prisoners, but it is gradually being worn away in cynical resignation and almost suicidal displays of personal charity. He has forced himself to visit the house because Freiherr von Rutta has begun to use it on his trips to Berlin in order to be able to get some sleep, despite the bombing. Serge's bad-tempered nervousness shows itself in a comical, stuttering search for words and the beginnings of sentences. A native of Krems, he speaks with the accent of the Wachau, whose phonetics, like the difference between Bavarian and Austrian, are hardly possible to notate: so he may speak here like a Viennese.

In a yellow party jacket, with black trousers and a swastika in a white circle on a red arm-band, is Regierungsrat (Administrative Adviser) Dr Pryzilla, of the Ministry for the Occupied Eastern Territories. A naturalized German, one of the spoils of war, with a strong Polish accent and a Hitler moustache, baldheaded, well behaved, and as small and squat as a bedside table. A man who would rather suffocate than contradict his superior . . . Even here, although indeed aggressive, he opens his mouth only when he is hot on the track of something to do with his own department. By the time he has become, in 1955, a high Civil Servant in Bonn, he has learnt fluent German.

The Doctor, who, even here, dandyishly holds the little cane with which he makes the selections in Auschwitz, never bowls. He appears, even in this philistine gathering, as the man behind the scenes, precisely because he takes so little part in anything. He resembles the others as the puppet-master his marionettes. He is not, like Gerstein, an uncanny figure. He is cold and cheerful – when not invisible. He has the stamp of absolute

18

evil, much more obviously than Hitler, whom – like everyone else, he no longer even despises. A being without interest in anything or anyone, it is not even worth the trouble for him to play with the species homo sapiens . . . with one momentary exception: Helga. He does not seem arrogant doing this, on the contrary, he is extremely charming. He captivates her immediately. We see this mysterious overseer at this moment in a light different to that which History will eventually shed on him. Characteristically, he was never caught – probably thanks to the 'suggestive sincerity' with which he used to promise children 'a nice pudding' just before they were gassed (vouched for historically), or ask the exhausted travellers on the platform whether they felt ill: anyone who, relieved by the sudden sympathy of this kind man, said he did, went to the gas chambers straight away. This comes in the report of Frau Grete Salus, a doctor's widow, the only one of her family to survive Auschwitz.

It was personally very moving to me when, a year after first writing the dialogue between Riccardo and the 'Selector' of Auschwitz (Act V), whom I had not yet been able to imagine as a person, I became acquainted with Frau Salus' report, and found there that the prisoners had also continually described this 'handsome and sympathetic' man as the Devil – even after they had learnt his name:

'There he stood before us, the man who made the decisions of life and death, the beautiful devil . . . he stood there, like an affable, elegant, dancing master, conducting a polonaise. His hands pointed left and right, right and left, with a casual gesture. The atmosphere about him, light and graceful, contrasted comfortingly with the brutal ugliness of the surroundings, soothed our frayed nerves and took all meaning from the whole . . . A good actor? A possessed creature? A cold robot? No, a master of his subject, a devil, with a joy in his work . . . nothing, no angel stood behind him, nothing to warn one. Quite indifferently . . . a tool of the master . . . the people went to right and left. Sometimes a daughter would not want to leave her mother, but the words "You'll see each other tomorrow" calmed her completely. . . .'

These are scenes of surrealism. It is scarcely believable that they were played out in the world we live in, but they are displayed in bald extracts and even photographs, for example in the book Der gelbe Stern (*The Yellow Star*) *by Gerhard Schoenberger.*

And because this 'Head Doctor' is so totally contrasted, not only to his companions of the S.S. but also to all men and to all things that, to my knowledge, men have yet experienced, it seems to me permissible, with this character, at least to hint that an age-old figure of the theatre and the Christian mystery play has once again stepped on to the stage. As this unholy apparition from another world is obviously only playing the part of a human being, I will avoid further attempts to fathom his human characteristics . . . for they can add nothing to the understanding of this incomprehensible figure and its actions. To all appearances a man, this apparition is, in fact, comparable to no one, not even Heydrich, whom Carl J. Burkhardt, also with stylistic exaggeration, described as 'the young and evil God of Death'.

Loud laughter as the curtain rises. Glasses in hand, the guests are watching young von Rutta take his Iron Cross off his neck and hand it to Hirt, who shows it round triumphantly: he found out long ago how Hermann Göring's officers, who from time immemorial permitted themselves every kind of extravagance in their uniforms, were accustomed to tie on their medals.

HIRT (*Swabian well to the fore*):
    Hullo, hullo, hullo . . . didn't I tell you?
    With a lady's garter, yes!
EICHMANN (*laughing*): The Iron Cross on a garter . . . impossible.
RUTTA JNR (*not, as yet, knowing how to react, he later compensates for his embarrassment by smart replies at which both he and his proud father can only be amazed*):
    That's been the way for ages: simply because
    It's more practical and safer
    Than press-studs on the ribbon.
HIRT: Now, dear boy, a few leading questions:
    Number one: Did you just get the Cross
    In enemy action, or the garter too?
    (*Laughter, cries of 'Pfui', 'Hand to hand fighting', etc. . . .*)
RUTTA JNR: Both, Herr Professor. And both on night operations.
    (*Jollity. They drink. Shouts of 'Health', 'Good hunting!', etc.*)
HIRT: And now, my second leading question: Which
    needed more courage . . . getting the
    Medal or the garter?
RUTTA JNR: Courage? I was scared both times . . . though

in the fight for the garter
there really couldn't have been any more blood.
(*Cheers. Rutta, confused by his own doggishness, puts his medal
on again.*)

EICHMANN: Attack on all fronts, eh?

RUTTA JNR: You could put it like that, Obersturmbannführer,
yes.

RUTTA SNR (*unnaturally, with an effort at jollity*):
Don't leave any souvenirs behind, Hans Bogislav.

RUTTA JNR: I'll be careful, father.

HIRT: Question number three: did the Cross
make the getting of the garter any easier?

RUTTA JNR: Let me ask you a question, Herr Professor
Do you usually wear your decorations
at such a moment?
(*laughter*)

HIRT: Damn me – I'm beaten. Baron, your son
is a bright, bright lad. But really, it's good
of you, Leutnant, to think an old fossil
like me can still manage it.

EICHMANN: Let's have three cheers for our guest of
honour and bowling companion Leutnant von
Rutta – and please, for his father as well, Baron
Rutta. . . .
Good old Baron Rutta, three cheers.
Hip, hip . . .

ALL: Hooray. (*Three times.*)

RUTTA JNR: Thank you very much, everybody. . . .
(*He has turned, and so have the others, towards the stairs, where
Helga has appeared with a tray – sure of her effect as the only
woman in the gathering.*)

EICHMANN: Fräulein Helga – to celebrate his Iron Cross,
will you give the Leutnant a dance?
(*She agrees. Rutta Jnr goes to her, bows. Fritsche runs to the arm-
chairs and works a gramophone. Eichmann takes the tray from
Helga and, as the waltz begins, he takes it to the counter, dancing,
as if he had a woman in his arms. Rutta and Helga begin to dance
rather woodenly, the circle spreads and then drifts off into the background. Some people are clapping in time.*)

HIRT (*to Rutta Snr*): So young – isn't that worth
more than all our dignity, Baron?

RUTTA SNR : Certainly – a charming creature. She was telling me,
when she brought me my breakfast this morning. . . .

HIRT : I wouldn't mind going into barracks myself, then.
Did she bring you breakfast in bed, Baron ?

RUTTA SNR (*laughing*): You want to know too much.
Yes, she said she was engaged to a
Lieutenant in the S.S. at Auschwitz.
Do you know him, Doctor ?

DOCTOR (*lazily*): But of course – he's a very good friend of mine,
her fiancé.

(*They go over to the arm-chairs, the dance comes to an end, Rutta
Jnr gives Helga his arm stiffly to take her over to the chairs, but she
pulls him over to the buffet.*)

HELGA : I have work to do, Herr Leutnant,
what are you thinking of ? Thank you so much.

RUTTA JNR (*shyly*): We should be able to dance more often.

(*He takes his leave of her at the buffet. Eichmann, who has put
up the blackboard with Fritsche, now pulls a deck of cards from his
pocket.*)

EICHMANN : Helga, pass the cards round, please.
Everyone to take one.

DOCTOR (*sits on the stairs and yawns*):
A German must either bowl or shoot.
Bowling . . . the sublimation tactics
of the German middle class, allowed by
the marriage-guidance bureau.

(*The Lieutenant laughs, equally bored, but draws the first card
immediately. Helga is holding out the cards, but the Doctor pushes
her hand away in a friendly fashion without drawing one and
says . . .*)

(*quietly*)
I'm going to ring Auschwitz later on,
and you can ask Günther at the same time.

HELGA (*frightened, moving away. Shortly*):
Oh please, don't go on with that. . . .

HIRT (*loudly from the arm-chair, towards which Helga now goes*):
What are we playing then ?

FRITSCHE : What about 'Knockout', Herr Professor ?

HIRT : I'd rather have 'Dead Man'; you only
have strokes, don't need to do
so much adding up. . . .

FRITSCHE: 'Knockout's' easier still, I think.
Each has three throws altogether. All nines
count as twelve points, tens fifteen.
We play it a lot at Auschwitz.

HIRT: Don't you set them up again after each throw, though?

EICHMANN (*to both*): Yes, after each throw. But I think
'Dead Man's' better still, Herr Fritsche.
And we can sing the chorus of
'Im schönsten Wiesengrunde' each time
someone falls out.
(*friendly, ironic*)
Since we have your splendid baritone
in our midst, Herr Professor . . . eh?
(*Laughter. Hirt begins to sing straight away, the others joining in.*)
Sie trugen einen Toten zum Tore hinaus
Dich mein stilles Tal,
grüss ich tausendmal,
denn sie trugen einen Toten zum Tore hinaus.
(*calls out*)
Hold your cards up. Helga. . . .
Didn't you keep one for yourself?
You've got to play, too.

HELGA: I don't know if I can.

DOCTOR (*still alone on the stairs, close to her, quietly*):
You would be amazed what you can do.
(*She turns away and goes to the sideboard. Downstage Eichmann
has written 'Helga' at the top of the board. Now he calls over to the
arm-chairs.*)

EICHMANN: Who's got the ace? Ace begins . . .

RUTTA JNR: Here, Obersturmbannführer, I've got it.

EICHMANN: Aha, the Lieutenant . . . Rutta Junior.
Right. All here with your cards.
(*He writes 'Rutta Jnr.' on the board, while Fritsche puts on a new
record, and turns down the music. One or two stay smoking and
drinking by the chairs, hold their cards up and call out the order in
which they have drawn. Most of them have formed a circle round
Eichmann at the board. It all happens with Teutonic discipline,
almost seriousness. Eichmann writes one below the other: 'Helga,
Rutta Jnr., Hirt, Fritsche,' etc.*)

DOCTOR (*gets slowly off the stairs and goes over to Helga, who can no
longer avoid him*):

23

Kitten, are you really afraid of being
nearer your fiancé? Get yourself transferred to Auschwitz.

HELGA (*laying cutlery and paper napkins*):
Stop it, leave me alone, will you: I *mustn't*
meet you any more, Doctor.
You are a devil . . . How did you
do that this morning – I am ashamed . . .
I've always been faithful to him . . .

DOCTOR (*sincerely, solicitous, his irony quite hidden*):
We *need* secretaries.
You can use the teleprinter . . .
and your loved one has you at his side.

HELGA (*threatening, without believing it*):
But he'll be on the look-out, I tell you that;
he'll protect me.

DOCTOR (*lazy*): Let's hope so. And when it all gets too boring . . .
I'm still there, I sleep with my door open.
(*He has picked up a plate and appears to be concentrating on
choosing his food.*)

HELGA: I . . . never again, I'm going to lock my door now.
I'm never going where you are, *never*.
Why pick on me, there's so many girls . . .

DOCTOR (*with charming wickedness*):
Because you can still be so wonderfully shocked.
The way you put your hands in front of your face
when I heaved you into the saddle – very pretty.

HELGA: I was so shocked, going behind his back . . .
He is so proper. He'd never go behind mine.
And I've only known you for twelve hours . . .

EICHMANN: There, all down – except you, my dear doctor. –
Haven't you got a card?

DOCTOR (*goes up the stairs and out*):
I have some official business – I'll be back right away.

EICHMANN: Helga, you have first throw . . .

HELGA (*after Eichmann has passed her a bowl*):
Oo, but it's so heavy . . .

HIRT (*giving her a smaller one*): Here, Fräulein, more your calibre:
small and light but hard all the same.
There, you can win first prize with that.

FRITSCHE: Right, come along then.
(*Silence as the bowl rolls. As it hits, cheers.*)

HIRT: Just the king still standing . . . the last
    in Europe.

EICHMANN: Don't forget the Danes, Professor.
    There's a chap who's giving us a lot of trouble.

RUTTA SNR (*seriously interested*): Really? What can he do to us?

EICHMANN: They don't have Stars of David in Denmark.
    The King has managed to oppose it successfully up to now.

FRITSCHE (*at the board*): Obersturmbannführer, your turn.

EICHMANN: Coming. Come along, Baron.

    (*The ones who bowled first are now at the buffet with Helga, then
    go over to the chairs. The bowling becomes automatic. One's atten-
    tion is focused mainly on the changing conversations in the fore-
    ground. Interest in the bowlers, who are not actually talking, is
    aroused from time to time by shouts at the starting-place and
    behind the stage, like:*

    'Come on, Fritsche, to the starting-place.'

    'You're dead soon.'

    'Your turn. No, not me yet, it's you.'

    'Another two lives and I'm a goner.'

    'Come along, tiredness is no excuse.'

    'Bugger it, nothing again.'

    'You forfeit one, one forfeited.'

    'It's going all to one side today.'

    'Penalty.'

    'Free throw.'

    *These and similar calls are spread over the whole scene. Everything
    stays on the move, without excessively disturbing the conversations
    which take place between the tables and the buffet, and even at the
    starting-point, when the speakers go to bowl or select bowls. Salzer,
    an insignificant officer, has come down to the bottom of the stairs.
    Eichmann sees him first and goes over to him genially.*)

    Heil Hitler, my dear Salzer. What's the news?

SALZER: Heil Hitler, Obersturmbannführer, not good.

    (*They shake hands. Eichmann brings him downstage, continues at
    the back.*)

EICHMANN: Excuse me a moment, gentlemen,
    just a few moments. Come over here, Salzer.
    Have you just come from Slovakia?
    I thought at first it was Gerstein coming: I am waiting
    for him here.

SALZER: Yes, your secretary said to go straight

to Falkensee . . . Nice place here.

EICHMANN: It was high time we got a guesthouse.
There'll be no bombs fall here.
So, what's happening in Pressburg – isn't it working?

SALZER: No, it is not, Obersturmbannführer.
The Church is making great difficulties for us.

EICHMANN: The Church! But that is out of the question.
It was in Pressburg where the Government
even put baptized Jews in with the others,
I assume only because the head of the Government
is a *priest*. Monsignor Tiso
is a reasonable man though.

SALZER: I know, Obersturmbannführer. The first train
to Auschwitz in March came from Pressburg, in fact.

EICHMANN (*nervously*): Well then, and it was the Hlinka Guard, the
Catholic people's party, who rounded the Jews up for us.
You must rely on these people, Salzer . . .

SALZER: They've got cold feet, because the Nuncio,
the Papal Nuncio, has forbidden them
to support the deportations . . .

HIRT (*calling out, as he takes his bowl*):
Don't be so official, Eichmann:
bowling's a service to the people, too . . .

EICHMANN: Just a minute, Professor . . . I'm coming.

SALZER: The Nuncio has notified Father Tiso
that we were burning the Jews in Lublin, so
now Tiso is demanding an investigation. That's
why he sent me to you. What do we do?

EICHMANN (*agitated, walking up and down*):
Investigation? Investigate what then? – ashes?
God damn it – the Nuncio in Rumania
has just this minute started to stir things up, too.
The foreign *bishops* aren't so dangerous,
but a *Nuncio* as representative of the Vatican . . .
There's nothing we can do about it; we'll just have
to leave Slovakia in peace for the time being. Shit!
All we need now is the German bishops, too. . . .
If they start shouting blue murder about the Jews,
as they did about the mental defectives . . . and
if the Nuncio in Berlin adds to the rumpus,
things *will* start looking black. Anyway, Salzer,

26

have something to eat first – Helga!
Where is Helga then? Come along. . . .
(*He takes Salzer to the starting-place. He introduces him; it all
goes very quickly, with the usual flourishes, 'Heil Salzer', 'Pleased
to meet you', 'Heil Hitler', etc. . . .*)
Gentlemen – may I introduce
Sturmführer Salzer,
Professor Hirt – Reichs University, Strassburg.
Director Freiherr von Rutta – Reichs Munitions Union.
Leutnant von Rutta – congratulate him
on his Iron Cross, Salzer.

SALZER: Many congratulations, Herr Leutnant, congratulations.

RUTTA JNR: Thank you, Sturmführer.

EICHMANN: Dr Fritsche from Auschwitz you know already?

FRITSCHE: Hullo, Salzer, nice to have you here.

EICHMANN: Colonel Serge of the Army High Command,
Regierungsrat Dr Pryzilla, from the Ministry
for the Occupied Eastern Territories.
There – and Dr Littke – on leave from Russia,
on the staff of the Central Army Group.
(*to Fritsche at the blackboard*)
So, Fritsche, put Salzer down, too –
Salzer, we haven't been bowling long:
when you've had something to eat,
you can catch up on your turns.
Helga, spoil Herr Salzer a little.

HELGA: What would you like then? – Good evening.

SALZER: Good evening. – Don't we know each other?

HELGA: We've seen each other, of course – I am
engaged to Leutnant Wagner at Auschwitz.
We met once in Prague.

SALZER: I knew it! Of course, at the Hradcany Palace.
(*They are at the buffet. Colonel Serge, who has bowled, is talking to
Rutta Snr who has also bowled and come forward.*)

SERGE: You're staying the night, Baron, did I hear? . . .
Herr Director, I'd like to say something to you;
that's why I came here, in fact . . .
It can't go on much longer, that
business with the Krupps, respectable firm,
mistreating their prisoners of war
in that way . . .

27

Perhaps you've heard already,
we're getting anonymous letters at G.H.Q. from
the civil population about the
way Krupp is behaving.

RUTTA SNR (*stung*):
But, Colonel, why are you telling this to *me*?
Surely the Directors of Krupp are the people . . .

SERGE (*angry, nervous, rather loudly*): I can't – can't get hold of
Herr von Bülow at all. Must General von Schulenburg
go to Essen, in person, to tell
Herr Krupp von Bohlen – that he will not permit
the beating of prisoners, yes, they get beatings
instead of potatoes . . . now! – now!
(*as Rutta is about to contradict*)
Baron – that – that is what I heard from a reliable source.
For six weeks now the prisoners at Krupp's
haven't had any potatoes to eat.

RUTTA SNR (*frosty and precise*):
Beatings only take place in the firm's work-training camps;
and anyway, only to the most notorious – the most notorious
food-thieves, who are caught in flagranti.
The creatures are downright greedy, you'd scarcely believe it.
Herr von Bülow has laid down very exactly . . .

SERGE (*who is so irritated, he can't listen any longer*):
Don't waste my time talking round the point, Baron.
If I don't f-f-f-feed my horse,
he can't carry me.
And all the rest of the stuff one hears about Krupp:
that they've transferred all the Ukrainian girls
to the Ruhr – they can't have been any too keen on it.

RUTTA SNR: I am somewhat taken aback, Colonel – these
are after all nothing but Bolshevists. The firm
plans, in point of fact, by bonuses to those
who work hard, and by organizing cultural activities for them,
to teach these people to enjoy their work!

SERGE (*with bitter irony*): Well, that's splendid now . . . Krupp
bringing culture to the Russians!

RUTTA SNR: Colonel, should the workers from the East
be any *better* treated? We are at war!
They're starting to breed in Essen, although
a doctor, a Russian, is there to do abortions,

because these women will persist in entering
into relationships which . . .

SERGE (*furious, without caution*):
Aha, relationships – relationships, Baron, yes, that
I d-d-*didn't* know about, I must admit:
when a young Russian girl has had the honour –
no, please – to be allowed to make guns
for Krupp for ten hours, day after day,
then certainly she doesn't need to sleep
with a Russian after that. Of course – of course,
Krupp's is a moral concern . . .

EICHMANN (*who has sidled up*):
Gentlemen, not so aggressive – let's
have some more bowling: we're here to enjoy ourselves!

RUTTA SNR (*with bitter gaiety, preciously*):
Colonel Serge appears to be very worried
about the hormone content of the Russian workers at Krupp's.
(*serious, firm, almost menacing*)
They get themselves pregnant, Obersturmbannführer,
simply in order to be allowed to shirk
six weeks off work each time: it's scandalous . . .
Krupp puts the children in a home in Voerde,
where they are exemplarily looked after, butter, milk, fruit . . .

SERGE: So, milk and fruit. – I wouldn't mind
sending my own grandchildren there to build them up,
if some liar, some story-teller hadn't told me, that out of
one hundred and thirty-two children at Voerde
ninety-eight had died . . .
They can't seem to take our climate, the Russians, can they?
Or do you think someone forgot the butter?
(*He laughs artificially, as he is, justifiably, afraid he may have gone too far.*)
It only struck me, most of the children are blond,
so let's not talk about it . . .

EICHMANN:
Krupp won't need to worry about *that* any more, Herr Director,
as soon as the new branch is set up
in Auschwitz: there will be no more complaints there.
I have yet to hear of
(*laughs complicitly, Rutta joins in*)
anyone getting in the family way there either.

FRITSCHE (*coming forward*): Gentlemen: it's your turn again –
come along, Colonel.

SERGE (*grateful, hurriedly*): Yes, coming, coming . . .

RUTTA SNR (*calls his son, who is at the buffet*):
Hans, take my turn, would you?

EICHMANN: And Helga mine, would you, please?

HELGA: I shan't be held responsible, Herr Eichmann.

EICHMANN: You'll bring me luck.
(*To Rutta, pointing at Serge, who is choosing a bowl.*)
Don't let yourself be put out by
caricatures of humanity like that, Baron.
I may say, they are gradually dying out,
even in the Army . . .

HIRT (*shouting to Serge*): To the side . . . the side, Colonel,
or you'll be dead soon . . .
(*Laughter at Serge, who is cutting an absurd figure.*)

RUTTA SNR (*to Eichmann, at the buffet*):
Actually, I wanted to ask you, Obersturmbannführer,
how the generals are
reacting to your measures in Russia?
My son's commanding officer, Luftwaffe of course,
is helping a lot in the Balkans . . .

EICHMANN: There you are, Baron, that bears out
what I keep telling my colleagues:
Don't make too much of the rivalry
between the S.S. and the armed forces.
Oh, I know this or that general
looks the other way – they try and make
out they see nothing, when we go to
work in their division's territory.
But others co-operate, as you said just now.
In fact, last year, before
Auschwitz had been started, we were able
to deal with three hundred and fifty thousand
Russian Children of Israel: and it was
the Army, let's face it,
who made it possible for us . . .
Between ourselves, it really is absurd
of Himmler to suspect Field-Marshal Manstein
of Slavic descent, just because he happens
to be called Levinsky or something.

RUTTA SNR: Yes indeed: that could have waited till
the war's over.

EICHMANN: Exactly! Manstein is certainly no
National Socialist – I find it all the more
praiseworthy that he should publicly order his soldiers
in the East not only to fight according
to the old rules of war, but to have
some understanding of the need for a severe
but just revenge on Jewry.

RUTTA SNR (*smiling*): Don't be in too much of a hurry, Herr Eichmann,
or our labour forces will be short,
when Krupp starts production in Auschwitz.
(*They are about to go, but stay where they are as the Doctor appears
on the stairs and is greeted by Hirt with a shout.*)

HIRT: Hey, Doctor . . . Give us a song.
They're all talking too much shop here.
Go on, cheer us up – you're not so proud
as to need asking ten times.

EICHMANN (*takes a mouth organ from his coat pocket*):
Yes, please, Doctor, a song –
I've got my mouth organ with me.

DOCTOR (*pointing to Pryzilla in his yellow coat*):
The canary should be the one to sing.

PRYZILLA (*extremely timid*):
Impossible, Doctor – even at school
impossible to sing.
. . . bad men, ha, ha,
says a poet, have no songs . . .

DOCTOR: Quite – that's why I've a whole book full . . .
(*to the large circle which has gradually formed round the foot of the
stairs: Serge is not among them*)
I'm getting claustrophobic, children, don't
crowd me! I was in Paris lately –
(*ironic*)
Germany's pleasure garden, as the Führer says,
no place for Christian souls . . . Eichmann, do you know
the tune of 'Brave Lenchen am grünen Bäumchen'?
Touching. Just right for Christmas parties
and little girls full of faith and beauty.
I have a song to it . . . which, alas,

has been arranged for the rising generation
by priests of both sexes,
I mean, both denominations. . . .
(*Unpleasant laughter. The Doctor hums a tune, Eichmann hums along with him, then improvises it. The Doctor begins with an appalling innocence. It is characteristic of him that with his rhymes he can still shock even these hard-boiled men – technicians, grown so cold-blooded that they could, as Reitlinger states, discuss the plans for the gas-chambers at daily luncheons at Headquarters. 'The horrible cynicism of these conferences exhausted Nebe so much that he had twice to go on sick-leave with a nervous breakdown'* . . .
and this Herr Nebe was no weakling : he was active as leader of an extermination troop in Russia, before he sided with the conspirators of the 20th of July plot.
His little cane in his hand, the Doctor speaks and sings, as he chooses, the first lines with diabolical piety : later with cynicism and such carelessness that he might be making them up as he goes along, slowly descending the staircase as he sings :)

She hadn't a room, she hadn't a tent,
'No room at the inn', (the usual refrain).
The parks were lit up to a shameless extent,
Where can we go, Madeleine ?

Her fear that a Frenchman might see her collaborate,
(Our intentions were primarily amatory)
inspired Madeleine her plans to elaborate,
so she took me off to a cemetery.

Père Lachaise! where the great ones of France – Héloïse,
Abélard, Balzac, even Verlaine,
have been laid to rest under the juniper trees,
and that's where I laid Madeleine.

With no sense of shame Madeleine starts to strip,
(all the while my passion increases)
she hangs up her stockings, her dress and her slip,
on Thorwaldsen's statue of Jesus.

With pagan simplicity, classical grace,
and an innocent gesture of prudery,
she hangs a scarf over the Savior's face,
just like St Veronica's sudary.

The thought of a crucifix over the bed,
where the sacred could watch the profane,
even in marriage she thought to be somewhat ill-bred,
(how could they be tellement sans-gêne?)
all this was beyond Madeleine.

Her innocence touched me, I fondled her heart –
she was wearing it down round her waist –
when all of a sudden, I woke with a start –
a joke in execrable taste –

Three spectres stood there, Proust, Chopin and Wilde,
– the Frenchman, the Pole and the Briton –
inspired, I rose up to fresh heights: – like a child,
Madeleine sank down, overridden.

(*The self-assurance with which he now provokes the gathering, to a
degree which only he could allow himself, indicates his mythical
stature – he is beyond comprehension, not to be controlled by any
earthly superior. During the song he goes up to individuals and
flings out a few words at them like a judgement. Baron Rutta
he dislikes particularly. It is entirely for Rutta's 'benefit' that he
has thought out this ugly blasphemy against Christ – sacrilege
would for him have literally no object. His careless treatment of
the song corresponds to his attitude to the criminals present, whose
master he is.*)

A vision of fire and ice the three of them granted
to me, as they stood there, grinning and clapping the rhythm –
don't ask me though, for the moral, now that the story has
    ended;
I keep it from you in mercy, however much you may want it –
Cassandra herself never had a more terrible vision.

For you, the Christmas tree's still hung with gold;
my soul hangs like a millstone round about
my neck – my tongue is simply hanging out.
As you might see it some day here
thirsting for draughts of German beer
(a German point of view)
or else protruding, swollen, thick and black,
on a tautened rope, the body swinging slack,
just like all of You!

(*At the end of the song applause is dumb. After the last line the
Doctor vanishes quickly. Eichmann has stopped accompanying. A
painful silence.*)

EICHMANN (*embarrassed*): He whips up excitement so he can
take it away all the more. – Come on, let's
have some more bowling.

RUTTA SNR (*extremely piqued*):
God knows, I couldn't see anything clever in it . . .
very poor taste, dragging in the artists of
three enemy countries, here . . . I'd very much like
to know what he meant behind all that.

HIRT (*turning the conversation*): My dear Baron, don't be so deep.
It was a joke, just a song,
he didn't mean anything with it . . . good Lord, no . . .
(*He has bowled; now he shouts, as Fritsche chalks his throw up.*)
Two lives, am I really two down?
One more and I'm a dead man.
(*He comes back downstage where Rutta Snr is standing on his own.*)
Still thinking about the Doctor's vision?

RUTTA SNR (*quite positively, coldly*):
Professor, is one able to speak at all openly
when this Doctor is about . . . is he
not perhaps an agent provocateur . . .
No *German* would put on a performance like that,
as long as his national pride . . .

HIRT: My good friend – a man's mind is always unfathomable,
if he wants it to be. Let actions speak:
(*confidentially*)
The Doctor does the sorting at Auschwitz
of the Jews on the railway siding,
who's going up the chimney – happy now?

RUTTA SNR: What? – and then sing that dreadful song?
    A riddle, that man, a riddle, Professor . . .
    (*Littke, Serge, Pryzilla and others have bowled.*)
HIRT: Come on, Baron – and don't worry any more.
    Now, Herr Fritsche, so quiet? What's up?
    (*Hirt claps Littke, who bowled after him, on the shoulder.*)
    Here, Littke . . . go and relieve
    Fritsche for a bit at the board . . .
FRITSCHE: Yes, I wouldn't mind a sandwich.
LITTKE: Sure, Herr Professor, of course, Fritsche.
HIRT (*comes downstage with Fritsche, then to the buffet*):
    Well? You're never all that chatty,
    but today – what's the matter then?
FRITSCHE: Nothing particular. I just have to go
    back – after a wonderful leave
    with the family at Tegernsee.
    I was thinking: maybe I'd rather volunteer
    for the Eastern front: I'm fed up with Auschwitz.
HIRT (*calmingly*):
    You're just having one of those days, Fritsche.
    Everyone has them. What good is it
    to your family, if you go and get yourself
    shot in Russia – no, you stay put
    in Auschwitz, my dear fellow. Better still:
    come and spend a week in Strassburg some time,
    visit my institute.
    Yes, we must fix up an official trip
    for you. You're sure to come across
    an interesting skull or two for me some time.
    Bring the creatures for my collection
    alive, then you've an excuse to make the trip.
    When I've taken photographs and measurements,
    then they can be liquidated in Strassburg.
    (*Points to Littke, who has just bowled and is coming back to the scoreboard.*)
    Littke's going to get me some Commissar skulls
    from his unit.
FRITSCHE: Of course, I'd love to come
    to Strassburg, Herr Professor, provided
    an official order for it could be arranged . . .
HIRT: What do you mean 'provided'? We'll take you out of yourself.

The *cathedral* alone – I'd give all Berlin
for it! You're fond of music, didn't
I once hear someone say, Fritsche?
FRITSCHE: I think I may say so. Heydrich on the 'cello –
(*he points to the death-mask; they go up to the photograph*)
myself viola. Just before the murder,
in March, we used to play quartets sometimes
in the Hradcany Palace.
HIRT (*lost in thought, looking at the mask, then softly*):
Yes, Heydrich – between ourselves, he had
the Jewish feeling for artistic quality,
strengthened, I need hardly add, by the power
of the Aryan constituents in his blood.
An exceptional man. I once heard him
reciting a story of Kleist's – masterly.
(*louder*)
Yes, wonderful: you come and see me.
Perhaps there'll be a concert in the Minster,
to hear the B Minor Mass there
is a real mystical experience. The words
are balls, but balls in Latin,
and they don't worry you.
But the Gloria – my dear fellow,
that takes the cake all right. That's how
I'd like to celebrate the final victory
in my own quiet way. Just the B Minor Mass –
but in Strassburg.
And no speeches, no speeches after the celebration.
Then just to show the Führer my collection
of skulls . . . Littke!
LITTKE (*eagerly*): Herr Professor?
(*to Rutta Jnr, who has just bowled*)
Would you take over, Herr Leutnant?
RUTTA JNR: Surely – give me the chalk, glad to.
LITTKE (*to Fritsche as he comes up to Hirt*):
Herr Fritsche, your turn . . . you too,
Herr Professor, your turn again in a minute.
HIRT: The next shot kills me . . . I've
not got the knack of it today . . .
(*Fritsche has gone to bowl, then returns downstage to Hirt and Littke.*)

(*firmly*)

Are you musical too, Littke, like Herr Fritsche?

LITTKE (*frightened, as he wants to make the best possible impression*):
  No, Herr Professor, I'm afraid not, hardly.

HIRT (*firmly*): You're not a medical one-track mind
  though, I hope . . . you have other interests?

LITTKE (*without anyone believing him*):
  I used always to be very fond of
  drawing before, Herr Professor. I used to . . .

HIRT (*reconciled*): Good, most important! Keep in practice!
  A surgeon must be able to draw, must have
  (*opens a bottle of beer*)
  or should have, let's say, a steady hand,
  a dead steady hand. You can
  draw my skulls and the cathedral,
  and the picturesque rooftops – Goethe has
  drawn them already – but first you must
  (*with the acquisitiveness of a philatelist*)
  bring me some more skulls. It's the only
  chance, the last chance:
  Littke, science hardly possesses a single
  Commissar's skull, in any sort of condition . . .
  What's the point of the Commissar Order in the first place?
  (*pours Littke a beer, too, and chews and talks*)
  You'll be getting a *direct* order from
  Reichsführer Himmler, which your unit will
  respect. I want everything you capture
  in the future, in the shape of
  Jewish-Bolshevist Commissars . . .

LITTKE: But they don't *have* to be Jews, do they,
  Herr Professor?

HIRT: Not necessarily, no: Commissar is the main thing,
  it doesn't matter whether Jews or Russians –
  Jews are more interesting, of course, aren't they?
  The main thing: in future don't kill
  any Commissars at once, but send them *alive*,
  to the military police at your unit H.Q.
  You've got your private car and chauffeur
  and you alone are responsible for the safe delivery
  of the material . . .
  And above all:

37

(*quite fearful, with extreme concern and insistence*)
above all, don't damage the heads – for God's sake
don't damage the heads. I'll give you
some forms on which you can put down,
as far as possible, it's understood, place and date
of birth and other particulars. Then
you take the measurements, photographic
and anthropological – and only *then*
is the Russo to be killed. Sever the head
from the trunk and . . .

LITTKE (*in a muck sweat of fear*):
Yes, Herr Professor. May I be allowed to
ask whether . . . whether I personally
(*he hesitates, fearful again of making a bad impression*)
have to perform the execution after the measurements . . .

EICHMANN: Professor: duty calls – you must have your turn.

HIRT (*to Littke on his way to the starting-place*):
No, no, no – the military police can look after that.
Don't worry, Littke – yes, I'm
coming, I'm coming – I'm afraid
this time it'll be my last life . . .
(*He bowls; great cheering as Hirt is the 'dead man'; shouts from
the back of the room*):
'Professor . . . a free round.'
'Dich mein stilles Tal, grüss ich tausendmal.'
'Not that war-time beer either – you might just as well pour it
straight into the piss-house.'

HIRT: 'Course, of course. Helga, what is there?
Still enough schnapps for everybody?

HELGA: You drinking, too? – but you're dead?
(*she pours: Eichmann begins to sing . . . most of the others join in*)
'Dich mein stilles Tal
grüss ich tausendmal
denn sie trugen einen Toten zum Tore hinaus . . .'

RUTTA SNR (*while the others go on bowling with increased concentration,
goes to Hirt at the buffet*):
I'm very glad, Professor Hirt, we have
met here, I am sick
of always just being a specialist.
Studium generale – that is basically
even today, during the war, still my aim.

We men of industry are much too much
taken up with material things and by now we
can only read production charts . . .
Tell me – what is your final purpose
in making your collection of skulls at Strassburg?
What does science hope to . . .?

HIRT: We are idealists, Baron, and don't ask
too much just yet about final purposes . . .
Even the real scientist nowadays
must not be too much caught up merely in
considerations of practicality.
But you know, with photographs and
head measurements and finally, the skull itself,
we at Strassburg are able to carry out
the *most precise* comparative anatomical research.
Racial classification, pathological characteristics
of the skull formation, and size – all brought
under *one* formula: our grandchildren will see, in years to come,
that the final solution of the Jewish question
was from a scientific point of view *as well*
irreproachably natural and necessary.

RUTTA SNR: That makes things a lot clearer, of course.

HIRT: Are you often in Auschwitz, Baron?

RUTTA SNR: Every now and then, to see the people from I.G.Farben.
The building for Krupp is still in the planning stage only.

HIRT: Good, good, I appreciate your interest:
the next time you are in Auschwitz
ask for Hauptsturmführer Dr Beger . . . Bruno Beger,
Yes, write it down . . . give him
my regards and ask him to show you
his skeleton . . . extraordinarily interesting.
And then the people he is still working on . . .
seventy-nine Jews, thirty Jewesses, two Poles and even
four real live Asiatics, in quarantine –
get him to show you – Aha, here comes
my good colleague, who reproaches me
because as a pathologist I . . . What's
the news, colleague?
He loafs around the table all the time,
looking as if he hadn't told us everything
he knows long ago – what *do* you know, then,

you tongue-tied old rascal?

DOCTOR (*very winningly, 'defeatist'*):
   I know nothing . . . only that my work has been
   as useless as all other forms of heroism.

HIRT (*ethically aroused, as he is well and truly drunk*):
   What's that? – Science is never –
   is never, never useless . . .

LITTKE: Baron Rutta – your go.

HIRT: Yes, go along – I'm finished.
   Blessed are the dead, good luck, Baron.

RUTTA SNR (*going to the starting-place with pretended indignation*):
   Hasn't anyone got all nine yet?
   What sort of heroes are we this evening?

HIRT: He was much piqued after your evil sing-song . . .

DOCTOR (*amused*):
   The stupid shit . . . that's what I hoped.
   I'd like to vivisect him with his own
   Ration-book scissors . . . What would a man like that
   be earning from the war per day, on an average, now?

HIRT: Let him alone, the old neuter. Of course, you
   stung the Catholic in him – Rhineland nobility.

DOCTOR: Endemically syphilitic since 1018, eh?
   Yes, he still writes in his ledger: 'With God.'
   'With God for Führer, people and profits' . . .

HIRT (*laughing*): You are in great form, this evening. Still,
   he's produced a splendid son. I'm still waiting
   for children from you, my dear chap . . .

DOCTOR: Idealist that I am, I sterilized
   myself recently. I wanted to see what it was like.

HIRT: Seriously: how far have you got with it?

DOCTOR (*factually, but without interest*):
   As far as I'm concerned, they can go ahead with the women,
   painless and en masse . . . it was
   intended for Jewesses married to Aryans.
   I could sterilize them on a conveyer belt.

HIRT: Is that a fact? – Well, congratulations.

DOCTOR: Congratulate the women – in fact, they were
   afraid to proceed at first. There were doubts in
   the Ministry of Propaganda on the 6th of March
   about forcing the annulment of these marriages . . .
   for fear of a possible protest from the Vatican.

HIRT: The Vatican . . . How so?
   (*Rutta Snr has returned.*)
DOCTOR: Remember that in many cases these marriages
   were celebrated by a priest of the Church.
HIRT: And Goebbels is afraid of the Vatican?
DOCTOR: An old Jesuit does not forget the power of Rome . . .
   (*They all laugh, then Rutta Snr, who does not care for the joke,
   says sourly:*)
RUTTA SNR: The Reich's armament industry has other problems.
   But I, as a Rhinelander, can still today
   remain a good Catholic, precisely because
   the Pope, by his sensible attitude, has spared
   me the need on that account to be a bad German . . .
   He takes no part surely – so I thought – in
   any way in German internal affairs.
   (*Eichmann comes up to them; the Doctor goes over to Helga, who
   has been talking to young Rutta and draws her over to the starting-
   place. Helga bowls.*)
HIRT: Of course, Pacelli is an aristocrat, Baron.
   His concluding of the Concordat after
   our rise to power, was of inestimable value.
   But look at Galen, that babbler:
   I was so furious that the Führer
   should have dropped the euthanasia programme . . . just
   because of that miserable pulpit-thumper . . .
EICHMANN: When we were taking him to be questioned, the
   old fox put on all his vestments, crozier
   in his hand, mitre . . . anyway, he's
   a hulking great fellow, like the Hermann Memorial . . .
   and said to the men: 'I'll only go on foot,
   I won't get into your car voluntarily.'
   So they withdrew the police.
   They were afraid of the congregation in the cathedral
   – and quite rightly –
   what a row *that* would have started.
   I think it is practical of the Führer . . . to protect
   people's religious feelings in wartime . . . take my father,
   for example, presbyter of the evangelical community
   in Linz: he did not even understand
   that the insane were to be disposed of.
   Provoking the people in wartime . . . what's the use?

We've got time . . . doesn't cost us anything.

RUTTA SNR (*laughing*):

Oh, it costs the national economy something all right,

Herr Eichmann, to go on feeding the imbeciles.

However, my own feeling is that a Jew,

as long as he can still work,

should be kept alive . . .

You see, gentlemen, we see it every day,

one Jew is worth more in the armament industry

than two Ukrainians, if only because he understands us.

He speaks our language, and doesn't go in for sabotage;

and he's cheaper, too: we don't have the expense

of bringing him three thousand miles first . . .

EICHMANN: Are they still bringing in Ukrainians? – But I heard

they were doing it the other way round now, Baron:

not taking Ukrainians to Krupp . . . but Krupp to the Ukraine.

RUTTA SNR (*sly, half apprehensive, half flattered, he points to the others*):

How do you know that, for God's sake?

Gentlemen, please . . . the greatest discretion.

You may imagine that young Bohlen,

and Flick, too, Röchling and the Union,

are, God knows, not all too keen

on the Russian idea.

That sort of sponsorship is an expensive business,

and what one has got to invest in it . . . I could tell you.

HIRT (*with a loud laugh, then quieter, when Rutta lays a finger to his lips*):

Well, Eichmann . . . we two couldn't mind

getting our paws on a bit of the Donetz basin . . .

(*Laughter. Pryzilla, who has bowled, is lurking behind Rutta's back at the buffet.*

Drunk enough to forget to be 'discreet', Hirt now drags Pryzilla down to them.)

There you are, he only needs to hear of a share-out,

and up he pops – Eichmann, for us,

no pickings . . . Come along, have some more to drink . . .

PRYZILLA (*with a hard, jabbing, abrupt intonation*):

Baron, did you fly with Alfried von Bohlen

and Councillor Röchling

to the Ukraine?

RUTTA SNR (*cold, ironic*):
>But, Herr Doctor, no, no, no. Don't overestimate
>my connections, I beg you, with these
>distinguished gentlemen . . . I have nothing
>to do with Krupp directly . . .

PRYZILLA (*aggressive*): Then I may tell you that Alfried von Bohlen
>is personally installing his own agents
>in the German official departments in the Ukraine.
>Personally. I know very well.
>And you know, too, what that means, Herr Baron.
>The name of Krupp is enough. Quite enough.
>Everyone is making a rush for the best plants.
>So that if there's to be a share-out later
>they will have certain faits accomplis to present.

RUTTA SNR (*with icy condescension*): But, my dear Doctor, I fail to see
>what is making you so angry . . . Herr von Bohlen . . .

PRYZILLA (*trembling with 'righteousness', spitting out each word*):
>Do you know, the Union . . . where it's already established?
>The Union's already set up in Stalino.
>Look at Krupp – in Dnepropetrovsk, of course,
>the Molotov-works – almost five thousand
>tons capacity – on a navigable
>river . . . ideal . . . i-de-al.

RUTTA SNR (*with measureless hauteur*):
>Yes, yes . . . but why not? . . . I fail to see . . .

PRYZILLA: We in the ministry . . . excuse me,
>we have an eye to the good of the country *as well*.
>The good of the country. It is the people
>who are paying for the war with their blood.
>The people should profit from it . . . not just private firms.
>If there is a share-out now,
>what will be left for the Göring state works?
>What will be left for the Volkswagen works, let's say,
>what will be left for the, let's say, for the . . .

EICHMANN (*loudly*): Just for a moment, quiet – gentlemen, please,
>quiet a moment – it's an alert.
>
>(*Sirens are heard in the distance. All listen, then several leave
>hastily. Now a loud wail of sirens starts in Falkensee itself. Eich-
>mann has come forward.*)

SERGE (*going to him*): Obersturmbannführer, may I thank you
>for your hospitality – it was very agreeable

to be – to be able to have a word or two with the Baron.
But now – my family's in the Wilmersdorferstrasse.
I must – I think I should say good-bye . . .

EICHMANN (*gives him his hand*): It's been a pleasure – but do
you want to go back in the middle of a raid, Colonel?

PRYZILLA (*quickly to Serge*): You can take me too, Colonel? I live in
Charlottenburg – and I must . . . Heil Hitler.
Herr Eichmann! . . . Baron, you're sleeping
here in Falkensee, are you not: may I ring you
tomorrow morning, about nine?

RUTTA SNR (*icy*): Please do, Herr Doctor. But as I said:
I have no information of any kind. Heil Hitler . . .
Heil Hitler, Colonel Serge – we shall see each other in Essen.

PRYZILLA (*corkscrewing round twice, squeezes out several times*):
Heil Hitler . . . Heil Hitler . . . Heil Hitler . . .

SERGE: 'Night everyone . . .
(*They both leave. Neither Littke nor Salzer have come back. The
Doctor and Helga disappeared as soon as the sirens sounded.*)

RUTTA JNR: They're on time tonight, Father. [*i.e. the bombers*]
– dreadfully smoky in here. I'm going
outside with Herr Fritsche. I'm interested in the way
they attack Berlin. Coming?

RUTTA SNR: Yes, just let me get my coat.
(*The three go out.*)

HIRT (*very drunk, calls after them*):
If you see where the Doctor and Helga
have got to . . . tell them not to catch cold.
(*laughs libidinously, claps Eichmann on the shoulder*)
I'm bowling again – there's no bomber
going to shoot me down.
No need to get excited – I'm going to bowl.

EICHMANN: Yes, you do that, Professor, I'll join you.
(*He turns and sees Gerstein, who entered the room as Hirt was
speaking of Helga and now announces himself.*)

GERSTEIN:
Sturmbannführer – reporting back from special mission
to Treblinka, Belzec Majdanek.
You wanted to have a word with me
right away, today without fail . . .

EICHMANN: Hey, man, Gerstein – where have you been?
I want to know all about it. Did it work?

(*to Hirt, who has approached, bowl in hand*)
Sturmführer Gerstein – Professor Hirt
of the Reichsuniversität at Strassburg.
Herr Gerstein is an engineer and doctor, head
of the technical side of the Disinfection Department.
He was the one who stopped the typhus
epidemic in our barracks last year.

HIRT: I heard all about it, my dear boy, you are
a technical genius. Very glad to meet you –
Heil, Herr Gerstein.

GERSTEIN (*enigmatic*):
Heil Hitler, Herr Professor – when are you finally
going to publish something for the profession
about your skulls?

HIRT: What are you thinking of? – It would be grand,
dream of my life. But, alas,
it must be kept a secret.

GERSTEIN: Oh, they are exaggerating: it would be quite safe.
Have a pamphlet brought out for the professors in the medical
schools.

HIRT: Glad you're interested: I must try to . . .

EICHMANN: Come, gentlemen, business first now:
Gerstein's been in Belzec, to see whether
or not the Final Solution can be reached
more smoothly and – above all – more quickly – with Cyclon B.

HIRT: I thought you used carbon monoxide?

GERSTEIN: Up to now, yes; but diesel exhaust
is useless: the generators are perpetually
(*very sharp, openly angry*)
going wrong. Obersturmbannführer, I have known people
have to wait almost three hours in the chambers
for the diesel motors to
start at all. And then . . . you can't imagine it:
it took half an hour before they were all dead.
(*Eichmann is speechless, appalled.*)

HIRT (*sounding off*): That's terrible, children. At least be humane.
Why don't you simply shoot them, out of hand,
like in Russia?

EICHMANN (*agitated, no longer pedantic at all*):
Shoot them! – It's easy for you to talk, Professor.
You try shooting forty

45

trucks full of naked, screaming people
out of hand.
In fact, they seldom scream. Most of them
just stand fatalistically in front of the graves, and
look amazed that it is being done
to them at all . . .
That's worse still. Their behaviour en masse is . . .
well, simply, Aryan. Even so:
there's a grandmother with a grandchild
in her arms: a girl, looking like
the first little girl one ever undressed
as a schoolboy. And the pregnant women . . .
The most hard-boiled rifleman
can't keep that up for long
not even if his blood is ninety per cent brandy.
No . . . shooting is impossible.
It makes one impotent and insomniac, Professor,
and we have a good eight million to treat
in Europe . . . by the end of the war at that.

HIRT (*complaining*): Well, an approved method *must* be found.
What Gerstein describes will never do.
Impossible.
You should leave it to us *doctors*, Eichmann . . .

EICHMANN: That's why Gerstein has been making these tests
with prussic acid. How did *that* work, Gerstein?

GERSTEIN: Obersturmbannführer: I was not able
to make the tests.

EICHMANN (*roused*): But, man, you were ordered to make them.
Didn't you even *try* to?

GERSTEIN: I couldn't, Obersturmbannführer: to begin with,
Captain Wirth at Belzec refused my request.
He was most insistent I did not suggest
to Berlin any alterations to his installations.

EICHMANN: But that is nonsense.
A *year* ago already I,
Yes, in September: I persuaded
Höss in Auschwitz to try out
Cyclon B on six hundred Russians.
We sealed the windows of the punishment block
hermetically, with clay,
and threw the crystals in through the door . . .

46

GERSTEIN (*pulling himself together with an effort*):
On that – occasion, Obersturmbannführer, though,
Captain Wirth told me yesterday,
and on the following afternoon,
several of the Russians survived.

EICHMANN: Good God, Gerstein. That was the
first time we'd tried it out.
We won't get results by waving a wand – anyway
the rooms were crammed full
like a bucket of fish. . . .
(*He falls silent, pointing to the loudspeaker at the back, which is announcing :*)

RADIO: Attention, please; attention, please; here is an air-raid announcement. The light formation of English aircraft at present in the area of Osnabruck on a south-easterly course is approaching the town of Hanover. The heavy formation flying south-west towards Berlin has reached the outer defences of the city.

EICHMANN: Now we'll have some fireworks.
How the others can go back to
Berlin like that – idiotic. Where's Helga then?

HIRT (*cheerfully*): Ask the Doctor where she is . . .
He wanted to give her a hand, taking her
cases down . . . to the cellar. . . .
They were going to go through her clothes first.
(*He yawns like a dustbin, unbuttons his jacket and lies in an arm-chair, his legs on a chair. He says very sleepily, more to himself than to anyone else :*)
Have they started already?
When are the others going to come down?

EICHMANN (*to Gerstein, reproachfully*):
So your journey was quite pointless?

GERSTEIN (*confident*):
Not at all, Obersturmbannführer. The prussic acid
had already decomposed . . .
so I couldn't have done the tests anyway.
It was buried . . . under my supervision . . .
However, in my own field, disinfection,
I was able to . . .
(*The rumble of attacking bombers from Berlin grows to a drone : if possible, we should hear the flak beginning, from the outer defences*)

of the city. The light flickers and goes out, then comes on again straight away. Eichmann has pointed tensely at the ceiling; neither says a word.)

EICHMANN (*with mistrust, even irony*):
Prussic acid, which you got only last *week*
fresh from the factory, disintegrates
as soon as that – remarkable, Gerstein.

GERSTEIN (*holding his glance, beginning laboriously*):
You see, Obersturmbannführer, when the acid
because of the heat and the travelling – travelling
on those terrible Polish roads, too . . .
was first . . .

EICHMANN (*putting his hand on Gerstein's shoulder*):
Oh, I am not doubting your description,
you're the chemist, not me . . . all the same –
(*laughing*)
Gerstein, you old jailbird, don't take it to heart –
you weren't exactly angry, were you . . . that
you couldn't carry out the experiments?

GERSTEIN (*with completely deceptive irritation, officially*):
Obersturmbannführer, if I am to take your reference
to my period of imprisonment as a further
expression of your lack of confidence in me,
I would like to apply for the institution
of a disciplinary investigation.
(*very fast, as Eichmann makes a shocked gesture, apparently deeply hurt*)
I imagined, on the basis of my work
in the disinfection service, that my probationary period . . .

EICHMANN (*without suspicion*):
Oh, come on, Gerstein, can't you take a joke?
Of course I trust you absolutely . . . Helga!
Let's not talk any more shop.
Have something to eat, Gerstein . . . Helga will be glad to . . .
(*Helga, in a summer coat, has appeared on the stairs with a suit-case, which Eichmann immediately takes from her.*)

HELGA: Were you looking for me? I was calling my fiancé
in Auschwitz . . . The Doctor had a call
booked through anyway, so I could talk
to Günther, too.
(*Smiles, points to Hirt, snoring luxuriously.*)

48

EICHMANN: Enviable . . . he can sleep like Napoleon.

GERSTEIN: Good evening, Helga . . . How are you?

HELGA: Oh, Herr Gerstein . . . all right, if I wasn't so
    scared of the bombing . . .
    (*She points to the ceiling, then quickly arranges a plate of food for
    Gerstein.*)
    The noise is terrible tonight . . .
    Herr Eichmann . . . my fiancé says
    I can go to Auschwitz, in the information section.
    I have to get out of Berlin, because of the raids. . . .

EICHMANN: What . . . well, your fiancé's wish is my command.
    But we'll be inconsolable here . . . Where,
    (*turns away nervously*)
    where is . . .

GERSTEIN (*to Helga*):
    Stay in Berlin! Auschwitz is no place . . . not for you.
    No bombs will fall here in Falkensee.
    (*Conversation languishes, the drone is uncanny.*)

EICHMANN (*beginning again*):
    Where are the Ruttas and the rest of them?
    They ought to . . . Donnerwetter,
    there's squadrons of them, hundreds . . .
    (*The light flickers briefly and goes very bright, the others come
    rattling down the stairs, except the Doctor. Not too far away is
    heard the sound of a landmine, the characteristic whistle, growing
    to a shriek.*)
    (*shouting*)
    Look out!
    (*As it falls, the light goes out completely.*)

                    Curtain

SCENE THREE

The following morning.
Gerstein's apartment, Berlin W.35.
Gerstein, in an old S.S. uniform, is standing on a pair of household
steps, busy re-plastering a long crack in the wall. He is messing about
with a plasterer's trowel and taking the plaster from an old jam pot.
He is smoking. There are old newspapers spread about under the steps.
The room bears many traces of the heavy air-raid of the previous night:

*the lamp has been knocked over and still lies on the floor; a broken
picture leans against the wall; the window upstage that gives on to the
street is blocked up with cardboard and is at the moment open, with a
view on to a ruined house opposite that has been there for some time.
The one on the opposite outside wall of the room, next to and to the
right of the door is completely undamaged even to its curtains. A large
carpet lies rolled up diagonally across the room; the simple bachelor
apartment furniture has been piled up together, as far as possible, to
allow the floor to be cleared of glass splinters, lime, plaster and shreds
of wallpaper. This is being done by a civilian of about thirty, who looks
older than he is: a Jew called Jacobson, whom Gerstein is concealing.
Jacobson speaks carefully, timidly, his movements are clumsy – one can
see he is a prisoner and also that he has not been in the open air for a
long time. Both work away in silence. Jacobson is smoking as well.
Outside one can hear the noises of a large city, though they are not very
penetrating, then, in the distance at first, the music of an approaching
parade of the Hitler Youth.*

GERSTEIN: Can we have the window shut now, Jacobson . . .?
JACOBSON: There's still a lot of dust. Let's wait a moment.
    (*He goes into the next room and brings in two buckets full of rubbish,
    then a shovel.*)
    Well, it's all clean in there again,
    as far as it can be. Herr Gerstein, please let me
    do the plaster, I have nothing at all to do now.
    The window is boarded up all right,
    no one will be able to see me on the steps.
GERSTEIN: Thank you. All right, if you want to. Fine.
    I'll take the rubbish down into the courtyard.
    (*He gets off the ladder and shuts the window, then gives the trowel
    to Jacobson, who climbs up and begins to work.*)
    Man, I was worried about you last night:
    not even being able to go down to the cellar
    during a raid like that.
JACOBSON (*smiling*): It's lucky my parents are still allowed to
    use the cellar where they live.
    Could you drop by later on,
    and see if the house is still there?
GERSTEIN (*turning away*): Certainly, Herr Jacobson.
JACOBSON: Thanks. It wasn't funny, not a bit,

with the windows flying about my ears,
but I'd rather they got me here . . .
than go to Auschwitz.
I'm sorry, that was very selfish of me:
how much longer can you put up with me here?
(*Gerstein gives him another cigarette.*
Conversation is no longer possible, as the music has got too loud, but
the march music is finished and as the parade comes roughly level
with the house they begin to sing, audibly, despite the closed
windows :)
Es zittern die morschen Knochen
der Welt vor dem grossen Krieg.
Wir haben die Ketten zerbrochen,
füruns war's ein grosser Sieg.
Wir werden weiter marschieren,
wenn alles in Scherben fällt,
denn heute gehört uns Deutschland
und morgen die ganze Welt.

GERSTEIN (*with great distaste, after a quick look into the street*):
They can do nothing without music – at Auschwitz
they have a little orchestra of Viennese Jewesses
who have to play Viennese waltzes
while they are choosing the next bunch of victims.
(*They are both silent. After a while Gerstein says reassuringly.*)
I'll have a passport for you
before the house is finally bombed to bits.
It is not likely that they will look
for you here in my flat – unless
I myself am suspected
as being a former concentration-camp prisoner.
(*smiling*)
Unfortunately you are a bit too dark
for a typical Swede –
but I haven't up to now been able
to get near the Spaniards or the Italians.

JACOBSON (*as he plasters the wall*):
The next time you go to the Swede,
in the Embassy here,
get a passport for yourself
to go to Sweden.
Only your wife will know where you have disappeared to.

At work they will just take you as missing.

GERSTEIN (*broodingly*): Just emigrate? Dear God, every hour
　　I watch people dying in the gas chambers.
　　As long as there is still the slightest hope
　　that I can save even one of you,
　　then I must risk becoming in the end
　　indistinguishable from the murderers.

JACOBSON: Your visit to the Nuncio was the last risk
　　you can allow yourself to take. Now go
　　via Sweden to England.
　　They've probably seen through you here already.

GERSTEIN (*smiling enigmatically*): Seen through me? No, not *me*.
　　No one has seen through me yet.
　　Possibly I am being watched;
　　I am often afraid so – above all
　　for my family and for you.

JACOBSON: You must ring your wife
　　before the War Office announces
　　that Berlin has been raided.
　　Don't tell her how the flat
　　has been wrecked.
　　She's worried enough about you as it is.

GERSTEIN: I'll ring Tübingen from the office;
　　I can get through straight away from there.
　　I hope to be able to go home over
　　the week-end – have you enough to eat?

JACOBSON: Yes, thank you. Quite.

GERSTEIN: You must really say if you
　　are hungry.
　　You're not taking anything out of my mouth,
　　you know that.
　　I get enough to eat at work.

JACOBSON: Thank you, Herr Gerstein. I know. However,
　　you could get me two new books.
　　Here is the money . . . (*He has taken out his wallet.*)
　　If you could possibly have another try
　　at getting me a Russian grammar.

GERSTEIN: Oh, don't bother about the money,
　　till I know what it costs.
　　I'll find one second-hand easily enough.
　　So, let's get on.

(*Jacobson takes the trowel. Gerstein picks up the buckets, to take them downstairs. Just as Gerstein is leaving, the door bell rings. They both show signs of nervousness. Jacobson, without a word, jumps off the ladder and vanishes into the next room. Gerstein closes the door after him. There is a second ring. Gerstein goes out and we hear him opening the door of the flat.*)

Heil Hitler – oh, it's *you*, Doctor.

DOCTOR: Gerstein – have you heard the news? Terrible . . .

GERSTEIN: Why, what's happened?

(*He has let the Doctor into the flat. The door is closed. We hear quick steps in the hall. The Doctor, highly elegant, in a black cape with silver buckles and chain, bursts into the room in front of Gerstein and now says breathlessly to him:*)

DOCTOR: Is your radio kaput as well, then?

Ah, then you don't know . . .

GERSTEIN: Tell me, Doctor. I've no idea.

DOCTOR: The attempt on Hitler's life? – Göring and Himmler
were on board as well, an air crash.

GERSTEIN (*disturbed by this turn of events, frankly shocked*):
For God's sake – all three?
But that can't be true, Doctor!
Was no one saved?

DOCTOR (*grinning diabolically*): Saved? – oh, yes. Guess who? . . .

GERSTEIN: Who?

DOCTOR: Germany!

(*His laughter sounds like the rattle of corrugated iron. Gerstein has sat down, first out of fright at the Doctor's appearance, secondly because he is unnerved by the disappointment of his denial.*)

GERSTEIN (*slowly*): Jokes like that, Doctor, I don't find very funny.

DOCTOR: Ah ha. Perhaps you find it funny
that they should do up your house so stylishly.
The house of my lady friend has been razed to the cellar.

GERSTEIN (*taking a second chair from the table*):
Sit down, Doctor, it's nice of you to call.

DOCTOR (*still with both arms in his cape*):
No, no, thank you, no time. I won't sit down.
I tried to call you,
but your telephone seems to have caught it too.
I'm going to Tübingen tomorrow morning
and thought I'd offer you a place in the car.
That way you will get to your family sooner,

and we can natter undisturbed for a bit.
You are the only one worth talking to.
GERSTEIN (*smiling to hide his fear*):
How do you mean, the only one . . . but it's very good of you.
DOCTOR: The only one. Our colleagues are, without exception,
good, beer swilling German dolts:
intelligent, only in the technical sense of the word –
I wanted to get off about seven. Agreed?
GERSTEIN: Fine. I'll be at the entrance door,
if it's still there tomorrow morning.
What's taking you to Tübingen then?
Do you want to become a professor as well?
DOCTOR (*has sat down, now stands again*):
Easy now, let's get a degree first.
GERSTEIN: Will you be able to use
the results of your experiments in Auschwitz?
I ask because of the security factor.
DOCTOR (*sunk in thought, looking at the broken picture*):
Aaaah – no, not as a *doctor*.
I am going to Tübingen as a philosopher.
Medicine is only my business, not my pleasure.
Apart from that, the experiments on prisoners
are not as secret as all that. Only last May
here in Berlin – but everyone was invited
who was anyone, army, air force, the lot.
Even old Sauerbruch added his stone to the cairn.
By the way, I couldn't bring flowers, so may I leave you
these brains . . .
(*He unexpectedly holds out his left hand from under his cloak. He is
holding a glass jar somewhat in the shape of a bombe glacée, which
he had under his arm. He displays the contents, a medical preparation of some whitish-grey, organic substance, the brains of twin
Jewish children, to the horrified Gerstein, who makes no secret of his
repugnance. Casually . . .*)
. . . the brains of a pair
of Jewish twins, from Calais, prepared in
formalin, extremely interesting comparative
sections. I brought them for a young lady
who's just started her first term in dissection.
Now her house has been bombed, and I've no idea
where the medical school has moved itself to.

54

I've already managed to get her a skull,
but that will be under the rubble by now . . .
GERSTEIN (*falling in with his conversation with some effort*):
What a charming memento . . .
DOCTOR: As soon as I know she is still alive,
she can come by and fetch it, can't she?
GERSTEIN (*picks up the jar hesitantly, hesitates to put it on the table,
then sets it down on a chair*):
Easier to come by in Auschwitz than flowers, eh?
DOCTOR (*apparently in a spirit purely of mockery*):
Revolts you, doesn't it, my dear Disciple?
GERSTEIN: I know what you're doing . . . it's horrible.
DOCTOR: Tell me one thing, it interests me:
how does one reconcile oneself nowadays,
to have understanding – and still be a Christian?
GERSTEIN (*with undiminished caution, slowly*):
Bismarck said something about that;
he too, after a wild, Byronic youth,
had to find the intellectual's detour
via Nihilism to God. – He said,
and I can add nothing to it, of course, myself –
I believe it is really the last word on the subject:
he said, I have stopped at a certain stage
of development, *fully conscious* of the fact.
DOCTOR: And is *that* supposed to have helped him
to plan three wars in peace of mind? – come, come! –
he knew very well that he was humbugging himself.
They were all of them aware of the illusionary
factor in their mental scheme, even Hegel.
And you – today, you are aware of it, too:
he who says what he means, loses his life;
he who means what he says, is off his head.
GERSTEIN (*laughing*):
Then I must be. I have always meant
what I have said to you, and always say what I mean . . .
DOCTOR (*close to him, satanic*):
Now and then, Gerstein, now and then . . . sly puss.
You don't humbug me.
Who exactly are you cheating? –
The Church and yourself,
or us – the S.S.?

GERSTEIN (*senses he is not up to this examination and therefore makes a display of putting all his cards on the table, in the manner of an unworldly idealist*):
How do you mean, cheat? I *do* say what I mean.
Leaving Christianity aside, Doctor, of course
I'm a Christian – with Himmler's blessing, at that.
But must one be a Christian then
to have a – one's doubts?
(*creating a diversion*)
Did you know, I got the news the day before yesterday:
my cousin had been murdered by partisans.
When we marched into Russia
there were no such things as partisans.
To stay loyal to the Führer . . .

DOCTOR (*to confuse*): Like you . . . loyal like you.

GERSTEIN (*slightly insecure*):
What? . . . yes, but I cannot tell him so:
racialism and imperialism are mutually exclusive.
I learnt that in the first form.
Either – or: never both at once.
Alexander married off his Macedonians
to the daughters of the conquered:
we exterminate the conquered.
Do *you* believe there is a future in that?

DOCTOR (*laughs, his hand already on the door knob*):
Believe? Who still believes in beliefs – or the future?
Don't look at me like that – I know
for you I am the embodiment 'of the principle of evil'.

GERSTEIN (*tries to fall in with the Doctor's frivolous tone*):
'Principle of evil'? Who said that?

DOCTOR: Otto Weininger. 'Evil is
at the root of despair, in order to give some direction to life.'

GERSTEIN (*laughing*): I must tell Eichmann
you read Viennese Jewish authors.

DOCTOR (*not without vanity*): Yes, and I incinerate them, too.
On Tuesday last I whistled Freud's sister up the chimney.
(*He laughs characteristically. He has left the room, and calls back from the hall.*)
Seven o'clock, then. I look forward to it . . .

GERSTEIN (*outside*): It's very nice of you, and we'll be able
to see a good bit of each other then, Doctor. Aufwiedersehen.

(*He comes slowly back into the room, leans against the door, breath-ing heavily, starts to go to see Jacobson and sees the glass container on the chair. He picks it up, but seems not to know what to do with it.*)

I couldn't bring flowers . . .

(*The bell rings again. Gerstein jumps with fright, and says, unable to calm himself:*)

What the hell does he want now?

(*He goes to open the door, but only gets there as the bell rings again. We hear him outside, saying:*)

Heil Hitler. Yes?

RICCARDO: Good morning, Herr Gerstein.

(*Gerstein has apparently let him in. We hear the flat door being shut, then steps in the hall. Riccardo enters the room in front of Gerstein and says with some embarrassment, in the face of Gerstein's marked reserve:*)

I see you were badly hit by the raid.

GERSTEIN (*coldly*): What brings you here? What is your name?

RICCARDO (*still more uncertain*): We met yesterday, Herr Gerstein, at the Nuncio's.

GERSTEIN (*interrupting him with asperity*):
Where? Where did you say?
I don't know you; I have never
seen you before. What brings you here?

RICCARDO (*spiritedly*): I told you yesterday at the Nuncio's
that I would come.
I would have liked to follow you straight away.
My name is Count Fontana, and I belong
to the State Secretariat of the Holy See.

GERSTEIN (*with undiminished caution, without looking directly at Riccardo*):
What do you wish to say to me?

RICCARDO: That the Vatican will help you;
you and the victims of Hitler.
I was ashamed, believe me,
to look the Nuncio in the face,
but his position
forced him to this neutrality.

GERSTEIN (*impersonally*): How am I still to believe the Vatican
will summon up any interest in the Jews?
Since the announcements from London

a good two months have elapsed –
without the Pope showing any signs of interest.
(*suddenly*)
Who did you just meet on the stairs ? –
Did you see an officer in a cape ?

RICCARDO :

Oh yes, I remember noticing him. Only in front of the entrance.
He was getting into his car.

GERSTEIN (*agitated*):

Good. Good, then he didn't see you on the stairs.
Do you know who it was you saw ?

RICCARDO : I had the feeling he was watching me.

GERSTEIN (*has to force himself to stay calm*): Oh, it's a large house.
You could be visiting any one of twenty families.
Let us come to the point, Count Fontana.
Doubtless, the Polish Government in exile
has also kept the Pope personally informed.
The Father General of the Jesuits in Rome
has for years been getting precise and exhaustive reports
from Polish agents –
for years . . .

RICCARDO (*embarrassed*):

A courier is taking a letter to my father today;
my father is one of the most important laymen in the Holy See.
I guarantee you, Herr Gerstein,
His Holiness will protest.
I have the honour to be personally
well acquainted with the Pope.

GERSTEIN (*almost cynically*): Careful with your guarantees;
they may make trouble for you.
Why did he not try to save old Lichtenberg,
the Prior of St Hedwig's ? They
threw him in jail, just because
he included the Jews in his prayers.
But your priests pray for the Führer as well –
how can the Pope just stand by and look on
when they are carted off for praying for the Jews ?
He does look on and has done so
since 1938.
Lichtenberg, whose sentence is now over, has proposed
to the Gestapo that he be allowed

to share the fate of the Jews in the Eastern provinces –
        had you heard?
RICCARDO: I have heard of Lichtenberg,
        Herr Gerstein – but please, you must
        understand that all these
        dreadful problems are new to me . . .
        but believe me,
        the Pope will help, the commandment
        of 'Love thy neighbour' . . .
GERSTEIN (*now sincere, his hand on Riccardo's shoulder*):
        I've become so frighteningly cautious
        as far as my hope in the Church is concerned.
        I myself belong to the Confessional Church;
        I am a friend of Pastor Niemöller;
        he's been nearly five years now in a camp . . .
        he said I was the saboteur incarnate
        and he understood very well
        why I wormed my way into the S.S. . . .
        One cannot fight the Nazis
        with pamphlets, as I used to.
RICCARDO: You mean you put that uniform on voluntarily?
GERSTEIN: Yes – I had to – but please sit down,
        if you can. . . . Here, please.
        (*He takes two chairs from the table, dusts them and they sit.
        Gerstein, however, soon gets up, as restless as a caged wolf.*)
        Yes, last year they discovered
        that I had been inside already, twice,
        for distributing Christian leaflets.
        The first time I went to prison, the second to a camp.
        I didn't tell them that when I
        entered the S.S. But a witch-hunt started,
        though on the very highest recommendation
        I was not touched. I had been forgiven.
        In 1940
        I stopped a typhus epidemic, in the barracks and prison camps.
        . . . That is my subject, medicine and engineering –
        that was what saved me. They think I'm off my head –
        in the eyes of that pack
        I am a mixture of technical genius
        and other-worldly idealism. Other-worldly –
        because Christian: they laugh about it

and leave me free to go to church in peace.
They also know I have many friends
in high Protestant circles. – All the same!
(*suddenly very restless, disconnectedly*)
Why, Count . . . what did you say your name was?

RICCARDO: Fontana . . .

GERSTEIN: Fontana – Count, why are you here?
We must have a story ready in case
one of my colleagues – splendid colleagues they are,
professors of murder –
should happen to call.
(*He ponders, then takes Riccardo by the arm.*)
Listen – you speak exceptionally good German.

RICCARDO: As a child I spent part of the time in Königsberg.
My late mother was German, Protestant.

GERSTEIN (*cold. Almost rude, but calm*):
Couldn't be better. You are an informer for the S.S.
Counter-Intelligence, Italian section.

RICCARDO (*gulps, sincerely offended, then coolly refusing*):
Well – that seems surely more than improbable.
I am a Jesuit father – do you think
anyone is really going to believe you?

GERSTEIN (*obscurely, perhaps with satisfaction at being able to say it*):
That is the most plausible explanation, Father.
You would not be the first priest
to turn informer for the executioners.
There's an informer in the Vatican, too.
Heydrich's closest co-worker told me
that he had been recruited into the Gestapo –
yes, by a Jesuit priest,
while he was studying in Bonn.
Himmler is a great admirer of your organization.
He founded the Order of the S.S.
on the rules of Loyola, and
he studied
pedantically, like everything he does,
a whole library on the Jesuits . . .

RICCARDO (*hurt*): Couldn't you find out which priest
is the S.S. agent in the Vatican?

GERSTEIN: Out of the question, as I don't belong to the Gestapo.
Anyway, they have no names there, only numbers.

(*suddenly uneasy again*)
However, all this will be quite pointless,
if *he* comes back, the man whom you just saw . . .

RICCARDO: The officer in the black cape?

GERSTEIN: Yes – I won't even try
to – humbug him, I could not.

RICCARDO: Who was that man, then?

GERSTEIN (*with nervous irritability*): Tcha. – Not a man, not a man.
You have seen the dark angel of Auschwitz.
He only comes to sound me out;
his ambition is to hand me to the hangman.
Don't let's talk about it, please. Now,
if the bell should ring –
go straight away into this room.
And don't say a word. Someone is there already.
(*superficially calmer*)
First I must explain – why do you
look like that? Are you so shocked to find
the game I play so underhand, is that it?
When playing poker with murderers,
one needs to cultivate the same expressions.

RICCARDO: But why, Herr Gerstein,
do you play with them at all?

GERSTEIN: Only the man at the helm can steer.
Dictatorships must be broken from within.
Let me state the facts. My visit to the Nuncio
and to the Bishop's legal advisers
was high treason . . .
(*grinning*)
That shocks you.

RICCARDO (*uncomprehending, reserved*):
How could I judge you? For you it must have been
a terrible decision; I mean – this treason.
You swore an oath to Hitler, did you not?

GERSTEIN: Father, I have to disappoint you.
It was no *sort* of decision,
no strain of conscience, nothing.
Hitler himself has written 'The laws of man are above
the laws of politics.' Therefore,
oath or no oath, a man who builds factories
which have no other purpose than that

61

of gassing human beings . . .
must be betrayed, *must*
be destroyed at any price, *any* price.
His murderer would only be his judge.

RICCARDO: But if one sets aside what Hitler
is doing to the Jews and to the Russian prisoners . . .

GERSTEIN (*furious*): One *may* not set it aside!
How can you, as a priest . . .

RICCARDO: I'm sorry . . . I did not mean it like that.
It is just that, what preoccupies me
as much as the terrible fate of the victims,
is how is it possible that this is done
by the same man, who is the last man in Europe,
and indeed with Europe, to follow
in the footsteps of Napoleon.
This man, who, at Kiev, won a battle,
the greatest in the history of the world –
six hundred thousand taken prisoner –
France overrun in six short weeks – Who can
deny this man the tribute of greatness?

GERSTEIN: Father, you are talking like the historians
of the future, who will perhaps dismiss
Hitler's victims in two sentences –
I cannot say *how* that appals,
revolts me . . .

RICCARDO: My father observes Hitler's victories with great
misgivings, too, of course – but recently
the Spanish Foreign Minister was with us,
having just come from Hitler, and he spent
a whole evening telling us about
what was happening in the Chancellory.
He was trying, by every possible device, to keep
his country out of this conflict – a patriot.
In short, he had no love for Herr Hitler.
But *how* he spoke of him!
Most impressive: a man who, with
the inviolability of a chosen being
followed his star, a Messiah –
and if he were to fail, then he would bring
the whole of Europe with him as he fell.
He has already achieved his own legend . . .

GERSTEIN (*unable to listen any more*):
    For the love of God, do not talk like that!
    There will be no myth attached to that name,
    believe me.
    (*uncertainly*)
    Guard against making a Lucifer out of
    this high-placed criminal, because – because
    foolish and indecisive contemporaries,
    ministers, politicians, generals and priests
    have given up all Europe for a while
    into the hands of this bandit chief.
    (*gradually more insistent, more convincing*)
    Let us not stray from the point: recall
    that every hour a thousand – please,
    just visualize it: every hour claims
    a thousand victims, fellow human beings
    cremated family by family after a horrifying death.
    Act yourself, go to Rome . . .
    if the Nuncio
    is still not to be convinced.

RICCARDO: Of course . . . But – don't misunderstand me –
    how shall I describe who you are,
    who is my informant?

GERSTEIN: I understand: a traitor is
    too suspect in the eyes of Rome to . . .

RICCARDO: I'm sorry, no, I didn't mean . . .

GERSTEIN: Please – I'm quite
    insensitive on that score, God knows.
    It is the traitors, and they alone,
    who are saving Germany's honour today.
    For Hitler is not Germany,
    he is only her despoiler – the judgement
    of history will acquit us.
    I will not survive my mission:
    a Christian in these times cannot survive
    if he is to be consistent.
    I don't mean Sunday Christians . . .
    beware of the assiduous churchgoer . . .
    I mean the Christians that Kirkegaard meant,
    the spies of God – I am
    a spy in the S.S.

but spies are hanged,
and that I know.

RICCARDO: No, please try to remain alive.
I will leave your name out of the conversation.

GERSTEIN: Don't protect me. But apart from me,
it will be better if you concentrate
on the reports from London and Warsaw.
There is no need to tell Rome anything new.
Stir up a protest against these murders;
the souls of their accessories are in danger, too.

RICCARDO: You may rely on me.
Now I must go, to endanger you no further.

GERSTEIN: No, please stay.
I still have something to ask you . . .

RICCARDO (*spiritedly*): I, too, Herr Gerstein, I, too,
am troubled by an unanswered question . . .

GERSTEIN: What is it . . .?

RICCARDO: How the German people,
the nation of Goethe, Mozart, Menzel . . .
how can the Germans have allowed themselves
to reach such depths of degradation?

GERSTEIN: We Germans are no worse
than other Europeans, Father.
As yet, the great majority, I know,
knows nothing definite about the murders . . .
Of course, many soldiers in the East
have seen the massacres; and the whole population
watches as Jews are driven from the cities
like cattle. But what can the willing do?
Who can judge a man for not wishing
to die for someone else?
Recently, the Jewish workers in
the Berlin factories were supposed
to be taken to Auschwitz. The police
did not act at once, but warned the firms
beforehand. Result:
four thousand Jews were able to disappear.
They were hidden by the Berliners, fed –
four thousand: and each Berliner
that helped was risking his life,
and the life of his entire family.

64

You see, not every German has forgotten
his obligations to the name of Germany.
And there are monsters everywhere: in Holland
the civil police helped most assiduously
to arrest the Jews; in France they helped,
not so assiduously, but still they helped.
In Hungary, as well, but mostly in the Ukraine . . .
The Ukrainians shoot their Jews themselves.
When recently in Majdanek
seventeen thousand Jews were shot, to celebrate
the day many Poles drank themselves
insensible. It is rarely that a Jew
can hide in Poland, outside the towns:
his good neighbours hand him over to the German hangmen –
for money . . . Let us say no more. The Germans
are most to blame, it was their Führer's programme:
but as for the country itself,
the other countries are not much better.

RICCARDO: I am appalled, Herr Gerstein . . . nevertheless,
I must, as an Italian and a priest,
argue with you: in Rome (*with pride, almost pathos*) that
would be impossible. From the Holy Father
down to the chestnut-seller in the piazza
the whole *nation* would rise against the terror
if Jewish citizens
were arrested, particularly
by the police of another country.

GERSTEIN: How moving, Father, how *enviable*
to be so sure of one's own countrymen.
I believe you . . . All the more bitter
(*cynically now*)
that the attitude of the Church
should be so questionable: Dr Edith Stein,
the most famous nun in Europe, was recently
gassed in Auschwitz, I believe. She was converted
years ago, a leading Catholic writer.
I ask you: how on earth could the Gestapo
learn that this *one* nun had Jewish blood?
She was dragged from her convent
in Holland . . . I cannot understand
how it is impossible to hide a nun

in a cloister of her own order. Poor woman,
she probably did not understand herself.

RICCARDO: Perhaps the invasion happened too suddenly.

GERSTEIN (*sarcastic*): You can see what a Jew can expect
when he goes over to Christianity, can't you?
Over a dozen people in orders
have been handed over by the convents in Holland.

RICCARDO: But under duress! Bishops
and workers in Holland have protested.
That only made the situation worse.

GERSTEIN (*irritated, violent*):
Made it worse? – you weren't consistent.
Rome left the bishops in the lurch!
I am not reproaching the *Dutch* at all.
But when they are deporting monks and nuns,
how can Rome keep silent, when it means
the world will never find out what is happening?
(*silence*)
The question which torments me every hour
is one that only a priest can answer.
Here are the facts: I must, by the end
of next month,
assemble, in a hangar, here in Berlin,
for some secret purpose,
over two tons of poison gas,
Cyclon B, the same as that with which
the Jews are murdered.
I do not know what they intend to do with it;
I don't believe they yet know themselves;
it is just that the poison must be ready to hand.
Possibly, they want to dispose at their convenience
of foreign labour or prisoners:
two tons, enough to kill two million people.
(*Pause. Riccardo is speechless.*)
Now I am faced with this question, Father:
should I let the firms
send the bills in my name
to this address?

RICCARDO: Not on any account! But why?

GERSTEIN: Only in that way will there be a chance
to supervise the poison after delivery.

Then, fairly soon perhaps –
perhaps I can arrange for its disappearance . . .
or its use as a disinfectant.
Part of the consignment I can say has decomposed.
I have already arranged for the poison *not* to be stored
in Berlin, –
because of the air-raids.

RICCARDO: Bills for *this* poison in your name.
Is there no other possibility then . . .?

GERSTEIN: Of course, I could simply escape to Sweden . . .
I have business in Helsinki soon . . .
But what becomes of the poison in the hands
of a criminal lunatic?

RICCARDO: That does not bear thinking of, I see.
What does your conscience tell you, then, Herr Gerstein?

GERSTEIN: Conscience – who can rely on that?
Conscience or God:
at no time does man rage so obscenely,
as when he appeals to God – or an idea:
the conscience is a highly dubious seat
of judgement. I am sure that Hitler
is following the call of his conscience, too.
No, I seek an answer outside myself.
We Protestants are too much turned in
upon ourselves; one cannot stand the strain
perpetually. We all have grounds for doubt –
answer me with the objectivity
of a priest: *must* I do this?

RICCARDO (*after a short pause*):
You are lending your name to horrible events . . .

GERSTEIN(*frightened, and therefore angry*):
My name . . . what is a name?
Do you think I am worried for my name?
Only the lukewarm,
who are no better than the murderers,
only they find it easy to come through
times like these with their good name
and hands as clean –
forgive me, Count –
as the Pope's vestments.

RICCARDO (*with an effort to hide the fact that he feels insulted*):

You asked me, Herr Gerstein –
then escape to England and
broadcast from London. You, Sturmführer Gerstein,
of the S.S. Health Department, ex-officio
and on oath, with figures, dates, receipts for poison and
all the details,
report exactly what is happening here.
(*enthusiastically naïve*)
You must say openly who you are,
what you have done, what prevented . . .
and what you have not been able to prevent.

GERSTEIN (*passionately*):
Good God – have you *any* idea what you are asking?
I would do anything . . . but this
I can't do. I am not an Abraham,
to sacrifice my own son.
One word from me over the B.B.C.
and my family in Germany would be wiped out.

RICCARDO: I'm sorry. I didn't know.

GERSTEIN (*calmer*): They would not only kill my wife,
my children – even my brothers,
they would torture to death in the camp.

RICCARDO: Forgive me . . .

GERSTEIN (*becoming colder*):
In any case, it should not be necessary to do it,
Father – it should not be necessary!
The British radio reported some time ago
what was happening in Poland. People already know,
at least every thinking man must have some idea;
and Thomas Mann recently repeated these
figures. Did he not also report
that Jews from Paris and Holland were being gassed?
I could only repeat all this, with details
that no one would believe.
Who am I? No one knows *me*.
I would be a dubious deserter, nothing more.
Why does not *the one* man speak
who is the only man in Europe today
still free from the suspicion of propaganda:
the Pope . . .
(*laughs hysterically*)

68

Oh God – God in Heaven. I am arguing
with him like a student. Did God
I wonder, only become a Christian
so that, like His Representative,
He could placate his conscience for not feeling
responsible for the Jews?

RICCARDO (*with understanding, but firmly*):
  Don't say that, Herr Gerstein . . .
  Do not lose faith in God as well, not now . . .

GERSTEIN: He must excuse me, after the education
  I have received at His hands in Poland . . .
  and since the Nuncio here has sent me packing . . .

RICCARDO (*with certainty, seriously*):
  The Vatican will act – God knows
  it will happen. I promise you.

GERSTEIN (*not reassured, warily*): How can I believe you?
  How can I have any confidence in you?

RICCARDO (*disarmed*): Herr Gerstein, please, did I deserve that?

GERSTEIN: I'm sorry . . . I saw in you
  only the representative of your organization.
  I did not have any doubts about
  you personally. My frankness has proved that . . .
  (*without pausing*)
  Would you put at my disposal immediately
  your cassock and your passport?

RICCARDO (*shocked*): What do you want with them? My passport?
  My cassock? I don't understand . . .

GERSTEIN (*obscurely*): A proof of your goodwill.

RICCARDO (*with growing distaste, then anger*):
  A proof . . . no, Herr Gerstein,
  I swore at my consecration never
  to lay aside my habit . . . What do you want?

GERSTEIN: I am no longer mistrustful . . . so,
  the truth: your passport and your cassock
  are to help a Jew over the Brenner Pass.
  As a diplomat, you can easily get
  a new passport from Rome.

RICCARDO (*very hesitantly, unwilling*):
  I see. – Yes. – Must it be right away?

GERSTEIN (*opening the door to the next room*): Herr Jacobson.
JACOBSON: Yes, Herr Gerstein?

(*He comes quickly in view, draws back instinctively, collects himself and comes into the room.*)
Good morning.

RICCARDO: Good morning.

GERSTEIN (*very deftly and quickly*): Count Fontana – Herr Jacobson.
Gentlemen, let's not beat about the bush:
black hair and approximately similar ages
are scanty prerequisites for changing passports;
on the other hand, Herr Jacobson – a cassock
and a diplomatic passport of the Throne of St Peter
is not an offer that I can repeat:
do you want to try to get over the Brenner with them?

JACOBSON (*not able to grasp things so quickly*):
What – do I understand there might be a chance here . . .
(*then eagerly to Riccardo*)
are you offering me safety?

RICCARDO (*at pains not to let his reluctance be noticed*):
Oh yes, of course – yes. When would you like . . .?

GERSTEIN (*rapidly*): This evening, I suggest . . . if we can
get a sleeper, Herr Jacobson.
I can get the ticket when I drop the Count
somewhere near the Nuncio's in my car.
You had better not go through the town
without a passport dressed as Herr Jacobson . . .
(*smiling*)
I was wondering, Jacobson, if you could
do without your glasses altogether –
when they check you at the frontier anyway. I hope
the collar fits. Could we get on with it . . .
Jacobson, what's the matter? . . . Man,
this is the end of your imprisonment.
(*Jacobson has sat down on a chair, done in. He produces a hand-kerchief, smiles, polishes his glasses . . . embarrassed.*)

JACOBSON (*halting*): It was just the surprise. I'm sorry.
Just now in there, in the room, when I
heard you talking out here . . . and then
last night's excitement . . . the raid:
I thought, if the house catches fire now
and the people come to put it out
and find me in your house . . . an officer of the S.S. . . .
you would be . . . they would lynch you . . .

GERSTEIN: But that is over now, Herr Jacobson.

JACOBSON: Yes . . . over. It's quite easy to say now.
Five minutes ago I still thought
that I would have to leave my hiding-place
when the next air-raid came,
so as not . . . you . . .

GERSTEIN (*to Riccardo*):
You see, he has claustrophobia already. It's high time . . .

JACOBSON: How am I going to thank you . . . you, too . . .
(*to Riccardo*)
now you are the one I am bringing into danger, you know that.

RICCARDO (*his mood completely changed . . . with sincerity*):
I thank God I can help – little enough.
I live at the Nuncio's and
Herr Hitler himself cannot touch me there.
You will send me a card from Rome, won't you?

GERSTEIN (*friendly but worried, looking at his watch*):
Jacobson will have to know something about your father, Count,
about his and your positions in the Vatican. It's important
that you're able to talk your way through the German frontier
guards;
the rest is risk. Change your clothes.
(*He gestures to the door of the next room.*)

JACOBSON (*who has pulled himself together*):
Is it essential . . . to have a sleeper?

GERSTEIN (*smiling, impatient*):
If possible – you are a diplomat, after all.

RICCARDO: Also, I think it will only be
inspected once, and very politely, at that.

JACOBSON: All right. Only I won't be able to leave
before tomorrow evening, in that case, Herr Gerstein.
I must go home tonight when it gets dark,
to say good-bye to my parents.
(*almost happily, not noticing Gerstein's uneasiness, with decision*)
Once in Rome I will get things moving
to get the pair of them into
the safe keeping of a neutral country.
Perhaps . . . their departure . . .

GERSTEIN (*with some conviction*):
Don't endanger your parents now . . . you must travel today.
I'll bring you to the station in the car.

(*less sure of himself*)
Do not go home first.

JACOBSON (*mistrustful, alienated*): Can't I say good-bye?
Herr Gerstein, you are not usually so timid –
(*looking at him aghast*)
Or – tell me . . . have they: please, the truth!
Have they already taken my parents?
Please, you must tell me now . . .

GERSTEIN (*quietly*): Yes . . . I could not get rid of
your Tuesday's letter . . .
(*He takes the letter out of his jacket, relieved to be able to report
something factual. He speaks hastily but haltingly.*)
But I could not tell you either, the door is sealed.
I almost didn't notice it and nearly
put the letter through the slot as usual.
The people in the shop across the road
saw me leave. They wanted
to tell me something. The woman beckoned
through the shop window . . .

JACOBSON (*fighting with his tears*):
Frau Schultze; yes, she was always good.
Otherwise my parents would have died of hunger already.
Did she . . . had she spoken with my parents?

GERSTEIN (*at first unable to reply, then . . .*):
I made myself scarce.
I was suddenly afraid.
I looked away.
I had to force myself to walk slowly.
(*grips Jacobson by the arm, beside himself*)
I'm sorry . . . I . . . I . . . thought, though,
I could go to the woman in the shop again
in a day or two, and ask what . . .
I'll go straight away after . . .
(*Jacobson turns the letter over and over in his hands.*)

RICCARDO (*to break the silence*):
Shall I try to discover where they have
been taken to? The Nuncio will find out.

JACOBSON: Don't bother. They all go to Auschwitz now.
Tuesday . . . three days . . . Herr Gerstein, do you think
it was on Tuesday, or . . . did they get them earlier?
How long does the train take? – Oh, questions.

(*to Riccardo, with an extreme effort to control his voice*)
There is nothing more to ask. They –
it's true, Gerstein – they will be . . . gassed at once.

GERSTEIN: – Not always, no.
Your father, as a First War veteran,
is sure to be taken to Theresienstadt . . .

JACOBSON (*changed, controlled*):
Germany – your gratitude! – Gerstein,
you have saved my life. But you do not need
to lie to me – I – understand me,
I – I do not *want* comfort now. I've known
quite well that it would have to come – a long
time now.
(*violent, tortured, but strongly*)
It will not kill me – I will not
do the murderers *that* favour. I will . . . now . . .
now I must – get out of here . . . out . . . out of here . . .
(*He crumples the letter, then tears it twice. His movements are con-
vulsively decisive, he is completely altered, unnaturally controlled
. . . and he speaks now with a quite Biblical hardness, while his
inoffensive, pale, librarian's face takes on a trait of ferocity.*)
Gerstein, consider once again
whether you wish to help me to escape,
for now – since this last news –
I am no longer German. Now,
whether you understand it or you don't,
all Germany, all Germans are my enemy.
This is no longer flight . . . I wish to go
only in order to return as an avenger. An avenger.
First to Italy – then to England.
(*wildly, frighteningly*)
No one shall say we Jews allowed ourselves
to be driven like cattle to the canning factories.
I will come back – a murderer myself . . .
as a bomber pilot. Murder for murder.
Incendiary for gas, fire for fire.
Gerstein, I *warn* you, that is the thanks you get
for hiding me. I tell you honestly,
it is an enemy you are helping to escape.
Now drive me as I stand into the street
. . . for I shall . . . shall never acquit

the Germans, every German, of the fact
that my parents – both of them good Germans –
were murdered here.
(*He has laid the scraps of the letter in a rubbish bin. Gerstein,
without a word, fishes them out and with his cigarette lighter burns
them one by one, letting them fall burning back into the bucket.*)

RICCARDO (*to Jacobson, objectively but sincerely*):
Do not harden your heart. You are oversimplifying.
(*he points to Gerstein*)
How many Germans are helping their brothers?
Do you wish to bomb their children?
Hate is never the final word.

JACOBSON (*putting him off, factually*):
Hate holds a man up. I must not fall now.

GERSTEIN (*hoarsely, gloomily, without looking at Jacobson*):
Every man to his post.
We shall neither of us survive the war.
Go and change. It is time . . .
(*He takes the two buckets and carries them into the hall. When he
comes back Jacobson is holding out his passport to Riccardo, on the
inner pages of which can be seen a large 'J' overprinted, and a
yellow star . . . a piece of material the size of the pa m of a hand.*)

JACOBSON (*smiling*): You're making a bad exchange, Father.
You are giving me a cassock and I –
here – this – this is all I –
I have no more to offer,
only the brand of an outlaw.
(*All three are silent. Riccardo holds the yellow star in his hands and
examines it. He looks at the star, then at Gerstein, at Jacobson. He
shakes his head and asks as he holds the star for a moment against
his cassock, over his heart, and the curtain rapidly descends :*)

RICCARDO: Here?

Curtain

Act Two · The Bells of St Peter's

Rome. 2 February 1943.
Palazzo Fontana on the Monte Gianicolo. A large drawing-room.
Beneath a conventional painting of the Madonna there is a narrow
Renaissance prie-dieu; family portraits, women of various periods,
soldiers, a cardinal. In the foreground, surrounded with flowers, a large
photograph of a middle-aged woman : Riccardo's recently dead mother.
Almost the whole width of the back of the stage is taken up by windows
reaching down to the floor, and a french window : we can see a garden
falling away steeply, with pines and cypresses, and beyond its walls,
chalk-grey, huge, and sharply silhouetted against the cold blue sky, the
dome of St Peter's.
The french windows are open. The bells of St Peter's are ringing loudly.
Count Fontana, 60 years of age, with rimless glasses and a stiff mou-
stache, belongs, along with other exclusive European aristocrats such as
Hitler's Vice-Chancellor, Herr von Papen, to the number of Papal
Chamberlains 'di spada e cappa', and it is his right and honour to be
allowed, on solemn occasions, to stand about in Spanish court dress in
the immediate vicinity of His Holiness.
As one of the foremost laymen in the service of the Holy See, Fontana
feels himself obliged to wear this costume, since it is certainly one of the
many picturesque trappings, and characteristic anachronisms that go to
make up the outward face of the Vatican. Fontana is a manager. He is
over-worked, clever, imaginative, capable of kindness and of suffering,
and even fairly perspicacious about the social demands of the twentieth
century. His discomfort at being at this moment obliged to be photo-
graphed in the mournful splendour of the court dress of Henry II, is
genuine. He is a sober, self-possessed finance expert, who knows very
well that he has been of great service to the Curia, and for this reason
has no wish to be dressed in any way like the other chamberlains, who
often are only allowed to wear their buckled shoes, silk stockings, knee
breeches, ruffs, balloon sleeves, lace cuffs, birettas, swords and orders
because they are members of erstwhile important families. The blood

of the Fontanas is not yet exhausted. Like the Pacellis, they were only ennobled at the end of the nineteenth century, and still have a capacity for serious work. They are therefore not taken seriously in their circle.

Nevertheless, His Majesty Victor Emmanuel III, on the recommendation of His Holiness Pius XI, who had early bestowed upon the 'ideal Catholic employer' the Order of Knighthood of the Holy Sepulchre, had been obliged to raise Fontana in 1939 to the condition of hereditary count.

As the curtain rises an old-fashioned photographer with a little beard and a velvet jacket, half hidden under his black cloth, is setting up his troublesome apparatus at the open french windows. Then he steps on to the veranda, where his subject will later be positioned, and looks 'significantly' into the camera. While he is standing there, making efforts to look like Garibaldi, he is surprised by the elderly servant who enters noiselessly and looks at him contemptuously, shaking his head, until the photographer busies himself once more with his apparatus.

SERVANT (*watering the flowers*): Don't keep His Lordship too long,
    or he will kick you out right away.
    He doesn't know yet that the young master
    has come home from Germany.
    He won't have any time for you,
    I can tell you straight.

PHOTOGRAPHER (*ridiculously aggressive, pathetic*):
    Who can stop me wishing my old patron happiness
    on his investiture in the Order of Christ?
    Apart from that – his portrait will be
    on the front page! Apart from that . . .

SERVANT: All right, but I'm going to close the door now.
    I'm not supposed to be heating the garden, and this noise . . .
    (*He closes the french windows. The noise becomes appreciably fainter.*)

PHOTOGRAPHER: You'll have to open the doors again right away.
    The Count must be photographed in the open
    so that the dome of St Peter's is
    right behind him.

SERVANT: I don't have to do anything of the kind . . . Here he comes.
    (*He leaves quickly. The photographer wipes his moustache and mouth while we hear steps offstage. He fingers his tie nervously and retires behind his apparatus, where he takes up a 'position'.*)

76

FONTANA (*nervous, happy, enters quickly*):
 Splendid, what a surprise. When did he
 arrive, Vittorio? Leave him to sleep.

SERVANT (*returning*): Just an hour ago, Your Lordship. But I was
 to wake him the moment Your Lordship came home.
 He is so happy too, the young Master,
 he won't have been able to sleep a wink.

FONTANA (*who has discovered the photographer, distractedly*):
 Yes, all right then, tell him I'm here.
 (*The servant goes out.*)
 (*to the photographer*)
 Do we have to? Good morning.
 Surely you have enough pictures of me already?

PHOTOGRAPHER: But none yet showing Your Lordship
 with the Order of Christ. Allow me, Your Lordship,
 to offer my most respectful congratulations.
 The front page tomorrow must have . . . definitely . . .

FONTANA (*has lit a cigarette. Not unfriendly*):
 Well then . . . where? Here? Well?

PHOTOGRAPHER (*quickly opens the french windows. The bells are very
 loud again*):
 Here, if I may suggest, here on the threshold,
 so that Your Lordship will get
 the dome right behind him.
 (*he stands around helplessly*)

FONTANA: Haven't you got everything ready?
 What are we waiting for?

PHOTOGRAPHER:
 Allow me, Your Lordship, if I may make so bold . . .
 whether the cigarette and the court dress . . .

FONTANA: What . . . do you want my hands
 in the picture, too? The whole paraphernalia?
 I thought just a head and shoulders.
 (*he puts the cigarette down*)
 All right, all right. As long as you're quick about it.

PHOTOGRAPHER: Perhaps the hand on the sword and the head
 a little higher and a little to the left.
 (*he presses the rubber ball*)
 My deepest thanks . . . perhaps just one more,
 at the desk, which will show Your Lordship
 for posterity, hard at work . . .

FONTANA (*making an effort not to laugh*):
> So, handed down to posterity. Posterity
> is capable of believing that I
> opened letters in this costume, with my sword?
> (*He points to the servant, who has come in again, takes his cigarette and says :*)
> Here, go on, take a picture of
> Signor Vittorio. He'll be seventy soon, and then
> he can give the picture to his wife. – Come on now!

SERVANT: But Your Lordship, I beg you, that is not proper.
> (*crossly to the photographer, as he shuts the doors*)
> Heating the garden. Keep the door shut.

FONTANA: Come along, Vittorio. Your wife will be very pleased.
> Stand there . . . don't make such a face. –
> My boy, what a surprise.
> (*Riccardo enters and embraces his father, who kisses him.*)

RICCARDO: Father, congratulations – and how grand!
> (*nervously*)
> Don't those bells ever stop?

FONTANA: How good not to be alone any more.
> How long can you stay?

RICCARDO (*now like his father, distracted by the scene in the background with the photographer and the servant*):
> That's very pretty, Vittorio.

SERVANT: It's a waste of money. And my teeth
> are at the menders . . .

PHOTOGRAPHER: One, two, three . . . just one picture
> of Signor Riccardo, Count Fontana. If I may suggest . . .

RICCARDO (*friendly*):
> Thank you, but I haven't shaved properly . . .
> Some other time.

FONTANA: Thank you, thank you. Put your things away now –

PHOTOGRAPHER (*while the servant is piling up his things*):
> The thanks are all on my side, Your Lordship.

FONTANA: My boy, are you unwell? You look very
> strained; yes, you do. We shall have to look after you.

RICCARDO: I couldn't get a wink in the sleeper.
> I'm just tired after the journey, Father.
> I'm quite all right in myself . . .
> (*nervous, irritable*)
> Why do they go on ringing?

FONTANA: Because this morning the Pope consecrated
    the world to the Immaculate Heart of the Virgin:
    very tiring ceremony. Then, on top of that,
    my audience . . . and there I was with an order.
    I had no idea.
RICCARDO: Mother would have been pleased . . . how we . . .
    miss her here at home, and everywhere.
    (*They both look at the photograph.*)
PHOTOGRAPHER (*packed up*):
    My most sincere thanks to Your Lordship,
    Your Lordship, good morning, good morning . . .
FONTANA: Thank you, too. Good-bye.
RICCARDO: Good-bye.
    (*Exit photographer.*)
SERVANT: God will reward you, Your Lordship.
FONTANA: Don't say anything to your wife.
    (*Exit servant.*)
    (*mixing a drink, sceptical, ironic*)
    Yes, my boy, by the end of the war
    we all quite seriously expect
    the dogma of the Assumption of the Virgin.
    In that way every history of the Popes
    will have to devote an important chapter to him.
RICCARDO (*sourly amused. He takes the glass from his father*):
    The things you think about in Rome . . .
    an example: poverty – in practical terms, that means
    the number of whores increases in the provinces
    with the number of the churches . . . Naples, Sicily . . .
    centres of vice on the Vatican's front doorstep . . . and
    instead of helping, we discuss how often
    a married couple should sleep together and if a widow
    may marry again.
    And now comes the dogma of the Virgin –
    has he really
    nothing better to do?
FONTANA: My boy, don't be so aggressive! An hour ago
    the Pope said to me, and he nearly always
    asks after you, that you could
    gain experience in Berlin today
    as at no other Nuncio's . . .
    have you more bad news from the Nuncio?

RICCARDO: None at all. I left without commission.
I could not stand any more. – You have known
(*with reproach*)
for months, the Jews of all Europe
are being systematically wiped out.
Every day – please, father, imagine,
every day, six thousand . . .

FONTANA: I read that, too . . . but that
must be appallingly exaggerated.

RICCARDO: What if it is?
(*desperately*)
I gave my word
the Pope would protest –
in an outcry that would excite
the pity of the whole world to action.

FONTANA (*agitated*): You had no *right* to do that.
What have you presumed to do?

RICCARDO: Presumption you call it? – Yes,
should I have presumed
that he would keep silence about it?
The children of a whole people in Europe
from Narvik to the Don, from Crete to
the Pyrenees are only born
today to be murdered in Poland.
Hitler is systematically reducing
Life itself ad absurdum.
Just read the terrible details that came out
of Poland and Rumania a fortnight ago.
How are we ever to excuse our silence?
and these bells!
(*He almost shouts it, putting his hands to his ears.*)
They ring and ring as if the world were paradise.
What stupidity, to consecrate *this world*
to the heart of the Mother of God. Is not the Pope,
who has five hundred million Catholics in his hands –
twenty per cent of them subjects of Hitler –
is not he *also* responsible
for the moral level of the world? How can he have the gall . . .

FONTANA (*loud, defensive*):
Riccardo, I forbid you to speak in this way.
Is this your thanks for the Pope's

    constant . . . constant preferment of you?

RICCARDO:

    Father, please. What has this to do with our private affairs?

FONTANA (*warningly*):

    You are very ambitious. Lucifer, the beloved
    of God, fell also by ambition.

RICCARDO (*sad, smiling*): Not ambition, disappointment
    makes me an adversary. Father,
    (*as intensely as possible, imploringly*)
    the greatest manhunt in the history of the world.
    Creation itself, shipwrecked. Faith
    locked in struggle with new ideologies,
    with the findings of science. Human wreckage
    on every land and ocean, human sacrifice
    on every front, in the fire, beneath the gallows,
    in the gas – and God's ambassador
    thinks to win without venturing? If God
    had destined that, in this hour,
    without a parallel in history,
    he too should founder,
    would not that tally now with what has happened?
    Has no one in the Vatican an eye
    for this? Here people cling
    to the hope that *everything* is
    predestination. But the greatest pyres
    that have ever been raised
    are thought the caprice of a transient
    dictator. Let us finally confess:
    these flames mean ordeal by fire for us as well.
    Who will ever again respect
    us as a court of morality
    if we today so lamentably defect?
    (*Both are silent, fought out. One can still hear the great bell of St
    Peter's ringing quietly. Fontana attempts painfully to control his
    agitation, and throwing aside his ludicrous sword, lights two
    cigarettes, gives one to Riccardo and says:*)

FONTANA (*reasonably*): Let us be realistic. I ask you
    as a member of the secretariat:
    how can the Pope
    force Hitler not to deport the Jews
    without revising his policy of neutrality?

RICCARDO: By exploiting the fact
  that Hitler fears his influence.
  It is not from piety that Hitler
  has forbidden all measures
  against the Church for the duration of his war.

FONTANA: That can change overnight. How many
  priests has he killed already?

RICCARDO (*with great passion*): Exactly! – and still Rome does not
  break off her friendship. Why?
  Because Rome does not feel herself attacked?
  That is the case: the Pope
  turns a blind eye, while there in Germany
  brother kills brother. The priests who
  sacrifice themselves there, do not act on orders
  from the Vatican – they act rather
  against its principle of non-intervention.
  Their deaths cannot be reckoned as atonement
  for the guilt of Rome
  since Rome abandons them.
  As long as Rome allows her priests to pray
  for Hitler . . . still to pray
  for this man – as long as . . .

FONTANA: Please, keep to the point: why do you ignore
  the protest of the Bishop of Münster?

RICCARDO: Oh, Father, Galen's example proves my point!
  He protested in the middle of Germany
  in the summer of '41, against the murderers –
  Hitler's star stood at its zenith, and look:
  he was allowed complete freedom of speech.
  Not for one moment was he arrested;
  and the result of his protest was that the sick
  were *no longer* liquidated.
  It needed just one bishop to stand up –
  and Hitler drew back at once.
  Why? – because he feared the Pope,
  the Pope who did not even
  support Galen's protest.
  Father, the Pope is the only man left whom Hitler fears.
  I met Herr von Hassel in Potzdam, he sends his regards;
  almost his first question was, why did Rome
  let Galen fight alone?

82

And my question, why did Galen
not intervene for the Jews as well?
Because the insane had been *baptized*?
A terrible question, Father,
let us admit it.

FONTANA: Riccardo – do not judge.
Do you dare to reproach a bishop
because he has set his life in hazard
more for the Christians than for the Jews? Do you know,
Riccardo, what it means, to set
one's life in hazard? *I* found out during the war.

RICCARDO: I admire Galen, I respect him.
Only, Father, we in Rome, in the Vatican,
unassailable, we must not
be satisfied with Galen's intercession
while in Poland . . .

FONTANA (*countering*): My boy, I find your arrogance surprising:
the Pope, in daily conference
with the world, with God – *knows* what he is doing.
He knows the reasons why he *must* be silent;
he will not be silent for *ever*.
Hitler's fortune is on the turn. Time
is on England's side. The moment
raison d'état allows the Pope
to protest against Hitler, without endangering the Church . . .

RICCARDO: Then every Jew in Poland
and Germany and France and Holland
will be dead. Once and for all, understand
it is a question of days. I gave my word,
I guaranteed this officer . . .

FONTANA (*beside himself*): And why did you do that?

RICCARDO (*breaking out, losing all control*):
Because . . . because I was not so cynical
as to go on talking
of raison d'état when I heard these things.

FONTANA: How you simplify – dear God,
can you believe the Pope
can see without pain
the hunger and suffering of a single person?
His heart is with the victims.

RICCARDO: And his voice? Where is his voice?

His heart, Father – is quite uninteresting.
Himmler, Hitler's Chief of Police, I am assured,
cannot bear the sight of his victims either.
It is all done through offices; the Pope does not see the victims;
Hitler does not see them . . .

FONTANA (*approaches Riccardo, threatening*):
Please, I must end this conversation at once.
If you mention Pius XII and Hitler
in the same breath . . .

RICCARDO (*contemptuously*): Confederates must expect that, Father –
aren't they negotiating with each other?
Pius XI would have
broken the Concordat long ago.

FONTANA: It is not your business to decide that . . .

RICCARDO (*after a pause, quietly, almost spitefully*):
Father? – do you think the Pope –
are you quite *sure* that the Pope
is involved in this conflict at all?
Raison d'état? – Love thy neighbour?

FONTANA: How do you mean, Riccardo?

RICCARDO (*forced to control himself*):
I mean, he does, after all, hold himself very aloof
from the fortunes of the world, of mankind. For forty years
he has been purely a diplomat, a lawyer. He was never –
or only for two years, and during the last century at that –
a keeper of souls, a priest among men.
He has never vouchsafed one word to any of the
Swiss Guards before his door.
Neither in his garden nor at his table can he
bear the face of a fellow creature . . . his gardener
is *ordered* always to turn his back on him;
Father . . . does he *love* anything whatever
outside his dictionaries and his cult of the Madonna?
(*suddenly full of hate, with flashing Roman mockery*)
I can just see him, cleaning his pen-holder with
that absolute precision – and this
is made a ritual as well . . . and I ask myself . . .
or, rather, I no *longer* ask myself, whether he has ever
in a single one of Hitler's victims
been able to see his brother in his own image.

FONTANA: Riccardo, please, that is unfair;

it's tub-thumping. However detached,
he still makes every effort to help and understand,
even if he is so self-centred that the victims . . .

RICCARDO (*interrupts quickly*): The victims . . . do you really
believe he sees them?
The world press,
the embassies, the spies – they all
bring dreadful details. Do you believe
that he studies more than statistics,
abstract figures,
seven hundred thousand dead – hunger,
gassings, deportations . . .
Or that he is involved,
that he has, even once,
turned his gaze inward – and looked?
The deportation train from Paris,
three hundred suicides already, before the journey started.
Children under five torn from their parents. . . .
And then Konin, near Warsaw:
eleven thousand Poles in travelling gas chambers,
their screams, prayers . . . and the laughter of
the S.S. guards. Eleven thousand . . . but imagine,
you, me . . . it could have been.

FONTANA: Riccardo, please – I know, you are upsetting yourself . . .

RICCARDO (*in the tone of an ultimatum*):
My question! Father, please answer this
question: the Pope – does he envisage
things like *that*?

FONTANA (*uncertain*):
Certainly, of course; but what follows from that?
He *still* cannot be prompted by his feelings.

RICCARDO (*furious*): Father! what you are saying there
cannot be – you just cannot say it.
Don't you understand here – you, Father,
you *must* understand. . . .
(*The bells stop. It becomes quite quiet. A silence. Then Riccardo
speaks, highly excited, yet stressing every word, very quietly at
first, then building up.*)
A Representative of God who has
such things before his eyes and still maintains
for reason of state a silence,

who wastes one day in thought,
delays one hour
to raise the voice of his suffering to a curse,
which the last man on earth
will hear and tremble at,
such a Pope is a criminal.

(*Riccardo sinks into a chair, wracked with sobs. Fontana goes to him with some hesitation. His anger, which was near to speechlessness, is mitigated at the sight of his 'prodigal' son.*)

FONTANA: You see what this leads to when you talk
like that. My boy, how can you . . .

(*The old servant comes in quickly but quietly with a card on a tray.*)

SERVANT: At last, Signor Conte, the . . .

FONTANA (*shouting. More uncontrolled than one would have believed possible*):
Leave us in peace.

(*While the servant, terrified, makes his way to the door, Fontana manages at least to say :*)

Vittorio, not now; I beg your pardon,
not to anybody . . .

(*Exit servant. Fontana, with powerful quietness, after a long look at Riccardo :*)

Your monstrous insult to the Pope
and also to all those in his service . . .

RICCARDO (*still confused*): My guilt – I am
guilty, too . . . gives me the right . . .

FONTANA: You are not guilty.

RICCARDO: Yes, guilty as any onlooker –
and as a priest . . .

FONTANA: Self-abasement can be pride as well.
You must *obey*;
you are much too – too insignificant
to bear this guilt . . . can you not grasp,
however hard you make it for yourself,
your view is superficial,
one-sidedly humane, compassionate and short-sighted.
In that way, you can *never* grasp
the point of this affliction.

RICCARDO: The *point*? . . . I would have to take on
the disposition of a ravening wolf
to find a *point* in all this.

(*jumping up*)
Am I, with the celebrated glass eye
of understanding . . . to drag in remote Hegelian arguments
to extenuate murder?

FONTANA: No sacrifice is wasted, even if history
does not record it. God will do so.
How can you doubt that, if only as a priest?
The Pope lives in this assurance, too.
He can only act upheld by this belief,
and in this way he can also avoid
blindly following the dictates of his heart;
for he *may not* endanger the Throne of St Peter.
(*after a pause*)
And do not forget one thing, Riccardo:
whatever Hitler is doing to the Jews,
he and he alone possesses the power
to deliver Europe from the Russians.

RICCARDO (*somewhat wildly*):
A murderer is no deliverer! . . .
This talk about the West, about Christianity.
We can all go to hell
if a mass-murderer
can be accepted by the Pope as a crusader.
The Russians have been defeated for a long time;
Hitler stands on the banks of the Volga.

FONTANA (*decisively*): The history of the world is not yet over,
the occupation of Russia not yet a victory.
The Pope knows that his intervention
would either be without effect or bring
the Church in Germany into the gravest danger.

RICCARDO (*violently*): He *does* not know, he *cannot* know.
Galen's success proves that a protest
from the Pope *could* bring Hitler
properly to heel for the first time.
He might well continue to abuse the Jews,
as slave labour for industry – but murder?
That is highly questionable. And setting aside simple
expediency. . . .

FONTANA (*quickly*): One cannot set it aside,
if one is answerable on this earth
for five hundred million believers.

RICCARDO: Nowhere is it ordained . . . that the successors
of St Peter should present themselves
at the Last Judgement as the largest shareholding
company in the world: if the Vatican were now
in its struggle with Hitler to forfeit
its power over finance, industry and politics –
Father, it could only result
in a more honest fulfilment of God's work.
Do you not believe that the suffering and
the defencelessness of the Fisherman
who first bore the keys,
are more appropriate to the Pope?
Some day, Father, it will come again,
the return to martyrdom of
the Representative of Christ.

FONTANA: You're dreaming, Riccardo. You despise
power . . . but what do we use against Hitler?
The Pope as poor fisherman – what would
Napoleon have made of him, let alone Hitler? –
No, the Pope
can only fulfil his charge
as long as he is on the side of the victors.

RICCARDO (*passionately*): On the side of Truth!

FONTANA (*smiling, cautious, dry*): Truth is on the side of the victor,
since he is ruler of the historians.
And as History – an old truism –
only reveals a sense of purpose
when historians give it one,
you may well calculate for yourself
how many footnotes Hitler the Victorious
will for instance concede to the Jews . . .
Riccardo, all this is bearable
if one holds on to the belief that
God will eventually make good the sacrifice.

RICCARDO: These consolations!
Would Christ have drawn back?

FONTANA: I am not a priest, but I know
the Pope, unlike you and I, is not an individual
who is able simply to follow his conscience and his emotion.
He must preserve the Church in his own person.

RICCARDO: But it is precisely the person

of *this* Pope, of Pius XII,
that Hitler fears: Pacelli's reputation
is greater in Germany than anywhere else.
No Pope for centuries, perhaps, has had
a standing such as his in Germany;
he is . . .
(*The servant has entered, still visibly sobered by his previous expulsion. He announces:*)

SERVANT: His Eminence, the most worthy
Cardinal . . .
(*We do not catch the name, as Fontana says very quickly and with slight nervousness:*)

FONTANA: Oh . . . please, yes. Show him up.
(*to Riccardo*)
Is it all right if he sees you here?

RICCARDO (*quickly*): He'll find out anyway that
there was no official reason for my journey.
Ask him to lunch.

(*Offstage we hear the sonorous sympathetic laughter of a fat man. Apparently it has pleased His Eminence to enjoy a mild joke with the staff. This prince of the Church, quite round and quite red, and yet nervous, indeed irritable, at work or in conversation, is a great gardener and apart from this, always concerned with the illnesses current in in his wide circle of acquaintance. At first glance, but only at the first, he looks like a member of a suburban sewing party, as with advancing age, though he is scarcely older than Fontana, he has become markedly more feminine. This is deceptive. The Cardinal is a polished, indeed unscrupulous diplomat, and his blue eyes can quite suddenly become as cold as the eyes of Göring or Winston Churchill, thus taking away from his chubby face all its effeminate cosiness. At that point his love of flowers seems as improbable as Göring's delight in model railways. For he is capable of saying nothing and of listening to his interlocutors, inviting them with his whole personality to say more than they can answer for.*
The Cardinal has succeeded in overcoming close relationships. He had considerable difficulty in avoiding women in the days when he was slim and straight, and when his still abundant black hair, combined with his large bright eyes, made up a distracting appearance. That he has had affairs is rumoured, probably incorrectly and certainly out of envy. As

*long as physical love disturbed him he was feared for his caustic wit.
Now, this malicious irony has softened into a bubbling jollity.*

*But the unusual intelligence of the Cardinal has always controlled his
sarcasms, and is even now too much awake to let him show his full
talents in the presence of His Holiness. The prince always remains
markedly in the shadow of the Pope, whom he calls 'The Chief', and for
whom he has little love. He would sooner show himself occasionally
dull-witted than at any time superior. He knows what he is doing.*

*One weakness, however, his intelligence has never mastered and, like all
ingrown peculiarities, it increases with the years: the Cardinal is a
great gossipmonger; bits of news fascinate him for their own sake, quite
independent of whether they are good or bad. And today he has a titbit
on the tip of his tongue, and is longing to share it, although unhappily by
this evening the whole world will know . . .*

*Like a lot of fat men, the prince is very sprightly, indeed nimble, and he
now enters laughing infectiously, with characteristic haste. His powerful
head is inclined to the right and he still wears his hat and light silk
cloak. He opens both arms heartily to embrace Count Fontana, who has
gone to meet him. In honour of the occasion he is wearing the red hat. In
his right hand he holds a magnificent orchid. The prince is still laughing
as he speaks a few half-finished sentences during their casual embrace.
He even continues to laugh between words, as he is not exactly unpleasantly, but still tiresomely surprised to find Riccardo there. His
noisy joviality wins immediate sympathy because it is completely
genuine. His Eminence is at this moment a very good man who is, on the
feast day of the Mother of God and of Count Fontana, quite uncom-
plicatedly happy not to be bothered by high blood pressure.)*

CARDINAL: My dear Count . . . mmm, what. God
    bless you . . . yes, we must . . . mustn't we . . .
    The right person for once, yes, mmm, what.
    I must try for the Order of Christ myself sometime, yes . . .
    No, really, it's – sincerely – yes . . .
    I had no idea, really not, yes.
    From the heart, mmm, what. Here . . . this.
    My Bletia verecunda, mmm, what.
FONTANA: Thank you, Your Eminence . . . how thoughtful.
    My most sincere thanks. What a beautiful
    orchid . . . *What* do you call it?

CARDINAL: Riccardo! No, what a pleasure! Yes,
  mmm, what. What a surprise: punctually in Rome
  to congratulate your papa, mmm, what?
RICCARDO (*who has bowed over the Cardinal's ring*):
  Good morning, Your Eminence. I wanted to request
  an audience with Your Eminence straight after lunch . . .
FONTANA: You will, of course, stay to lunch, Eminence?
CARDINAL: What . . . yes, oh yes, delighted. Look here, Count:
  the boy has got high blood pressure again . . .
  Riccardo, yes, you're quite red in the face,
  I say you are. Don't they have doctors in Berlin any more?
  (*As he gives his hat and cloak to the servant he stands between
  father and son rapidly throwing out remarks and not waiting for
  answers to the questions he raises.*)
  How nice, isn't it? How surprising.
  And today of all days, yes – ah, and particularly
  now that your father is so much alone –
  The Nuncio gave no warning of your arrival?
  – Yes, do you like the orchid, Count,
  yes, mm, what, that is my beloved
  Bletia verecunda – oh, don't let it stand
  in a draught, lots of light, mmm, what, and *no* wind.
  Yes, I so seldom succeed with them . . . usually only
  at investitures of the Order of Christ.
  We've had them here for some time,
  they were first bred in 1732 in England, mmm.
FONTANA (*very polite, obviously uncertain what on earth to do with this
  noble blossom*):
  That was very friendly, very thoughtful,
  Eminence. And very interesting. But wasn't it
  painful for you to cut it for me?
  But please . . . let's sit down, please –
  Eminence, please . . .
  (*They remain standing. Fontana gives the orchid to the servant,
  with an instruction. Exit servant. Fontana passes the Cardinal a
  cigar. His Eminence manipulates the cigar . . . pierces it with
  ritualistic delight. Riccardo lights it for him – all during the following dialogue.*)
CARDINAL: Riccardo looks quite exhausted, does he not?
  But Berlin has such wonderful clean air,
  when no one here can any longer move

– in September, mm? I always wish
I was Nuncio in Berlin . . .
How high is your blood pressure?

RICCARDO (*with very cautious irony*):
But, Eminence, I'm really very healthy.
I haven't been to the doctor for a year.

FONTANA: Then you should. – He gets too
excited in Berlin, Eminence.

CARDINAL: He's much too young for that! No other complaints,
heart, stomach – sure there's nothing?

RICCARDO: Fit as a flea, Eminence.

CARDINAL: Then it's the change in the weather today,
the difference in temperature – no feeling of congestion on the
train?

RICCARDO (*polite*):
Yes, a little, in point of fact, but I'm sure only
because I was lying down the whole time.

CARDINAL (*calmed*): That's what I thought – mmm?
Now . . . you must restore the balance.
How is your gall-bladder, my dear Count?

FONTANA: Oh, nothing to speak of – but, please,
Eminence, let's sit down.
Lunch will be quite a while yet.

CARDINAL (*puffing at his cigar . . . takes hold of the Count's arm*):
Yes, let's sit down, let's sit down – I often recall
a party I was at in Paris, I was
Riccardo's age then, and no one was taking
any notice of me, I just stood in the corner.
Eventually
the hostess called, 'Haven't you anything to sit on?'
'Certainly I've got something to sit on, Madame,'
I called through the room, 'but no chair.' – mm, what?
(*His Eminence is amused for quite some time by this joke, which is
respectfully received by the Fontanas. While the older men are
deciding where to sit, Riccardo shows signs of increasing unease.
The old servant brings champagne and a precious Venetian glass
jar for the orchid.*)
Riccardo, your uneasiness, mmm, what,
supports my theory of high blood pressure. Come
and sit down here with us . . . Ah ha,
there's a fine sight on a cold morning,

yes, mmm, what. Well then, Count,
once again, may you wear that order for a long time,
for a long time.

FONTANA (*while the drinks are being poured*):
It really is most amiable of you to have
come at once, Eminence . . .

RICCARDO: Eminence . . . Father, your health.
· (*bowing*)

FONTANA: Thank you, my boy.

CARDINAL: Your very good health, Riccardo.
(*The Cardinal empties his glass before putting it back on the table,
where it is immediately filled by the servant. Now the Cardinal
brings out his bit of news, effectively underplayed.*)
London has just announced, and Moscow
said yesterday, . . . yes, mmm, what, the battle for
Stalingrad is over. A German field-marshal
Stalin's prisoner. The Volga will not be crossed . . .
Yes, that's . . .

RICCARDO (*violently surprised, delighted*):
Surrendered? Really? . . . and everybody
in Berlin thought it would happen
as the propaganda said –
no German would ever surrender.

FONTANA: The poor fellows. What were they to do?

CARDINAL: Moscow says ninety thousand Germans
have surrendered – yes, Hitler's field-marshal
with the whole of the rest of his twenty-two divisions.
That's a slap in the face, and not only for Hitler.

FONTANA: From a military point of view
it's not totally disastrous for Hitler,
psychologically though . . .

RICCARDO: Psychologically miraculous for us.

CARDINAL (*crossly*): Riccardo, you are being frivolous.
Who can predict today whether
the victory that has been won at Stalingrad
will not soon prove a most serious threat to us Christians.
(*with emphasis*)
Mmm, what, the West . . .
Hitler's whole Southern Front will waver now.
He needs the oil from the Caucasus. Well, perhaps
he will make himself master of the situation once again.

RICCARDO (*cautiously . . . not to spoil his chances*):
But surely Your Eminence must also
want Hitler brought to his knees?

CARDINAL (*jovial, with an effort to conceal his impatience*):
But not by the *Russians*, Riccardo . . .
he should be thrashed by England and America,
until he understands that he cannot
rule the entire world on his own, mmm, what.
Punished, yes certainly. He must no longer
afflict and murder
the Poles, the Jews, the Czechs and even the priests . . .
otherwise, peace is unthinkable.
(*Fontana gestures the servant to leave.*)

RICCARDO: Eminence, peace with Hitler
will always be unthinkable.

CARDINAL (*laughs at first, amused at Riccardo's solemn enthusiasm,
then as if he was crying with rage*):
Never? – *never* use that word in politics!
Count – just listen to this son of yours –
such a clever boy, and now, mmm, what, he, too, is
infected with this Casablanca lunacy, what.
Holy Mother of God, who is *ever* going to bring
Hitler to the point of unconditional surrender?
And anyway, must we
today, on such a lovely morning, mmm?
I wanted to *congratulate* your papa, Riccardo.
(*One cannot impute the Cardinal's withdrawal to indolence: he
simply finds it unfitting that his youngest employee should want
to read him a lesson.*
Fontana, an old man himself, sees this better than Riccardo.)

FONTANA (*diplomatically*):
Yes, Eminence, let's have another drink . . .
To what now? . . . that Stalingrad
will teach Hitler a lesson . . .

CARDINAL: Yes, indeed – good luck, good health.
(*Riccardo raises his glass.*)
(*more relaxed*)
The Chief . . . the Chief has
quite unmistakably
let Mr Roosevelt know
that he considers America's demand

for Hitler's unconditional surrender
to be totally anti-Christian.
FONTANA: And ridiculous into the bargain, Eminence.
America is being bled almost to death by Japan.
And in Europe? – They won't get
a look in. While at any rate Hitler
can set half a dozen victories like Crete
against this fiasco at Stalingrad,
they *will* negotiate with this man, definitely.
CARDINAL: I certainly hope so, mmm, what.
Although Crete proved clearly
that winning a battle does not
decide a war. The Germans, this time as well, may
easily ruin themselves by their victories because
they have such an extended field of operations
instead of concentrating on a single front.
Their megalomania, once our greatest fear,
is today our strongest hope, yes.
It's cost them so much blood already
that even Hitler must become more moderate.
Limitations are very good for dictators, mmm, what?
Even the Kremlin, Heaven help us, in November,
just as the battle of Stalingrad began,
made its peace with the Church. Ha!
Hitler knew at the very beginning of the war that he
could not do without the Church,
if soldiers are going to die.
FONTANA (*seeing his chance*):
May one hope, Eminence, that the Pope
will exploit Hitler's awkward position
to threaten him with the breaking of the Concordat,
if he continues to murder the Jews?
I heard from New York yesterday the most terrible reports
about Poland and Rumania . . .
CARDINAL (*smiling. Suddenly nervous, rising*):
Has Riccardo been attacking you as well, my dear Count?
Well now; Fontanas père et fils showing a united front.
FONTANA: Not entirely, Eminence, but Hitler's defeat
on the Volga now encourages me to ask
whether his ruthlessness might not be denounced.
CARDINAL: Mmm, yes . . . mmm, what. Riccardo, I already *said*,

during the summer when you and then the Nuncio
in Pressburg and in Bucharest . . . and then the Poles
in London told us, mmm, yes, the terrible
things that were happening. I said then,
The Concordat is there for the protection
of our fellow Catholics . . . the Chief will not
put himself in a false position
to help the Jews.

FONTANA: Not even now, Eminence, when Hitler
would be forced to accept it?

CARDINAL (*with growing seriousness and irritation: the huge cigar glows strongly*):
Of course we are helping, under cover, yes.
The League of Raphael has already
financed the escape abroad of thousands, mmm, what.
However three events in recent weeks
must alarm every Christian:
first, the unscrupulousness with which America
abandons Europe to Stalin's divisions;
secondly, Hitler's defeat on the Volga;
thirdly, the reconciliation of Stalin
with the Orthodox Church, which proves to me,
proves unmistakably, mmm, yes . . . that Communism
for Stalin is only a pretended solution.
Communist or not, he is the *Tsar*,
the orthodox soul of all Russia, the Slav who, with
the nation firmly behind him, will realize
the dream of Peter and Catherine
for absolute domination.
Therefore he *had* to reconcile himself with those elements
apostate to the Church of Rome,
schismatics, anti-Latinists, pan-Slavists, what.
The Eastern temperament is quite foreign
to the Latin. If this war, mm, what,
does not bring the realization
of the dream of a Holy Roman Empire
nearer to the old Continent
then the last Christians, mmm, what,
can crawl back into the catacombs.

RICCARDO: Eminence, a fire-raiser like Hitler,
who is simply gambling away the power of Europe,

who allows himself quite pointlessly
to be drawn by Mussolini into adventures
in Greece and Africa – *cannot* be the man
to unite the West.

CARDINAL : You imagine then, these dubious
parliaments and debating societies à la Geneva
would still have the strength to do it ? Did not
the League of Nations die of insincerity ?
Oh, those vested interests from Warsaw
to Paris, from Rome to London –
they were *talking* Europe into her grave.
Ask your father, hm, what.
No, this continent is much too old,
too much streaked through and stirred up with prejudice
to be able to find unity again by peace.
Even the cities of Ancient Greece,
after their numerous disagreements, did they still
have the strength
to unite on their own ?
Riccardo, what if God were now to use
Herr Hitler, in his megalomania,
so to degrade the European nations –
just think of France –
that in the end they would never again
be able to erect those frontiers
that Hitler overran, how about that ?
Wars always produce other results
than those for which they were fought.
One does not need to be a general, mmm, what,
to be able to see that such
a tremendous idea as the unification
of Europe, can only be achieved
upon the battlefield, with blood and suffering –
certainly not by discussion among broad-minded democrats
who, anyway, always represent particular interests.
The fact that Scandinavians,
Italians, Croats, Rumanians,
Flemings, Basques, Bretons,
Spaniards, Finns and Magyars are forming a single front
with the Germans against Stalin, mmm, what,
(*furious*)

should have prevented Mr Roosevelt
from promising the Kremlin that they
could occupy Berlin – and it is, may I say,
a reckless, empty promise into the bargain;
megalomania, mmm, what . . .

RICCARDO: Eminence, allow me, but the Russians
are without question morally in the right.
They are fighting a good and just war.
They were overrun, their country laid waste,
their people dragged off and murdered.
If they are now threatening Europe,
it is Hitler alone who is to blame.

CARDINAL (*cold, impatient*): Maybe – but if one's house is on fire
one must put it out: the question
who started the fire can be asked later, can it not?
(*he laughs*)
Our Riccardo – careful, my dear Count –
is an idealist. One might even say
a fanatic, mmm, what. In the last resort,
an idealist will always spill blood
in his mania for doing good – more blood than any realist.
(*He laughs, very much the prince, and seeks both to distract and to
become more reasonable. Then he says with a remote irony, which
makes Riccardo look a fool:*)
Riccardo – you idealists are *inhuman*.
We realists are more humane because
we take people as they are.
We laugh over their failings, for we have them, too,
An idealist does not laugh . . . *can* Hitler laugh?
Has he himself a single failing? No.
He cannot laugh at the world;
he wishes to improve it.
Anyone who opposes his ideals is exterminated.
I'm afraid, for this reason, he will not compromise:
first he will ruin the world, in order then
to present it with his version of peace. Thank you very much.
We realists are for compromise, conformity – yes, of course
we make concessions;
and why not, what? Either
one is consistent *or* one stays alive, yes.
Let us not forget, God put

98

devils as well as saints into the world.
And in between stands man, with a perpetual choice, only
between two evils, mmm, what, Riccardo?
(*casually*)
Your fanaticism does not help the Church:
Hitler is a fact . . . we have
to live with him, mmm, what?
And be careful – an old man
can allow himself to say this – be
careful Riccardo, of making valuations,
which in the light of History will make
your contemporaries look ridiculous. You say
Hitler *invaded* Russia: your father and I
say, mmm, what, my dear Count . . .

FONTANA: You are absolutely right, Eminence.

CARDINAL: We prefer to say: Hitler entered Russia,
entered, yes. Let us not quibble, though.
Do you think the clever chess player
would willingly have marched on Moscow? He
could not have done otherwise – not in '39,
when he signed the non-aggression pact with Stalin
before the British could do so . . .
nor in '41 when he broke it.
You have no idea, mmm, what,
how much a ruler becomes the slave of
the events that he has brought about, yes.
When Hitler made that pact with Stalin,
so he could attack England,
he woke the sleeping tiger at his back. He *couldn't*
know how long Russia would sustain the role
of corn-chandler to him; the price –
the Baltic, the Straits, and Bessarabia –
was beginning to amount to blackmail.
But Mr Churchill, mmm, what, was sure
of his provisions from the U.S.A. Certainly
Stalin did not threaten Herr Hitler directly,
just as Alexander did not let Napoleon
force him to take the offensive.
But let us confess, hardly anyone
had an idea how long
Stalin could resist the German army – Hitler

was not the only one who was mistaken.
A *quick* victory in the East
would indeed have rendered him invulnerable, yes.
It is a blessing that he cannot win;
a blessing too, mmm, what, that he will not collapse, yes.

RICCARDO (*greatly troubled, but with as much friendliness as he can muster*):
Eminence, the Holy Father should protest, though,
at the fact that hundred of thousands
are being literally slaughtered . . . murders
that in no way influence the course of the war.

CARDINAL: Should ? . . . How do you mean exactly, mmm, what ?
Composure disarms the fanatic, nothing else will.
The Chief, mmm, what, is risking a great deal
if he intervenes for the Jews.
Minorities are never popular
in any country and the Jews have been
provoking the Germans for years, have they not ?
They have overdrawn the credit balance they had there.
Pogroms don't just happen . . .

FONTANA (*cautiously, seeing that Riccardo's intervention is only having a negative effect*):
My own opinion exactly, Eminence – but
one can scarcely talk in terms
of pogroms where Germany is concerned. Hitler's lawyers
have constructed whole systems of statutes
to take away the rights of the Jews so they
can then exterminate them physically.

RICCARDO (*quietly, not missing his effect*): We Christians were once
in a minority, too; perhaps we
shall be again soon: I believe that God
has chained us Christians indissolubly
to the race to which his son belonged.

CARDINAL (*laughs for some time, then with great adroitness*):
But, good gracious . . . my good Fontanas,
whom are you saying all this to ?
Count, do you take me for an enemy to the Jews ?

FONTANA (*quickly*): Certainly not, Your Eminence . . .

CARDINAL: Well then. I only say, the share
which the Jews had in the leading
professions before Hitler's rise to power

was certainly unhealthy: they had too many
doctors, lawyers, bankers, industrialists,
and newspaper owners, mmm, what . . . of course,
because they were more industrious:
members of a minority are always
more industrious; even at school –
they get punished for the others, yes. –
Makes a man disconcertingly hardworking, mmm, what?

FONTANA (*wishing to save the situation at all costs*):
Too much so, at any rate, for a country
with over six million unemployed.

CARDINAL (*spontaneously, with gratitude*):
Certainly . . . that was all I meant to say.
The main problem, Riccardo, is the
terrible popularity of Hitler, is it not?

RICCARDO: Your Eminence must consider – since his entry
into Paris, two whole years have passed.
Years of war. The country is tired
and frightened; the allied bombers . . .
Berlin has a nasty taste in its mouth.

CARDINAL (*lively, glad of the diversion, walks up and down*):
A people loves a ruler it can fear.
Nero – no, I'm not joking – Nero was
adored by the rabble in the same way.
'The people of Rome worshipped him' . . . yes, terrible.
Another 'Master Builder'. The Circus, party congresses . . .
the burning of Parliament . . . and then the persecution,
not the Christians this time, but the Jews,
the Communists – parallels, terrible, mmm, what.
(*half cynical, half downcast*)
Society, it may be, Riccardo, sees
Hitler as a parvenu . . . but it's still very happy,
mmm, what, for its sons to win his Iron Cross.
But I should like very much to see
the people that did *not* worship a ruler
who provides them with so *many* scapegoats.
Where would the Church be, gentlemen, if it
had not lit up the stakes for the *canaille*
in the Middle Ages; panem et circenses,
confiscation, indulgences, burnings: one must
offer the people *something*. And Hitler, mmm, what,

gave them *bread* as well . . . let us not forget.
Bread and a uniform and daggers.
Most of his beer-hall rowdies had been following
a red flag long before he pinned a swastika on to it . . .
And let us not ignore the fact, mmm, what,
the people gave him half their total votes
or nearly half, indeed . . . in '33
in the last remotely free election.
Admittedly, the noble Krupp and his sort
gave Hitler's cabinet at the time, three million marks.
– That brought the mob round to him.
And then the bishops – the bishops in the Reich!
One mustn't say it too loudly here,
but between ourselves, my dear Fontanas, between our-
    selves . . .
(*with definite physical pleasure, tasting each word like an oyster*)
that touched the Chief on his 'point d'honneur'.
Pacelli, the great diplomat, mmm, what.
Hitler looked like a hairdresser – the Concordat
gave him the entrée to the best drawing rooms, urbi et orbi,
and is the Chief now supposed
to anathematize him ex cathedra?
(*He laughs, as does the old Count Fontana.*)

RICCARDO (*wanting to defend the Pope*):
Eminence, did not the Concordat *have* to be signed
for the protection of our brother Catholics?

CARDINAL (*with a hearty laugh, claps him on the shoulder*):
That's how history is written, Riccardo.
Let's hope that's how it looks eventually.
No, ask your Papa: no one here
at any time thought Hitler capable of the wickedness
that he had already announced in his book . . .
it was there to read, mmm, what, in black and white,
how he would like to poison, as he said,
ten thousand times ten thousand of the Hebrews –
he has a hearty appetite, I must say.
I would have had a closer look at him myself.

FONTANA: His late Holiness Pope Pius XI, Eminence,
told me the Concordat with Hitler was
a stage from which a protest could be launched –
if it should become necessary. It is now.

CARDINAL (*another diversion*):

    The old Chief was a great fire-eater, yes . . .
    However, Pacelli wanted above all things
    to have a grand finale
    to all his Concordats, yes.
    So the Holy See advised the unhappy
    German Democrats to cave in
    of their own accord, mmm, what.
    People saw in Hitler another Mussolini,
    with whom one might do equally excellent business . . .
    (*he laughs*)
    Ah, yes, the Democrats . . . Years ago, do you know,
    I met one of Hitler's forerunners in Paris . . .
    Yes, a very famous man, now exiled and soured up.
    'But we were going to do that,' he said, meaning
    the end of unemployment, and the building
    of the autobahns, the plans were his, yet . . .

FONTANA: Why did he not execute them?

    I think I know, Eminence, who said that.

CARDINAL (*laughs*):

    Yes, why not indeed . . . I wondered that too, myself;
    just like the Vatican choir in former times, my dear Count . . .
    They knew jolly well how it was done . . .
    they just couldn't do it, what.
    (*serious again, with steely opportunism*)
    As long as Hitler is victorious and therefore popular . . .
    and Stalingrad alone won't bring him down . . .
    The Chief is only going to make himself unpopular
    if he makes open intervention for the Jews.
    Brother Innitzer has already shown that, yes, what.
    The Cardinal was Hitler's deadliest enemy
    until the day the clever scoundrel
    actually walked into Vienna.
    The nation ran to him . . .
    A negligible quantity, sixty thousand I believe,
    were put behind bars . . . but the man in the street
    was cock-a-hoop.
    Then the Cardinal did the only sensible thing:
    after the parade in front of the Hofburg
    he was the first to offer Hitler his congratulations, ha.
    Riccardo, if the Chief came out for the Jews

he would be much discredited.

RICCARDO: In Germany . . . perhaps.
But what about America, Eminence?

CARDINAL (*decisively, conclusively*): Not only in Germany,
but also in Poland, Holland, France
and the Ukraine . . . *everywhere*, mmm, what,
where they give active help with the persecution.
They have very militant anti-Semites
in America, too, you know. Mankind is prone
to slaughter, God help us,
and when he is about it he is not amenable
to reason . . . Riccardo,
I cannot at this moment advise the Chief
to challenge Herr Hitler.
The defeat on the Volga will give
him quite enough trouble for the moment, what?
How would it be if our Nuncio in Berlin
were to speak to Herr von Weizsäcker?

RICCARDO (*bitter*): Oh, Eminence, there would simply be a very
polite conversation. The Secretary of State
would certainly know nothing of the exterminations.
He could easily overlook
the fact that the Jews are being carted off
like criminals,
even in the streets of the capital,
and as no one would ever dare suggest
to Herr von Weizsäcker
he might be lying in his Führer's name,
and as he always likes to say that threats
would only aggravate the situation . . .

CARDINAL (*sharply, as he finds Riccardo's irony a bit much*):
Can *you* guarantee that threats
will *not* aggravate the situation?

RICCARDO (*his last, already uncontrolled and much too loud, attempt*):
Eminence, a hundred thousand Jewish families
in Europe are waiting to be murdered:
the situation, Eminence, cannot be aggravated.
(*quieter, pressing*)
No, Eminence, please attempt nothing through
Weizsäcker, nothing through the Nuncio:
the Pope to Hitler . . . direct and now.

FONTANA (*agitated, as Riccardo's tone is ruining everything*):
>   My boy, please – are you giving
>   orders here? I must ask . . .

CARDINAL (*lays his hand on Riccardo's shoulder, without significance*):
>   He is worn out, poor lad . . .
>   Riccardo – I don't like hearing Weizsäcker
>   slightingly spoken of.
>   He is a man of honour, mmm, what, and the
>   tried and trusted trait d'union
>   between the Nuncio and the Wilhelmstrasse, yes. In '39
>   he was the one man left we could still talk to.
>   Even he, however, could not save the peace.

FONTANA (*with a weak attempt at reasonableness*):
>   Yes, Eminence, that is to his eternal credit.
>   But Hitler has a talent for exploiting
>   many men's virtues for discreditable ends.

CARDINAL (*smiling*): It is always creditable to talk of peace, Count.

FONTANA: With the sealed cattle-trucks of deportees
>   rolling towards the crematoria? I am,
>   as you well know, Eminence, not a cynic . . .

CARDINAL: Yes, mmm, what a difficult, insoluble . . .
>   (*The servant has entered, and announces to Fontana:*)

SERVANT: His Eminence, the most worthy Lord Cardinal
>   is being asked for urgently. An officer . . .

CARDINAL: Please . . . show him up.
>   (*to Fontana*)
>   May I? I will, of course,
>   go through all this once more with the Chief.
>   (*An officer of the Swiss Guard has entered, and salutes very
>   smartly.*)

OFFICER: Eminence, His Holiness requests
>   Your Eminence's urgent presence in the palace.
>   My orders are to accompany . . .

CARDINAL (*most unwilling*): Now? . . . Before lunch? Well then,
>   my hat, Vittorio . . . what a pity.
>   The Chief's not going to save Stalingrad
>   simply by talking about it, what?
>   (*While he puts on his hat, and Riccardo takes his cloak from the
>   servant to help him on with it:*)

FONTANA: A great pity . . . Can we wait lunch for you?

CARDINAL: Quite out of the question, my dear Count. What a pity.

(*laughing intimately, apparently appeased*)
I already asked outside,
before you actually invited me,
what you were having today . . . mmm, yes,
I am uncouth à ce point-là, mmm, what.
And now, instead of specialità della casa Fontana . . .
debates on Stalingrad – melancholy indeed. Riccardo,
(*He goes to him; Riccardo kisses his hand again.*)
you should take lemon juice for that blood pressure of yours.
If that's no good, foot baths, as hot
as you can stand. – Till this afternoon?

RICCARDO: Yes, Eminence, many thanks. What time?

CARDINAL (*casually*): Well, now. Round about five. I think
you ought to have six months in Lisbon.
(*quickly, without connection*)
My dear Count, enough of politics for today:
this is a special day for you. God bless you. Arrivederci.

RICCARDO (*moodily*): Arrivederci, Eminence.

FONTANA (*bowing him out*): It was so nice of you to call,
Eminence, and I must above all . . .
(*The servant shuts the door behind them. Riccardo is alone.*)

RICCARDO (*shattered . . . to himself*): Lisbon . . . dead end.
(*He lights a cigarette nervously and opens the french windows. His
father returns and says quickly, even before the servant has shut
the door behind him:*)

FONTANA: He's getting rid of you. He did not even ask
why you left Berlin.
Lisbon: the reward for going too far.

RICCARDO: Father, I did not reveal the worst,
so that he may at least *try* to move the Pope
to *some* expression of opinion.

FONTANA: Well, what, then?

RICCARDO: Weizsäcker is coming to Rome. He will very soon
be asking for his agrément.

FONTANA (*disbelieving*): Hitler is making his Secretary of State
Ambassador to the Vatican?

RICCARDO: He will expect decisive action from him.
First: he is to concern himself with Mussolini,
they are afraid that Italy will soon
abandon Fascism.
Secondly: . . . and this above all, Weizsäcker,

as Hitler's immaculate shop sign, is to spoonfeed
the Pope personally with all
the old arguments: mutual non-intervention;
no discussion on fundamentals, no negotiation.
For Hitler knows what it would mean for him
if the Pope were to associate himself
with the protests of the Allies against his crimes;
then he would have no further hope
of making a separate peace
with the West and thereby gaining a free hand
in the East . . .
(*Silence.*)
(*sincerely*)
I am so grateful to you for siding with me.

FONTANA: Stalingrad is the turning-point that allows us to negotiate.
You have right on your side, my boy,
but not power.

RICCARDO: Father, I beg you:
We must act *before*
Weizsäcker reaches Rome; at once, father . . .
(*The bells begin to ring again loudly. They both look up and then at each other. The father makes a gesture of resignation*)

SERVANT: Luncheon is served.

Curtain

Act Three · The Visitation

> The world keeps silence. The world knows what is happening
> here – there is no doubt about it, and it keeps silence. In the
> Vatican, the Representative of God keeps silence. . . .
>
> FROM AN ILLEGAL POLISH LEAFLET, AUGUST 1943

SCENE ONE

Rome. 16 October 1943. Early evening.

*The attic flat of Dr Lothar Luccani, a young university lecturer, and
his family, in the lively Via di Porta Angelica, which begins in the square
of St Peter's in the colonnade of Bernini and leads to the Piazza del
Risorgimento, bounded on the left by the precipitous wall of the Vatican
City and on the right by tall office, café, and apartment buildings.
Luccani's apartment has, on the street side, a restful outlook on the
Pope's palace standing opposite, with His Holiness's private apartments on the third floor. It thus happens literally in this scene, as Herr
von Weizsäcker, by then German Ambassador to the Holy See, reported
to Berlin on the 17th October, that 'these things had taken place, so to
speak, under the very windows of the Pontiff'. If possible, we should be
able to see the upper stories of the Renaissance palace through the
window of the living-room and through the tall narrow door which
leads to the flat roof of the building, but the same purpose will be served
if we retain the image of the Dome of St Peter's, familiar to us from
the preceding act, to illustrate . . . as Gerald Reitlinger writes in*
The Final Solution *. . . how Jews were 'being herded to their death
from the very shadow of St Peter's'.*

*The stage is divided into three rooms: left, a small hallway with the
passage door in the background, and a door, right, leading to the living-
room, the large main part of the set. The living-room is sparsely furnished, and is superficially recognizable as the home of an educated
man by an ancient fragment of bas-relief let into the wall and two
walls of bookshelves. On the right is a colourful nursery, the same size
as the hallway: two little cots one behind the other and a pram in the*

*middle of the room. There is no connecting door between the nursery
and the living-room; to reach it one has to go out of the living-room door
into the hall and then across the stage in front of all three rooms.*

*In the living-room there are about four suitcases, ready packed, a small
skip standing open, a cardboard carton and a school satchel. Over the
sofa are spread coats and hats. A little girl about 5 years old is bringing
out of the nursery one doll after another and laying them on top of the
suitcases. Her brother, about 8, is lying on the floor of the nursery,
looking through an album. Dr Lothar Luccani is standing at the window
of the living-room. His wife, Julia, is at the table, busy getting a baby
ready for the night. The baby cries at first, then begins to whimper, but
is soon quieted by its mother. Her father-in-law is reading the* Osservatore Romano *with a magnifying-glass, beneath a standard-lamp.*

LOTHAR: I've no more to do. Half past four
    and still quite light.
    It gets dark late. I'm beginning
    to get impatient.
JULIA: Why are you still getting so excited?
    Everything's packed.
    The Father told me specially
    not to appear before it got dark.
    Be glad we're being hidden at all.
LOTHAR (*nervous*): Do you want to walk? Yes, you're right,
    we'll all go on foot. Once we are
    safe, then Simonetta can get
    the luggage over to us. She can
    take a taxi from the square.
JULIA (*tries to calm him*): But, Lothar, that has all been arranged
    for ages. I've given her money
    and she's got the key, too . . . you will just have to leave her
    a little money for the rent.
LUCCANI: I've taken care of that. The rent
    is paid up till April.
GIRL: Daddy, can I take all of them?
LOTHAR: Thank you very much, Father.
    (*to his daughter*)
    You can take two dollies,
    and the Teddy, or Puppy – not both.
LUCCANI: You don't need Simonetta.

I can wait for the taxi here
and hand the luggage out.
Then we're sure the flat
is properly shut up. Why
should that woman be able to snoop around
the rooms when we're away . . .?

JULIA (*crossly*):
Oh, Grandfather . . . we're asking her to look after Pippa.
Won't you ever trust her?

LOTHAR: (*leafing through a book without concentrating, undecided whether to take it or not*):
And don't you stay behind here either.
There's no point in waiting longer than absolutely necessary.
I don't like it . . .

JULIA (*still busied with the baby*): Lothar, stop being so nervous,
it's getting into the children.

LOTHAR (*very nervous, irritated, rather loudly*):
But I'm *not* nervous.
Anyway, they warned me.
I'm angry with myself for not having
gone yesterday, as soon as
the Father had been here. This damned packing.

JULIA: The Germans have been in Rome for weeks already.
No Jews have been arrested up to now;
why today all of a sudden?

LOTHAR (*violently*): Why? Why? Huh – because it is only today
that they have been ordered to. The gold
was not enough for them. They have
plundered the synagogues, too – now
it's *our* turn.
(*after a pause*)
Do you still
not believe what London says?
Everywhere where the Russians are
regaining ground
they are coming across mass graves
full of murdered civilians . . . Jews.

LUCCANI (*lays the newspaper crossly aside and says very decisively*):
I know the Germans better than you do.
I don't believe these fairy-stories. Who shot
the five thousand officers in Katyn,

the Germans or the Russians?

LOTHAR: I don't know. I can believe it of both.
In any case, it was German ammunition
they found with the corpses.

LUCCANI: That proves nothing. The Germans
dug up the Poles . . . a sign
that they were sure of themselves. Stalin
murdered them – like he did his own General Staff
six years ago.

JULIA: Please, Grandfather, can't you talk about something else.
We are not in Poland.
The Pope is our next-door neighbour; he won't
just let us be carted off.
(*She points to the window, smiles and gives her husband a kiss.*)
He need have no fear of Hitler; the Americans
are in Naples already.

LOTHAR: My dear girl, we are not Catholics.

LUCCANI: Yes, indeed – I am a Catholic – that's enough.
Apart from that, we're going to a monastery.

LOTHAR (*ironically*): That *will* impress the Germans . . .
Oh, don't be naïve both of you . . . All right,
change the subject.
It's getting darker now.
(*The little boy has brought his album into the living-room and asks
his father:*)

BOY: Daddy, can I take my stamps, too?

LOTHAR: Yes, you can. Sit here
at the table and take them
out of the album carefully.
The album will take up too much room.
Put them in the box with the ones
that haven't been sorted out yet.

BOY (*furious*): Then they'll all be muddled up.
(*to his sister*)
Don't you touch the stamps.

LOTHAR: Do as I say – or the album
will be left behind.

GIRL: They're my stamps, too.

JULIA: Now do as you're told and be quiet,
so Pippa can get to sleep properly . . .
then we'll take her over in the basket.

Lothar, be a dear and take
all this here to Simonetta.
(*She lays a couple of bath towels and a pile of nappies over her
husband's arm and puts bottles, powder, toys and a little jacket in a
baby bag.*)
We can leave the pram down below. –
(*after a pause*)
Couldn't we take Pippa with us?

LOTHAR (*impatiently, unfairly, snatches up the bag from her hand*):
Why do you always go back on what we've decided?
Squalling infants aren't quite the thing in a monastery.
You wouldn't even be able to bath her,
let alone get the proper food for her.

JULIA: You're quite right, Lothar, it's just that
it isn't easy for me to leave Pippa behind.

LOTHAR: Anything else? – I'll be back in a moment.
(*friendly*)
I don't find it easy either, Julia.
(*He kisses her on the brow, then kisses the child and goes out of the
apartment.*)

JULIA (*calling after him*): Tell Simonetta I'll bring
Pippa over to her in half an hour.
(*The passage door stays open and we hear Lothar go downstairs;
Julia takes the child, after its grandfather has petted it, over to the
nursery and lays it in the basket. The old man also goes out, saying
to himself:*)

LUCCANI: I'll just check the meter and turn off the gas.
(*to the children*)
Behave yourselves now.

GIRL: Grandad, the stamps belong to me, too.
(*But she is not looking at the stamps at all, with which her brother
is busy at the table, but, following the example of her mother, is
putting a nappy on one of her dolls.*)

LUCCANI: I'll buy you another doll
which can really talk,
or a fairy-story book – what would you like?

BOY: Some American stamps for me!

LUCCANI: Just be good children when you're with the monks
and I'll get something for both of you.
(*to himself*)
I hope we'll be able to have the carpets brought over,

those stone cold floors in winter . . .
(*He goes off left down the passage. While he has been talking to the grandchildren, Lothar has come back and gone into the nursery. Julia has put the baby in the basket. They look at the child and then come forward away from the basket. Lothar takes her arm.*)

LOTHAR: Don't be angry with me for being so edgy.
(*He buries his face in her neck and kisses her passionately.*)

JULIA (*tenderly*): It won't last for ever . . . it will soon be over.
The Allies have crossed the Volturno already.

LOTHAR (*violent again*): Good God, why don't they land at Ostia?
You rely on the Americans, Grandfather on the Pope . . . and I
on nothing at all. If only
the convent doors were already shut behind us . . .

JULIA: Lothar, admit you always
look on the black side, mm?
Isn't it something that we can at least
stay together?
(*She kisses him and strokes his arm.*)

LOTHAR (*very gloomy*): Separation from one's work, one's books,
is bad enough. And then, all those people . . .

JULIA (*smiling resignedly*): My misanthropist.
Your books are still more important to you
than I am . . . aren't they?
You find me a nuisance sometimes.

LOTHAR: But, Julia, how can you . . .

JULIA: Yes, yes . . .
In the first years together, before the children came,
I was often unhappy about it . . . I don't believe
you even noticed *that*,
you selfish old man.
(*She shakes her head and embraces him.*)
We quarrelled too often, that's the terrible thing.

LOTHAR (*upset*): But, Julia – you know how much I need you!

JULIA: A little bit – every now and then.

LOTHAR: We're still young, we'll make up for it.
Just wait till this bloody war is over.

JULIA (*smiling*): One can never make up for things – you gave up
a lot on my account. For a man,
you tied yourself down very young.

LOTHAR: Yes, but to *you*, Julia. You are
the one woman who includes all the other women

I didn't have.
(*He has turned away, uneasy again.*)
Which suitcase are the papers in and the
bankbooks? We should have
drawn the rest of the money out.

JULIA: With your manuscripts. But . . .
(*She disengages herself.*)
I nearly left my ring in the bathroom.
(*She goes off right, Lothar off left down the passage into the living-room. The old man, who meanwhile has just come back into the living-room, has begun a completely supererogatory job of sorting out the old newspapers from the rack and checking the dates pedantically with his magnifying-glass. He says to his grand-daughter :*)

LUCCANI: Why have you brought all your babies here?
They should be asleep.

GIRL: I've got to wash them, though,
if I'm going to take them with us.

BOY: Taking all of them? Daddy said only two.
Daddy, is she going to take all her dolls?
Then I'm going to take my pistol, too.

LOTHAR (*taking two suitcases into the hall with a feeble attempt at joking*):
To the monastery? . . . Julia, do you hear that?
He's going to hold up the monastery at revolver point.
Not even the Nazis do that.

JULIA (*comes into living-room*):
You mustn't have any guns in the monastery.
Grandfather . . . *who* on earth are you sorting out
the old newspapers for? You're getting nervous, too.

LUCCANI: Not at all. It's just that
I've nothing else to do.
(*He consults his pocket watch.*)
Still, you're quite right.
I'd better see if the windows are shut.

JULIA: Yes, they are.
(*But the old man still goes out.*)
(*to her husband*)
I'll give Simonetta the keys to the cellar
as well. She can bring us
a jar of the home-made jam

to the monastery every now and again.
(*sadly*)
But she must bring Pippa at least every three days,
otherwise she won't know me
after three months.
(*Loud ring.*)
There she is now . . .

(*Another ring . . . continuous now. Lothar goes out, meeting his father in the doorway, who looks shaken. In answer to Julia's glance of inquiry he shrugs his shoulders and says nothing. Lothar closes the living-room door and only then, while the bell goes on ringing all the time, opens the passage door. The four people in the room stand very close together.*

A German Platoon Leader of the Waffen-S.S. and two Italians of the Fascist militia barge in. The Sergeant's name is Witzel and he looks, in 1943, like most of his compatriots of about 35, just as in 1960, as Inspector-General of the Municipal Government of D., he will look like most of his compatriots of 50. Perhaps one should mention that he is very correct . . . the coarse, dirty-minded swaggering tone, which he uses when dealing with Jews and other defenceless people because it is the custom, does not suit him. Witzel has, without noticing it, absorbed this brutal garrulity from his superiors, even to the extent of whole un-digested sentences, with the same speed as he will lose it the moment his superiors change. In 1959 he is a reliable citizen – his love of order makes neo-Nazi activities as disagreeable to him as a wage strike or a burst pipe.

The Sergeant is such a typically average man of our time that he is only recognizable by his uniform. In this way he can play the priest in the first scene and the Jewish Kapo in the last: should he double these roles, he should not even put on a moustache or a pair of glasses. The two Italians are likewise the consumer-product of contemporary history – representative of the type that would have set up the stake for Joan of Arc without thinking twice. One of them carries under his arm a weapon at the ready, yet carries it so carelessly that one has the feeling that if the thing were ever to go off it would be by accident. More important to him is what he has in his other hand, a little straw-covered bottle out of which he drinks at regular intervals. His comrade has a strong, narrow face and slightly pop-eyes. He is formal, 'smart' and vain as a drum-major in the piazza. He carries a list of names and makes un-necessary play with various coloured pencils. He carries a pistol-holster and a bandolier. His cap is set with precision. He is clean-shaven; his uniform is clean and pressed with a coloured sash around his waist; he is wearing boots, while the other one has a filthy pair of trousers that he probably only takes off in bed, and even then only when he is not alone. Witzel has no control over him. He is already incensed by the frivolous moustache of this delinquent reprobate.)

SMART ITALIAN (*with the list*):
> Dr Lothar Luccani? Wife Julia?
> Two children: one boy, one girl?
> You will be going to a labour camp.
> Get your things packed quickly.
> (*Witzel and the Italian with the bottle have pushed past them into the living-room, the door of which Julia has just opened.*)

WITZEL (*he speaks in no particular accent, just in a completely cor-rupted German. The louder he speaks the more his speech takes on a sloppy Kassel intonation. Amiably*):
> Get packed . . . Ah, the stuff's
> all here together.

LOTHAR (*quietly to Julia*): Too late.
> (*He stands, quite resigned, against the doorpost until Witzel, who has shut the passage door again, gives him a brutal shove which sends him stumbling into the middle of the living-room.*)

WITZEL: Go on, get your traps together.

LUCCANI (*the first to recover*): What has my son done to you?

WITZEL (*taking no notice of the old man*): You've got ten minutes –
> five anyway: get packed! Los! Avanti!

LUCCANI (*walks over to him with great decision*):
> We are Catholics. We have all been
> baptized. You have no right
> to arrest us. Where are your orders?

WITZEL (*amiably*): Where is your Star of David?
> Catholic are you? I was Catholic
> once upon a time, it doesn't last long.
> Ten minutes, because you're Catholics.
> (*looks round, points at the ready-packed suitcases*)
> All ready to go? How did you know

we were coming?
Whole family here?
JULIA (*controlled*): Yes, the whole family. We had
no idea. We were just going on a trip.
WITZEL: Ah, a trip . . . which monastery?
(*He laughs to his companions, who are looking about idly and
smoking, the one with the bottle sitting on the table. The smart one
laughs dutifully; the delinquent takes in the room and the furniture
with an enterprising glance. Amiably to the little boy:*)
Which monastery were you
going to so suddenly?
(*The boy, very shy, does not answer, but clings to his grandfather.
Lothar is not yet completely controlled, but says nevertheless:*)
LOTHAR: My father is here on a visit. He has
been a Catholic for donkeys' years.
Anyway, he's not on your list.
Leave him here, or there'll
be trouble with the Vatican.
(*It is very dark in the room. Over the way, on the third floor of the
Pope's palace, the lights go on.*)
WITZEL: He won't have to complain to the Pope,
he can complain direct to God the Father, when
he gets to see Him in the near future.
(*Witzel looks at the old man, who can say no more; then Witzel
spins round on Julia and Lothar and shouts:*)
Do you think I've brought a whole flying squad out
just for you?
(*He strides across in front of the suitcases still standing in the middle
of the room and throws the hats one by one from the sofa on to the
floor.*)
Twenty-five kilos of luggage per Yid . . . just
clothes and eatables.
Everything else to be unpacked, double
quick – los! avanti!
JULIA (*hardly able to speak with fear*): Where are you taking us?
WITZEL (*amiably*): To build roads, up there
in the Apennines.
LOTHAR (*suddenly active – significantly to Julia and his father*):
And our *two* children – here,
they're on the list.
JULIA (*understanding immediately*): *Both* the children . . . yes.

(to Witzel)
Please can't you leave the children here?
They'll only be in the way.

WITZEL *(takes the list, with great good nature)*:
We've a lot of family feeling, you know,
so the two children had better come too.
And you – you aren't down on the list at all,
but you can come too.
Those who can't work get preferen – . . .
get special treatment.

(Lothar and Julia are unpacking and repacking in great haste. The little girl has crept on to her grandfather's lap and the boy has gone to him as if for protection. Factually, to the old man:)
You can't have been in Rome long,
or why didn't the Duce
notice you when he had
the Jews registered?

LUCCANI *(contemptuous)*: First, I'm only here on a visit;
secondly, I'm a Catholic.

JULIA *(standing up)*: Please let my father-in-law stay
and my two children.

WITZEL *(spins round, brutal)*:
You get on with your packing. We Germans aren't interested
in your religion.

(He goes over to the bas-relief. Lothar and Julia go on packing, otherwise it is very quiet. Witzel gives Lothar, who is kneeling in front of a suitcase, a cautious prod with his foot.)
Art collector, are you? Worth quite a bit?

(Nods towards the relief. Lothar, in the unfounded hope of starting a conversation and perhaps achieving something for the children, says:)

LOTHAR: Yes. I'm an archaeologist. That relief comes . . .

WITZEL: I don't give a toss
where it comes from. They can
worry about that Göring's end.
(to the smart Italian)
Give us the other list . . .
(The Italian takes it out of his briefcase. Witzel makes a note and asks the men:)
What's this street called?

MEN: Via Porta Angelica. 22. Fourth floor.

(*Witzel gives him back the list, goes over between Lothar and Julia who are repacking a suitcase on the floor, bends down and takes from one of the suitcases a figurine and a purse and holds them in front of them. The Italian with the bottle becomes very attentive, but says nothing. Witzel, scornfully, then with an unpleasant laugh, puts the little bronze on the table and rummages in the purse.*)

WITZEL: The things people have to take
with them on a trip . . . All old
coins, or what . . . ? Worth much?
We'd better make a note of these two.

(*He has the other list passed over again, makes a note, then notices that the delinquent sitting on the table cannot take his eyes off the coins as he rolls a cigarette. He sends him out, roughly:*)

Don't loll about here, you,
gawping at me,
and keep your eyes off the antiques.
Go and have a quick look in the other rooms instead –
there – and over there.
Maybe we'll find another little rabbit
to add to the day's bag . . . like Grandad.

(*As the Italian gets off the table with insolent slowness and reluctance, without his gun, pushing his cap on to his forehead and scratching the back of his head, Julia, still on her knees, looks up fearfully. She bites her lower lip in an agonized attempt not to cry out, and clutches Lothar's arm. Her husband takes her hand away and busies himself ostentatiously with the packing. Julia is so little able to conceal her fear that she rises to her feet as the Italian leaves the room. Witzel, who is behind her, immediately grabs her by the back of the neck and pushes her to the floor again, while he says stupidly trying to calm her:*)

WITZEL: There's no need to worry
about your countrymen making off
with the teaspoons, just get on
with that you're doing . . .

(*Julia begins to cry soundlessly. In the background the grandfather tells the children, by laying his finger to his lips, not to say anything. He whispers to them, then at the moment of maximum tension, in order to occupy the children and get a grip on himself, he begins to speak to Witzel.*)

LUCCANI : Can the boy take his box of stamps with him ?
Look . . .
(*He takes the box out of his grandson's hand and shows it to Witzel, who answers amicably :*)

WITZEL : Of course he can, as far as I'm concerned.

LUCCANI : Now, Claudia, ask if you can take
your dolls and teddy . . .

WITZEL (*impatiently*):
Oh, for Christ's sake . . . All right, come along.
Well ? – Rooms empty ?
(*He looks questioningly at the returning Italian, who has been in the nursery, looked in the baby-basket and, after a short pause for reflection and a reassuring look into the passage, has left the room with a smile on his face of which no one, not even himself, could tell whether it refers to the saving of the child or the deceiving of Witzel.*)

DELINQUENT : Nobody else there, not a soul.
(*He looks first at Julia, then steadily at the bag of coins. Lothar takes Julia comfortingly by the arm and stands up at once ; he is now in a great hurry to get away.*)

LOTHAR : We're ready.
(*He throws his coat over his shoulders, takes two suitcases and leads the way. Julia, more controlled, is putting on the children's coats.*)

WITZEL : Wait. Just one little thing more.
Show your hands, not the children.
You . . . you there: the ring . . . take the rings off.
Jewellery is confiscated. Hurry up.
(*Lothar breaks the silence with painful irony as he takes his wedding ring off, not without difficulty, while his father and Julia show no reaction.*)

LOTHAR : Our wedding rings might get in the way at 'work'.
(*enraged, as Witzel lays hands on Julia, who in her nervousness cannot get her ring off without help*)
Have you specific orders to rob us ?
(*The children cluster round their mother.*)

WITZEL : Rob ? Just don't get cheeky now.
Now your watches . . . los! . . . your watches.

JULIA : You were right, Lothar.
(*Witzel has given the watches and the rings to the smart soldier, who has noted them down and put everything into his briefcase.*)

*Now he turns to the old man, who is sitting there as if he was
witnessing some incomprehensible happening on another planet; his
eyes clouded, wide open, immobile, his hands spread out in front of
him on his slightly parted knees – without any external reaction, he
allows his pocket watch, his gold chain and his two wedding
rings to be taken away. The rings are not so much drawn off as
torn off.)*

WITZEL: You're a sound sleeper, aren't you? . . . Come on,
let's catch the post. Get the children dressed.
*(He has said this to Julia, and now briefly, but not brutally, takes
hold of her hair to look at her ears.)*
No earrings, then. Good. Ready. Let's go.
*(Julia passes the grandfather a little case, takes a rucksack herself
and leads the children out.)*

GIRL: I want to go with Grandad . . .

LUCCANI: That's right, you stay with me . . . *(to the boy)* You too.
Come along.

BOY: What about Pippa? Isn't she coming, too?

LUCCANI *(putting his hand over his mouth)*:
Never mind that now.
*(He pulls the children out quickly with him. The Italian with the
list has already opened the passage door. In the crush in the little
hallway, the boy asks the sergeant timidly:)*

BOY: Are we going to the monastery now?

WITZEL: We're going straight to Heaven,
straight to Jesus . . .
(He pushes them out. Outside stands Simonetta, crying.)

SIMONETTA: Oh, Signora Luccani, oh my God.

JULIA: Good-bye . . . Just have another
look in the nursery and see
whether I shut the window.
*(She begins to cry and goes out quickly. Witzel is the only one left
in the apartment.)*

WITZEL: Out. 'raus.
*(He pushes Simonetta out and slams the door so loudly that the
baby begins to cry. It is now almost completely dark in the flat, for
the elder Luccani has not forgotten to switch off the standard-lamp.
A little light is shed into the room from the Pope's palace. A
trample of feet on the staircase, then silence. We hear the motor of
a heavy lorry being cranked. Simonetta opens the flat door and
goes on tiptoe, but quickly, into the nursery and bends over the baby.)*

SIMONETTA: Ah, then . . . have they taken your mama away then.
Come on, my precious, poor little thing.
Come on.
(*taking the child out*)
Devils!

(*She calms the child until it is quiet, lays it on a cushion, looks around the room nervously several times, then goes to the window, which is closed, and looks down. She begins to cry. The deplorable Fascist who 'overlooked' the child earlier has just stolen back quickly and quietly through the open door into the living-room, where he tries to stuff the bagful of coins into various pockets. This takes a moment, then he takes the figurine and tries to put it into his trouser pocket, sees it will not go, eventually undoes one or two blouse buttons and puts it in his blouse. He looks fearfully towards the door the while – and at this moment Simonetta comes out of the nursery along the passage. They both stand petrified, unable to speak. The soldier looks at her in great confusion, but with complicity: the figurine is not completely hidden inside his blouse. He points to the child then pats his pocket, laughs . . . takes the figurine once more from his blouse, shows it, as he has been caught anyway, then replaces it slowly and comes out into the hall grinning. Simonetta has been unable to say anything except 'Oh'. With a large gesture and theatrical relish, the soldier sways his hips and holds his arms like Simonetta, as if he had a child at the breast . . . putting the statuette under his blouse.*)

DELINQUENT: Madonna mia . . . I,
I saved it.
(*He hurries out.*)
SIMONETTA (*leans against the wall, exhausted and relieved, but unable to move another step*):
You bastards.

Curtain

SCENE TWO

The workroom of the Father General of an Order.
A few styleless pieces of office furniture, a crucifix, and not far away and slightly larger, a picture of Pius XII praying, in profile. Four

Scene Two

Renaissance chairs, copies, like the ones in the guardrooms of the Swiss Guard. A prie-dieu. A large map of the world lit by a neon strip, showing in red dots the positions of the not very numerous missions of the order. The long wall of the room is taken up by an enormously large and heavy baroque cupboard with two great doors.

In the foreground by the telephone an aged monk is reading his breviary. On the door, catching the eye, hangs a black cardinal's hat and red cape. The plain office clock strikes ten: it is evening. Then we hear steps echoing loudly, as if someone was walking over the thin floor of an empty loft. The monk looks up, then rises. Now we hear the sonorous sympathetic laughter of a fat man, muffled, as if it was coming out of a barrel – in fact, it is coming out of the cupboard, the doors of which are now opened creakingly and suddenly from within: His Eminence, already familiar from his visit to the Fontana palace, comes fussily into view in a mood of man-of-the-world cheerfulness; with his left hand he holds up his cassock – he is wearing red stockings and high-heeled black-laced shoes – with his right he leans on the monk, who has hurried towards him to help the prince descend. He coughs, laughs, talks over his shoulder to the Abbot, who is still in the cupboard replacing the false back wall. Then the Abbot emerges and closes the cupboard doors: an old white-haired man, a typical general staff officer, slim, mean, obedient.

CARDINAL (*with one foot still in the cupboard – with princely amusement*):
Jonah – what . . . Jonah
in the belly of the whale. Thank you, my friend, thank you.
(*He comes out. The monk brushes a little dust off his cassock, then fetches a clothes brush from the desk drawer and goes to work on the Abbot as well.*)
Yes, splendid, mm, this hiding-place.
And you negotiate, my good
Father General, with Hitler's minions
right next to this cupboard?
(*laughing again*)
Perfect. Yes, mm, what? But what
if one of your flock – up there,
(*he points to the ceiling*)
were to run amok . . .
if he couldn't stand it any more,

123

hidden away there, and ran out,
mmm, what, yes – screaming and bawling and
ran right out of the cupboard
just as you were drinking Frascati
with the head of the Gestapo, eh ? – mm, what ?
(*This picture amuses and horrifies him in equal measure ; he laughs
questioningly, anxiously.*)

ABBOT (*grinning*): Don't worry, Eminence:
The Germans know perfectly well
I have a house full of deserters,
Communists, Jews, Royalists . . .
They respect sanctuary.
(*to the monk who is brushing him off*)
Thank you, brother, thank you – any telephone calls ?

MONK (*bows and goes*): No calls, right reverend Father General.
(*kneeling*)
Eminence!

CARDINAL (*without interest*): God bless you, friend . . .

ABBOT: Bring us a glass of wine . . .
Red, Eminence ? The local stuff ?

CARDINAL: Thank you, no . . . I have
my coach and horses waiting in the Piazza, mmm, yes.
I mustn't linger, mmm, what.
Oh, well, a thimbleful, red, mmm, yes.
(*to the monk*)
But, please, my friend, not the local brew, hm ?
(*Exit monk, after bowing.*)
And how is your rheumatism, my good Father General ?

ABBOT: Thank you for asking, Eminence. I'm afraid
it's come with the November fogs
as it does every year. No sooner
but, alas, no later. I am not to
be spared this year either.

CARDINAL: Tomorrow morning I shall send you, mmm,
my cat's fur, yes. Put it on straightaway,
don't wait until the pain's already there.
(*The Cardinal has sat at the desk. The Abbot brings a chair up for
himself.*)

ABBOT: Very kind of you, Eminence, but do you not need
it yourself ?

CARDINAL (*with a wide gesture, very seriously*):

Not at all, I take the water-cure and then
the warm atmosphere in my greenhouse, what,
disease can't make much headway against that.
(*He points again to the ceiling and coughs – coughs himself into a
violent fit of coughing.*)
But up there – the attic is very dusty.
How do they get fresh air, then,
the poor stowaways? The dust . . . ah.
(*He gradually stops coughing.*)
Yes, the dust up there, what.

ABBOT: Quite simple, Eminence, they go
on to the roof at night, all night
if they have a mind to it.
By day, they go *singly*
into the garden, help in the kitchen,
and in the library . . . why ever not?
In point of fact, Eminence, the cupboard's
merely decorative: it will only become necessary
if the Gestapo cease to be so admirably
respectful as they have so far shown themselves
towards the extra-territorial houses
in Rome. In that case we would
wall up all the doors leading to
the hiding-place and the cupboard
would be the only entrance.
(*The monk brings, in silence, glasses and a straw-covered bottle
and leaves again.*)
(*pouring*)
Thank you, brother . . .

CARDINAL: Well, Father General, to your protégés.

ABBOT: Many thanks. God protect them.
Your Eminence has, with your visit and
your kind words, brought
a wonderful cheerfulness and a new
feeling of comfort to our refuge.
Please, Eminence,
come as often as you can to see them.

CARDINAL (*moved*): Yes, mmm, what, and I must visit
the stowaways in the Campo Santo
and at Santa Maria del' Anima
mmm, what – the wine

is welcome, it was too dusty
up in the attic. Among the *Jews*
(*he points to the ceiling*)
up there, my good Father General, we may
make several converts to the Church of Christ, yes.

ABBOT: That would be an excellent thing, Eminence.

CARDINAL: Yes – and have no fear
for your guests: Herr Hitler is no more likely
to attack the monasteries of Rome than he is
to attack the Chief:
he is a lot too foxy
to offer the world that sort of entertainment.
Although the Germans know that several
of the monasteries are being used to send radio messages from –
of course, that shouldn't be happening.
Herr von Weizsäcker, in fact, actually asked me
to make a statement on the front page of the *Osservatore*
for the benefit of the occupying forces, mmm, what,
about the excellent way in which the Germans
behave towards the Curia and its property
and its property, yes – we'll do that,
mmm, what – they've deserved it.
Nevertheless, not quite for nothing, eh?

ABBOT (*smiling*): Good. Eminence – tomorrow morning I shall
make the head of the Gestapo a bargain:
We make the statement –
he gives me a Communist,
the son of a well-known scholar in Milan
who came to us for help . . .
The Pope attaches great importance to it.
I think I will be able to pull it off.

CARDINAL: Fine, fine.
(*The telephone rings. The Cardinal passes the receiver over to the
Abbot, then stands, puts his hat and his cloak on while –*)

ABBOT (*speaks into the telephone*):
Yes, speaking – who? Hm. Just a minute.
Eminence, Father Riccardo is asking
to be received immediately
with an officer of the S.S. Shall I . . .?

CARDINAL (*curious. Irritated*):
Riccardo Fontana? Oh, certainly . . . please, mmm, what.

But only if it's no trouble to you, yes.

ABBOT (*into the telephone*): Bring him up, brother.
  (*He hangs up and says to the Cardinal, who is walking up and down nervously but unable to make up his mind to leave :*)
  Father Riccardo, Eminence, has already importuned
  me several times to ask His Holiness . . .

CARDINAL (*offended and irritated*):
  Yes, yes, yes, what, it's Riccardo's
  eternal theme; we've got to know it by degrees.
  At the fall of Stalingrad six months ago,
  I had to get him away from Berlin
  because he was acting too much on his own responsibility.
  What is he up to back in Rome already?
  His place of work is Lisbon. He should be there.
  His father's position has spoilt him, yes,
  and being a special protégé of the Chief's,
  who treats him like a favourite nephew.
  He's too ambitious. Incapable of obedience, yes.
  (*A knock at the door. The Cardinal has positioned himself so that
  he is not immediately visible to anybody entering. The Abbot opens
  the door. Riccardo and Gerstein enter with the old monk, who
  immediately withdraws. Riccardo almost jumps the two steps
  down into the room, Gerstein stays by the door.*)

RICCARDO (*even before he has introduced Gerstein, shouts*):
  So we have let it go as far as this:
  This evening they started picking up the Jews
  in Rome as well . . . it's infamous . . .
  (*He sees the Cardinal, starts, goes to him, bows over his ring.*)

ABBOT: *What* did you say? – This is terrible.

CARDINAL: Ah, Riccardo, what. Has the Nuncio
  sent you from Lisbon? And who might this . . .?
  (*He goes to Gerstein, who makes a deep bow. Gerstein is very
  uneasy and extremely mistrustful.*)

RICCARDO (*quickly*): This, Eminence, is our informant
  in the Reichsführung S.S. – we will leave
  his name out of the conversation.
  It was he who first asked the legal representatives
  of Bishop Count Preysing to report to the Vatican
  on the gassings in Belzec and Treblinka.
  (*angry*)
  That is now over a year ago . . .

CARDINAL (*fairly genially. Shakes Gerstein's hand*):
    Oh, yes, what, thank you –
    Herr Leutnant, we were very deeply moved.
    God will reward you for performing
    this service for the victims, what.
    But what – Riccardo, what did you say just now?
    It really *is* happening in Rome, now, what?
    (*uncertain, nervous, angry*)
    We thought those banditti – good Father General,
    we really did think the Jews here in Rome
    would not be arrested.
    Let us hope most of them have been able
    to get over to the Allies by now.
    They're in Naples already, yes.
    (*to Gerstein in justification*)
    And there are hundreds hidden in the monasteries . . .
    (*The excitement allows the four of them to talk at once. The Abbot greets Gerstein; the Cardinal speaks to Riccardo and the others, the Abbot to Gerstein alone, trying to calm him.*)

GERSTEIN (*nervous*): May I ask you, Monsignore,
    to make absolutely sure that – that beside myself
    no other German is allowed in here.

ABBOT: Don't worry. As long as you
    were not noticed coming in from the street –
    no one will see you here: none of
    your colleagues visit me at this hour of night.

GERSTEIN: Colleagues . . . Monsignore,
    I only wear the same uniform.

ABBOT (*understandingly*): I know. I have already heard of you –
    although, please rest assured, your name
    remains unknown to me . . .
    (*Now they listen to the Cardinal and Riccardo.*)

RICCARDO (*begins while the Abbot is talking to Gerstein*):
    Eminence – it has come to this:
    citizens of Rome outlawed!
    Civilians hunted under the windows
    of His Holiness – is no action
    to be taken even now, Eminence?

CARDINAL (*aware of being in the wrong and therefore very angry*):
    Action *has* been taken, Riccardo,
    (*with emphasis*)

we have given asylum even to unbaptized Jews.
Father General, show Riccardo your attic, please.
(*threateningly to Gerstein*)
You Germans, yes. You terrible Germans.
I am so fond of you, mmm, what, the Chief
is fond of you – but stop this
business with the *Jews*, mmm, what. Eternal
disturbers of the peace and Protestants.
Now you have gone so far, that even the Pope
must expose you to the world.
Here, under his very window . . .
you are dragging off women and children, and
every one knows, mmm, what, not one will return.
You are forcing us, and now you force the Pope,
to public recognition
of these atrocities, yes.

RICCARDO: Thank God. Now, at last . . .

CARDINAL (*flies out at Riccardo, who receives it with a challenging expression of mockery*):
I will not tolerate that, Count Fontana.
Are you so narrow-minded as to overlook, yes,
that every execration of the Curia
against Hitler sounds a clarion
of victory for the Bolshevists, mmm, what?
Stalin is marching on Kiev.
Hitler's summer offensive has come to grief . . .
(*to Gerstein, almost in tears*)
Just what are you up to, you Germans?

ABBOT (*to Riccardo*): Let me take you up to my protégés.
You must see we are really helping . . .

RICCARDO: I know that already, Father General.

CARDINAL (*cold, commanding*): Even so, go up with the Father General.
(*While Riccardo is shown into the cupboard by the Abbot, the Cardinal turns to Gerstein. The cupboard doors stay open until the Cardinal leans against them.*)

GERSTEIN: Eminence, perhaps Hitler
might draw back if His Holiness
were secretly to write to him and threaten him,
with the revoking of the Concordat.

CARDINAL (*evasive and reserved*):
Possibly, yes, what, quite possibly.

I am speaking to the Chief again this evening, yes.
Tell me one thing, Herr Leutnant – how on earth
could the Germans forget the mission that God
has given them in the centre of the West . . .?

GERSTEIN (*quietly*):
Eminence, that cannot be. God would not be
God, if He used such a man as Hitler . . .

CARDINAL: Yes, yes, most certainly He would . . . indeed,
was not Cain, his brother's murderer,
also the tool of God? Cain spoke to God:
My sin is greater far than you
will be able to forgive. And still the Lord set,
mmm, what, a mark upon Cain,
lest any, finding him, should kill him, yes.
And what does your Luther say?
That worldly power stems from Cain, mmm, what.
Cain has his purpose in the world, Noah his,
what can we know of the terrible ways of God?
(*enthusiastic*)
But one thing we do know, mmm, what,
the West, yes, the culture of Christianity,
that God does not want to destroy.

GERSTEIN (*repelled*): And why not? Eminence, if God
did not wish to destroy us, why has he
struck us Christians blind in this terrible way?
The Church, Your Eminence – may I be frank?

CARDINAL: Of course, why yes, certainly, say what you like.

GERSTEIN: For sixteen months now Rome has known
what Hitler is doing to Poland: why does
the Pope say not one word about it?
There where the towers of his churches stand,
stand also Hitler's smoking chimneys.
Where the bells ring on Sundays,
the ovens burn on weekdays:
that is the look of the Christian West today.
Why, Eminence, should God
not send another flood?
Only the tanks of Stalin are now able
to free Treblinka, Auschwitz, Majdanek . . .

CARDINAL (*appalled, in extremis*):
What are you saying? – Surely, though,

you love your country, mmm, what, Herr Leutnant?

GERSTEIN: Do not ask me to answer that, Eminence.
In my country Hitler is
a very popular man. Many Germans I love
will die when the Red army invades.
I will probably die myself – and yet . . .

CARDINAL: And yet – you're not a Communist,
are you? – You want the Red army
here? Can you not see ahead then, mmm,
how altars will be ransacked, priests beaten,
women violated, mmm, what?

GERSTEIN (*brutal*): Yes, Eminence, it will be the Apocalypse.
Nevertheless – the barbarities of a troop of soldiers
in the dormitory of a nunnery would not be
more terrible
than what the lawyers and the doctors and the brigands
of Hitler have been doing
under cover of this – my uniform – for years,
for *years*, Eminence,
to Jews and Poles and Russian prisoners.
Eminence, you can check this for yourself,
tens of thousands of Jewish families
from Western Europe, tens of thousands,
have been carried off: where to, Eminence, where to?
What do they think of that in Rome, then?

CARDINAL (*helpless, because overwhelmed*):
Of course, yes, naturally . . . nevertheless, my dear sir,
the horror of the crematoria
has blinded you, too, to the fact
that there still must be, *must* be
an alternative to the saving of these victims
by the Red army, *must* be,
for the sake of the West, mmm, what. . . .
Perhaps a landing in Normandy . . .
The entry of Stalin into Berlin – yes, good God,
that is a price which Europe
cannot, no, *must* not pay.

GERSTEIN: Eminence, when Napoleon had senselessly
destroyed his Grande Armée, he then invented,
in the course of a conversation with Caulaincourt
(who did not believe a single word of it)

the legend of the Russian Colossus who,
ostensibly, had wished to annihilate Europe.
This legend, about which Bismarck,
Frederick the Great, even Wilhelm II,
would only have laughed maliciously,
Hitler was already exploiting
when he invaded Russia. –
And every European criminal, who looks with greed
towards the East will, in the future, reiterate
it is his duty to save civilization. . . .
The Vatican must never support this, Eminence!

CARDINAL (*gladly taking advantage of this diversion*):
We are not anticipating any sort of aggression, what.
But you're simplifying, Herr Leutnant: Frederick
of Prussia and Bismarck too were all *too* well aware
of the Russian Colossus, what. And because the king –
like Napoleon, like Hitler –
could see no other way around the question,
he whipped up the ambitions of the Russians
towards expansion in the West *himself*.
Like Napoleon, mmm, what, like Hitler; the offer of
collaboration in the ruins of divided countries, yes.
Always the same as long as things go well.
They never *do* go well for long, mmm, what.

GERSTEIN: But Russia has never threatened the West
as strongly, Eminence, as Hitler
and Napoleon have threatened it.
Both would have entirely subjugated Europe,
had not their marches on Moscow
called Russia into the field first.
Europe has been *saved* by Russia . . .
and she can only defend herself
against this dangerous deliverer
by living in agreement with her.

CARDINAL: With the Bolshevists as well?

GERSTEIN: With every leader in the Kremlin . . . it doesn't matter
whether his name is Alexander or Stalin . . .

CARDINAL: Easy to say, hard to do . . . mmm, what . . .
(*Riccardo and the Abbot come back through the cupboard. The
Abbot closes the doors.*)

GERSTEIN: It has always been hard, Eminence; even for Bismarck

it was a tight-rope act.
But still he never even allowed himself
the *idea* of a preventive war against Petersburg . . .

CARDINAL: Neither has the Chief personally ever called
for a crusade against Russia, mmm, what, yes.
I understand the distress you feel, Riccardo, yes.
But have you now seen up there
that the Holy See is playing its part, what?

RICCARDO: Eminence, these are the lucky ones,
very few amongst millions –
who reach the sanctuary door.
If the Pope assures them a hiding-place,
he is only doing what many families
are doing for the hunted
in Berlin, Paris, Amsterdam and Brussels.
Except, Eminence, that the doctor, the businessman,
the worker, who hides a Jew,
risks execution.
What does the Pope risk?

CARDINAL (*with an effort to control his once more rising temper*):
Riccardo – today, here, yes, what,
the arrests in *Rome*, that changes everything, yes.
The Chief will speak now as Bishop,
as others have spoken.
But we are losing time, while outside
the terror rages. . . . Had you not better stay
(*He has laid his hand on Gerstein's shoulder.*)
here in the house, for your protection –?
My good Father General, mmm, what, is that all right? . . .

ABBOT: I guarantee your safety
as long as the monastery is not bombed . . .

GERSTEIN: Eminence – Monsignore, I am touched.
But I still have a family in Germany.
I cannot leave them on their own.

CARDINAL: May God protect you and your family.
Thank you, gentlemen. Let us pray
for the persecuted, mmm, what . . . My
dear friend, I'll find my own way out
with Brother Irenäus, please stay here
with your guests . . . yes, good-bye!
(*The Abbot rings for the monk, who appears at once.*)

ABBOT
RICCARDO } (*all together*): Eminence.
GERSTEIN

CARDINAL: Good-bye.

> (*Goes with the monk, but turns immediately, very nervous, to Gerstein.*)
>
> Just one more quick question, Herr Leutnant,
> not out of curiosity but desperation, yes:
> London *and* Madrid and Stockholm
> and several visitors here speak optimistically
> of an anti-Hitler movement inside Germany itself . . .
> What is there in that? Anything at all?
>
> (*The Abbot gestures the monk to withdraw, which he does.*)

GERSTEIN: Oh, Eminence, a few defenceless people,
> priests, Socialists, Communists,
> Jehovah's Witnesses. On one day
> in September, a hundred and eighty were
> hanged in Plötzensee, the women beheaded . . .
> a hopeless struggle . . .

CARDINAL (*agitated, with great sympathy: it is the first he has heard of it*):
> *Women*, did you say? Women as well!
> Oh, Mother of God, intercede for them.
> And the army? London mentioned generals, yes –
> would these officers be in any way able
> to coerce a populace
> still in love with Herr Hitler?

GERSTEIN: Only if they announced that *Himmler*
> has murdered the Führer! – in that case, they could.
> The anger of the people must be turned
> against the S.S. and the Gestapo . . .

CARDINAL: Diabolical . . . mmm, what. Yes . . . diabolical.

GERSTEIN:
> It would be the only way, Eminence, that revolutionaries might
> perhaps get control.
> Perhaps.
> But I do not think the officers
> are prepared to sacrifice themselves. It is not the German
> army that will do away
> with Hitler, but the *Russian*.

CARDINAL: Hitler along with everything else, may be.

But that is terrible, mmm, what . . .
Thank you. Arrivederci. Good night, gentlemen, good night.
(*The Abbot accompanies the Cardinal to the door, behind which the monk is again visible and accompanies the Cardinal off. The Abbot returns and speaks to Riccardo, who is leaning hopelessly against the wall.*)

ABBOT: I agree with you: this calamity had to come
even to Rome. Hitler
will now learn the price
of challenging the Holy Father.
(*Riccardo says nothing as yet.*)

GERSTEIN: Monsignore, are you *sure*
that he will intercede now?

ABBOT: Absolutely. – Aren't you, Riccardo?

RICCARDO: Not so sure as all that.
If the Pope reacts as usual,
– that is to say, not at all,
(*passionately*)
Father General, what do we do then?

ABBOT (*curt*): We must obey, you know that.

RICCARDO (*stubborn*): That would be too easy. Look at him –
an officer: if he had not disobeyed, broken his oath of allegiance,
he would be a murderer. What about us?
(*insistently, enlisting sympathy*)
Father General, you have saved the lives of hundreds.

ABBOT: It was the *Pope* who made it possible.
Don't forget that, Riccardo!

RICCARDO: I do not forget it, but think:
this good Samaritan's work the Pope has done
without making the smallest sacrifice,
apart from financial,
without the shadow even of a risk . . .
and, if I know you, you will not be *able* to stand by
and do nothing
when the victims
are loaded into cattle trucks – tomorrow! – here! –

ABBOT: Good God – a priest may not shoot!

RICCARDO (*quietly, almost to himself*):
No, but go with them. He can go with them.

GERSTEIN (*with no idea how long Riccardo has been thinking about this*):
That would be quite pointless.

ABBOT : And would not save one single Jew, not one.

RICCARDO (*more to himself*):

No, not one Jew, but our – superiors.

When I visited Prior Lichtenberg

in the prison hospital,

he was tormented by the fact that none of us was with the Jews.

'I will go with them' – he said – 'the Nazis

had already given permission.' Then they

broke their word, as ever,

and dragged Lichtenberg off to Dachau.

Now not one of us is with the Jews.

GERSTEIN (*with certainty*): The S.S. could never allow

an Italian priest to accompany the deportees.

It would be too interesting for the Allied propaganda.

RICCARDO: And if the priest himself should be a Jew –

like the Dutch monks who were deported

to the East.

(*He looks at his watch ; then, smiling :*)

He's sure to be in Naples by now,

with Eisenhower's soldiers, the Jew

whom I exchanged passports with this morning,

and I still have

the Star of David from your lodger.

I have only to be seen with that –

and I'd be arrested straight away.

GERSTEIN (*greatly disturbed*):

Riccardo – you would not be treated as a priest,

you would be gassed as a Jew.

ABBOT (*frightened and irritated at the same time*):

Burn the star *and* the passport –

it's dangerous for you to have them.

RICCARDO (*to cause a diversion*):

How do you account for the fact, Herr Gerstein,

that we have heard

no more from your friend Jacobson ?

GERSTEIN: The death of his parents turned him against us.

RICCARDO: But not against me, surely!

GERSTEIN (*shrugging*): Perhaps they caught him after all,

and killed him on the spot.

RICCARDO (*after another look at his watch*):

Father General, please tell me –

you *must* know – what are we to do
if the Pope does not protest?
(*Pause. A helpless gesture from the Abbot. Silence, while Gerstein
looks at the map of the mission stations. Almost with scorn :*)
Nothing? Nothing at all?

ABBOT (*hesitating. He must say something*):
In individual cases . . . we can help
as we have . . . up to now . . .

RICCARDO: And *look on* – ? No! Most Reverend Father,
that is not . . . that cannot be . . .
your final word: look on and do nothing,
when tomorrow evening at Termini Station
our fellow citizens – not forgetting
the Jewish-born Catholics as well – are herded
into cattle trucks. *We – we –*
stand there and –
(*he laughs suddenly*)
wave to them with our handkerchiefs,
if the good Germans will allow us.
(*again this not quite normal laugh, and he proceeds with the rising
tension of his anger and his argument*)
And then – then do we go home?
And confess – confess what?
That we have spoken the name of God in vain?
And read in the newspaper
how far the excavations in St Peter's
have progressed . . .
And then on Sunday, we ring the bells
and we celebrate mass . . . so devoutly
that we are not indeed led into the temptation
of thinking of those who, at that moment,
are being driven, naked, into the gas
at Auschwitz.

ABBOT (*unnerved, despairing*): God in Heaven . . . what is there
left for us to do then?
(*Silence . . . Then . . .*)

RICCARDO: Not to be against them – that is as bad
as to be with them.
It is – I don't know, perhaps still less forgivable.
(*a shout*)
We are *priests*. God could not pardon it

in a hangman,
but a priest, *a Pope* . . .
(*Silence. Then quietly, calculatingly, factually :*)
Father General, please – tell me: if God promised Abraham
He would not destroy Sodom if ten righteous men
were found in the city – do you believe,
most reverend Father –
that God will still spare His Church
if even a few of her servants –
like Lichtenberg –
stand by the persecuted ?

ABBOT (*surprised, but with understanding*):
Many of us help, as well as they can,
But I do not see what this question . . .

RICCARDO : You see as well as I, Father General,
you must see:
the Pope's silence on behalf of the murderers
is laying on the Church a burden of guilt
which we must expiate,
and as the Pope, although too, only a man,
can actually represent *God* upon earth,
then a poor priest could – and will –
(*Gerstein understands and tries to interrupt. Riccardo does not let
himself be sidetracked.*)
if need be,
represent the Pope . . . *there*,
where he should stand today.

ABBOT (*more shocked than angry*):
Riccardo, I shall regard your – monstrous accusation,
as a secret of the confessional –
(*to Gerstein, who is making a gesture of agreement*)
Herr Leutnant, I would ask you to do so to . . .
but I am afraid for you, Riccardo.
What gives you the right to use these words,
which should shame every single one of us
to the depths of his being . . .

RICCARDO (*very alarmed*):
No . . . for God's sake, no! Father General,
you, and how many other priests besides, some of whom have
died already on the scaffold – have
done their duty, you have . . .

ABBOT (*sharply*): And not the Pope?

RICCARDO (*strongly*): Not to the limit of his powers! No!
Perhaps tonight still or tomorrow
he will make good, what has long been his duty,
as the mouthpiece of Christendom.
Or else . . . or else one of us in Rome
must go with them.
And if he dies . . .

GERSTEIN: He will die all right.
He will be gassed and burnt.

RICCARDO (*unmoved*): Then perhaps the fire that consumes him,
if God accepts the sacrifice –

ABBOT: Riccardo.

RICCARDO (*very quickly*): Will purge the guilt of our superiors.
The idea of the Papacy . . .

ABBOT (*violently*): . . . will survive Auschwitz. Why do you doubt,
why do you torment yourself like this, Riccardo? You go too far.

RICCARDO: It is not a question of Auschwitz now! The idea
of the Papacy must be kept pure for all eternity,
even if it is temporarily
incarnate in an Alexander Borgia
or in a . . .

ABBOT (*grips him almost brutally by the shoulder*):
Not one syllable more. That is –
Do you know so little of Pius XII?

RICCARDO: Ah, Father General, the picture
of Cardinal Pacelli has hung
above my bed since I was twelve years old.
Because of him I became a priest, even though
my . . . my mother begged me not to do so.
For the rest of tonight I will pray
that I may have been mistaken in the Pope;
that by tomorrow evening he will have freed the families
– I pray for it, I am afraid –
(*very quiet, almost inaudible*)
I have such dread of the camp.
(*The Abbot is going to him, fatherly, when Gerstein steps in between
them decisively.*)

GERSTEIN (*with energy*): You make yourself guilty, if you abandon *us*.
Stop thinking of the salvation of the Church –
you will not help one single human being.

You would be making yourself guilty, Riccardo.

RICCARDO (*with aversion*): I would only be honouring my word.
　　I cannot be of help here,
　　I have tried – for more
　　than a year: all I did was talk.

ABBOT (*one cannot tell whether he believes his own words*):
　　Tomorrow morning, Count, you will see:
　　it was not all in vain. The Pope will help.

RICCARDO (*points to his watch*):
　　But he *knows* what has been happening
　　here in Rome for hours now.
　　You are his go-between with the Gestapo.
　　Why has he not said anything to you?

ABBOT (*unsure of himself*):
　　He won't negotiate with the Gestapo in Rome;
　　he will negotiate only with Hitler himself.
　　I think he will send him an ultimatum.
　　(*Silence. They walk up and down. Gerstein looks for a long time at
　　Riccardo, then says hesitatingly, cunningly:*)

GERSTEIN: I see just one last chance, but . . .
　　no, no, I must not say it.

RICCARDO: But tell us.

GERSTEIN: Gentlemen, who am I
　　to lead two priests
　　to disobedience . . . no, I must not . . .

ABBOT: What do you mean by that?

GERSTEIN: Monsignore: if you, together with
　　Father Riccardo, were for half an hour
　　to take over the Vatican broadcasting station . . .

ABBOT (*mistrustful*): What do you mean 'take over'? I go
　　in and out of the station all the time.

GERSTEIN (*quickly, but one sees it is no sudden idea on his part*):
　　Then, Monsignore, order
　　every priest in Europe to follow the example
　　of Lichtenberg . . .
　　and call on their congregations,
　　from Narvik to Sicily, to save the Jews.

ABBOT (*angrily*): You suggest a priest should presume
　　to speak in the place of His Holiness?

RICCARDO: Yes, when the Pope forgets
　　to speak in the place of Christ.

ABBOT: But, gentlemen, this is infamous!
    A priest, as Pontifex Maximus, to order,
    ex cathedra, his brothers in office in Europe
    to martyrdom?
GERSTEIN: Monsignore, it will not go as far as that.
RICCARDO: Certainly not, no: Hitler's fronts are weakening.
    He will not alienate the Catholics
    of all Europe, for the sake of the Jews.
    Millions upon millions of us,
    in industry . . . the army . . .
GERSTEIN: Yes, Monsignore; Hitler will withdraw –
ABBOT: But, gentlemen, the idea that the Holy Father
    himself had called the congregations to resist
    would not survive a day, a single day:
    the Pope himself would issue a denial.
    (*to Gerstein, more angrily, still excited*)
    Be realistic: if a shock troop
    seized Berlin radio today, and told England and America
    ostensibly in Hitler's name
    they were ready for peace: how long
    would Hitler let the deception continue . . .
    Half an hour, a whole hour?
GERSTEIN: Monsignore –
    I am thinking about the Pope, you are talking about Hitler;
    there . . . there is no parallel.
ABBOT (*offended, irritated*): Certainly not. But both of them
    would, of course, deny immediately . . .
GERSTEIN: I see . . . In that event, Hitler would have to be
    prevented from denying it:
    first do away with him, then the announcement:
    that the S.S. have murdered the Führer, so that
    the anger of the people . . .
ABBOT (*self-righteous, disgusted . . . he is incapable of lying, decisively*):
    You have already suggested that
    diabolical plan once: but we are priests, Herr Leutnant,
    we have no means of hindering the Pope
    from making a denial. A priest,
    I feel I have to inform you,
    'hinders' the Pope from nothing. It is absurd!
GERSTEIN (*as casually as possible*):

Of course not, Monsignore, though
any 'hindrance' suffered by the Pope would,
be laid automatically by everyone
at the door of the S.S. as long as they
are taking victims for Auschwitz from Rome . . .

ABBOT (*rises, bringing the conversation to a definite close*):
Gentlemen, please: let us end this
conversation at once. You cannot,
in this house, and with priests, discuss
acts of violence against His Holiness . . .
it would be monstrous

GERSTEIN (*apparently offended*):
Monsignore, what are you imputing to me?

ABBOT: I wish to impute nothing.
Your own implication is quite clear enough:
that anything that might be undertaken
against the Pope at this moment . . .
I dare not ask you what you have in mind –
would automatically be laid at the door of the S.S.

GERSTEIN (*hastily*): But I never thought
of recommending the application of force
against the *person* of His Holiness . . . Monsignore.

ABBOT (*ironically*): Did you not? . . . Aha!

GERSTEIN (*quite in control of himself again*):
But a *denial* over the radio
could be hindered by a priest,
in that he could temporarily
destroy the *radio station – that* is what
I meant just now – the whole world would, of course,
hold the S.S. responsible for *that*,
especially if the jamming were to come
after an official radio protest
by the Pope against the S.S. . . .

RICCARDO (*fascinated by Gerstein's plan, as if waking up*):
Father General: at a moment like this
this could mean deliverance for thousands,
for hundreds of thousands, the final deliverance.

ABBOT (*cold*): You will not, Father Riccardo, be able to
get to the microphone by yourself . . . I am relieved to say.
You are very tired and nervous; please,
before we finally get a little rest,

I must speak to you further alone.

GERSTEIN: Monsignore, I must thank you,
and take my leave.

ABBOT (*more moderately*): Live more carefully . . . Don't
take it amiss, it is well meant advice from an old man
who would like to pray for you, though he cannot follow you.
God be with you.

GERSTEIN: Monsignore, thank you – from my heart.
Count – auf Wiedersehen, good night.

RICCARDO: Come to us early, before my father
goes to the Pope at nine tomorrow morning.
(*The monk is waiting for Gerstein.*)

GERSTEIN: I will come around eight. Good night.

RICCARDO: Good night.
(*Gerstein goes out with the monk.*)

ABBOT (*after watching Riccardo a moment without speaking*):
I was frankly scared, Riccardo,
to send you out into the night
with that uncanny man. His eyes. He is
hypnotizing you; he has been singled out, that man,
he bears the mark of Cain. What is his name?

RICCARDO: Let us leave his name out of this, Father General.

ABBOT (*not offended*):
You are quite right, excuse me. Tell me,
you didn't want to go with him either, did you?

RICCARDO: Because I still have something to ask you.
And because I must then make confession.

ABBOT: First I have something to ask you: I am alarmed
to see you wax in the hand
of this strange ambassador, Count.
Go carefully with him, I beg you.

RICCARDO: No need to worry.

ABBOT: Riccardo, I would believe that man capable of . . .
(*extremely agitated*)
Why, please: *why* did he twice,
quite superfluously, quite unnecessarily,
entertain the idea of that Satanic betrayal:
to murder Hitler . . . and put the blame on the S.S.?

RICCARDO: A very moral intention.

ABBOT (*provoked, violently*):
Which leads to Civil War! 'Moral' – please:

143

you are dog-tired.
But that is not what I was thinking of, my dear boy;
nor was he. This uncanny man, believe me,
I watched him closely, *he*
did not find it unnecessary
to bring it to our notice.
(*His aversion grows, the more he follows his thought to a conclusion.*)
Riccardo, this man would be prepared to
consign you or himself
to Hell, by suggesting to you –
more by his looks than his words –
that – I – I simply *cannot* say it –
it is so execrable . . . so –

RICCARDO (*still inhibited from speaking the truth*):
He suggests nothing to *me*, Father General.

ABBOT: *He did, he did.*
He suggested to you that humanity,
that the whole world could never be stirred,
more irreconcilably against Hitler,
than by charging Hitler's bodyguard, the S.S.,
with the . . . the assassination,
(*almost inaudibly*)
the *murder* of
the Representative of Christ on earth.

RICCARDO (*groans, in his excitement using Gerstein's name, which the Abbot does not notice*):
You are thought-reading, most reverend Father . . . but
they are *not Gerstein's* thoughts . . .

ABBOT (*unable to control his voice with horror. Whispering, as he turns brusquely away*):
Riccardo – what . . . I have nothing more to
say to you. Go away.
(*Silence. Then, frankly pressing:*)
You do not know, you do not know
what you are saying . . . Come into the chapel,
you said you wished to make confession, now you *must*.
(*With trembling hands he lights a three-branched candelabrum, puts out the desk-lamp, takes the candelabrum and goes ahead, till he notices Riccardo is not following him. The room is now lit by the candles only.*)

Why are you not following me, Riccardo?

RICCARDO: I cannot . . . I can . . . not make confession now.
You would have to withhold absolution,
for I cannot make true *repentance*.
Just understand, Father General,
for three months, since Rome has been occupied
by the Germans . . . I have been hoping that, once and for all,
the S.S. and the Vatican would meet in bloody collision.
But now the most terrible thing is happening
that could possibly happen: they do not even
disturb each other . . .
They live *together*
in the Eternal City – because the Pope
does not forbid the hangmen of Auschwitz
to load up their victims,
here under his windows.
(*madness in his eyes*)
How do we know – that God
is not sending a murderer to the Pope
to save him from complete damnation?

ABBOT (*totally uncomprehending, no longer capable of reaction*):
Riccardo . . . you are in sin, in sin.

RICCARDO (*as if driven*): He who said, I bring not
peace, but a sword,
(*emphatically*)
must also have reckoned with the fact
that it would one day
be turned against the foremost of His followers.
And the Church must know it, too,
as she has always used the sword herself.
(*tormented*)
Must I draw back most reverend Father?
Do not resist evil . . . is this our duty now
because it will destroy us?
No soldier is allowed to save himself . . .
why then a priest? Could Judas have declined?
(*in great terror of the consequences to himself*)
He *knew* he would be damned to all Eternity . . .
His sacrifice was greater than that
of Our Lord.

ABBOT (*annihilating*): Riccardo . . . Judas has not

deserved to be compared to *you*:
for you *want* to do this thing yourself . . .
and lay the blame on *others*.

RICCARDO (*with wild passion*):
Not I. Every man, the whole *earth*
would accuse Hitler with the S.S.
And it must be so. It must be so . . .
Therefore I will atone . . .
on earth and before God.

ABBOT: You are struggling, but God holds you still . . .
or why should you have told all this to me?

RICCARDO (*objectively, yet fanatically. The Abbot only listens because
he is incapable of speaking*):
Because I cannot do it alone.
Because I need *you*. You must go to the radio
and say, the S.S. committed the murder
because the Pope wished to save the Jews.
Once spoken over our radio,
once *known* from Iceland to
Australia: and for the rest of his days
Hitler will stand before all mankind
as the contradictor of creation
that he is, its most degraded outcast.
No one, not Goebbels, not the Cardinal,
could publish a believable denial
before the crematoria of Auschwitz
had been extinguished . . .
(*He throws himself on his knees before the Abbot.*)
Help me, most reverend Father,
you *must* help.

ABBOT (*with cold horror*): Leave me – go.
Outcast of creation, you said:
that is you, yourself.
Repent . . . get away . . . get out of my sight,
or come to confession.

RICCARDO (*shouting*): I cannot do it without you.
(*as he rises, with a final effort*)
If you do not help me, Father General . . .
Then *I* must pray for *you* as well . . .

ABBOT: Go away. Go away now,
if you persist in this

criminal madness. Go away.
(*He has turned away completely. Hoarsely :*)
Go . . . get out . . . murderer.
(*Riccardo goes, the door stays open, the candles flicker wildly, then the draught extinguishes them. The Abbot falls on his knees before the prie-dieu.*)

Curtain

SCENE THREE

The grey dawn of 17 October.

The Roman Headquarters of the Gestapo, in the former Cultural Section of the German Embassy in Via Tasso. The entrance hall is arranged as a large office, which has access on one side to the cellars – the cells – and opens on the other side on to a dark courtyard, the gate of which we are unable to see. A heavy lorry is heard driving into the courtyard; people are loaded off it and led to the cellar behind the stage. Shouted orders like :

'Runter! 'raus da! Fuori! Los, los . . . subito!

Dogs bark. A command :

Get off. Stop that row.

Then Witzel is heard counting away :

Forty-six, forty-nine, fifty –
fifty-two – ah, with them there – and then
the two kids brings it
to sixty.
Take them to the others.

Before the Sergeant appears on the staircase that connects the house and the courtyard, we see in the foreground an officer of the Waffen-S.S. rising from an arm-chair in which he had been asleep, his boots beside the chair, his feet on another chair covered with a light great-coat – Salzer. He yawns like a dog with his whole body, cranes his neck and stretches luxuriously, runs his hands through his hair and over his cheeks, drinks from a bottle of mineral water, walks in his stock-inged feet to the glass door and looks down into the courtyard till Witzel appears and reports.

Salzer is an officer like many others : tall, stout and insignificant, in vigorous good health, in his middle thirties, and more devoted to Adolf

Hitler, the leader, than most, since it is precisely this devotion he has to thank for the fact that he is hunting defenceless civilians in the occupied territories instead of having to risk his life on the Russian Front, like the great majority of his contemporaries.

Just as the Father General in this play bears only a slender resemblance to the historical Abbot of the Salvatoriani, so the character of this officer is only slightly taken from the historical Obersturmführer Kappler, who belonged to those S.S. officers whose actions were not anonymous and who could, unfortunately, in 1945 be accused of definite acts. Kappler is currently paying for his activity as German Chief of Police during the years 1943–44 with a sentence of life imprisonment: in his position of absolute authority he had hanged 335 hostages instead of 330 – as Berlin had ordered him. We would like, however, to carry over to our Chief of Police a remarkable quality which Consul Moellhausen describes Kappler as possessing: it has a bearing on the sequence of historical events, and, apart from that, it is typical of most people who today, at one time or another, have to exercise similar functions: this intelligent, unquestioningly obedient officer did not even have a negative relationship with his victims. If ordered, he would have been similarly punctilious in arresting the whores or the nuns of Rome; he was no fanatic and worked with as little passion as a guillotine. That the cellars of his prison were ruled by terror is nevertheless an established fact.

WITZEL (*appearing at the top of the stairs, enters the room and reports*):
Obersturmführer, report operation
completed: 1,127 arrests.

SALZER (*beginning to pull on his boots*):
Thank you. A gratifyingly small number.
There used to be eight thousand Jews in Rome.
They've all buggered off
to the South, to the Yankees. Well, let them feed them.
I said right from the start it wasn't worth it.

WITZEL:
And there's hundreds in the monasteries. We caught about thirty
trying to slink off there. The Italians
from the mobile battalions,
they've been into the monasteries already,
where you can be sure that out of a hundred

monks twenty are fakes,
Communists, Jews, Badoglio traitors . . .

SALZER (*with growing impatience; an uncontrolled dogmatist, the more unsure he is of his ground, the more domineering he becomes to his subordinates*):
Off your head, Witzel. You are completely off your head.
Why not exterminate the Pope as well?
Idiot – can you still not understand
(*shouting*)
we are not in the Ukraine?
(*threatening*)
Witzel, I hold you responsible – you will be
on the next train to the Eastern Front
if you don't see that
these idiotic Fascists behave themselves.
These spaghetti-eating hangers-on, always
so god-damned tough when it's
to do with civilians . . . they really would be capable
of raiding a monastery,
better still a nunnery, the filthy-minded scum.
(*He clutches his forehead.*)
You are right off your head.
(*firmly*)
No provocation to the Catholics, understand?

WITZEL: Yes, of course, it's just we have to . . .

SALZER (*screaming*): Do you understand . . . or not?

WITZEL (*sobered*): Yes, Obersturmführer.

SALZER (*quite quietly*): Good . . . What else had you to report?

WITZEL (*confused*): Just that we kept strictly
to the list, Mussolini's list.
So, a lot of the kids weren't on it yet of course.
And then, in general, if someone, for example –
what I mean to say, was on a visit,
he wasn't, of course, on the list.
But they're all Jews, guaranteed.
Just a few got a bit cheeky
and threatened us with the Church,
because of being Catholics – some of them – according to
them –
from birth, and anyway, what I mean to say –

SALZER (*has got his coat on, stops in the middle of buttoning it up,*

extremely agitated):
What are you jabbering about – idiot!
Why didn't you tell me that last *night*?
I would have had a chance
to squash the whole stupid proceedings.
Arresting Catholics in Rome – I –
(*quietly, at a loss*)
perhaps one of them really
isn't a Jew.

WITZEL (*cautiously*): But, Obersturmführer, even you would not
have been able to find that out.
How is one to know which of them is lying?
(*more confidently*)
Obersturmführer, I had no other orders,
and if I may say so,
we can always blame the trespassing –
I mean, if he complains –
I mean, the Pope – then we can
always blame the trespassing on the militia,
on the Italians . . .
They go at it happily enough; it's just one can't
stop them making mistakes, I'm afraid.

SALZER (*resigned*): Very well then, Witzel, the fault is mine –
I should never have put such faith in your intelligence:
take yourself to the photographer
after this heroic act – you ghoul.
Witzel, you have been watching me working here
for weeks: now when we were in Poland
can you recall me ever having dealings with a priest?

WITZEL (*meekly*): No.

SALZER:
And you never considered, did you – why here in Rome I
have to allow our friend the Jesuit,
to visit me every five minutes
to ask me to release one of the troublemakers
that we have happily incarcerated, eh?

WITZEL: Of course, Obersturmführer. Yes, I did.
Only he doesn't come about *Jews*;
the Pope sent him
because he, he . . .

SALZER: *Jews* – you blockhead,

we didn't bring them in before today –
oh, never mind:
get out and bring me
in about five minutes everyone from
that bunch in Cell One, who says
he's a Catholic. Understand?

WITZEL: Yes, Obersturmführer.

SALZER: And another thing: that lot is getting
double rations today: when we've got them
safely over the Brenner
the rations will be cut down once again.
And no beatings, and enough
fresh air in the cellar. Understand?

WITZEL: Yes, Obersturmführer.

(*Exit Witzel. Salzer opens the glass door on to the courtyard, in
which it is gradually getting light, gives a whistle on four fingers
and gestures to the two militiamen who arrested the Luccanis with
Witzel to come up. They appear: the smart one quickly, saluting
punctiliously, the delinquent slouching, after some delay, up the
stairs and into the room, grinning and munching noisily on a huge
slice of melon, which he balances with both hands in front of his
pretty, dirty face, like the sickle of the new moon. Once in the
room he clicks his heels together strongly but with an ironic
coquetry – amused by all the German 'discipline'.*)

SALZER (*indifferent*):
'Morning. At ease. What are you grinning at?

DELINQUENT (*in a voice of moving complaint*):
No joke, Commandant, duty very hard.
No sleep, no food, no money.
Night duty very bad.

SALZER (*amused*):
You are impossible . . .
(*to the smart one*)
Has his girl been waiting up all night for him?

SMART ITALIAN (*offended that Salzer should pay so much attention to
the other one*):
I don't know, but mine has.
Permission to dismiss, Herr Commandant.

DELINQUENT: Nice Jewish girls, Commandant.

SALZER: You can get along now, and don't you
lay a finger on them.

One other thing: you're good Catholics, aren't you?

SMART ITALIAN: No, I'm not a Catholic any more.

DELINQUENT (*simply*): Not good Catholic – ordinary Catholic.

SALZER: Never mind. You can take a look at
these swindlers who say they are Catholics.
We'll see whether they
know anything about the good old customs
of your Church. Will you do that?

SMART ITALIAN (*laughs unpleasantly*):
They must pray. Will they have to pray?

DELINQUENT (*cheerfully*): Sing, singing is better.
Or we baptize them in the Tiber.

SALZER (*serious*): No one is to be hurt, understood?
No beating-up, is that clear?

SMART ITALIAN: And if they don't want to pray?

SALZER: They'll want to, if they can.
Order some coffee and rolls, will you?

SMART ITALIAN: Yes, Herr Commandant.
(*Exit smart Italian.*)

DELINQUENT: We make physical inspections, Commandant?
Very nice, very nice young girls, with the Jews.

SALZER: You keep your hands to yourself.
In an hour's time you can go home
and screw your girl senseless. You aren't
one of the old monks who could always
get a pretty woman arrested as a witch
if the problem ever got urgent for them.

DELINQUENT: Me – monk – oh no.
I would not make a very good monk.
(*now sincerely unhappy, with a gesture of throat cutting*)
The young girls with the Jews,
Commandant . . . they go, too, to Poland?

SALZER (*finishes his toilet, doing his hair*):
None of this lot is going
to Poland; they are going to work
in Austria . . . We have a
holiday resort in Mauthausen.
Aha, Witzel . . . with the godly folk.

(*Witzel marches through the door to the passage with Carlotta, a girl
of about 20, a 40-year-old man and the elder Luccani. None of them*

wears the Star of David. They are all exhausted, the men unshaven, without shoelaces, belts or ties, the girl still very beautiful, but pale and untidy.)

WITZEL (*to the Jews, shouting*):
Faces to the wall! – About turn! – That's
the three from Cell One, Obersturmführer. There's
a lot more say they're Catholics,
but not according to their papers. That one,
the tall one there, I'm not sure about either.
He just says he's an arms manufacturer.

SALZER (*quietly, in the foreground*):
I see . . . that's a nice bunch you've collected . . .
My God, Witzel, it is incomprehensible.
I shall send you to the Eastern Front . . . you idiot, you.
(*louder, uncontrolled*)
I don't want to see them before breakfast!
(*The delinquent looks at the girl, and now goes to her quietly and
quickly ; he separates her from the men, speaks urgently to her, tries
to put a cigarette in her mouth, etc. . . .*)

WITZEL (*very timidly, points to the 40-year-old of whom he has just
spoken : an exceptionally well-dressed man, as far as one can still
tell*):
Him . . . that one, he said . . .

SALZER: I don't want to know what he said.
All I want, for Christ's sake, is to drink my coffee.
(*quietly*)
Did they get a tailor,
a good uniform tailor ?

WITZEL: Herr Obersturmführer, not a tailor;
a shoemaker, though. They took one
out of a shoe shop, and a barber . . .

SALZER: Rubbish, barbers . . . but that reminds
me, I haven't shaved yet. This dirty rabble
keeps me awake all night
and I let myself go to rack and ruin.
After breakfast you can get that Latvian
to come and give me a shave. Understand ?

WITZEL: Yes, Obersturmführer . . . Here comes
the coffee now.

(*He hastens to spread a tablecloth. The smart Italian has brought a big*

*tray with coffee and rolls. Witzel takes it from him eagerly and lays the
table. Salzer, still standing, takes a roll straight away. He now looks
across to the delinquent in the background, who is trying to kiss the girl.
He has her round the shoulders and the waist. She is defending herself,
repelled – then she tears free and fetches him a slap across the face hard
enough to send his cap flying into the room. Salzer, who was about to
intervene, laughs out loud, laughs until he cries. Even the smart Italian
is entertained, but Witzel, with the mania for discipline of the spiritu-
ally ill provided and his National Socialist feeling of honour, grabs
the delinquent by the scruff of the neck.)*

WITZEL: You filthy swine. Haven't you got any self-respect?
Get out. Mucking about with Jewish girls,
are you?

*(He pushes him out into the courtyard, helping him out with a boot. For
a long time he cannot calm down. His idea of discipline is so strong that
he picks up the delinquent's cap, even dusts it off with one hand, then
opens the door again and chucks it out after its owner. He shouts :)*

You can't buy self-respect for ten lire, you know.
Animal – I showed him.

SALZER *(still laughing)*:
The Italians don't understand, Witzel.
They look just like the Jews themselves.
*(He has a roll and a cup in his hand and goes towards the girl,
friendly, impressed.)*
Donnerwetter! Are you always so much on the defensive
when a man gets close to you?
(The girl does not answer.)
You don't look as if you would be, I must say.
Of course, you'd have a young man. Is he perhaps
down there, too, in the cellar?

CARLOTTA *(coldly)*: My fiancé was killed in Africa.

SALZER *(pained, speaks quickly)*:
What? – When, then? How was he killed?
On the English side? Or what?

CARLOTTA: On the German side, of course. He came
from Rome, after all.

SALZER *(in an effort to change the subject)*:
Since when have they allowed Jewish girls
to marry Italians here?

154

CARLOTTA: That's why I became a Catholic.

SALZER: I see. All the same, I'm afraid we must
    send you to an armament factory in Austria, with the rest.
    Since you were not yet married to this
    Aryan, legally you are still
    a hundred per cent Jewish. Your religion is unimportant. We Germans
    are tolerant. Anyone can pray however he likes.

CARLOTTA (*fearfully*): But I would have been married long ago
    and therefore only half Jewish under the law,
    if my fiancé had not
    been killed – for Germany. Please
    let me go. I am already
    registered with the Sisters over the way
    to enter the convent as a novice
    on the first of November.

SALZER (*in a difficulty, very seriously*):
    Your case is complicated. I can't
    decide it here . . . and now . . .
    (*He gestures to the smart militiaman.*)
    Keep your hands off her, understand?

SMART ITALIAN: Yes, Commandant.

SALZER: Take her back to the cells.

CARLOTTA (*in great fear*): Oh, please . . . no. Please not . . .

SALZER: It'll all be settled by the first of November.
    (*The soldier takes the girl away. Salzer is visibly more at ease the moment the girl is no longer in front of him. In the foreground Witzel is drinking coffee. He stands up as Salzer approaches him.*)
    Sit down, man. Listen, Witzel.
    If that shoemaker you spoke of before
    can make boots himself, good ones, to measure,
    then he – and his family,
    as far as I am concerned – can be Aryan, for the present,
    is that clear? He can stay here.

WITZEL: Yes, a good cobbler is worth quite a bit.

SALZER: I must have a pair of boots
    in which I'm fit to be seen.
    You could use a pair yourself.
    Something soft, and at the same time firm.
    A leather you can clean.
    That gives a shine. This crap

(*He points to his boot.*)
here belongs on the rubbish heap.
Every step I take reminds me
of four years of war. It doesn't shine at all.
WITZEL: Yes, Obersturmführer.

(*Witzel has finished his breakfast and goes out. Immediately after speaking to Witzel, Salzer, altering his voice as suddenly as a musical box, shouts in a coarse voice at the two men still standing facing the wall. What happens now is in no way contradictory to Salzer's intention to treat the Jews well as long as they are in Rome. The 'treatment' of Jews arrested in other countries, with one or two exceptions, could not be shown upon the stage.*)

SALZER: You baptized Hebrews there – about turn!
Los! About turn! Come on, los!
(*Only now does the elder Luccani turn towards the audience.*)
Now show me that you're Catholics.
Give me your passport.
(*The 40-year-old shows his passport.*)
How did you get in here? You aren't
any sort of Catholic! Witzel?
(*He turns round. Witzel is not there. The smart Italian returns, collects the crockery and tidies up without speaking. Meanwhile the examination continues.*)

MANUFACTURER (*eagerly, as if rehearsed*):
I make equipment for you. I have big textile works.
My family is Catholic,
Catholic nobility. I am only
here in town by chance, quite by chance; I was
pulled in during the raid.
I tell you, my arrest
will have the severest consequences.

SALZER (*nettled*): You must work like your brothers.
After all, you are Jewish – the most I can do
is inform your family . . .

MANUFACTURER (*plunges eagerly in his briefcase and brings out an address book*):
Oh, please. Here – this
is the address, my telephone number, please . . .

SALZER (*laughs dirtily. He snatches the address book out of his hand and throws it right across the room; then, with a sneer*):

And how is your family going to protest
if they don't even know
that we've arrested you?

MANUFACTURER (*frightened*):
What? But . . . but it's common knowledge
that you have seized us.
The whole of Rome knows it, the whole of Italy!

SALZER (*now, against his intention, as unpleasantly as possible*):
If you threaten me, Herr Manufacturer,
with your great big textile factories, understand,
then you will quite simply *disappear*
for good and all.
Disappear . . . how would I know?
Fell down a sewer,
or got knocked off by a tart on the Appian Way,
one hole or another, how would I know?

MANUFACTURER (*loquacious with fear*):
But please . . . since 1941 I have been working
for the German forces. All my factories . . .

SALZER: Will go on working for us.
You are going with your brethren . . .

MANUFACTURER (*steps ostentatiously away from Luccani*):
They are not my brethren and
never have been. My marriage was
Catholic. A cardinal performed
the ceremony in St Peter's.
It's more than sixteen years since
I had anything to do with the Jews.
My arrest is a mistake
which will have the most severe consequences for you.

(*Salzer is extremely irritated, as it is precisely of the consequences that
he is afraid; because he knows that whether the Pope protests or not,
this Jew, witness of the happenings in the Gestapo cellar, must not be
allowed to open his mouth again. Witzel has entered. Behind him,
smartly, the S.S. soldier Katitzki, a tall blond Latvian. He is carrying
a shaving mug.*)

SALZER: There you are, threatening again – oh, I
am really very much afraid of . . . the consequences.
Right, Katitzki, lather away.

KATITZKI: Very well, Obersturmführer.

(*Witzel has pushed the arm-chair in which Salzer was sleeping into the middle of the room, with a chair in front of it, on which Salzer puts his feet.*)

SALZER : If your factories are working for our armies,
      then you would naturally sympathize with
      our measures concerning the Jews.
      Do you sympathize, or do you not ?

(*He lies back in the arm-chair, but pushes Katitzki aside again. Witzel sits at a table and carefully stamps a heap of forms, breathing on the stamp each time as if he wanted to swallow it ; then he undertakes a thorough excavation of his teeth and ears while he watches the interrogation.*)

MANUFACTURER : Sympathize, yes. But
      at least since my marriage
      more than sixteen years ago . . .

SALZER : I'm not interested in your marriage.

MANUFACTURER : I'm just saying that for years now,
      I have been, both inwardly
      and outwardly, antagonistic to Jews. For years now.
      In accordance with Mussolini's
      Anti-Jewish laws I immediately
      dismissed, and I can prove it,
      all the Jews in my works who held responsible positions.
      Count Ciano is personally . . .

SALZER (*amiably*): . . . Awaiting execution in Verona.

MANUFACTURER : And the Duce himself
      treated me as an exception . . .

SALZER : As a good tax-payer ?

MANUFACTURER : No, as a good Fascist. I could
      have emigrated ten times over . . .

SALZER : Once would have been enough.

MANUFACTURER : I wanted to do my bit
      for the victory of the West over
      Bolshevism. I would think . . .

SALZER (*stands up*):
      Yes, yes, yes, you talk like a book. You would think
      our struggle is good and just, of course, aha ?
      And you welcome the fact, too,
      that we have made the Jews responsible
      for instigating the war ?

MANUFACTURER:
    Disturbers of the peace should always be punished.

SALZER: You are generalizing rather.
    What I want to hear is a clear statement:
    do you declare yourself against your race
    and for Adolf Hitler who wishes to free
    the world of that race?

MANUFACTURER: My behaviour during this war
    is proof enough of that.

SALZER: Behaviour from which one earns
    as much as you do from this war
    is no proof of any kind. Stop quibbling:
    do you approve of the extermination of the Jews?
    Yes or no?

MANUFACTURER: The Führer knows what he's doing.

SALZER: Yes or no, man? Stop wasting my time.

MANUFACTURER: Yes.

SALZER: That sounded a bit thin. Here –
    here's a Jew – spit in his face.

MANUFACTURER: But, really, the old man
    is a Catholic. Anyway, he has done
    nothing to me personally. No!

SALZER: Has he done anything to me personally?
    Go on, spit at him.

MANUFACTURER: No, I will not.

SALZER: Very well – Witzel! Take this giant of industry
    back to his brethren.

WITZEL (*standing up*): Right, into the cellar . . . come on, los!

MANUFACTURER (*almost relieved at being taken away*):
    Herr Obersturmführer, look out for
    protests from the Duce and the Pope.
    I wouldn't try . . .

SALZER (*now quite sure he must kill him. He stands up*):
    There you go again, man.
    You aren't even a Catholic . . .
    so you must give me every proof,
    every possible proof,
    that you have, at any rate inwardly,
    renounced your Jewish boyhood:
    what justification could I possibly have
    (*with extreme cynicism*)

in letting you go? But don't expect
anyone to look for you here.
When your widow finds you missing, where
is she going to look?
In the brothels on the Via Veneto, of course. She'll look
there, for a while, for a while.
But people soon forget other people.
We are like matches, for wholesale delivery,
one just like another, you as well.
We are taken out of the box,
we flicker a little, set fire to something . . .
chucked away. No one notices.
And your widow won't search for long.
If you behave properly – well and good.
But threats! – It is ludicrous
of you to threaten me. Go on, spit
at that old man, then you won't have to go back
to that cellar, word of honour. Go on, spit;
that will be proof enough.

(*The Manufacturer is finished. He has understood that even he, with his special privileges, could actually disappear in this house 'like a match'. What happens to him now is not pleasant, but it is human: only after this deep self-abasement does he regain his full dignity. . . . Later, on the ramp at Auschwitz, we see how he stands by old Luccani. Now, after Salzer's last words, he delays no longer, but claps his hand quickly in front of his eyes and, his face distorted with pain, spits on the old man's coat. Salzer, Witzel and the Italians laugh, each in his own way, Witzel longest and nastiest.*)

SALZER: Pity. It would have made a good photo for the *Stürmer*.
Right, take him away, not to the cellar – we keep our word.
We'll put this gentleman
in the dog kennels.
(*Somebody laughs again, but not Salzer.*)

MANUFACTURER (*crying out*): No! Swine!

WITZEL: Get on, to the dogs. Take your
trousers off now. Come on . . .

MANUFACTURER (*suddenly regains control*): To the dogs, see.
(*imploringly, to Luccani*)
Forgive me . . . just forgive me . . .
(*Luccani looks at him without speaking. Despairingly:*)

Please do not despise me.
The fear . . . this terrible . . .
I am ashamed.

LUCCANI: I do not feel it any more. You must pray.
(*Witzel drags the manufacturer brutally away, shoving him out.
Salzer, now in full swing, momentarily forgets what he is afraid of
here in Rome. He lets fly at Luccani right away.*)

SALZER: Pray yourself. Go on, pray. Pray.
Prove you are a Catholic.
Sing something, go on, sing an Ave Maria.
Go on, hurry up, sing.

LUCCANI: No, I will not take God's name in vain.

SALZER: In vain? My dear good man, if you don't sing now
you'll be singing with the angels soon, in Heaven,
or with the children in the fiery furnace.
(*He calls the soldiers.*)
Your last chance: your brothers in Christ
will see if you can sing
an Ave, without making one mistake.
Go on, you altar boys,
proceed with the examination.

LUCCANI (*pathetic, with enormous contempt*):
I will not speak to traitors . . .

SMART ITALIAN (*shouts*): Traitors?
(*He gives Luccani a badly aimed push in the chest. The old man
tumbles, staggers, rights himself quickly.
Salzer grips the soldier by the arm, holding him back.*)

SALZER: Come here. You are not to strike him.

SMART ITALIAN: Commandant . . . insult.
Traitors,
I do not allow anyone to say that.

SALZER (*with dangerous interest to Luccani*):
What did you mean by that?

LUCCANI (*very sharp and clear*):
An Italian who hands over a former
officer to the Germans
is a traitor. I may have lain beside
this coward's father, at the Isonzo . . . here . . .
(*He feels in his pocket and brings out two medals. Salzer pauses
and says quickly:*)

SALZER: Why didn't you say straight away

that you were an officer?

LUCCANI (*to the soldier*): Have you no shame, you coward?
We fought at the front against
the Austrian mountain troops, they were
sharpshooters – and whom are you fighting?
Civilians, your defenceless neighbours. Traitor!
(*Salzer is silent, permitting this insult to the soldier, whom he despises, as he does all Italians, without noticing that Luccani's words apply to his own war work. The old man has turned his back on the soldier and says to Salzer, very controlled:*)
As consul-general in Innsbruck,
and as a soldier in the First World War,
I learnt to respect the Germans . . .
and I still do not want to believe . . . Please,
allow me to ask you a question,
a favour . . .

SALZER (*now inwardly extremely anxious; the old officer has touched him on a sentimental nerve, particularly because Salzer himself has avoided active service*):
Of course, I respect
the officer in you. Naturally,
you won't be taken to Auschwitz but to
Theresienstadt, where you will be interned
till the end of the war.

LUCCANI: Thank you . . . for this indication
of your fairmindedness. But what I wanted to ask . . .
I am seventy-two, don't give me special treatment.
Just leave me with my son and daughter-in-law –
down there, in the cellar. You too
are only doing your duty. But perhaps you
have children of your own . . . My grandchildren are down there,
a boy of nine, a girl of six. Let them go.
I know some nuns, they'll come and fetch them,
and bring them up as Catholics, please . . . I . . .
(*gradually losing control*)
I have never in my life begged any man
for anything, but now I'm begging you . . .
Think of your own children . . . I . . . I . . .
(*stutters, in tears*)

SALZER (*hoarsely*): The children won't be touched.

What can you be thinking of us Germans?
They'll be taken to Theresienstadt.
The younger Jews must build roads,
up in the Apennines.

LUCCANI: But not the children – they were
taken away from their parents yesterday evening.
Then we really are to believe what
we hear of your camps in Poland . . .

SALZER: All lies, propaganda lies of Churchill.
Don't listen to the British radio.
If it were true, what those agitators
say . . . do you think the Pope
would be receiving thousands of
German soldiers in audience so friendlily?
Go now . . . we won't hurt you.

LUCCANI (*more controlled, but in great terror, which is why he uses
such big words*):
As an officer, you are a man of honour:
how will you ever be able to look your wife
or your children in the face again?
I ask you in your mother's name . . .

(*Salzer has turned his back on him, touched to the core, revolted.
While Luccani speaks, Witzel has come in with the cobbler, who carries
a briefcase: a chubby, middle-aged Jew, who stays timidly standing by
the door till Witzel indicates, with a movement of his hand, that he
should turn and face the wall.
At Luccani's last words, Salzer suddenly begins to scream like a lunatic
at the soldiers and Katitzki, then at Witzel as well. His own shouting
increases his loss of control. Eventually he yanks his pistol out, as if this
ridiculous grasp at a weapon could protect him against his feelings of
humanity.*)

SALZER: What are you all staring at like idiots?
Take him away. I said take him away . . . Don't
hurt him. Everyone get out of here . . . That one too.
(*pointing at the cobbler*)
Take him away, there.
Go on, what are you waiting for? Take them away.
Witzel, are you ever there when anyone
really wants you?

WITZEL: This is the cobbler, Obersturmführer.
    He's brought his kit with him, too.

SALZER (*still shouting*): I don't give a damn. I don't want
    to see anyone now. You, too.
    Now get out of here, everyone, out.

WITZEL: Obersturmführer?

SALZER: If any of the others still object,
    take their trousers off and see
    whether they're circumcised.
    Catholic or not . . . I don't care.
    Are they circumcised . . . that's all I want to know.

WITZEL: Yes, Obersturmführer – and the women?
    How do we know with the women?

SALZER (*shouting again*): Don't drive me mad – idiot!
    Once and for all, get out! I don't want to see you again.

WITZEL: Yes, Obersturmführer.

(*While they are all going out, Gerstein has entered, almost stealthily,
from the courtyard, behind Salzer's back. He is in time to see Witzel
and the soldiers taking the two Jews away. He puts his hand on
Salzer's shoulder, while his expression, which was showing extreme
exhaustion, completely changes; his face is now full of energy and
wakefulness, which he seeks to hide behind an artificial-looking grin.*)

GERSTEIN: You need some sleep, don't you?
    Heil, Salzer! You're looking pale.

SALZER (*annoyed*): Gerstein – man, you gave me a fright.
    You always come in so stealthily, so quietly.
    Where were you all night?

GERSTEIN: What was going on here, then?

SALZER (*still put out*):
    Enough to drive you off your head . . . That idiot
    of a sergeant of mine, out of sheer stupidity
    picked up a whole bagful of
    Catholics in tonight's raid.

GERSTEIN (*hardly able to hide his satisfaction, he exaggerates*):
    What . . . have you been arresting Catholics, too?
    You've put your foot in it there all right.
    The Führer is in no position at the moment
    to afford trouble with the Pope.

SALZER: That's what I was afraid of. And I'm all in;
    Gerstein, I had an old officer up here,

showing his medals, begging me
for the lives of his grandchildren.
I'll never let it happen again, never again.
The moment you treat the scum that we're supposed
to parcel up and pack off to the gas chambers
as if it was made up of human beings,
they make a bloody fool of you. I'm not
hard-boiled enough to stick it out. Anyhow
I'm full to here with it: you weren't in Posen
ten days ago, on the 4th, when Himmler said
our work for the
benefit of the Children of Israel was –
how did Reichsheini put it now ? – he said
it was a page of glory in German history
which has never been written, and is never
to be written – yes, Gerstein
that's our reward, unsung and terrible.

GERSTEIN (*seeing immediately a chance, he behaves as if angry and overawed at the same time*):
I see, so Himmler thinks like that as well.
That supports my feeling, Salzer, that the whole
course of things will soon be changed. I see, a
'page of glory never-to-be-written'.
One might think that the Reichsführer S.S.
was openly admitting that the Final Solution,
the most violent expression of the will of the century,
perhaps of the millennium . . . that it should
never be admitted to the scrutiny of history . . . Yes,
(*darkly, apparently very much the possessor of special knowledge*)
it's not only rumours, it is beginning
to dawn on me . . .
(*apparently changing the subject, as if he had already said too much*)
Got a roll and a cup of coffee for me ?

SALZER (*most interested*):
What ? What are you talking about ? . . .
Of course you can have some coffee –
Gerstein, man, tell me. You
know things, you're always in Berlin . . . I
never hear anything. What's going on ?

GERSTEIN (*mysteriously, significantly*):

Salzer, I can't say anything definite,
only a word of advice among friends:
now and then a diplomat goes to Stockholm
to have discussions with the most surprising
people: it would be *very* dangerous
at this moment, if the Pope, of all people,
were to open his mouth at all wide. Don't
offer him provocation: the Führer *knows*
what he's doing when he leaves the Vatican alone,
spy centre or not, instead of occupying it.

SALZER (*excited*): Stockholm? . . . Who are we dealing
with there? . . . With the Russians or . . .?
Word of honour, I can keep my mouth shut.

GERSTEIN (*who has no idea, but only hears what the foreign radios have
been inaccurately and exaggeratedly repeating during the last
few months*):
Not another word, Salzer, not a syllable.
You've always been a good fellow, that's why I'm giving you
a warning: don't do anything in Rome
which might stir up international feeling
against Germany. It just isn't worth it,
not for the sake of a lousy Jew or two.

SALZER (*angrily*): Why does Berlin *order* me
to arrest the bastards then?

GERSTEIN: What do you mean, Berlin? It's Eichmann gives the
orders.
He likes to feel important; always talking
about 'orders from the Führer' because he won't
risk anything on his own account. He'll drop you
like a hot potato, if the Führer
has a fit because the Pope has protested
and ruined . . . all his plans in Stockholm.

SALZER (*furious, insecure*):
Am *I* supposed to understand politics?
Why should I? I am simply given orders.

GERSTEIN (*shrugging*): They are bound to say you should have seen
the impending dangers from the Vatican.

SALZER (*very agitated*):
But I *do* see them, Gerstein. Don't make
me completely confused. I tried,
twice I tried, to get out of doing

this idiotic operation. At the end of September
the order came to make the arrests on the first of October
Moellhausen, the Consul, said it
would be politically inopportune, and hauled me off
to Kesselring. The Marshal, God be praised,
claimed that he had no troops available
for the raid. I could shelter behind that.
Berlin gave way, but ordered us instead
to demand a hundredweight of gold
as ransom for the Jews. Which I did,
three weeks ago now. The Pope
knew about that. He was even prepared
to guarantee the ransom, if the Jews
couldn't get the whole hundredweight together.
This readiness of the Pope's –
we thought *then*, he was going to make a fuss –
encouraged us to go ahead,
and deport the Jews.
It will probably be all right . . . If the old man
could keep his trap shut
at a demand like that – then why not now?
And he's very fond of the Germans too,
a very decent man, really.
Gerstein, you should see
the kindness with which he gives audiences
to our soldiers – thousands of them.
Berlin does not like it . . .
But go and see for yourself. It's quite an experience.

GERSTEIN (*taken aback. He cannot answer for some time, then*):
Your conclusions are too optimistic for me, Salzer:
the fact that the Pope wanted to guarantee
the ransom for the Jews – proves conclusively
he is on their side. If he held his tongue
three weeks ago, it was because he thought
the Jews had bought their freedom with the gold.
Now you have well and truly betrayed him:
just wait and see, he will be on the air tomorrow,
to tell the world what you have been doing tonight.

WITZEL (*entering, to Gerstein*):
Heil Hitler, Obersturmführer!

GERSTEIN (*tired*): Heil und Sieg!

SALZER: Bring some more rolls and coffee, Witzel.

WITZEL (*leaving*): Yes, Obersturmführer.

SALZER: It's quite possible the Pope *will*
     protest today. The main point; no one can
     hold *me* responsible. Not me.
     Next: Berlin will certainly not risk,
     Gerstein, cooking the Jews from Rome
     straight away: the first consignment will
     be going to Auschwitz
     via Mauthausen. If the Pope protests,
     we can always send them
     back home again. They need only be put
     into the ovens when we're really sure
     he's no longer interested in them.
     (*He offers Gerstein a cigarette. Gerstein tries once more to intimi-
     date Salzer.*)

GERSTEIN: Thank you. That was an extraordinary speech
     that Himmler made in Posen: *that* must be
     the reason Colonel Blobel has been having
     to dig up our mass graves in Russia, ever since August,
     and burn the bodies one by one . . .
     A nice job. *You* don't know when you're well off.

SALZER: Is that true? Why we give ourselves so much trouble
     I can't understand – can you?

GERSTEIN: Just look at the map: in August
     Blobel fired the graves at Kiev . . .
     Russian low-flying planes witnessed it, stupidly enough.
     Yes, Salzer, I can see it all: the Führer,
     does not appear to reckon with the fact
     that Kiev is the future capital
     of a *German* Ukraine. Ironic . . .
     the tide has turned – I have said nothing.
     (*He says no more because Witzel has appeared with coffee and
     rolls. Then to Witzel:*)
     Thank you – thank you.

WITZEL: That's all right, Obersturmführer.

SALZER (*worried*):
     Is *that* why they're going to Stockholm, Gerstein?
     Damned depressing, what you're saying there.
     (*Gerstein puts his finger to his lips behind Witzel's back. To
     Witzel, trying to find a neutral topic of conversation:*)

What's our cobbler up to then, Witzel?
(*to Gerstein*)
We roped in a cobbler
who's going to make boots for us here.

GERSTEIN: Oho! I could use some new ones, too.

WITZEL: He's got his kit with him. I asked him.
Just no materials. We'd have to get
them from his place. But the kit he has,
a great big bag full. 'What you want with that?'
I says to him. He says, 'I've got to take
care of my kids, even in Poland.'

(*Witzel is amused. Laughs with complicity. The paralysing bestiality of the whole proceedings is expressed here at its frankest, in the squalid humorousness of Witzel's remarks, made cruder still by the comfortable ugliness of the sloppy Kassel suburban accent.*)

WITZEL: So, I says, you want to take care of your kids?
Then take care of yourself. You're a craftsman.
We'll fix you up your own little workshop
in Auschwitz . . . nothing but the very best,
with plate glass windows, or even, maybe, I says,
a great big shop in Warsaw, just for you.
You can look after your family there . . . silly, isn't it?

(*He laughs delightedly. Gerstein cannot eat another mouthful; he has risen and is making an effort not to notice. But even Salzer has been touched on the raw by Witzel's commonplace, weak-minded cynicism, and says with annoyance :*)

SALZER: All right, Witzel – here's a cigarette.
Now take yourself off. We're still talking.

WITZEL (*takes the cigarette, leaves*):
Thank you, Obersturmführer.

SALZER: You're not eating a thing, Gerstein . . . You were
hungry and thirsty when you came in.

GERSTEIN (*turns round*):
I can't stop thinking of that speech of Himmler's:
it's going to change the whole course of events soon.
And then
we'll be the inquisitors whom they'll be ashamed of.
Just as the Church today is ashamed of its witch burners.

SALZER (*feebly*):

Yes, the fact that Blobel had to make the exhumations
leads one to suppose the Führer thinks
he's going to lose the Ukraine again.
Dammit.

GERSTEIN (*takes a piece of bread, tries to introduce the next words as
casually as possible*):
And that's why *you* must not provoke the Pope
to turn against the Führer yet.
Hold up the deportations till the day after tomorrow.
He is sure to protest – and you'll end up with the short straw.

SALZER (*tired, sentimental and somewhat worried*):
Oh, Gerstein, it's easy for you to talk.
I wish I was here in Rome
just to look at churches and museums;
I'd like to bathe at Ostia with the children
or buy something nice for my wife in the Via Veneto . . .
instead of which – good God,
am I supposed to be more Catholic than the Pope then?
If he keeps quiet till this evening it's too late.
Unless he protests within the next twelve hours
I'll have to put them on the trains tonight.
(*The telephone rings. Salzer points significantly at the apparatus,
saying as he goes towards it:*)
Talk of the devil . . .
nowadays: wait for it,
this'll be the Pope already . . .
(*into the receiver*)
Yes, put him through.
(*to Gerstein*)
The Town Commandant.
Yes, Salzer here. Heil Hitler, Herr General – I see,
Aha, we were *just* talking about it – really, yes!
God almighty, then there *has* been a protest!
(*He beckons to Gerstein, who has come up to Salzer in extreme
tension, so that he can follow the conversation.*)
I thought of that at once, yes . . .
Have you . . . I beg your pardon. Thank you, yes . . . yes.
Are you in possession of the full text sir?
I see – already on its way to me – good.
Thank you very much, Herr General.
Aha . . . I see, that isn't quite so dangerous.

Then it doesn't actually come from the Pope himself.
But there is a definite threat though.
My own opinion? . . . You are well aware, sir,
I only carried out the operation against my better judgement.
Unfortunately, however, the Bishop's letter
in no way absolves us from
making the deportations . . . very well.
He won't stand by it? . . . I'm afraid of that, too.
Of course, Herr General, very good,
as long as I still have them in the cellar,
the Jews will be particularly well treated.
We must wait and see . . . of course,
my deepest thanks, Herr General.
(*He hangs up and looks at Gerstein.*)

GERSTEIN: You'd better report to Berlin right away.
      If there's an outcry they'll hold you responsible.

SALZER: Confound it! What am I supposed to do?
      (*then very loudly*)
      If only this damned Pope would say
      once and for all, clearly and definitely
      just where he stands. If he is leaving us
      (*quiet again*)
      a free hand, as he has done up to now,
      is only trying, with the Bishop's letter . . .
      to fulfil his obligations as a Christian . . .
      the deportations must begin this evening.

GERSTEIN: For God's sake, Salzer – that *is* the protest!

SALZER (*almost mistrustful*): Gerstein, how can you say that?
      The comment of a single Bishop?
      That isn't any sort of protest. They'd laugh
      in my face in Berlin if I let
      this bunch go free for that.
      I wouldn't dream of releasing . . .

GERSTEIN (*somewhat more cautiously*):
      I don't want to confuse you, Salzer, but
      I can't for the life of me believe the Pope
      will allow you a free hand here in Rome.

SALZER (*annoyed again*): But Gerstein, I don't think he will, either.
      After this letter of the Bishop's
      I'm absolutely sure that Pius is going
      to raise a hue and cry about his flock . . . and

the Führer will give in, naturally.
What do eleven hundred Jews matter, after all?
But, Gerstein – that's none of
my business; *I* have no desire to stick my neck out again.
As long as the Church is just going to issue
vague generalisations . . .

(*Gerstein has, during Salzer's last words, become extremely uneasy. He looks continually at his watch and walks up and down. He wants to get to Riccardo as soon as possible. He now takes leave in a manner almost conspicuously abrupt. Outside it has become quite light.*)

GERSTEIN: Well, Salzer, hm, it's time for me to go.
Good-bye. Take care how you treat the Pope.

SALZER (*without mistrust, smiling, more and more amused*):
I never saw a man as nervous as you.
Like a wolf in a cage – walking up and down the whole time.
As if you were in the zoo.
Look at you now, Gerstein. You don't even notice it.
Why this sudden non-Aryan haste?

GERSTEIN (*angrily, then relaxed*):
What do you mean? Am I really that nervous?
I must see something of Rome . . .
(*a hint*)
Who knows whether I will ever again be able
to stand as a German on the banks of the Tiber?
You have depressed me a great deal . . .
(*He behaves as if it was Salzer who had been holding this 'defeatist' talk.*)
What you've told me, Salzer . . . and then,
what with the Americans in Naples,
and the Russians in Kiev already: your bad mood is contagious.

SALZER: Good God, I was just a bit put out
by the interrogation.

GERSTEIN (*gives him his hand*): And thank you for breakfast.

SALZER: Ah, Gerstein, what a pity you're going.
The thanks are all on my side . . .
You know the way to the aerodrome, don't you?
Give my love to Finland . . . Heil!

WITZEL (*entering and announcing*):
Obersturmführer, the Abbot is outside
wanting to speak with you urgently.

SALZER (*as Gerstein starts back violently*):
    He's all I'm short of . . . Oh well,
    what can we do but wish him
    a friendly good morning? Oh, all right.
    (*Witzel leaves.*)
    (*to Gerstein*)
    You were right. Here comes
    the protest. The man
    comes every other day, a stubborn old
    so and so, always winkling something out of me.

WITZEL (*announcing officially*):
    Obersturmführer . . . the very Reverend the Father General
    Monsignore . . .

(*Salzer has quickly done up his belt and put his cap on. Now he turns towards the door and looks at the Abbot, who enters quickly and confidently. Gerstein, behind Salzer's back, shakes his head in denial, and, as soon as Witzel has closed the door behind the visitor, lays his fingers to his lips.*)

ABBOT (*in no way indicating that Gerstein left him only a few hours ago*):
    Good morning, Herr Salzer . . . I'm sorry I must
    disturb you this early.
    But you have a visitor already . . .

SALZER (*laughing amiably*):
    Good morning, Father General. Yes,
    a visitor from Berlin: a colleague . . .
    this is the Father General of the Salvatorians,
    who comes once a week, sent by His Holiness
    to steal away a Communist
    from the wicked Nazis.
    (*All three laugh, Gerstein from relief.*)

GERSTEIN: I'm delighted to meet you,
    Monsignore . . . My friend Salzer has already
    complained what a hard bargainer you are . . .

ABBOT (*flattered*): Really? Does he say that? Yes.
    Well, that is a compliment. I've come today
    again about a Communist . . . or what you would
    call a Communist: I am talking about
    the eighteen-year-old Tagliaferro – good God,
    if he's a Communist then I'm a Mahommedan.

(*he laughs*)
His father is the leading lawyer
in Milan and he went yesterday
to the Pope: let the young puppy go.
If he goes on distributing leaflets, his father
will give him a clip on the ear,
the silly young rascal . . .

GERSTEIN (*as disappointed as Salzer is relieved that the Abbot has not come about the Jews. He says quickly*):
Please excuse me, Monsignore . . .
Salzer, I really must go now . . .
auf Wiedersehen, auf Wiedersehen.

ABBOT (*sly, holds Gerstein's hand tightly and asks inexorably*):
Auf Wiedersehen, Herr . . . What did you say your name was?

GERSTEIN: My name is Gerstein. I am just
flying back to Germany.

ABBOT: Aha. Herr Gerstein: I see . . . I didn't quite
catch just now, as usual.
Well, have a good flight, I hope it stays fine for you.

GERSTEIN: Thank you, Monsignore . . . Wiedersehen.
(*Salzer takes Gerstein to the door.*)

SALZER: Don't you think your worries
(*with a movement of his head towards the Abbot*)
are a bit exaggerated?
(*calls to the Abbot*)
I beg your pardon, Father General, do sit down.

GERSTEIN (*quietly, then with a gesture towards the Abbot*):
I hope so for your sake, Salzer . . . but,
no, it won't yet have got around to him.
Well, gentlemen, good morning to you both . . .
(*Salzer and the Abbot simultaneously: 'Heil, Gerstein!' 'Auf Wiedersehen', 'Bon voyage', etc. . . .*)

Curtain

174

Act Four · Il Gran Rifiuto

And I who straightway looked, beheld a flag,
Which, whirling, ran around so rapidly,
That it no pause obtained: and following came
Such a long train of spirits, I should ne'er
Have thought that Death so many had despoiled.
When some of these I recognized, I saw
And knew the shade of *him*, who to base fear
Yielding, abjured his high estate. . . .
DANTE *Inferno, Canto III* TRANS. CARY

In the Pope's palace.
A small throne-room, almost empty, frequently used as a room for private audiences and business conversations. It is hung in scarlet – the colour of the robes of the Cardinals, which, as is well known, symbolizes a readiness to stand up for the faith 'even to the spilling of their own blood'. The Pope wears white, of course. His cassock is as white as the dove with the olive-branch in his coat of arms, embroidered on the tapestry above the throne, along with the triple crown and the two crossed keys.
This tapestry rises upwards to a canopy, that in turn, rises gently up to the ceiling until it is out of sight. The throne is only slightly raised, and on each side of it is a tall, narrow door, also hung in scarlet and gold. On the left-hand wall is a baroque console table with an astronomical clock and writing materials. Over it hangs a large crucifix of beaten brass. A few golden stools stand round the walls. There are no guards. The Cardinal is in conversation with the elder Count Fontana. The Count is wearing dress-clothes, with the Order of Christ, and carrying a document-case. His Eminence, though quite at home here, is more impersonal than he was either on his visit to the Fontanas or in the monastery, more chary of, and subdued in word and gesture.

CARDINAL (*complaining*): . . . at all events, what,
  it was not until September, Herr Hitler . . .
FONTANA: Ah, as recently as that . . .
CARDINAL: Yes! He let the Chief know

quite confidentially that he regarded the bombers
like any other weapon, what, and that
the German Government had been the first
to make use of this weapon, and expected
to retaliate quite soon very strongly
against the present counter-attack of the Allies.
We shall see, shall we not?

FONTANA: Pride, of course, prevents Hitler
from sending the Pope as emissary to the White House.

CARDINAL (*not without malice*):
The Chief is extremely offended, as always
when his services as a go-between are rejected.
He so enjoys writing letters
to Mr Roosevelt that say absolutely nothing.

FONTANA (*with feeling*):
It's *Hitler* he should be writing to, Eminence.
I had a terrible time with Riccardo last night.
He was determined to go with the Jews.

CARDINAL: Holy Madonna, Count, you must prevent
your son from doing anything so stupid.

FONTANA: No one could have prevented him.
Then, about dawn, his friend in the S.S.
brought word the Pope had finally protested.

CARDINAL (*astonished, in fact frightened*):
Protested? . . . Out of the question.
The Chief most certainly has not protested, Count.
Here he comes. No, I know nothing of this.

FONTANA (*surprised*): But yes. This morning he . . .

(*The Cardinal and Fontana have whispered the last words, for the
right-hand door has been noiselessly opened by a Swiss Guard. The
moment the Pope has entered, rapidly, without speaking, the door is
closed again. His Holiness, at first nothing but a tall white shining
figure, now stands in front of the two men, who kneel and kiss his ring.
The Cardinal rises first, the Pope raises the Count up graciously, closer
and closer to his cold smiling face. After the Holy Father's first words,
which treat without preliminaries of business matters, Fontana gradually retires a few paces. While His Holiness addresses himself increas-
ingly and in the end almost exclusively to the Count, and when he later
sits on the throne, polishing his glasses, the Cardinal comes in to the left*

of the Pope. The actor who plays Pacelli should remember that His Holiness is much less a person than an institution : big gestures, a vivid movement of his exceptionally beautiful hands and a smiling aristocratic frigidity are enough, with the addition of the icy fire of his eyes behind the gold spectacles. The rest must be left largely to the Pontiff's recondite, ceremonious way of speaking. We see him here, in no way an old man, in his sixty-eighth year, and at the height of his powers.)

PIUS: My good Fontana! We are delighted to receive you,
    to hear your advice and also that of our honourable brother –
    filled, as we are, with burning concern
    for our factories. Power stations,
    railway stations, dams,
    every undertaking demands supervision and protection.
    We estimate, of course, the chances of finding a hearing
    on matters of industry and mining, realistically . . .
    With our Eternal City things are different:
    it is no one's wish to offend Rome again.
    Herr Weizsäcker was so co-operative as to ask
    Marshal Kesselring to reduce the German garrison
    to something in the neighbourhood of a thousand men.
    It must be said, the Germans, on this point,
    have shown considerably more friendliness
    than the destroyers of San Lorenzo.
    But at the White House, too, they will take care
    not to provoke us again. We have declared
    with resolution that we, as Bishop of this city,
    the mouthpiece of 500 million Catholics
    who look towards Saint Peter,
    will energetically protest – directly. Monte Cassino!
    (*complaining*)
    The bombing of armament factories is, however,
    the right of war.
    You have recommended, Count Fontana,
    that the men round Roosevelt, industrialists and high-ranking
    military men in America . . .
FONTANA: And in London as well, Holiness . . .
PIUS: Yes, indeed . . . should be approached to purchase shares.
    But how, my dear Count, are we to bring
    financiers of influence to take an interest in Italian

industry, which is in such a perilous situation?

FONTANA: The best investments we have,
and they are very good ones,
are as much in demand as ever, Holiness.
I am thinking here particularly of the shares in the possession
of the Society of Jesus, which . . .

PIUS (*as if he was warding off physical danger*):
No, my dear Count, no – no.
We must take care not to begin a new quarrel
with the Jesuits – no, most unprofitable.

CARDINAL: May God forbid, the Order of Jesus, indeed.
Why do they hide their records from us, what?
Eight thousand fathers in America are refractory, that's the
trouble.

PIUS (*immediately interrupting*):
Only as far as money is concerned,
of course, Count. Otherwise they are
the devoted servants of our affairs. The Lord
forfend that we should not see that, Eminence.

CARDINAL (*respectfully*):
Yes, of course, mmm, indeed, in other ways.
And they are certainly not miserly:
. . . the diocese of New York alone,
simply the diocese of New York
brings more into the Holy See than all
the Old World put together, yes indeed.
Still, not to let us see their books, mm, what?

PIUS (*maliciously*): The moment to apply pressure on them will
come some day, Eminence.

FONTANA (*smiling, taking two cheques from his document folder*):
Holiness, it is far from my intention
to show ingratitude towards the Jesuits,
my own son's order; one of the two cheques
which I have to present to Your Holiness today
comes from the Society of Jesus – a sum
which may do something to appease Your Eminence's anger
at the arbitrary behaviour of the Fathers.
(*gives the cheques to the Pope, who takes off his glasses to read the
figures*)

CARDINAL (*smiling, highly curious about the cheques*):
I look as unbending as all that, do I?

(*Without batting an eyelid Pius gives the cheques back to Fontana.
Fontana gives him a pen and holds the folder out for the Pope to
endorse the cheques ; he then passes the cheques on to the Cardinal.*)

PIUS: My dear Count – Eminence: you must both of you thank
    the donors, in our name, for these Peter's Pence . . .

CARDINAL (*who has added up the total at a glance, looks at Pius and
    Fontana*):
    Oh yes . . . that certainly makes . . . yes, what ?
    I shall thank Brother Spellman.
    (*gives the cheques back to Fontana, who puts them in his folder
    once more*)

FONTANA: The first amount, Holiness, can only be explained
    by the fact that the donors have a holding
    in the four largest aircraft factories in America.
    I think it suffices that they should earn so much
    by making bombers. But they cannot be allowed
    to use these aircraft to destroy Italian industry.
    The Jesuits would be cutting their own throats.
    They must unload their Tuscan holdings
    as quietly as they can, to members of the U.S. Government,
    and influential men in London, too.

PIUS (*trying not to hear what he knows already*):
    The Fathers, you say, acquire dividends
    from the bombers: my dear Count !
    Let us not regard things in that light.
    The aeroplane is a blessed invention.
    That they are now, at this sad time,
    loaded with bombs, instead of passengers,
    that is not the fault of the good Fathers, is it ?
    They have invested their money, bona fide,
    in these factories.
    The innocent are easily abused.
    If such sums are forthcoming by such means,
    then we must resign ourselves,
    according to the word of the Apostle:
    where sin abounded, grace did much more abound.

FONTANA (*obstinately, not without very respectful irony*):
    Grace, Holiness, will still abound,
    in any case, if you would recommend
    the Society in all kindness
    to unload its shares in Tuscany.

PIUS (*mistrustful*): At a loss?

FONTANA: Not at a loss. The Fathers took the shares
over at a nominal price, for the most part,
and will still make a profit on them.

CARDINAL (*with feeling*):
In the event of their declining, Your Holiness
must absolutely forbid them
to sell the mercury from their mines in Almadén
to Stalin, mmm?

PIUS (*irritated: he does not like being reminded of this*):
But Eminence, that is unthinkable.
At the moment Stalin is a very good customer
of the Society of Jesus.
The Order has the monopoly.
To whom is it going to sell
if Russia ceases to be a customer?
America buys from the Jesuits in Texas.
With the best will in the world, they can't buy up
everything the Society digs up in Spain as well.
And since the Germans, and we Italians,
absorb the mercury from the mines in Tuscany,
we are not able to *forbid* the Order
to supply Stalin as well: or they would be
forced to sell way below the market price.
(*The Cardinal is much sobered. Fontana interrupts the outbreak
and suggests with caution:*)

FONTANA: It would not be necessary for Your Holiness to exercise
constraint in person upon the Society of Jesus.
Señor Franco could put a curb on the Fathers,
since Almadén is, after all, in Spain.
In any case, why does he allow the Jesuits
to sell the mercury to Moscow?

PIUS (*contemptuously*):
Ah, Señor Franco. . . . Just as he sold Hitler
a division, that is bleeding to death in Russia, for coal and iron –
in the same way he would allow the Order to pay for the licence
to supply Stalin's arms factories.
We are *in no way* happy about this – all the less
since the Russians depend urgently on these deliveries;
their own mines in Nikitovka are well nigh exhausted.
Quite apart from the fact that,

until a short while back, the Germans
still occupied the Donets Basin.

FONTANA (*complaining, then imploringly*):
Something *must* be done, Holiness, or the mines
belonging to the Society in Tuscany will be bombed.
I must be permitted to ask the Jesuits
to allow their securities in Idria and Monte Amiata to be –

PIUS: Try it! You are free to try, Fontana.
For we are deeply concerned
for the families of the workers,
particularly in the mining communities,
who, if the factories are destroyed,
will become not only poorer, but more radical –
they will become anarchists – it does not bear thinking of.

CARDINAL (*honestly displeased*):
Yes, what? – Now, since the fall of Mussolini,
who whatever else he did always took a stand
against Communism, and was a guarantee
of social stability, there has arisen a vacuum
which fills me with great alarm, mmm, what?
Praise God, the Germans are still in the country,
they won't permit a strike, nor any idleness.
But what happens when they withdraw their troops, mmm,
what?

PIUS: Then we shall have the Americans here, Eminence.
This afternoon we shall be receiving the President's
Envoy in audience.
Unfortunately, Mr Taylor comes again and again
with Mr Roosevelt's plea that I condemn
Hitler's atrocities ex cathedra.
It was not the Germans who bombed San Lorenzo.
The Germans brought every book and parchment from
Monte Cassino in safety to Castel Sant Angelo,
(*careworn*)
then Mr Roosevelt's bombers came and
left that citadel of peace
in dust and ashes. – All the more – *tactless*
that the Germans should
now be dragging the Jews out of Rome, too.
(*highly indignant*)
Have you heard about this, Count? . . . Eminence?

It is most ill-behaved.

FONTANA: Rome is aghast, Holiness.

CARDINAL: Yes, an infamous piece of impertinence, what?

FONTANA: May I be allowed, in the name
of those Jews who have sought refuge
in my house, to express a word
of deeply felt thanks to Your Holiness . . .

PIUS (*all goodness, spontaneous, heartfelt*):
But my good Fontana – surely it goes without saying
that we shall do, as always, all that God
has given us the strength to do,
to stand at the side of the unfortunate.

FONTANA: It is a true deliverance that Your Holiness
should now have made so definite a threat
as a public statement. – May I ask,
in all humility, whether there has been
any reaction from the German Town Commandant as yet?
(*The Pope looks mistrustfully and uncomprehendingly at the
Cardinal, then at Fontana.*)

CARDINAL: The Town Commandant? – Reaction to what?

PIUS (*mistrustful*): Reaction? – To what, Count?

FONTANA (*somewhat unsure. He suspects what is to come*):
But – I heard from my son
that Bishop Hudal this morning
threatened the Town Commandant that
Your Holiness was going to protest
for the first time since the outbreak of war.

PIUS (*sharp*):
The Bishop threatened that? – In our name?
Eminence, did you give Hudal authority
in the name of the Holy See, or in our Name,
for that matter . . .?

CARDINAL: God is my witness, Holiness. I only just
heard of the protest, here, from the Count . . .
I don't believe, I can't believe, mmm, what . . .

FONTANA (*agitated*):
I don't know the wording. The Bishop
may not have protested actually *in the Name*
of Your Holiness, but only announced, at first,
that a public statement from the Holy Father
was to be expected.

My son says . . .

PIUS (*much annoyed*):

Your son, Count Fontana – where
is your son? Shouldn't he be in Lisbon?

CARDINAL (*frightened, but assiduous*):

The Minutant is waiting for me below
in the Secretary's office, Holiness.

PIUS (*extremely angry*):

Get him up here. He shall be good enough to inform us
by what authority he permits himself,
as a member of our Foreign Service, to poke
his fingers constantly in these affairs.
The Jewish and German questions are the business
of the two fathers we ourselves appointed
to deal with them.

(*The Cardinal has gone straightway to the door and whispered
an order to the Swiss Guard. In the face of the Pope's anger, his
duty of obedience now makes him turn a face of stone to the elder
Fontana as well.*)

FONTANA: I must ask you to forgive my son, Holiness.

His eagerness is born of despair. He was
an eyewitness in Berlin, as the Nazis
were loading Jewish children on to lorries . . .

PIUS (*a gesture of dissatisfaction, and he now speaks naturally and
impulsively*):

Eyewitness! – Count, a diplomat
must see a great deal and – say nothing.
Your son has no discipline.
The Nuncio in Pressburg knew already
in July of last year, that they had sent
the Slovakian Jews to the gas-chamber near Lublin.
Did he on this account leave Pressburg? No.
He continued to do his duty, and – look now:
the result is, not another Jew, not even
the unbaptized, is being sent to Poland.
We are leaving it to the bishops in each place
to make their own assessments of the possible extent
to which, in cases of episcopal proclamations,
retaliatory measures are to be expected.
If we are silent, my dear Count –
then we too are silent

    ad maiora mala vitanda.

FONTANA: Your Holiness's Nuncio in Pressburg,
    nevertheless, by his protest, has saved
    the lives of countless victims
    without the murderers taking reprisals.

PIUS: Think back to our last Christmas message, Count –
    what an appeal we made for brotherly love –
    with what result? The murderers took no notice.

FONTANA: Holiness, I too was much dismayed
    to see the message having no effect.
    Nevertheless Your Holiness did not
    make any mention of the Jews, expressis verbis,
    in the message and to me it seems
    that with Herr Hitler nothing but the bluntest clarity
    can ever serve Your Holiness's turn.

PIUS (*turning away impatiently*):
    Your son – here he is, the young hothead.
    (*Riccardo has entered in the belief that the Pope has protested, and
    therefore with the feeling that he was much mistaken in him the
    previous evening. He kisses the ring; the Pope smiles.*)

RICCARDO: Holy Father . . .
    (*He bows to the Cardinal, who coldly indicates the Pope.*)

PIUS: We have joy in you, Riccardo,
    and look upon your zeal with love. Whoever
    intercedes for the persecuted, always speaks with our voice.
    Only we hear, with no little concern,
    that you or Bishop Hudal, in our name,
    have protested against the deportation of the Jews. Is this so?
    Eminence – please – the Father General.
    (*The Cardinal gives an order to the Swiss Guard at the door.*)

RICCARDO (*politely, not understanding*): I? – No, Holiness, I heard
    from my informant in the S.S. that
    Your Holiness had issued a protest through Bishop Hudal.

PIUS (*annoyed*): What presumption is this of yours,
    conspiring with the S.S.?

CARDINAL (*angrily*): The Holy Father, mmm, what, has only just
    heard the first mention of this alleged announcement . . .

PIUS: Let him alone, Eminence.

RICCARDO (*as if destroyed, turns to his father, and says, but not softly*):
    Then: there has – nothing has been done.
    (*He does not yet believe it.*)

But Your Holiness has threatened to protest?
I don't understand . . .
(*He understands at last, and says passionately, almost in a shout:*)
Holiness, the Jews are being deported, murdered . . .
CARDINAL: Be quiet . . .
PIUS (*smiling*): But not at all. – God bless you,
Riccardo, speak, you have a good heart.
Only you must not have dealings with the S.S.
The Father General will tell us what has happened.
Control yourself – discretion, at your age,
is the only course you may pursue with honour.
RICCARDO: It is not a matter of my honour, Holiness,
it is the honour of the Holy See,
and that is dearer to me . . .
FONTNAA: Riccardo.
(*The Pope is silent, the Cardinal answers quickly for him.*)
CARDINAL: Oh, it's the honour of the Curia he fears for!
Have you never heard, mmm, what,
that we have established whole departments, yes,
offices, committees,
simply to help, to save – yes,
but I think we have already
discussed it several times, mmm, what?
RICCARDO (*gradually losing control of himself*):
This help reaches just a few Jews in Italy, Eminence;
that has been discussed often enough, too.
(*turning now to the Pope as well*)
But the terror is raging now in every country.
One million eight hundred thousand Jews
in Poland alone
have been murdered already – and since this figure,
was given officially to the Papal Legate
in Washington this July by the Ambassador
from Warsaw to the White House,
it cannot be God's wish Your Holiness
should utterly ignore it.
CARDINAL (*furious*):
Leave the room, mmm, what,
talking like this in the presence of the Holy Father.
Count, please forbid your son . . .
(*During Riccardo's last speech the Pope has risen, but now sits*)

again. It is a moment before he is able to speak, which he does with extreme effort.)

PIUS: 'Ignore'. It is not our intention
to account for ourselves to Riccardo Fontana
– does his father have nothing to say?
Nevertheless, we should be glad
to put a word in here ourselves.
(*with growing asperity, in an attempt to change the subject*)
Are you aware, Minutant, exempli causa,
that we were quite prepared some weeks ago
to help the Jews of Rome, whom they wanted to arrest,
out of their difficulty? With gold, a great deal of gold.
Hitler's bandits promised freedom for the Jews
against ransom.
Then they blackmailed us with sums
beyond all bounds of realism:
and *still* we paid it.

RICCARDO (*has turned to his father, astounded. Now he says quickly to the Pope*):
Then Your Holiness has known –
for some weeks –
what the S.S. intends to do to the Jews?

PIUS (*agitated, elusive*): What do you mean? The Father General
can bear witness to what has been done already.
The convents and the monasteries stand open . . .
(*The Father General enters; the Pope turns quickly to him. The Monsignore kneels, kisses the ring, bows to the Cardinal, and is straightway drawn into the conversation. The Cardinal avoids looking at Riccardo, who has gone over to his father's side. Before the Guard has time to withdraw, the Cardinal claps his hands and has four stools brought out from round the walls, and grouped round the Pope. The Cardinal sits, his example being followed by the elder Fontana, who is extremely nervous and tired.*)
Father General: I am seeking information
about what Bishop Hudal has undertaken
in our name against the deporting of the Jews.
Did he happen on this praiseworthy idea himself?

ABBOT: No. Herr von Kessel of the German Embassy
visited me secretly at dawn this morning
and asked me, through His Excellency the Bishop,
to threaten the Town Commandant

with the official protest of your Holiness.

PIUS (*delighted and relieved*): There now! A German to do that –
    how sympathique.
    What an age this is when high treason
    is the last weapon of the righteous!
    A German is ashamed of the S.S.
    So, Kessel was the name, we must remember it. –
    This letter of the Bishop's now will do its part,
    and save whatever there may be to save.

RICCARDO (*with the recklessness of a man who has nothing more to
    lose*):
    That letter will save nothing, Holiness.
    Only you yourself can . . .

FONTANA (*steps in between Riccardo and the Pope*):
    May I speak for my son, Holiness?

PIUS: What is it, Count?

FONTANA: Holiness, if I may ask, in all humility:
    threaten Hitler, say that you will *compel*
    500 million Catholics to Christian protest
    if he continues with this bloodbath.

PIUS (*sees that he must answer this valued adviser objectively. He is
    displeased, irritated, and speaks as if he had often explained
    before. Nevertheless he brings himself to go to Fontana and lay his
    hand on his shoulder*):
    Fontana! A counsellor of your acuteness.
    How bitter that you, too,
    should misunderstand me. Do you not see
    that for Christian Europe
    the catastrophe is coming, if God does not
    make us, the Holy See, the Mediator?
    The hour is dark; although we know for sure
    the Vatican will not be touched.
    Herr Hitler renewed his guarantee a short while ago.
    But our ships upon the open sea, which we must steer?
    Poland, the Balkans, yes, Austria and Bavaria, too,
    into whose harbours may they not be driven?
    They might easily vanish in the storm,
    or be driven helpless on to Stalin's shores.
    Hitler *is* Germany today, and those who still maintain
    the fall of his régime at home would *not*
    bring about the collapse of the front, are talking nonsense.

For Hitler's generals, who wish to do away with him,
we have no respect whatsoever.
They wanted to act in the year of 1940.
And how did they act?
They let Hitler cover them with medals and they went and
made mincemeat out of Europe.
We are acquainted with that sort, from our days in Berlin:
most of the generals have no opinion;
if Hitler falls, they'll pack up and go home . . .

CARDINAL: And Stalin would have a clear road to Warsaw,
Prague, Vienna even . . . mmm, through to the Rhine, what?

PIUS (*has sat down again*):
Is the President quite clear on this?
Stalin won't listen to a word he says.
Since Casablanca reason has not been
wielding the sceptre in the White House any more.
And Mr Churchill is too weak. He, too, seems
unwilling to open up a second front
in the West. He would be delighted
if the Russians were first completely to exhaust themselves
fighting the Germans, and vice versa.

CARDINAL:
We cannot be too cross ourselves about that can we, what?

PIUS (*emphasizing every word by beating on the arm-rest of his throne*):
Hitler alone, my dear Count,
is now defending the whole of Europe,
and he will fight until he dies
because a murderer can expect no pardon.
Nevertheless, the West should let him have a pardon
so long as he is useful in the East.
In March, we publicly declared that we had nothing,
absolutely nothing, to do with the war aims
of Great Britain and the United States.
They must first settle their differences with Germany.
The Spanish Foreign Minister has unfortunately
already broadcast that to all the world.
But come what may: *Raison d'état* forbids
us to denounce Herr Hitler as a bandit:
We have no choice.
Understand, once and for all,
we have no choice!

Hitler's Intelligence Service here in Rome
has spoken with the General of the Jesuits
– a pity, Signor Minutant,
that you should be unaware
of the efforts of your Superior. . . .

RICCARDO: I am not unaware, Holiness,
but can we even consider
using Hitler as a tool?

PIUS: A tool we shall discard
as soon as . . .

CARDINAL: God be praised, your opinion, Minutant,
is totally without significance.

RICCARDO (*with enmity*):
The Holy Father asked me a question, Eminence.
Am I to answer, Holiness?

PIUS (*coldly*):
To the point, of course, to the point. To the point.

RICCARDO (*an attack, whose only result is that not one single word of
his finds a real audience*):
Holiness, it should be remembered, we Jesuits
have for years been training specialists
for Russia, who following in Hitler's train,
following the German army, that is,
were to proselytize the Russians.

CARDINAL (*furious*):
Yes – well? Would you, Minutant, have guessed
before the invasion, then,
that Stalin could have held out so long?

RICCARDO (*to the Pope again*): The commentaries too, of some
of the bishops on this so-called crusade
of Hitler's are . . . blasphemies.
It is the fault of the Vatican *as well*, Holiness,
if the red storm is now approaching Europe.
He who sows the wind . . . Russia was not, after all,
the aggressor.
(*The Pope makes a couple of fidgety movements of the hands. He is
silent, either because he is so agitated that he is, as before, bereft
of speech, or because he considers it beneath his dignity to answer.*)

CARDINAL (*without pausing*):
Holiness – I beg you, break off this conversation.
It is quite unheard of, mmm, what, what the Minutant . . .

(*to Riccardo*)
I took you for a gifted boy, certainly. But *controversialists*
we can do very well without in the Secretariat, mmm, what.
You talk
like – a London newspaper, mmm.

PIUS (*his voice sounds as if it had rusted over, then, with caustic irony*):
Count Fontana, your son appears to us . . .
sorely in need of a holiday . . .

FONTANA: Holiness . . . what Riccardo heard
in Berlin, from Prior Lichtenberg,
and from what he saw himself . . .

PIUS (*sarcastic, but still trembling with anger*):
Yes, we are extremely sorry for him – Riccardo,
go out to Castelgandolfo, for three months
put our library in order – if your nerves
are up to it. Above all, get plenty of exercise,
good long walks, and look
at the Campagna and at water.
A morning by Lake Albano puts one in good humour.
The cool clear October days
opening up the view across the water
open up vistas into one's own inmost being . . .
Go straight out there, today.
You have our most glad permission . . .

CARDINAL: Yes, mmm, what, and not too much reading,
so you can rest your nerves – read the new
masterpiece of Ferrero's on the Congress of Vienna –
disturbingly up to date, mmm, what.
(*seriously to the Pope, somewhat verbosely, to remedy the situation*)
The gentlemen in Washington and London
should be made to read it, like schoolboys, what.
That is what they must preserve in Germany: –
a man like Talleyrand, who, admittedly, had blood on his hands
like any other servant of Napoleon,
was *nevertheless* accepted as a man
with whom one could negotiate. The way
he split the alliance of the enemies of France
in Vienna, and ranged Austria and England secretly
against the Tsar: *that* is the cleverest
advice to give a diplomat today, mmm, what.
Another thing: Minutant, I may in all kindness tell you,

as you are so concerned about the welfare of the Kremlin:
it was a good thing for Russia that
her territorial ambitions were restrained.
Peace in Europe lasted for decades,
the Balance of Power for a century, what.
(*Riccardo bows to the Cardinal with scarcely noticeable irony.*
The Pope speaks spontaneously, as if the Fontanas were no longer
in the room, delighted to have a new subject to talk about.)

PIUS: Yes, Eminence, *they* were diplomats in those days,
at the Congress of Vienna. When one compares their wisdom
with the demands made at Casablanca –
this primitive unconditional surrender!
The only thing the Allies achieve by that is
to make the Germans identify themselves
more closely than ever with their wretched Hitler.
Why does not someone explain, we will make peace
as soon as Hitler is discredited?
That would be a basis which would allow us
to accuse Herr Hitler without necessarily directing
our protest against Germany.
The *Germans* must at all costs remain
negotiable with, even if Herr Hitler does not.

CARDINAL: Surely, Holiness, I have no doubt at all
a German Talleyrand must exist:
Herr von Hassel, for example, or . . .

ABBOT: Even with *him* there will be no negotiation, Eminence.
The Germans have made themselves too much disliked.

PIUS: Very true, Father General – nevertheless:
no peace in Europe without the Reich
as centrepiece of the Continent, keeping
East and West a sufficient distance apart.
Great landlords only stay friends
when their lands do not march . . .

CARDINAL: Yes, if the Reich is simply
divided as the spoils of war,
the result will be the same as Hitler
and Stalin's partition of Poland, or the
Peace of Tilsit in 1807.
The seeds of the next war will have been sown.

PIUS: That is what we keep telling the American Envoy, Eminence.
Herr Hitler can only be allowed to fall if the Reich

survives as a buffer between East and West,
a *small* autonomous military power,
not strong, but strong enough, so that it cannot
be completely overrun and torn in half.

CARDINAL: What do the Germans think they're doing here,
here and now, mmm, what? –
Now even Catholics are being arrested . . .
But let this impertinence be a lesson to us:
to keep the Germans on their knees.

FONTANA (*bitterly*):
For years to come, Eminence. For ever, for ever,
the Germans must be kept on their knees.

CARDINAL (*coolly to Fontana. His first sentence is directed equally to
Riccardo, whose mother was, as we know, German. Then he talks
himself into a passion*):
Yes, mmm, what; protestantism –
that is: megalomania and good music,
that's what they give the world: and we must treat
them carefully, or they'll be hanging round
our necks again in no time, what.
If their war against Moscow has no other effect
than to allow the Russians to – to
march on Silesia and Stettin,
– and it looks very much like it already –
then they have forfeited the right
ever to carry arms again.
Then we . . . as in the days before
Bismarck, their *barbare de génie* . . .
we must not let them have more weapons than
are absolutely necessary for them to
indulge their passion for war and slaughter
in a little mutual blood-letting.
For millenia it has been
their chief amusement: Europe has got along
quite well considering, mm, what . . .

PIUS (*with impatience*):
Tempi passati, Eminence – and some time ago.
Certainly this reign of terror against the Jews is disagreeable,
but we must not allow it so to incense us
that we forget the obligations
which the Germans have to honour

in the very near future
as Protectors of Rome.
Germany must remain viable.
Capable of maintaining an independent existence,
not only for the preservation of the Eastern frontiers,
but also to preserve the balance of power in Europe.
The balance of the Continent
is more important than a unity
which hardly corresponds to the old tribal pattern.
On the few occasions that God has caused the rivers of Europe
to flow in one direction, in one bed:
then the stream has swollen to a torrent
sweeping aside and flooding the old order:
so under Philip II, under Napoleon, under Hitler.
No, each land must have its own stream,
its own directions, limits and frontiers:
that is both healthier and easier to control.
Alliances, to be sure – but never unity.
What was in the mind of God
when, in the winter of '39,
he prevented London and Paris
from supporting Finland in her war with Moscow,
as had been planned?
It had been planned, then nothing came of it.
At that moment, hardly noticed,
the fate of the world was decided:
France and England against Stalin – *that*
would have brought Hitler, who knew even then
that he would break with Russia,
to the side of Britain. Under Hitler's leadership
the Continent could
have emerged from the struggle united.
Great Britain would have preserved her Empire.
Why did not God want this?
Why did he let it come to this,
that the West is now tearing itself to pieces?
For a long time we could see no sense in it –
but today we know that
Hitler, as World Conqueror,
would subjugate *everything*, everything, us as well.
He is therefore only to be tolerated

if he barely survives.
But God was with us, even in that hour.
It was His will that we should not be harmed.
God be praised . . . We must finish;
our beloved congregation is awaiting us.
It is our wish to urge forward the canonisation
of Innocent XI.
It is most important to us, that this
great precursor of ours should once more enter
the field of vision of the thinking European.
Under his leadership Christendom formed
an alliance, to make a stand against the Turks.
God grant this new agression from the East
will founder in its turn, because Europe
has recognized in time that in the presence
of this threat she must
bury her internal squabbles.
(*He makes as if to go, then, after taking a few steps, when he sees
the Fontanas wish to stand in his way, he continues :*)
And pray, beloved in the Lord, also
for the Jews, of whom many
will soon be standing before the face of God.

FONTANA : Holiness – with all due respect
for those reasons which impose silence on you:
I humbly appeal to you, I beg you . . .

PIUS (*who has collected himself after a momentary embarrassment*) :
Did you really believe, Fontana,
we would allow this wanton sacrilege
under our very windows
to pass entirely without comment ?
Certainly not! It is self-evident
a protest will bear witness, that the Pope
extends his deepest sympathy to the victims . . .
Eminence – *that* we will have time for, let us do it
at once! The Writer, please . . . no one shall say
we sacrificed the law of Christian love
to political calculation – no! Today
our feelings are, as always, with the poor . . .

(*As if he had never meant to do anything else, the Pope now looks as if
he is going to protest publicly against the arrest of the Jews. The Cardi-*

*nal has called in the Writer, a tall, Gothic, spidery-limbed monk, who
appears as obedient and characterless as a fourth-generation official
and whose exquisite good manners would put any normal man to shame.
In Germany he wrote a thesis on the symbolic use of the lily in the late
Pre-Raphaelite painters. While this refined Benedictine is transforming
the three prescribed bendings of the knee into a ritual quite peculiar to
himself, prior to sitting at the console table and taking up his pen, the
Representative of Christ collects himself. The coldness and hardness
of his face, lovingly described by the propagandists of the Church as
'unearthly spiritualization', have reached freezing-point simultaneously
– he looks out, past all those around him, outward and upward, as he
liked to be photographed.*

*It is inevitable that this scene should have an unreal, even fantastic
effect. Words, words, speech totally debased into a perfect method of
talking without saying anything – it is a relief that with the stage
arranged as it is it is impossible to show a few of the victims in
the background – ragged families, from infants to grandfathers, a few
of the hundreds and thousands of families in Europe, Catholics
among them, a few of the nuns and monks – on their way to the gas
chambers, abandoned by all, abandoned even by the Representative of
Christ on Earth. This happened in Europe from 1941 to 1944.)*

PIUS (*dictating*):
  The Holy Father hears . . . with growing compassion
  the increasing echo . . . of the misfortunes
  which are intensifying . . . daily . . . due to the . . .
  continuance
  of the present conflict.

CARDINAL: That will most certainly annoy the Germans, yes.
  (*The Fontanas look at one another without speaking. The Father
  General's face is motionless.*)

PIUS: Since the time when the Pope, as is known, attempted
  to prevent in vain, the outbreak of the war,
  in that he . . . in that he . . . warned the leaders of the
   nations
  against the step, today so terribly potent,
  of taking arms, he has not ceased
  to use all means within his power
  to allay the sufferings which . . .
  which in . . . *in whatever* form,

are consequent upon the universal disorders.
With the increase of so much suffering,
the Pope's world-wide and fatherly work of succour
has itself further increased . . . semicolon. Further increased;
it knows
. . . this to be printed with double spacing . . .

WRITER (*in a thin voice*):
Very good, Your Holiness: to be printed
in double spacing.

PIUS (*with a large gesture, raising his voice*):
Knows no frontiers, comma, neither of
nationality, comma, nor of religion, comma,
nor of *race*.
(*to the Fontanas*)
Satisfied, beloved in Christ?

CARDINAL (*visibly impressed*):
Nor of *race*, Holy Father, yes.
That is burningly relevant, mmm, what.
But should one not append – add here, if I may
in all gratitude and humility suggest, mmm, what . . .
(*turning to the Writer, with pathos*)
This many-sided and unsleeping
activity of Pius XII
(*he bows, as does the Father General*)
has, recently, increased still further
due to the present arrests
undertaken in Rome itself,
in the Eternal City,
against the Israelites, who . . .

PIUS (*violently, shaking his head*):
No, Eminence, not that, no!
Not so direct, not so specific: that
would be expressing a direct opinion
on military events. The Holy See
must remain a sanctuary of the spirit of *neutrality*.
(*with impatience*)
Not so direct . . . well, then, Writer:
what did we say before Rome and the Jews
were mentioned directly?

WRITER (*stands, bows, in his thin voice*):
This many-sided and unsleeping

activity of Pius XII
(*kneels, stands up again*)
has recently increased still further
due to . . . that was the last word, Holiness.

PIUS: Now let us say: Due to the aggravation . . . yes –
due to the aggravation of the sufferings
of so . . . so *many* unfortunates.
Eminence, we find that more *comprehensive*
than if we mention the Jews alone.

CARDINAL: No question, mmm, what, Holiness;
more comprehensive certainly.

PIUS (*appeased*): If, dear Eminence and brother,
you are to mention here our humble self,
then it is only just and right
to mention with joy
the prayers of all believers – so, Writer;
(*he dictates very fast now*)
may this blessed activity, comma,
above all things, be, by the prayers of believers
throughout the world . . . My dear Count!

FONTANA (*approaches the Pope, who is standing downstage, and speaks coldly*):
Holiness?

PIUS (*friendly, intimate*): One of the cheques, Fontana, which
you brought us today, reminds us
of our Hungarian Railway holdings:
you will, of course, make it your business
to see that we incur no loss in that direction,
even if the Red Army should occupy Hungary.

FONTANA: I am offering the shares in Zürich, Holiness,
through third parties:
part of the holding has been sold already,
and not too unfavourably at that.
Only it must not be noised about
who is the selling concern, who is unloading.

PIUS: We understand. Get rid of them quickly. No actual
profit is to be made: just get rid of the shares.
Who knows whether Hitler can defend Hungary . . .
What were we saying . . .?
(*Riccardo has meanwhile turned to the Father General and is trying to draw him away from the Cardinal, down right, while*

Pius goes on dictating and Fontana retires into the back-ground.)

WRITER (*bows, then almost singing in his thin voice*):
. . . Prayers of believers throughout the world.
I thought, if I might suggest a form of words
to Your Holiness . . .
(*the Pope waves his hand in agreement*)
who unceasingly, unanimously and
with burning ardour, raise their voice to Heaven . . .

PIUS: Very much what we have in mind. Good.
What did you say ? Raise their voice to Heaven – yes,
comma, to achieve in the future
still *greater* results, and, soon,
to bring about the day, when
(*with great emphasis, liturgically, almost singing*)
the *light* of *peace* shall shine once more upon
the earth, and all men shall lay down their arms,
all discord and all anger shall be extinguished,
and man shall once more find his brother man,
and work together at the last in justice
for the common good of all Mankind, full stop.
(*During the long last sentence the Pope has gone over to the
Writer. After the words 'lay down their arms' he goes towards the
Cardinal and Fontana, almost singing the concluding phrases of the
dictation. Meantime Riccardo passionately importunes the Abbot.*)

RICCARDO: These clichés! Father General,
you know as well as I do, Hitler is not even *supposed*
for one minute to take them seriously.
You must help! Today I must . . .
. . . we must *both* broadcast . . .

ABBOT (*as he turns away from Riccardo, quietly, tensely*):
Are you mad ? Be quiet . . .

CARDINAL (*while Riccardo is still talking to the Abbot*):
This protest, Holiness, will be of great comfort
to the persecuted . . .
(*The Pope has heard the Abbot talking to Riccardo. He turns away
from the Cardinal and says, smiling, but without friendliness.*)

PIUS: Now, Signor Minutant, still
not satisfied with us ?
(*The Cardinal, too, turns to Riccardo. Before Riccardo, in his
intense agitation, can answer, his father says :*)

FONTANA: Holiness, this Article,
which does not in one syllable mention the arrests,
cannot be understood
as having specific reference to the Jewish question.

PIUS (*at the end of his patience*): Have we not, expressis verbis,
spoken of men *of all races*,
Count Fontana?

CARDINAL: The protest will go down in history, yes.

ABBOT: We do what we can.

FONTANA: Father General – the Holy See has,
as we well know, other means than this
of getting itself a hearing.
Holiness, issue an *ultimatum* to Hitler,
or a letter that Herr von Weizsäcker
can deliver to him.

(*The Pope, agitated, gestures to the Writer to leave.*)

WRITER (*bowing*): If in humility I may remind him,
Your Holiness has . . . not yet signed.

(*While he goes to the Pope, who fumbles for the proffered writing-case in extreme irritation, Riccardo affixes the Star of David which he has with him to his cassock. The Pope now sees it. Words fail him. His gaze fixed on Riccardo, he reaches or rather gropes for the golden pen the monk is holding out to him, to put it in the ink-well. It should be a goose quill, like the one with which the Pope, on November 1st, 1950, signed the Dogma of the Assumption of the Virgin. Absently, he dips the nib in the ink, and as he signs:*)

CARDINAL (*his breath taken away, appalled*):
Signor Minutant . . . now you forget yourself!
Remove that – thing! Leave the room!
What are you thinking of, in the presence of the Holy Father!
Blasphemy . . . on a sacred habit . . .
Blasphemy.

FONTANA (*imploringly*): Riccardo – don't, please . . .

RICCARDO (*unmoved, passionately*):
Holiness, what you are signing there is
a power of attorney giving Hitler freedom
to do with the Jews
as he has been doing for . . .

(*As the Pope in great agitation is rapidly signing, the pen slips from his fingers and covers his hand with ink. He holds out his hand reproachfully, so they can see it.*)

CARDINAL (*breaking in on Riccardo's words*):
    Be quiet! Holy Father,
    I beseech you in all humility
    to end this conversation!
    (*The Pope has controlled himself sufficiently to be able to continue speaking. He does so haltingly, though without the stutter which afflicted Pacelli frequently as Cardinal, though seldom as Pope.*)
PIUS: In the name of the victims – this . . . this . . .
    sacrilege, too! – And this impertinence there –
    the Star of David on the dress of a servant of Christ.
    (*He looks again at his inky hand, usually so painfully clean, and with deep vexation shows it to the others, like a wound. The Cardinal orders the Writer to leave, and turning to Riccardo, points angrily to his chest, where the Star of David is pinned.*)
RICCARDO: This star that every Jew must wear
    from the moment he is six years old
    as a sign of outlawry,
    I shall wear, until . . .
PIUS (*shaking with fury*): That he shall not.
    We forbid him – forbid him –
    to wear . . . on a soutane . . . that – this . . .
    (*He breaks off, his voice about to fail.*)
RICCARDO: I shall wear this star until
    Your Holiness in front of all the world
    curses that one man, who
    is slaughtering the Jews of Europe
    like cattle.
    (*The Pope is silent, apparently at the mercy of Riccardo and of his own powers of speech.*)
CARDINAL: Sacrilege and folly – leave the room!
RICCARDO (*his voice rising*):
    FOLLY? . . . No, Holiness: the King
    of Denmark, a defenceless man,
    threatened Hitler he would wear the star,
    along with *every member* of his house,
    if the Jews in Denmark were
    forced to do so . . . They
    were not forced. When, finally,
    will the Vatican act so that
    it will be possible once more for a priest
    to admit without shame that he

is a servant of *that* Church, which sees
in brotherly love its first commandment?
CARDINAL: In obedience! Unconditional obedience
is where the Jesuit sees his first commandment, Minutant!
RICCARDO: Yes, in obedience to God.
CARDINAL: . . . Who works through the voice and through
the will of His Holiness, yes. You will obey!
(*Pius maintains an ostentatious silence.*)
As a member of the Society of Jesus, you took
a vow of special obedience to the Pope.
RICCARDO: Eminence, forgiveness; does not every cardinal,
true to the colour of his scarlet robe,
promise to stand up for his faith
to the last drop of his blood?
Our faith, however, Eminence, rests
on brotherly love . . . before you judge me
think of those who are being deported.
CARDINAL: I do not judge you, I pray for you, yes, mmm, what.
But that obscenity there – on your soutane . . .
Once and for all
leave the presence of the Holy Father.
PIUS (*makes another attempt to leave, sincerely shattered, extremely
agitated*):
Uproar in *these* rooms,
disobedience and presumption, Protestantism . . .
Pah . . . is this the thanks we get for all
the benefits we have conferred on this young man?
FONTANA: I must ask your permission to withdraw, Holiness.
PIUS: You will stay, Count.
Your son is tribulation enough for you,
you do not need to do penance for his folly.
FONTANA: I beg Your Holiness, allow me to withdraw.
PIUS (*majestic, cold*):
You will stay and there's an end. – You, Father General,
(*He turns to the Abbot. The Writer has entered soundlessly, now
carrying a large brass or copper basin of water and a handtowel.*)
are responsible to us, that this misconduct . . . there
will find an end. Accompany the Minutant
to his house. – God protect him, he knows not
what he says, we have forgiven him.
Of course he cannot go back to his post,

nor can he return to Lisbon . . .

(*Riccardo is standing as if for some time all this has ceased to concern him; one cannot even tell whether he is listening. The monk carrying the bowl goes towards the Pope. Fontana, a broken man, falls on his knees in front of the Pope, while the monk looks as if he will die of fright on the spot.*)

FONTANA: Holiness, please . . . I beg of you, Holy Father . . .

PIUS (*irritated*):
Please, Fontana, rise, what can *you* do about it?
Your son's behaviour cannot, after all,
estrange the two of us. Non possumus,
(*finally, glassy and hard*)
we cannot and – shall not – write to Hitler.
He,
and in his unhappy person
the German nation, in corpore,
would only feel themselves
denounced and provoked. But they must see in us,
and so must Roosevelt, a fair-minded negotiator.
Now, finally, a stop to this, ad acta.
(*During the last sentence he has turned back to the throne and makes as if to wash his hands in the basin that is proffered to him . . . when Riccardo, already at the door, says quietly and strongly*)

RICCARDO: God will not forsake His Church
simply because a Pope forsakes his office.

(*The Pope rises, incapable of speech. He cannot hide the fact that these words have hit him deeply. All look towards the open door through which Riccardo has left quietly and abruptly. Each is shocked, but betrays it by gesture and expression, not in words. Fontana feels that for him it is more than a question here simply of an unforgivable 'offence'. He goes helplessly three steps towards the door, in great trepidation, as if he was going to follow Riccardo – then he turns, utterly demolished. He looks at the floor and holds himself upright by leaning on the console table. A Swiss Guard with a halberd appears at the door; the Cardinal in great agitation gestures him to close it. Now the Pope sits and begins to wash his hands. He can say nothing, and it is fortunate for him that he is able to conceal the shaking of his hands by the action of washing. The Cardinal watches him, deeply affected,*)

*then goes towards him and says in the intimate tone of voice which he
seldom uses :)*

CARDINAL: Holy Father, you must not allow yourself . . .
   to be so upset by the silliness . . .
   They are merely *impertinences*, mmm . . .
   (*The Pope smiles at him sadly and gratefully. Now he can speak.
   He says to the Abbot, and it soothes his troubled conscience some-
   what :)*
PIUS: My good Father-General, in the monasteries
   for the refugees, is there enough bread ?
ABBOT (*consolingly, as if to a very sick man*):
   I'm sure for the first few weeks, Holiness,
   all the monasteries are doubtless adequately supplied.
PIUS (*exasperated at being so misunderstood*):
   Summa iniuria.
   As if we were not ready to give our help to all, *to all* . . .
   What it was granted to us to do is done.
   We are . . . God knows . . . innocent of the blood
   that has been spilt . . . As the flowers
   (*his voice rises in declamation*)
   wait in the earth, beneath the thick blanket
   of the winter snow, for the warm winds of spring,
   so must the Jews in prayer and confidence
   learn to await the hour
   of heavenly consolation. – In conclusion
   (*he has dried his hands and now rises to his feet*),
   since we are gathered here in the name of Christ,
   let us pray . . . Fontana, please,
   you, too, must come into our circle.
   (*Fontana, against his will, comes in between the Abbot and the
   Cardinal, who have sunk down on the steps up to the throne, left and
   right of it respectively. The monk has placed the wash-basin and
   towel on the table, and kneels also. The Pope comes down, too,
   bends down to Fontana and says kindly –*)
   Fontana – who would know better than we,
   to be a father means a crown of thorns.
   (*Fontana is forced to kiss the ring on the Pope's extended hand.
   Then the Pope, once again completely master of the situation,
   steps back towards the throne. 'The haggard noble frame is drawn
   up . . . the eyes – turned to Heaven . . . in his outstretched*

arms the Pope seems to wish to draw all mankind together in a fatherly embrace.'
The curtain starts to descend after he has spoken his first words:)
Exsurge, Domine, adiuva nos, et libera nos
propter nomen tuum –
sit super nos semper benedictio tua –

Curtain

Act Five · Auschwitz
or the Question Asked of God

If there was bad weather or a strong wind, the stench of burning
was carried for many kilometres and led to the whole surrounding
population's talking about the burning of the Jews, in spite of the
counter-propaganda of the Party and the Government offices.
Apart from this the Air Raid Defence objected to the fact that the
fires could be seen from the air at night from a long way away. It
was, however, necessary to continue the incinerations by night, in
order not to have to stop the incoming trains. The timetable of the
separate actions, which had been drawn up with precision by the
Reichsministerium in the course of a meeting for the purpose, had
to be adhered to, in order to avoid any hold-ups or confusion on
the railway lines involved, particularly from a military point of
view.

I was struck by a young woman, who was helping the small
children and the older women to get undressed, continually run-
ning to and fro. . . . She did not look in the least Jewish. Up
to the last moment she lurked among the women who had not yet
finished undressing with several children, talking encouragingly
to them, calming the children. With the last of them she went into
the gas chamber. At the door she stopped and said: 'I have known
from the beginning that we were coming to Auschwitz to be gassed.
I avoided being selected for the labour squads by taking the
children under my protection. I wanted to experience the whole
process, consciously and completely. I hope it will be over quickly.
Farewell!'

FROM THE STATEMENT OF LIEUT.-COL. HÖSS,
COMMANDANT OF AUSCHWITZ

*It is common to the most momentous events and discoveries of our time
that they make too great demands on the human imagination. No power
of invention is great enough to bring before our eyes Auschwitz, the destruction of Dresden or Hiroshima, research flights into space or even
industrial progress and high-speed records. Man can no longer grasp
what he can achieve.*

*For this reason, the question whether or how to bring Auschwitz on to
the stage in this play occupied me for a long time. Documentary naturalism is no longer any sort of stylistic principle. A figure as over-lifesize*

205

as the Doctor, who doesn't even have a proper name, the monologues, and other things, make it clear that an imitation of reality is not being striven for – nor should it be striven for in the setting. On the other hand, it seemed to me dangerous to proceed in this play on the lines of Celan in his masterly poem 'Todesfuge', which transposes the gassing of the Jews into metaphors, e.g.

'Black milk of the dawn, we drink you each evening,
We drink you at noon, in the mornings, we drink you at night.'

For however great the power of suggestion emerging from word and sound, metaphors conceal the infernal cynicism of the real thing. This in itself is such an immeasurably intensified reality that the impression of unreality which it gives off, even today, fifteen years after the events, supports our already strong temptation to treat it as a legend, an unbelievable apocalyptic fairy story. This danger is only increased by the use of alienation effects. If one clings as closely as possible to the historical tradition – then the diction, the scene and the happenings on the stage immediately become unrealistic. For even the fact that we can today visit Auschwitz as we do the Colosseum is hardly enough to convince us that, seventeen years ago, in the world in which we live, this huge factory with its regular train service was once erected so that, by the agency of normal human beings who now earn their daily bread as postmen, district judges, youth workers, sales representatives, pensioners, secretaries of state and gynaecologists, other human beings might be done to death.

SCENE ONE

The stage is as dark as possible. It would be as well if the guardroom in the left foreground were not yet visible.
It is immediately evident from the sound-track, without the speakers themselves coming forward, that the monologues are being spoken or 'thought' in the interior of a truck: we can hear a goods train in motion and then being shunted. A livid early morning light illumines the scene sparsely, so that just the outlines of the deportees are visible, crouching huddled together on the floor among cases and boxes. Apart from the monotonous beat of the wheels of the truck, which remain audible during the monologues as well, there should, for the time being, be no realistic effects such as talking, crying children, etc. . . .

The Monologues

THE OLD MAN: Not to die in the truck,
  not in the sight of my grandchildren.
  A long while back fear wiped their faces away,
  stifled their questions. They sense, what I now know:
  this journey's end is our end, too. . . .
  Wherever it may be, you terrible God,
  your Heaven is above us, and the hangmen
  are men, whose power comes from you.
  Are you watching, too? Yes, you will be . . . So truly
  I served you, among the many who despised you,
  so sure was I of your omnipotence:
  how could I doubt, inconceivable,
  that you would have your hand in this as well?
  Was not the comfort of my old age, the surety
  that no one, no one, would snatch the reins from your hands?
  It is this faith in You that now destroys me. –
  Be warned, for Your Name's sake:
  do not show your greatness by burning children
  before their mother's eyes so that
  in the cries of the tortured you may hear
  your name repeated.
  Who in the smoke of the crematoria
  could trace your finger pointing toward repentance?
  Oh, you measureless God . . . is man most like you
  when himself measureless? Is he
  such an abyss of ruthlessness, because
  you have made him in your own image? –
  I cannot quarrel any longer, my Dreadful God,
  nor pray, but only still implore:
  let me not die in this truck,
  not in the sight of my grandchildren.

THE WOMAN: They leered when they found the little jackets and
  the nappies in my case. They listened politely.
  I was in my eighth month.
  And, friendlily, they asked after my husband. –
  As if they had never, just two days before,
  dragged you from your workbench and flung you
  down the stairs, till blood came out of your mouth.
  As you looked back . . . your face; oh, if I knew

what you were wanting to say. Did you mean
our child? What was it you meant?
And they laughed, they laughed when you cried out to me
you would be back.

How happy we were with our daily life
and being no one's enemy: we loved
the narrow kitchen balcony, and sought the sun
in the piazza beside the grapesellers,
and the cool in the park. And on Sunday,
relaxing at the cinema.
And now . . . never a family, never the three of us.
Never to eat, to talk at our own table,
no room to protect us . . . nor paths that are safe and dreams
and daily milk and light by night and a bed
and a man who loves his work
and gives me comfort and warmth in the night and a shield.
We had forgotten the menace of the world.

The child menaced already in its mother's body.
The old man still menaced, wanting just to die
in his own room, like a wounded animal in a bush
after the man-hunt of life. – We talked all the time
of you, thought of names for you and month by month
we bought your first clothes, your little cradle. We were happy.
It cannot be, this cannot happen.
You are alive . . . I feel your hands, your heart.
In a month you will come into the world
defenceless!
Madonna, Mother of God – don't let it happen!
Leave me my child still – let us live!

THE YOUNG GIRL: No hope, my darling, that you will find me.
God is as cold as the splendour in San Giovanni.
He is not moved, that the pregnant woman next to me
will never be a mother, or that I shall never belong to you.
God is cold, my hands grow stiff when I fold them to pray.
And the Gods of old are as dead as their legends
and the antique rubble in the Vatican museum –
the charnel-house of art – or there might
still be a hope you would find me yet,
as Orpheus Eurydice.

But this truck is no boat to Hell,
the railway track to Poland not the Styx.
Even the underworld has been snatched from the Gods
and peopled with guardians whom no song will move.

You will not find me any more, however long
you search. Do not search for long. Take a girl
who will give you more than I. Forget. Be happy.
And don't hesitate with love. Those who love are hunted,
and always in danger.
Do not miss your day
as we missed ours in the Campagna.
Don't miss the evening on the shore
when the beach, the black sand of Ostia,
is still warm, a cradle for you both.

Don't forget it quite, not too fast:
dark around us, and shelter, and
the breakers flooding our hearts
and your words
that drew forth those tender sounds,
where no one could hear. I shrank so
close to you, hidden as never again, hidden –
and your mouth broke me open. Oh, not even the night
that was given us was ever ours.
Why – forgive me, my darling – did I put away
your hands? If you were only with me now, I am left
so terribly left alone. But we missed our hour.
If I were with you on the shore! A flood could hurl
us out into the waves, so long as we were together.
I am so alone. Once more take
sand from Ostia in your hands
and throw it in the sea,
my ashes, and call my name,
as you did then, in Ostia –

(*After the last monologue there is a loud noise of shunting, the train
stops, and now with the opening of the sliding doors there begins the
noise, well known from numerous descriptions, with which the Kapos
found it necessary to unload the trains: oft-repeated orders to be reproduced very realistically, such as:*

> 'All out, come on, come on, come on.'
> 'Leave the luggage here.'
> 'Faster, faster.'
> 'Any sick to stay behind.'
> 'Stay behind.'
> 'Out of it, get a move on, there.'

Children crying. A woman shouts: 'Rachele, Rachele . . . where are you, Rachele?' *In between, the barking of dogs, blowing of whistles . . . and the release of steam from the engine. The frightened people are dragged off with great speed and brutality by the Kapos from the imaginary truck and vanish in the darkness of the stage.*
Silence.)

SCENE TWO

During the whole scene it never gets light, only twilit. The 'cloud' visible on almost all the extant drawings done by its inmates lay permanently over Auschwitz, along with the pestilent stench of burning flesh and the myriads of flies, and was noticed by the population of the neighbourhood and the travellers on the stretch of railway between Cracow and Katowice, who crowded to the windows as the trains passed by the camp.

The mephitic smoke, the glare of the fires and the shower of sparks from the crematoria and the ten gigantic pyres, visible thirty kilometres away, on which something like a thousand corpses could be burned at one time in the open air, this constitutes the infernal atmosphere which shrouded the death factory, even on the railway sidings and in the outer courtyards. What happened in the interior of this underworld is not even to be imagined, let alone evoked atmospherically.

The stage setting is throughout ghostly, dreamlike, even if 'reality' is technically possible. A few indications suffice.

On the forestage, far over to the left, is a guardroom, to the right of which are a few inhumanly tidy flowerbeds and a bench. The rear part of the stage is raised and falls away slightly upstage right, so that the deportees on their way to the unseen gas chambers remain in sight as long as possible. A ramp on the right of the stage joins the rear stage to the forestage. In the background is the often photographed gate-house, still undamaged today (1959), through which the trains with the pri-

soners entered Auschwitz: a mournful, stable-like, extended building with few windows and a low watch-tower in the middle, reminding one of a silo.

A couple of steps lead up to the guardroom, which is open to the audience. There is a very large window in the back wall, at present still blacked out, in front of which are a typewriter, a telephone, office chairs. On the far left side of the room is a narrow camp bed, and next to it a short-legged table with coffee things, bread rolls and those numerous bottles of drink which were never far away when murder was being committed on the orders of the teetotaller Adolf Hitler.

This whole setting is only characteristic of Auschwitz if we can feel the gruesome background of smoke and fire lowering over it. We must be able to feel that this dreary hut with its little garden is, by way of comparison, still the human façade – a façade however which reveals more than it conceals of what takes place behind it.

One cannot, alas, console oneself with the idea that a camp like Auschwitz was run by the mentally deranged, or by criminal lunatics. These were normal fellow creatures who had their 'place of business' here. To remind ourselves of this fact, let us begin in detail with Helga.

A loud old-fashioned alarm clock rings. Helga, now an S.S. information clerk (Blitzmädel), switches it off at once, throws back the blanket and sits up in the camp bed, where she had fallen asleep with the table-lamp on. She is as young as she is pretty, and dressed only in gym clothes: on the vest, just below her well-developed left breast, there is sewn a sports badge, and the short white pants are adorned on the left-hand side at the top with the S.S. device. However, she probably still has her back turned to the audience; then slowly her right, then her left leg, very pretty bare legs, come into view; finally she stands in front of the bed and begins right away to hum sadly Hans Leip's 'Lili Marlene'. She goes, barefoot, over to the electric element, puts it in a jug of water, and then takes a pair of stockings, from the revolving chair in front of the typewriter, which she pulls on luxuriously, for they are rare in the fourth year of the war. Now she is wide awake and brisk. After putting on her blouse and black tie, she puts on her mannish suit, which emphasizes her fashion-plate figure, opens the door, briefly sniffs the fog and smoke outside, then puts a forage-cap on her blonde head. Her night shift ends at 7 a.m., in other words, very soon.

She folds up the blanket, pours hot water into a coffee filter, and is about to start reading again over breakfast from the thick book which was lying by her bedside, when Obersturmbannführer Dr Fritsche appears with two gentlemen from the industrial plants.

A little more about Helga. The specifically feminine abilities, first to be completely in agreement with the opinions of those who make an impression on her and, secondly, the ability to ignore anything that might disturb the view, are powers which she has not even needed to develop particularly. Like any markedly feminine characteristics, they are inborn in her to such an extent that if she were ever actually to reflect on the subject she would find even Auschwitz to be 'quite in order'. Of course, she never does reflect on the subject. For this reason, she is a particularly attractive kind of sleeping pill for the men here, who are from time to time troubled at night by ghosts. She has nothing in common with the termagants who become wardresses in the camp, although she is well aware of the nature of what she transmits over the telephone and the teleprinter. More so even than Höss, the Commandant, Helga proves, by her unconscious simplicity, warmheartedness and womanly charm, how 'human' a human being can still be even when he is a professional criminal. She proves also that 'human' has become a totally meaningless word because it is all too ambiguous . . . Helga's favourite occupation, when she is not involved with some man or other, is daydreaming about being far away from this place, say on the Lüneburger Heide. She wants, in fact, to be a faithful, happy bride, instead of constantly betraying her fiancé, a good-looking but unimaginative crematorium filler with the rank of Lieutenant, with the Doctor, on whom she is so totally dependent that she overcomes all her fears and scruples for the sake of an hour in bed with him in the middle of the day. She loathes this medical man, because she is susceptible to his lascivious charm . . . and because she loathes anything which is wicked and too intelligent. In her passion for cleanliness and respectability, she might even be disgusted at the slaughtering of the Jews if it had ever entered her head that it was in any way as reprehensible as, say, marital infidelity or listening to the B.B.C. But, like all young girls, she is completely manageable, not simply pliable material in the hands of a lover, but in the way that many secretaries, even in their deepest likes and dislikes, are nothing more than parrot-like repetitions of their

*bosses. For this reason, in two years' time, in 1945, she will grasp
immediately and quite without opportunism the fact that what was done
to the Jews was 'not nice' . . . since it will be a distinctly virile (and
Jewish) officer of the occupying forces who will make it clear to her.
Even in bed she will not, for safety's sake, confess to having known
about the more appalling details of the happenings at Auschwitz
to which she was party . . . 'obviously' she knew nothing whatsoever
of the fact that human beings were systematically exterminated there.
The American believes her, not only because she is pretty: he quite
seriously believes what she says to be possible, just as his judicial
colleagues in Nuremberg were to give consideration to Julius Streicher's
statement that he was totally unaware of murder operations.*

*The Doctor is given a hand not only by sweet young girls with no charac-
ters, but also by soured-up bourgeois with lots of character, bearing
out the incontrovertible statement of Prince Talleyrand that a married
man with a family is always ready to do anything for money . . . To
whom God gives an office, to him also He gives fellow workers. The
gentlemen who are here on their way to see Helga, although 'imaginary',
are not only known to us from the second scene of the first act . . .
they have been known to us for a long time, whether we observed them
daily on the switchback of the German Economic Miracle or in our
own bathroom mirrors.*

*Even this morning we can see that they will survive the war, to their own
bodily and financial satisfaction. Every one apparently indispensable
in his job and therefore protected from being drafted to the front, they
are, in fact, as interchangeable as motor tyres. For this reason, it will
be enough for us to look at one of them to stand for all three.*

*Let us take the one in uniform: Herr Doctor Fritsche, pale and bespect-
acled, resembling his Reichsführer Himmler much as a retouched snap-
shot resembles a studio portrait. His job is to share out, having obtained a
receipt, to the various industries which have settled in the neighbourhood of Auschwitz like vultures round gorging lions, healthy 'prisoner-
material' of both sexes, taken off the goods trains . . . and after a few
months to take back, again on a receipt, from such reputable firms as IG
Farben the pitilessly exploited husks of the workers and deliver them to
the gas chambers. Herr Fritsche has never felt scruples about this
activity, since he was originally a lawyer, and knows that nothing is*

happening here which is not in order from the point of view of his terms of service. It would never occur to him to beat a prisoner, and he hopes that his subordinates, too, would only carry out whippings if a prisoner, by malingering or idleness, had made himself liable according to the regulations for physical punishment. The proof that a sickness is not faked is final only when the prisoner is dead.

Herr Fritsche does not, in principle, watch or listen to the carrying out of disciplinary punishment, and also avoids being a spectator at the crematoria as well, as he is frankly afraid of 'losing backbone and falling back into our bourgeois ways of thinking'. He fights such tendencies by taking extensive walks in the protection of two wolfhounds, and by reading National Socialist party directives, although Herr Fritsche is in no wise politically committed. He has climbed by dint of study, with great self-denial, and married a girl with no money, so he makes efforts in his career towards speedy financial progress, but would never enrich himself illegally: the gold wristwatch, the property of a cremated Jew from Amsterdam, has arrived on his forearm through the proper channels. Seeing that the Führer recently denounced all lawyers with the deepest scorn, saying they were all out of date, Dr Fritsche too sees little point any more in the career of a judge, while the activity of a solicitor appears totally absurd to him. Not, be it said, because he has any feeling of the grotesqueness of people of precisely his kind – as was often the case in Western Germany after 1950 – being set in judgement over men who may, for example, have stolen a bicycle. All that Sturmbannführer Fritsche says to himself is that after the final victory modern jurisprudence will probably only have room for two forms of penalty – death or transportation for a term to the occupied Eastern Territories: the Greater German Reich must not burden itself with prisons full of 'useless mouths'. Consequently, and because it is readily listened to, Herr Fritsche talks of the entailed estate which he will doubtless get for his services and which he and his family are intending to work in the, alas, now momentarily reoccupied Ukraine. It goes without saying that he has no knowledge of farming. He finds it particularly hard to make contact with living creatures, e.g. Helga. He even avoids approaching horses too closely, for fear of being kicked. By 1952 he will have become financial expert to one of the most important German building societies, by 1960 a chief county court judge

*entitled to a pension . . . a change of profession, which, as his heart is
not sound any more, he effects out of concern for his family, despite
temporary financial sacrifices. . . .*

*As far as possible, despite fog and stinking smoke, it has got lighter.
While Helga is making herself coffee, Fritsche appears in a winter
greatcoat, with cap and earmuffs, and is about to go straight into the
guardroom to get warm when a menacing-looking officer appears
from the left, complete with steel helmet, whip, lantern and wolfhound,
and comes towards him.*

OFFICER: Sturmbannführer . . . a report
    (*He ties the dog up to the bench.*)
FRITSCHE: So early in the morning? – What's up?
OFFICER: Sturmbannführer, a great surprise on the outer platform:
    the Pope has personally sent us a priest . . .
FRITSCHE: *What* was that about the Pope?
OFFICER: The Pope has sent a priest as travelling-
    companion for the baptized Jews.
    It's the Jews from Rome after all! He was to
    travel with them, to look after their souls, of course.
    And . . .
FRITSCHE: And what?
OFFICER: And some benighted idiot in Rome
    loaded the man up just like the mob.
    Packed in along with them,
    right there in the truck, although he
    was wearing a cassock, an Italian, not a Jew,
    and apparently a relation of Pacelli's into the bargain . . .
FRITSCHE: Goddam. God-damned idiots.
OFFICER: He spoke to me; it was still dark,
    it's only luck I didn't set the dog . . .
FRITSCHE: Where's he got to now?
    Has he seen anything of the camp yet?
OFFICER: Not of the camp, *so far*. He's still outside
    on Platform One. I handed
    him over immediately to the police
    who took over the train at Passau,
    and the railway people,
    to get him back.
    He's having breakfast with them at the moment and . . .

FRITSCHE: This is a muck-up. Don't watch him too closely.
    Till he goes he must be able to move about
    on the outer platform enough not to arouse
    his curiosity too much, so he won't expose us like
    the gentlemen from the Red Cross.

OFFICER: I'm only afraid he may have seen a lot
    too much already on the train.

FRITSCHE: We need a drink after a shock like this.
    (*They go through the little garden; Fritsche knocks almost timidly.*)

HELGA: Come in.

FRITSCHE (*shyly*): Ah, Heil und Sieg. May we come and get warm
    with you just for a minute, Fräulein Helga?

HELGA: Yes, of course. Good morning. Cold, isn't it?
    Cigarettes there, Heinz, help yourself.
    Herr Fritsche, please.

OFFICER (*takes a cigarette*): Thanks, Helga. How are you then?
    I don't need a drink now.
    I'm just going off duty.

HELGA: What about you, Herr Fritsche? Coffee?

FRITSCHE: No, thank you, just a brandy, I must be off to the station.
    (*to the officer, as Helga folds up some blankets*)
    Just get him away, get the priest away from here.
    I will call Berlin at eight sharp.
    Does he want to go back to Rome? –
    He's certainly all we're short of here.

OFFICER: He wants to go to Breslau, with German money.
    He has to see the Bishop there,
    then he's going on to the Nuncio in Berlin.

FRITSCHE:
    What for? To put in a complaint or something?

OFFICER:
    No, he didn't say anything about that. He used to work there.
    Of course, he was furious with the idiots
    in Rome or Northern Italy
    who carted him off like some Jewish urchin.
    He's calmed down now.

FRITSCHE: Whoever did that will be finding himself in
    a nice job on the Russian front pretty soon.
    Irresponsible moron!
    Behaving as if he was in the Ukraine,
    especially now, with our position

in the South precarious enough as it is.
Unbelievable, with the Führer only a short while back
saying again the Church would not be touched
till after the Final Victory,
and Himmler – did you hear about that?

OFFICER: No, Sturmbannführer.

FRITSCHE: Himmler recently had his mother laid to rest
with the blessing of the Catholic Church! – Wasn't that nice?
Well then, get that black man away, get him out of here.
Get him off to Berlin, they know how
to treat people from the Vatican there.
Well – one more drink after a fright like that.
Helga, be an angel, and pour me a bit of consolation.

HELGA: You console me, I'll console you. –

FRITSCHE: There – then I'll ring Berlin.
Well, Helga, heil and thank you!

HELGA: Wiedersehen.

OFFICER: I'll come with you. I have to get some sleep.

HELGA: Heil, Herr Fritsche. Heil, Heinz – have a good sleep,
I've got to catch up on last night, too. . . .

(*She yawns and laughs. Fritsche and the officer leave. Helga
switches off the table-lamp and pulls up the blackout blinds on the
window at the back. A circular saw is singing: this noise comes
from one of the workshops in the camp, underlining from time to
time some of the Doctor's more particularly significant utterances.
From the right, springing elegantly over the beds of the little
garden right up the two steps to the door, cane in hand, a book
under his arm, comes 'the beautiful devil'. He is already in the
room, laughing and genial, malicious, winning, very tall and slim.
Helga is frightened to the bone, but we see it is a fear she prefers to
peace of mind. She steps back, but he has already pulled her to him
and kissed her on the mouth, as she says:*)

You! – go away, leave me alone, you devil!
I hate you, I *hate* you – let go!
If anyone sees us, no, don't!
The window, . . . you beast, . . . go back to your Jewess!

(*After the first kiss, she has tried to push him away. He laughs
softly and tenderly and pulls her to him in a scuffle, while she beats
at him, angrily but helplessly, held in his arms as in a vice.*)

(*tortured, weak, clings to him while he bites her ear*)

You'll ruin all three of us, all three.

Go and sleep with the prisoners – till someone hangs you.

DOCTOR (*with tender irony at which she is eventually forced to smile*):
Jealous of a wretched girl like that?
But I do not hate you for going
to do your premarital duty with Günther every night.
You still have time for me in the middle of the day.
This afternoon? – Who knocks at my door,
who slips into my room to ask,
just to ask if the Herr Doctor can
lend her his copy of *Anna Karenina*?

HELGA: Well, you've got your Jewess now.

DOCTOR: But you only come to ask, my kitten,
whether I've got some stupid book or other . . .
There's nothing wrong with that!
How can you possibly help it if I happen
to be under the shower at that moment.

HELGA (*wrenches herself free, goes three steps from him*):
Leave me alone – people will see.

DOCTOR: Exactly, then get away from the window.
(*He takes her by the arm; she kicks out; he spins round with her a couple of times.*)
You've got stockings on for the first time.

HELGA (*now clinging to him contentedly*):
It was so cold this morning. Oh, you –
(*He lays her quickly on the camp bed and puts his left knee between her feet.*)

DOCTOR (*tenderly*):
I'm looking forward to lunchtime. Look here . . .
(*He has taken a pearl necklace out of his pocket and lets it swing above her face. She takes no notice, but says tormentedly:*)

HELGA: He'll report you, he'll kill us.

DOCTOR: For the last time, be quiet. Your Günther will be
only too glad not to have to kill anybody.
He's on crematorium duty this afternoon,
and we'll be getting warm in bed.
Well then . . . you will be very frightened,
and very small, my little naked kitten . . .
(*quietly*)
and wild all of a sudden, so wild that you
can even forget who you are wild with.
Look here.

(*He swings the necklace.*)

HELGA: You frighten me.

DOCTOR: Don't you like the necklace? I found the pearls
yesterday morning when we opened up
a big fat Jewish oyster.
I'll give them to you as a wedding present.

HELGA: I don't want anything to do with it.
What would I tell Günther!

DOCTOR: You've just inherited them.
They can be consecrated this afternoon.
(*He stands up, walks nervously up and down the room and says
with ironic charm:*)
Then you won't need to feel ashamed any longer,
in broad daylight. I'll put the pearls on you
and your left hand won't be naked either –
with your engagement ring . . .

HELGA: How can you go on laughing at me!
I don't *want* to. I don't *want* to do it any more.
I don't *want* to do it.

DOCTOR (*very relaxed*):
It does you good, I can see it in your face,
like polishing a dirty mirror.
(*She shakes her head violently, yet cannot help smiling; then she
puts her arms round him and pulls him on to the bed.*)

HELGA: You are a devil!

DOCTOR: How do *I* look after these entertainments?

HELGA: Very peaceful, no longer nervous and
not so wicked; above all, not so wicked.

DOCTOR: Wicked? What do you mean, wicked?

HELGA (*embracing him tighter*): That little laugh of yours
is no more real than my fidelity
to Günther – and my love for you, which is so terrible.
I really don't know whether I love you at all.
It nearly drives me mad, at times, I know.
But then comes hate and I hate you
then with all my heart, really . . .
Oh, please let us be honest – and break off the engagement.

DOCTOR: But you're still sleeping with him every night!

HELGA (*starting to cry*): Oh don't – it isn't every night!
And only so I can be with you during the day.
Why do you always send me away? I don't want

to know whether I love you – all I know
is that I'm in your hands, I *must* be with you.
Please, can't we get married . . . ?
DOCTOR (*who has freed himself from her, stands up and walks up and
down again, discomposed*):
Married? Procreate children? . . . Dear God,
that is the one sin I shall *not* commit,
never, *that* I can promise you.
Sweetheart, you just stick to your Günther;
my climate is a bit harsh for you,
Günther is better.
Present the Führer with soldiers and
good male-producing girls.
(*with considerable self-cynicism*)
By the time your daughters are ready to be bedded out,
I'll have seen enough of the twins here
to see how they are made. Then I can
prescribe for our blonde master-race (the animals!)
the basic formula for twins,
and they can breed like rats.
My name will be in the encyclopedias:
my final ambition and my stupidest.
Isn't that enough, my darling?
Am I obliged to plough, sow and reap
the marriage-bed myself? I'm doing quite enough
for the cause of Mankind's racial purity.
I bring death
and I bring life. . . .
And always I bring *suffering*.
Suffering when I push them into the gas,
suffering when I pull them into the world.
However, your uncle-doctor
loves his own children far too much to think
of throwing them on the mercy of the world.
(*He pulls her to him and says almost with passion:*)
And whatever gymnastics we may get up to,
don't be afraid, I won't give you a child.
HELGA: Please, stop, you seem so strange. . . . Oh,
(*quietly, then hesitantly; she can hardly get the words out*)
tell me, why have you done it with
this Jewess of all people, whose . . .

but she had two children. Does she know
that *you* sent her children . . .

DOCTOR (*lets go of her, but without agitation. Objectively*):
I don't come here to talk about my work.
Don't be childish and jealous . . . Ah,
bread-rolls, small and white, like you,
and just as fresh and wholesome. I'm hungry.
(*He kisses her, takes a roll, bites into it, goes towards the door.*)
Let's go and sort out the Italians.

HELGA (*stands in his way. She shows for the first time a certain firmness,
but not for long*):
I'm not jealous, if you'll tell me
why specially this woman . . .?

DOCTOR (*bored*):
I just find it exciting, for Heaven's sake, simple as that.

HELGA (*with inane femininity*): And don't I excite you enough?

DOCTOR: You little fool –
don't you understand? I want to see
whether this wretched woman will go on sleeping with me
when I tell her what has happened to her children . . .
And that I am the lord of life and death
here, that's what I want to see.

HELGA (*freeing herself from him*):
How horrible you are. If you want
to spare her life, then at least do so properly . . .

DOCTOR: What use is it to her? Her family is dead.

HELGA (*loud, angry*): But she still hopes.
That's why she comes to you. The *only* reason!
Any woman would, I would anyway.

DOCTOR: Maybe she only came for that at first;
perhaps to have a hot bath and some
supper – maybe.

HELGA: But, if you know that, what do *you* get out of it?

DOCTOR (*smiling*): Things are no longer quite so simple.
Now she comes for. . . .
(*laughs and breaks off*)

HELGA: I find you stranger every day – you. Yes –
(*the words are drawn hesitantly from her*)
if you're like you are with me when you're with her,
then she *must* be in love with you,
even if she damns you – and herself –

to all eternity.

DOCTOR: Eternity.

HELGA: I'm not coming to you any more. Never again.

DOCTOR (*kisses her, smiles*): Fine then, as usual, half past two.
I want to bury myself in your fur, little kitten.

HELGA (*screaming, tears in her eyes*):
Never again, I said, never again.

DOCTOR (*has her again in his arms. Quietly, tenderly*):
Have a good sleep first . . . and don't knock,
just look behind you. If anyone's following you
simply go on walking – once round the house
and try again.

HELGA (*faintly*): I'll have to think about it seriously.

DOCTOR (*smiling*): We can think about it together then. 'Bye.

(*Helga has taken him to the door. He is standing outside the hut. He
bites into his bread-roll and speaks his concluding sentences to her while,
unnoticed by them, upstage left, a shadowy wall of deportees has accu-
mulated. They have no luggage, as it always had to be left at the
station. Our only departure from historical accuracy is that here the
women and children have not been separated from the men, whereas in
fact the families were separated on the platform itself, that is, even
before 'selection'.*

*We hear the 'incidental music' which accompanies the victims when-
ever they are led off down the ramp off right: the peaceful and quiet
rumination of a cement-mixer. Now from the right we hear a whistle
blowing – just about where we can see the reflection of the fire, which
must not be naturalistically represented. A Kapo detaches himself from
the group waiting in the background, and without speaking, counts off
six deportees of various ages and types, and sends them down off right.
Helga and the Doctor glance for a moment at these first victims who
shuffle forward almost paralysed with fear, until they have disappeared
off right. The glare of the fire grows brighter; the sound of the cement-
mixer grows quieter. Its monotony reflects the stereotyped procedure of
the murders.*

*Helga is now in a hurry to get away from here. Suddenly she points to
the left and says:*)

HELGA: Hey! – look! there!
Back there – the priest.

DOCTOR (*as he frees himself and goes two steps to the right*):

222

Well? – Go and get some sleep, Helga.

HELGA: No, listen . . . Fritsche
gave orders, the priest
– I suppose it must be that one –
wasn't to be allowed into the camp.
He was deported by mistake.

DOCTOR (*turning back*):
There's nothing special about that – they *all* were.

HELGA: Apparently he's not a Jew!

DOCTOR: I shall decide who is a Jew or not –
as Göring says. Don't worry, I know all about it.

HELGA: Till later. – How strong the smell is today. Horrid.

DOCTOR: The fog isn't letting the smoke rise.
Sweet dreams, bread-roll.

(*Helga goes quickly through the garden, round the hut to the left and disappears, after we have seen her head pass the window. The Doctor, slapping his little stick on his elegant, soft leather riding boots, looks at Riccardo, who is standing with Signora Luccani, her father-in-law, and the children, still hardly distinguishable. We hear the sharp noise of an approaching lorry. The oppressive 'light', the gaseous smog and the glow of the fire, all concentrate the gaze of the spectators on the Doctor who is standing with his back to the audience, feet planted four-square and yet graceful. He stares fixedly at Riccardo, who suddenly, shy and fearful, as if he felt the gaze, looks over towards him and then quickly takes Luccani's little daughter in his arms.*)

DOCTOR: You! Your Holiness!
The black one, come over here a minute.
(*Signora Luccani holds her son closer to her, and all the deportees look at the Doctor except Riccardo. It has become very quiet.*)
Get a move on! Over here!
(*He goes impatiently upstage to the group and gestures to Riccardo, who can no longer evade him; he steps hesitantly out of the line, with the little girl on his arm. The Doctor retires silently as far as possible downstage, and gestures Riccardo to follow him. Riccardo follows hesitantly. Signora Luccani watches him and her child walking away and screams uncontrolledly.*)

JULIA: Don't go away! Stay here, stay with us!
(*She weeps. Her father-in-law takes her by the arm soothingly and speaks to her. Riccardo has stopped at her scream and looks back. He is afraid.*)

DOCTOR (*threateningly, as if to a dog*): Come here, I say.
> (*Riccardo follows him a little farther. They are now standing face to face right downstage. Riccardo is bleeding from the forehead, there is blood on his face. He has been maltreated.*)
> (*friendly, ironically*)
> Do it yourself?

RICCARDO (*angrily*): The Germans beat her father to death.
> They thought it was funny that he should wear glasses.

DOCTOR: Terrible people, these Germans.
> (*He taps Riccardo briefly and almost amicably on the chest with his little stick.*)
> What happened to the star?

RICCARDO: I got rid of it because I wanted to escape.

DOCTOR: I hear you aren't a Jew, but you told them
> on the platform that the Pope had sent you
> to look after the Jews.

RICCARDO: I said that just to get away I played
> the representative of the Vatican;
> they believed me and let me go free.
> I am a Jew like the others.

DOCTOR: Congratulations. A nice piece of Jesuitry.
> They caught you again, all the same. How?

RICCARDO (*with contempt*):
> Nobody caught me. I went along with the rest of my own accord.

DOCTOR (*mocking*): Well, well, isn't that noble?
> We're short of volunteers. And priests.
> Just in case anyone should happen to die here.
> The climate here in Auschwitz has its drawbacks.
> Of course you aren't a Jew . . .
> (*Riccardo says nothing. The Doctor sits on the bench and continues with deep irony.*)
> A martyr then. . . .
> So why did you run away?

RICCARDO: Wouldn't *you* be frightened
> if you were brought here?

DOCTOR: Frightened? Of what? . . . of an internment camp?
> When a man is as close to God as you
> already?

RICCARDO (*very insistent*): Human beings are burning here . . .
> The smell of burning flesh and hair –

DOCTOR (*with more politeness*):

You don't know what you're talking about.
What you see here is simply industry:
lubricating oil and horsehair,
drugs, nitrates, rubber, hand-grenades.
We have a second Ruhr Valley growing up here.
Buna and I.G. Farben both have branches,
and Krupp in the near future.
The air-raids don't affect us this far out.
Work personnel are valuable.

RICCARDO: For a year I have known what was happening here.
It was just that my imagination was not strong enough.
And suddenly today I no longer had the courage . . .
to go along.

DOCTOR: So . . . you know all about it . . . Splendid –
I understand your wanting to be crucified,
but I give myself the pleasure of deflating
your self-importance, in the name of God the Father,
God the Son and God the Holy Ghost.
I have quite other plans for you.
(*Riccardo has put down the child he was carrying. It clings tightly to him.*)
(*to the little girl*)
Would you like your uncle-doctor
to give you a sweetie? Come here. . . .
(*He has taken a paper bag out of his pocket. The child snatches at it greedily.*)

CHILD (*shyly*): Grazie.
(*The Doctor takes the child and tries to sit it down beside him on the bench, with the bag of sweets in her hand. But the little girl now begins to struggle and clings once more to Riccardo.*)

DOCTOR (*mocking*): Such fidelity.
(*friendly, to the child*)
What's your name then?
(*the child says nothing*)
A pity she hasn't got a little twin brother.
Research on twins is my hobby.
The other children here never live
more than six hours, even at our busiest,
nor do their mothers: we've got enough working animals,
and we're kind enough to gas
the children under fifteen

together with their mothers.

That way we save ourselves a great deal of hullabaloo –
what's the matter?

I thought you said you knew what happened here?

RICCARDO (*hoarse with horror*): Keep it short.

DOCTOR: What? Surely you don't want to die too, not just yet?

That *would* be convenient for you, wouldn't it?

A quarter of an hour's deep breathing – and there you are
sitting as a saint at the right hand of God. *No!*

I cannot do you such a favour
while all the rest of your contemporaries
go up in smoke without this consolation.

So long as you are able to *believe*, my dear good pastor,
dying is just a joke.

(*A scuffle in the background: the deportees are to be moved on. The
crocodile moves forward. Signora Luccani tries to back away to
Riccardo. She cries:*)

JULIA: Leave us together! I won't go. – My child!

(*A Kapo darts forward, trying to push her back into the line.
Luccani attacks him clumsily.*)

LUCCANI: Don't hit the women. Don't hit their children.

(*The child tries to drag Riccardo back to its mother. Riccardo
hesitates. The Doctor steps forward.*)

DOCTOR: Let her go!

(*to the women*)

Who will weep then if you are separated?

(*The deportees shuffle on. The old man tries to stay behind, but is
pushed on. He calls in a tired voice:*)

LUCCANI: Julia – Julia – I'm waiting . . . come along.

(*He is pushed off. The back of the stage is empty when this group,
which includes the Manufacturer, who is supporting the old man
and a pregnant woman, have gone off. Soon the concrete-mixer falls
silent.*)

JULIA (*imploringly to the Doctor*):

Let us stay with the priest. Can't you see
how the child clings to him. He was so
good to us on the train. Please let us
die together, the priest and us –

SON (*whom she has dragged out of the line with her, frightened of the
Doctor*):

Come on, Mamma . . .

DOCTOR (*to Julia*):

> Now come now, no one's going to *die* here.
> (*to Riccardo*)
> Tell the woman the truth!
> These are factories here, look at the chimneys!
> You have to work here, work hard;
> but no one's going to hurt you. Come along,
> (*he strokes the boy's hair to calm him*)
> young man. We'll get you something to eat now
> and a nice pudding.

ULIA (*even though still half crazy with fear, now full of confidence in the Doctor*):

> Do you know where my husband is?
> Where's my husband been taken to?

DOCTOR: Run along now.

> Here – take your little sister with you.
> Your husband? – well, he must still be in Rome.
> Or maybe in another camp.
> I don't know everybody here.
> (*to Riccardo*)
> Go on, give the woman back her child.
> (*to Julia*)
> Here, take your child – we've still got things to talk about.

JULIA: Stay with us, please stay!

> This morning you were suddenly gone for such a long time.
> I was so glad when you came back again.

RICCARDO (*strokes the little girl, kisses her and gives her to her mother*):

> I'll come on afterwards. I will come –
> as God is with us.

DOCTOR: Good, then. In a quarter of an hour

> your friend will be with you again . . .
> (*he calls a Kapo and hands the family over to him*)
> Anyone who lags behind
> gets no more to eat.
> Get along now – quick!
> (*Exeunt all except the Doctor and Riccardo. Riccardo staggers.*)
> (*solicitously*)
> You're very tired, I see.
> Sit down then . . .
> (*He points to the bench and ambles back and forth. Riccardo sits, exhausted.*)

RICCARDO: What sort of devil are you?

DOCTOR (*hugely delighted*):

> Devil? . . . Excellent! I am the Devil,
> and you my private chaplain.
> A bargain: you save my soul . . .
> But first let's patch you up. Allow me.
> Come here – where did you get that scratch?
> (*While the Doctor goes into the little hut, Riccardo stays sitting,*
> *holding his bloody handkerchief to his forehead to wipe away fresh*
> *blood.*)
> (*in the doorway*)
> Come along, come along. I have a lot of plans
> for you yet, – chaplain . . .

RICCARDO: What is it you want from me?

DOCTOR: My offer was meant quite seriously,

> you know what to expect, otherwise?
> (*He is standing inside the hut and fiddling with a medicine chest.*
> *Riccardo has dragged himself up the steps and drops on to the*
> *nearest chair.*)
> (*sticking a dressing on him, almost seriously*)
> These bestial idiots here lately amused themselves
> by torturing a Polish priest for ten days in the hunger cell,
> because he volunteered like you to die
> in the place of a prisoner with a family.
> In the end they even did him up
> with a crown of barbed wire.
> Good. He got what he wanted, what you all want:
> his agony in Christ – and Rome is sure
> to canonise him sooner or later.
> Quite a special death –
> a good old-fashioned martyrdom.
> But you, my dear fellow, will just be gassed.
> Quite unpretentiously gassed,
> and *no one*, neither man, nor Pope, nor God,
> will ever know. At best you will be "missing"
> like a lance-corporal on the Volga,
> or a submariner in the Atlantic.
> You will die here, if you persist in this,
> like a snail beneath a motor tyre . . . die,
> die like the heroes of today, anonymous,
> snuffed out by powers that he cannot even recognize,

let alone struggle against. In other words, pointlessly.

RICCARDO (*with scorn*):
Shall God not mark a sacrifice simply because
it is not made with pomp and pathos?
Your ideas surely cannot be as primitive as that.

DOCTOR: Aha, God marks the sacrifice! Indeed?
Basically, my whole work is devoted
entirely to this question. . . . Yes, I do
my best: since July '42, some fifteen months ago,
weekdays and Sundays, I have been sending men to God.
Has He shown any sign of recognition?
He hasn't even aimed a thunderbolt at me.
Can you understand that? Of course you *must* know . . .
nine thousand in *one* day not long ago.

RICCARDO (*groaning, says against his better knowledge*):
It's not true, it *can't* be . . .

DOCTOR (*lazily*): Nine thousand in one day. – Pretty
little creatures like that child you were carrying . . .
Even so, in an hour unconscious or dead.
Either way, ready for the oven. . . . Little children
often go into the ovens unconscious,
an interesting phenomenon, infants particularly.
Oddly enough, the gas doesn't always kill them.
(*Riccardo has been holding his hands in front of his face; now he
dashes to the door, but the Doctor pulls him back and laughs.*)
Now you can't be doing good all the time;
stop shivering like that. Word of honour:
I'll let you live . . . what earthly difference
can it make to me, one article more or less
up the chimney?

RICCARDO (*shouts*): Live – to be *your* prisoner!

DOCTOR: Not my prisoner. My partner.

RICCARDO: Can you imagine that to leave a world
in which both you and Auschwitz can be possible –
is harder than to live in it?

DOCTOR: A martyr would always rather die than think.
Valéry was right. He said, The angel –
maybe you are an angel –
(*laughing*) differs from me, differs from the Devil,
purely through the act of thought
which lies ahead of him.

I shall expose you to this act of thought
as a swimmer to the ocean.
If your soutane still keeps you afloat,
then I will let myself be brought by you
home to the bosom of the Church of Christ.
(*laughs*)
Who knows, who knows? But you must practise first
the celebrated patience of Negation.
First you can watch me here for a year
in this, the most audacious experiment
that Man has ever dared to undertake.
Only a theological nature like my own –
(*he taps Riccardo on the collar*)
I also wore the neck irons once –
could risk taking such a burden of guilt upon himself.

RICCARDO (*beats his forehead in despair, cries*):
But why? . . . why? . . . Why are you doing it?

DOCTOR: Because I wanted an answer – an answer!
And so I risked what no man had
yet risked since the world began to turn . . .
I took an oath that I would provoke
that Old Man so measurelessly,
so totally beyond measure, that he would have to give an
answer.
Even if it was only the negative answer, which
as Stendhal says, is all that *can* excuse Him:
that He does not exist.

RICCARDO (*sarcastic*):
A consulting-room joke . . . paid for by
millions with their lives. Are you not . . .
not even . . . a criminal then?
Are you just a lunatic? As primitive
as Virchow, when he said he had dissected
ten thousand corpses, but had found no soul in any one of
them . . .

DOCTOR (*hurt*): Soul. Isn't *that* a bit primitive?
Isn't it monstrously superficial
hiding behind these figures of speech all the time?
(*he imitates a praying priest*)
Credo quia absurdum est . . . still?
(*serious*)

Listen to the answer;
not a sigh from Heaven,
not a sigh for fifteen months,
since I have been sending tourists on this Ascension.

RICCARDO (*ironic*):

So much savagery . . . and all for something
which any harmless schoolmaster can do with much less fuss,
if he is so unimaginative as to try:
to prove away the incomprehensible . . .

DOCTOR: Do you find it more comforting that God in person
turns Mankind on the spit of history?
History! A vindication of divine providence,
the final theodicy – really?
(*he laughs like a torturer*)
History: dust, altars, suffering, rape,
while every reputation mocks its victims.
Creator, creation, creature, all these three
Auschwitz negates.
The *Idea* of life is dead.
It could be a great turning-point,
the redemption from suffering.
By this reckoning there is but
one guilt: accursed be he who creates life.
I dispose of life, that is today's
humanity – the sole salvation from the future.
I am quite serious about it, even in private,
out of pity I even buried my own children
right from the start – in contraceptives.
(*Silence.*)

RICCARDO (*trying to make fun of him, but he shouts so as not to break down completely*):

Redemption from suffering! A course of Humanitarian Studies
given by a homicidal maniac: just – just save
one single child,
so one can see you are a human being.

DOCTOR (*indolent*):

And what gives *priests* the right to look down on the S.S.?
We are the Dominicans of the technological age.
It is not chance so many of my kind
have sprung from good Catholic backgrounds.
Heydrich was Jewish, admittedly.

Eichmann and Göring – Protestants.
But Hitler, Goebbels, Bormann, Kaltenbrunner . . .?
Höss, the Commandant here, was to have become a priest . . .
And Himmler's godfather – Suffragan Bishop of Bamberg.
(*he laughs*)
The Allies have solemnly declared
they'll hang the lot of us, if they can catch us.
Logical: at the war's end an S.S. uniform
will be the condemned man's winding sheet.
But Holy Mother Church, who for centuries
has practised in the West the murder of heretics,
now sets herself up as *the* last court of morals.
Absurd! – St Thomas Aquinas, a god-intoxicated
mystic, like Heinrich Himmler,
who also talks a lot of well-meaning nonsense,
persecuted the innocent just as here
these idiots persecute the Jews . . .
and yet you do not purge *him* from your temples!
In that case, why should not anthologies
in years to come, include all Himmler's speeches
in praise of mothers of large families . . .?
(*He is hugely amused.*)
A civilization which gives its children's souls
into the hands of a Church that has
the Inquisition to its credit – ends logically
when the brands that fire its funeral pyre
are snatched from our crematoria.
Do you agree? – Of course not.
(*spits and drinks a brandy*)
One of us is honest . . . the other credulous.
(*angrily*)
It was your Church first showed
that one could burn a man like coke.
In Spain, alone, and without crematoria,
you incinerated three hundred and fifty thousand,
and nearly all alive: for *that* one needs –
the support of Christ.

RICCARDO (*loud, furious*):
I am as well aware as you, or I would not be standing here,
how often the Church has been at fault
and how often still today. . . . And I have nothing

232

further to say to you if you make God
responsible for the crimes of His Church.
God is not master of history, but in Him
our final destiny lies. In Him all man's
suffering is concluded.

DOCTOR (*interrupts*): Yes, yes, I learnt all that once, too.
His suffering here
on earth has bound in chains the principle of evil.
Just how? When have I . . . when was I *ever*
bound in chains? Luther was less presumptuous:
he said it is not man
who hangs and tortures, strangles and makes war
but God . . .

(*He claps Riccardo on the shoulder, laughing. Riccardo draws
away.*)
Your anger amuses me: you are a partner,
I saw it straight away.
You can help in the laboratory,
and in the evenings we can quarrel
about that product of neurotic weakness
that you, for want of a better word, call God,
or about some other philosophic trifle.

RICCARDO: I have no intention of being your court jester,
to cheer the hours in which you
are delivered up to yourself.
I never saw a man so deep in suffering:
you *know* what you are doing . . .

DOCTOR (*at pains to be accurate*):
There I must disappoint you yet again:
just as your whole faith is a self-deception,
so is your hope that I should be in torment.
I am always plagued by boredom, that is true.
That's why I find our argument so refreshing,
and that is why you are to stay alive.
But torment? No. I am studying, at close quarters,
homo sapiens: yesterday I watched
a workman in the crematoria.
As he was hacking the corpses apart,
to get them through the oven doors,
he came upon the body of his wife.
Now *how* would he react? . . .

RICCARDO: You do not look as if this study
    makes you as cheerful as all that. . . .
    You yourself are no happier
    than the workman . . .
DOCTOR: No? Then I have my books, too.
    I am reading just now how long it took
    after Napoleon's death for this gangster,
    who once remarked to Metternich that
    the death of a million men meant nothing to him,
    to become the idol of posterity.
    Quite interesting with regard to Hitler . . .
    Of course that odious vegetarian
    didn't seduce his sisters, like Napoleon.
    He lacks that sort of popular appeal.
    But, even so, he is more *sympathique*
    (*He picks up a book with 'Hegel' on the cover.*)
    than the philosophers, who sit and sift
    the horrors of world history through the sieve
    inside their twisted brains, until the moment
    they can be looked at with forgiveness.
    I re-read Nietzsche lately,
    the Eternal Schoolboy – a colleague
    had to deliver Hitler's present
    to Mussolini, on his sixtieth birthday . . .
    (*He gives a ringing laugh.*)
    Nietzsche, Complete works of, on *Bible* paper! . . .
RICCARDO: How can Nietzsche help it if the beasts
    and the fanatics – and the murderers –
    have broken into his garden. Only madmen
    would ever take him literally . . .
DOCTOR: Correct, only the madmen, only the men of action.
    Them it suits, that he
    measured men's virtues by the beasts of prey . . .
    probably because he felt so little of
    the beast in himself, not even enough
    to get a girl into bed.
    Grotesque: The Blond Beast or The Consequences
    of Pathological Shyness:
    the massacre of millions.
    (*He laughs as if tickled.*)
    What fascinated Hitler, though, was not

the most refined critic in all Europe.
He was excited by the animal,
the beautiful beast of prey,
because the discoverer of this glorious monster
wrote in a German so high-sounding,
so princely, and so arrogant, as if he dipped
his pen in champagne.
(*without pausing*)
You can have champagne, here, and girls as well.
This afternoon, when that family you came with
is cooking in the crematorium
I shall be somewhat heated up myself
between the legs of a nineteen-year-old.
That is a comfort that outweighs your faith,
simply because one '*has*' it,
'has' it with heart and mouth and hand.
And has it here on earth, where one most needs it.
But you know all that . . .

RICCARDO (*casually*): Of course, a great comfort – but
not one that lasts very long . . .

DOCTOR (*pulling on his gloves, almost with triumph*):
We understand each other splendidly. You will
have two nice girls in the laboratory,
but the latest books will be more interesting to you . . .
Habent sua fata divini – the blessed saints
fall on their arses,
and the light of Reason falls on the Gospels.
I made a pilgrimage to Marburg last year
to hear Bultmann. Clever for a theologian,
how he spring-cleaned the New Testament.
Even the preaching of the Gospel
no longer demands that men
should take the mythical world-picture
for sober truth. . . .

(*Already, during the last sentences, the noise of the cement-mixer outside. No more deportees are yet visible. But in the background on the extreme right the reflected glow of a huge fire shines out again, high and menacing. The noise of two lorries. Whistles blowing. Riccardo springs to his feet, tears open the door, points to the light of the underworld and cries with scorn, while the Doctor slowly crosses over to him.*)

RICCARDO: There . . . over there . . . I am there . . . amongst them.
What need do I have to believe
in Heaven or Hell any longer?
(*closer to the Doctor, quieter*)
You know that. You know, even for St John
Judgement Day was no cosmic happening.
(*loudly, flinging the words out*)
Your grimaces of lust, and filth and idiocy
sweep every doubt aside . . . every one.
If there is a devil then there is a God:
or *you* would long ago have won.

DOCTOR (*grips his arm, bubbling with laughter*):
That's how I like to see you. The St Vitus dance of the fanatic.
(*He grips his other arm, too, since Riccardo is about to fly to the
back where another bunch of deportees has come in sight, waiting
silently. Only a Kapo stalks round them. The Doctor forces
Riccardo, whose strength soon fails him, down on to the bench.
Riccardo hides his face in his hands and rests his arms on his knees.
He puts a foot up on the bench by him and says with camaraderie:*)
Quite tense. You're trembling. You cannot
stand on your feet for fear.

RICCARDO (*draws back, the Doctor's face was too near. Wearily he
says*):
As if I had ever denied it.
Courage or not . . . finally it *is*
only a question of vanity.

DOCTOR (*while Riccardo hardly listens to him, and he is watching the
waiting victims*):
I gave my word, nothing would happen to you.
I have other plans for you . . .
The war is lost, the Allies will hang me.
You find me a place in Rome, in a monastery.
The commandant will be grateful, too,
if I arrange for the Holy Father's guest,
who is not exactly here by invitation,
to leave. – Agreed? – Just a minute . . .
(*He goes into the hut and looks around.*)

RICCARDO (*as in a dream*):
To Rome . . . I am . . . to go back to Rome?

DOCTOR: We'll have a nice trip by car to Breslau,
(*goes to the telephone, dials, listens, hangs up, meanwhile saying,*

236

half to Riccardo, half to the receiver)
With a girl, fair as the sun . . .
and the Representative of Christ – Helga, hello.
Helga ? . . . Asleep already . . . and Pius has you again.
(*He leaves the hut. Riccardo is highly excited.*)

RICCARDO: No . . . never. You only want
me to run away again, that is all.
I wouldn't get a hundred yards. I would
just be shot trying to escape . . .

DOCTOR (*fishes out a wallet and shows him a passport*):
I quite understand that you might have
doubts about my offer. But look here:
is that a passport of the Holy See ?

RICCARDO: It is . . . where did you get it ?

DOCTOR: Only the dates are missing . . . I'll fill them in
as needed. . . . Now, our agreement:
you find me a niche in Rome, until the time
when I can get away to South America.

RICCARDO: How can you expect to desert ?
Rome is under German occupation.

DOCTOR: And how else could I make the pilgrimage
to Rome so easily ? I only need
a perfectly legitimate travel warrant.
I could be there within a week –
then with your help, I go to earth – agreed ?
(*Riccardo is silent.*)
(*impatient, insistent, convincing*)
Yes. – Just think of yourself then,
and your soul or whatever you call it.
You go to Rome and hang up your message
on the bell of St Peter's . . .

RICCARDO (*hesitant*):
What could I tell the Pope that he doesn't know ?
Details, of course. But the fact that Jews
are being gassed in Poland . . . has been known
for a full year already.

DOCTOR: Yes . . . but the Representative of Christ
must *speak*. Why is he silent ?
(*eagerly*)
Something you can't yet have heard:
Last week two, three bombs

237

which killed no one, fell in the Vatican gardens:
for days the great sensation of the world.
The Americans, the British and the Germans
are all falling over themselves to prove
they could not *possibly* have dropped them.
You see again: the Pope's a holy man
even to heretics. Exploit the fact –
challenge him – what is the matter?
Sit down.
(*He takes Riccardo by the shoulder. Riccardo has sunk on to the bench.*)
You're whiter than the walls of a gas chamber.
(*Pause.*)

RICCARDO (*on the bench, with difficulty*):
I have already asked the Pope to protest,
but he is playing at politics.
My father stood by me . . . my father.

DOCTOR (*with the laughter of Hell*):
Politics – yes, that is his level,
with the gift of tongues.

RICCARDO (*for a moment as if he were somewhere else. Then, still sunk in thought*):
Let *us* not be his judges.
(*During the last lines the cement-mixer has stopped. From the back, from the direction of the fire, comes the blowing of whistles. The Kapo drives the waiting victims off right, a procedure that should not be different from the last walk of the Luccanis and the other Italians. The Doctor summons the Kapo to him with a whistle; the deportees disappear off right, down the ramp. The glow of the fire flickers up fiercely.*)

KAPO (*returning, stands at attention*): Sturmbannführer.

DOCTOR (*points to Riccardo*):
This man will go along to the crematorium.
No games with him, understand.
He is my personal patient.
He will be working there –
(*ironically to Riccardo*)
I shall not forget you, Father.
You get enough to eat there and a normal
working day of nine hours more or less.
You can prosecute your studies, investigating God.

In a fortnight's time I'll take you into the laboratory
as my assistant, if you like.
And you *will* like.
(*to the Kapo*)
On your own ashes: not a hair . . .
not a hair of his head is to be touched. I will have
a word with your commanding officer. Right, get out.
KAPO: Very good, Sturmbannführer.
(*He goes off with Riccardo, down the ramp. The Doctor watches motionlessly.*)

Curtain

SCENE THREE

The same setting. Again early morning, about a week later. It is snowing. The cement-mixer is working again.

Helga stands in the guardroom, combing her hair in a hand mirror; Fritsche enters with the civilian Baron Rutta and the engineer Müller-Saale, both carrying briefcases.)

FRITSCHE: You're certainly very early. I can't take
you into the officers' mess yet, I'm afraid. Please.
(*He lets the civilians pass in front of him.*)
RUTTA: We have the whole day before us, Sturmbannführer,
and we're looking forward to the visit.
Herr Müller can explain the contract to you.
You can make your corrections, then we can
have it all ready and correct by lunchtime.
FRITSCHE (*at the door, where the civilians are still standing*):
We'll find a table and some drink in here. –
The winter came on so suddenly. I hate to think
what it's like on the Eastern Front.
(*He knocks and opens the door almost shyly.*)
HELGA: Come in.
FRITSCHE (*modest*):
I beg your pardon . . . I've brought some visitors from Essen.
The gentlemen are going straight over to the mess . . .
we just wanted to have a drink together.
They've had a long journey – may we?

RUTTA (*with charm*):
    Are we being a great nuisance? Good morning. I hope you
    slept well.

HELGA: I was on night duty, not much sleep, but not so bad . . .

MÜLLER: 'l Hitler, Fräulein – 'morning to you.

FRITSCHE: Herr von Rutta and Herr Müller-Saale . . .
    and Fräulein Helga, our most attractive inmate,
    if I may put it like that. We're on duty
    and freezing, Helga dear.

RUTTA (*with exaggerated charm*):
    Haven't we met before though? In Berlin!
    Where was it now? Oh, really, how annoying . . .

HELGA: In Falkensee, the Jägerkeller . . . of course.

RUTTA: But of course! And now here we are in Auschwitz.
    Do you like your job?

HELGA: A job's a job, as usual.
    But my fiancé's here as well, though.

MÜLLER: Aha, it was love that drew you here.
    Your fiancé's a very lucky chap,
    I must say. Definitely . . .

HELGA: Shall I put on some coffee? – or a drink?

RUTTA: Most attentive of you, Fräulein Helga.
    Herr Müller'll have a drink, if I know him?

MÜLLER: That's a fact. It's got bloody cold
    during the night.

RUTTA (*laughs meaninglessly*):
    Without wishing to be a wet blanket
    I'd rather have a cup of coffee.

HELGA: Of course. The water will be hot in a moment.
    (*Fritsche smiles at her somewhat inanely, trying hard to be
    charming, but without knowing how. She arranges cups and
    glasses; the men have removed their coats. Rutta was wearing a
    fur coat and leggings. Everyone finds a seat, Müller-Saale takes
    an index file from his briefcase, Rutta a ground plan which he
    spreads out on the bed. He points to Helga.*)

RUTTA: Congratulations, Herr Fritsche. I hardly
    expected to find such talent in Auschwitz.

FRITSCHE (*smiles as if Helga was his fiancée*):
    Yes . . . Strength Through Beauty.
    (*The telephone rings. Helga answers*)

HELGA: Inner Platform One – yes. He's here – hold on.

Herr Fritsche, for you . . .

MÜLLER (*facetiously, as Fritsche goes to answer the telephone*):
  I should think you could use a view
  like that after work.

FRITSCHE (*completely disinterested, listening to the conversation*):
  Yes, we're lucky to have a few women . . .
  Excuse me . . . thanks . . .
  (*He has taken the receiver while Rutta spreads the ground-plan
  out on the camp bed.*)
  Fritsche here – yes, Commandant. *Gerstein?*
  Oh, *he's* collecting him?
  I've got visitors here from Essen, though –
  I can't bring the Father to you.
  I suggest we have him called over here,
  and Gerstein can take charge of him himself.
  Yes indeed. Of course. Need never have happened.
  Unheard-of carelessness.
  That's what *I* said all along. Thank you.
  (*He hangs up and murmurs:*)
  There's a nice thing.
  (*immediately, turning to the camp bed, with great respect*)
  Good God! The detonator factory.

RUTTA: There we are . . . ideal, isn't it? Capacity
  five hundred thousand detonators a month.
  So when in your opinion can Krupp
  begin production here in Auschwitz?
  You certainly aren't short of personnel.

FRITSCHE: Indeed not! – Just a moment.
  (*He listens, as they all do. Helga goes on brewing coffee. In the
  distance a loudspeaker says:*)
  Attention please, here is an announcement. Internee Riccardo
  Fontana, number 16670, report immediately to the guardroom
  on Inner Platform No. One. End of announcement.

FRITSCHE: It is a priest from Rome, an Aryan.
  The Church sent him along for the Italians,
  because there were some Catholics. Now he's getting out.
  He's been here ten days . . . by mistake.

MÜLLER (*incredulously*):
  And we're . . . you're letting him out now?
  Isn't that a bit risky?

FRITSCHE: We've got a couple of Polish priests interned,

as spiritual hostages for him.
He talks . . . they die.
He'll keep his mouth shut all right.

RUTTA: Oh . . . yes, they use hostages
in Essen, too: workmen from Belgium
or France, who can't be refused a journey home,
have to provide
the firm with a surety, a fellow countryman.

MÜLLER: Just like Schiller.

(*Laughter.*)

FRITSCHE (*idiotically*):
Haha . . . 'The Surety' . . . yes.
The workers from the East,
Polacks, Ukranians, can they get home, too?

MÜLLER: That'd be the last straw – what would become of us?

(*Coffee is now ready. The announcement comes over the loud-
speaker a second time. While Müller-Saale chats with Helga,
Fritsche makes a telephone call.*)
What part of the country do you come from, Fräulein Helga?

FRITSCHE (*to Rutta, as he takes off the receiver*):
Please excuse me, Herr Baron – hallo?
This is Sturmbannführer Fritsche: I want bundle number
16670 brought to the guardroom on Inner Platform One, at once,
it's a soutane. What? The black coat of a Catholic priest. Not
find it quickly? Are you off your head? 16670, brought in last
week. I expressly ordered it *not* to be chucked on to the big
pile. Well, kindly look for it. I should think so, too. Good.
Right away then.

MÜLLER: Is your mother from Saxony? Somebody from Saxony
must have taught you to make
coffee like this.

HELGA: Glad you like it. We know how to make it
in Hamburg, too, you know.

RUTTA: Really excellent . . . Herr Müller, be so good
as to read the draft over to us. Then we
can go to the office with Herr Fritsche . . .

MÜLLER (*reading*): Well then: short and sweet. The S.S. –
as basic condition of this contract will agree to rent
the buildings at Auschwitz, 120 metres by 118,
to Friedrich Krupp Limited.
Two: the generator station,

built and installed by Krupp,
will be assigned to the S.S. authorities.

FRITSCHE: To *us*?

RUTTA: Just the generator station, Herr Fritsche. The machines
remain the property of Krupp, correct, Herr Müller?

MÜLLER: Yes. Point three
machinery to remain the property of Krupp.
Fourthly: the period of notice one year
effective from 1st January. –
I think it is in your interests, Herr Sturmbannführer,
if we don't actually mention in the contract
the daily rental which Krupp will be paying
the S.S. per arrestee.

FRITSCHE: Naturally, Herr Müller, of course not.

RUTTA: Anyway, our Lieutenant-Colonel, that is
Doctor von Schwarz of the Army High Command,
has already seen the plans last week
and has approved them.

FRITSCHE: Fine, that's it then. One more cigarette
and I must be off.
(*They smoke and drink.*)

RUTTA: First of all, many thanks. My colleague Streifer
of I.G. Farben wasn't exaggerating
when he went on about the splendid
relations between the S.S. and industry
in Auschwitz.

FRITSCHE: Yes, Siemens is using forced labour
from some of the camps, too.

MÜLLER: Alfried von Bohlen wanted to send someone
to Auschwitz even in September.
And Herr von Bohlen knows that his office in Breslau,
the technical head office, is in closest contact
with Auschwitz . . .

RUTTA (*unexpectedly*): The people here are easy to control.

FRITSCHE: Here, yes. But how does Krupp
manage to keep twenty thousand
foreigners in Essen under control?

RUTTA: Many of them are docile. If not:
the Gestapo – your Friend and Helper –
they pull in someone every now and then.
Then some of them get letters, even send them –

the post for the workers from the East is burnt
twice a week.
They're a great nuisance, that rabble.
We don't like having to take them.
(*Jollity, in which Helga does not join. Gerstein, in a steel helmet,
has appeared outside, restlessly looking for something. His face is
dark and gloomy. He looks cautiously into the hut, and hesitates –
he knows the most dangerous moment of his life is approaching.
Now he puts on an idly thoughtful expression, knocks, enters,
salutes.*)

GERSTEIN: Sturmbannführer . . . the Commandant sent
me to you; am I in the way? I have orders
to collect a Father Fontana from here.

FRITSCHE (*friendly*): Heil Hitler, Gerstein . . . gentlemen . . .
I'll follow you . . . Fräulein Helga
will be good enough to show you the way . . .
That's all in order, Gerstein.

HELGA: Yes, all right . . . 'morning, Herr Gerstein.

GERSTEIN: Ah, Fräulein Helga, how are you, good morning.

RUTTA: Many thanks, Herr Fritsche.

MÜLLER (*while they are all helping each other into their coats*):
It was delightful in your wigwam, Fräulein Helga.
I wish you would make my coffee
every morning. 'l Hitler!

RUTTA (*to Gerstein*): Heil Hitler!

GERSTEIN: Heil Hitler!

HELGA (*calls as she goes*):
There's still some coffee left, Herr Gerstein.

FRITSCHE (*to the civilians*): I'll be right along.
(*to Gerstein*)
The black man will be here soon – our Doctor
(it's unbelievable) – he had the idea
of putting the Father to work in the crematoria,
as dentist. Just for a joke! He said
he wants to give him his second communion.
Mark you, the Doctor is to blame, that he
was allowed to get into the camp at all.
I wanted to send him back home at once.

GERSTEIN: Where is the Doctor now, then?

FRITSCHE (*laughs disapprovingly*):
He was well under way just now.

Still asleep, they're all still asleep. I can
hardly stand on my feet myself:
We gave a farewell do for Höss last night
(*confidentially*)
till four in the morning – but you know about that?

GERSTEIN: Yes, but we shan't hold it against him.

FRITSCHE (*sniggers*):

The Doctor says, from now on Höss should wear
his Iron Cross with fig leaves and two brass balls.
Seriously: they have actually promoted him . . . he's
to be Deputy Inspector of all concentration camps in the
Reich. Even so,
it is a bit bold for the Commandant here
to sleep with a Jewish girl.
That was his little bit of consolation –
he supervised at the ovens every day,
and basically he is a *terribly* nice fellow.

GERSTEIN (*without the least attempt at irony*):

Yes, Höss has a good heart: you'll miss him here.
He's at his desk already, today as usual.
(*as casually as he can manage*)
Have they liquidated the Jewess?

FRITSCHE (*eagerly*):

No – use your head – still alive. Suspicious, eh?
I should think Kaltenbrunner
is probably looking after the shickse,
so he can get a permanent hold over Höss.
Well, bring the priest across, then, will you?

GERSTEIN: To you, Sturmbannführer?

FRITSCHE (*with vehemence*): No, not to me. I don't want
(*decisive*)
anything to do with this business . . .
Take him to Höss,
he can sign a statement that he's seen
nothing but flower-beds.

GERSTEIN: He'll keep quiet, as long as he gets out of here.

FRITSCHE: It's never happened before, that anyone has been let out.

GERSTEIN: I was surprised, too.
Oh well, they must know what they're doing.
I just happened to be by the phone
when the Nuncio rang through.

Then I went straight to Eichmann.
He got as much of a shock as I did.
FRITSCHE: It was idiotically careless of the Doctor
to let him in in the first place.
He really goes too far sometimes – yesterday evening
he was doing imitations of Dr Ley and Heydrich
I thought it was disgusting.
There's a limit to everything, after all.
GERSTEIN: Heydrich – yes, that is certainly in bad taste.
Ley does look like a sugar pig, but Heydrich . . .
(*A Kapo, frightened and woebegone, brings on a bundle tied with
string, with a number hanging from it: 16670.*
*Fritsche and Gerstein leave the hut, the Kapo takes the clothes
inside.*
A factory siren sounds. Fritsche looks at his watch and sets it.)
FRITSCHE (*laughs*):
Sugar pig is good. And always pissed. Just leave it
there in the hut; so Gerstein, the priest . . .
KAPO: Very good, sir.
FRITSCHE: . . . will be here at once. After all, it's a good
two kilometres from the crematoria.
GERSTEIN: And the smell of flesh still so strong?
What do the local people have to say?
FRITSCHE: They know what's happening, of course.
though what you're smelling isn't coming from the ovens.
That's from the open pits.
We can't manage with just the ovens any more.
I must be off now, I don't want *anything*
to do with this business.
It can only cause trouble.
(*Carlotta enters with a bucket and scrubbing-brush and goes
timidly past the two men in uniform into the hut, where she kneels
and begins to scrub the floor. Seeing Helga's handmirror on a
chair, still kneeling, she pushes back her headscarf a little and
looks at her shaven head, her dirtied and miserable face. For the
first time since the deportation it seems to her to be possible, and
she begins to cry silently. When Gerstein enters the hut later she
tries hard not to show it.*)
Please tell them in Berlin,
I am quite without blame in this business.
I saw at once he could not stay here;

(*points to the bundle of clothes*)

that's why I didn't have the clothes thrown on the main pile.

(*going*)

Well: it's not my fault. Heil Gerstein.

And go and get a bite to eat

afterwards in the canteen. Heil.

GERSTEIN: Thanks. Heil Hitler, Sturmbannführer,

thanks very much.

(*grinding his teeth*)

Stupid shit . . .

(*He walks up and down nervously; he lights a cigarette, then notices the girl scrubbing and goes into the hut to get away from his own uneasiness. As he comes in the girl starts back, every movement betraying fear of men in uniform. Gerstein takes a piece of bread from his pockets and hands it to Carlotta.*)

Where are you from? – Here, eat this.

Been here long?

CARLOTTA (*without rising, without taking the bread*):

Rome – thank you, a week now.

GERSTEIN: Rome? Then do you know the Father

they were calling for, Father Fontana?

Go on, take the bread.

CARLOTTA: We all know him.

(*refusing, afraid of being pumped*)

How can you be giving me bread?

GERSTEIN (*puts the bread on the chair*):

How can I! – You're hungry, aren't you?

Do you want me to deliver a letter for you?

CARLOTTA (*pause, then coldly*): No, thank you.

GERSTEIN: You don't trust me.

Give the Father a message –

he's being released – going back to Rome.

CARLOTTA (*overjoyed, then sadly*): Released? – Oh. He doesn't

really belong, properly . . . not to us.

GERSTEIN (*takes a piece of paper and an envelope from the typing-table, uncaps his pen, and puts it all on a chair*):

Write in here, so no one sees you.

The Father will take the letter to Rome.

CARLOTTA (*still refusing, then with Latin pathos her voice breaks, in tears*):

Who am I going to write to then?

My lover died in Africa – for Germany,
at the capture of Tobruk. In gratitude
you deported my parents and myself, all of us,
my sister and her children.
Just tell me, are they – already dead?
Tell me *that*. We came here on the 20th October.
We were separated at the station. Only about a hundred
came into the camp here. They took the others off
in lorries. Where to? Lorries with Red Crosses.
You must know where to!

GERSTEIN (*helpless*): I don't belong to the camp staff, really,
I don't know. I never go into the inner camp.
(*The cement-mixer begins grinding; she listens to it a moment. He
changes the subject*)
Was your fiancé not Jewish? – Then write
to his parents. They can try, through the Vatican . . .

CARLOTTA: No, my parents-in-law are to blame
that I became a Catholic.

GERSTEIN: And you regret it – why?

CARLOTTA: It was *Catholics*, Catholic fascists,
who handed me over to the Germans,
who took the last picture I had of Marcello
and my engagement ring – perhaps it was
a punishment for leaving my own people
and going over to their Church.

GERSTEIN: You mustn't say that. Catholics are being
persecuted, too – many priests
have already been murdered in Poland and Germany.
And Father Riccardo, going of his own free will . . .

CARLOTTA (*dismissing this*): But they are single cases. Outsiders . . .

GERSTEIN: Of course. And yet – the majority of Italians,
the great majority, disapprove of the terror, Church and people.

CARLOTTA (*as she turns back ostentatiously to her work*):
Disapprove – like you? Isn't that right?
But do little or nothing to stop it, like you.
Christians! – every one a Christian.
Marcello – was a Christian, but he could
respect another's faith. He left me mine.
But I used to listen to his family
tormenting him, till I became a Catholic.
(*bitterly*)

248

I felt safe as a Catholic – in Rome;
that's the only reason I didn't hide.
Can't you find out if
my family is still alive?

GERSTEIN: Really, I can't. I don't know.
At least write your name down for Father Riccardo.

CARLOTTA (*her mood suddenly changing, begins hastily to write a letter, crouching on the floor, using the chair as a desk: later, alone in the hut, she begins to cry again and just before Gerstein comes into the hut with Riccardo she tears up what she has written and gives Gerstein the torn scraps*):
Yes, I would like to write a letter.
Thank you. And forgive me.

GERSTEIN (*smiles at her, goes to the window, and says quickly but aloud to himself*):
Here he comes – but – it's – Jacobson!
(*He tears the door open and runs to Jacobson. As he sees that Jacobson, in his astonishment at finding him here, can only speak his name, his 'death mask' split by a smile that threatens at any minute to turn to tears, he cannot bring himself, in spite of the great danger, immediately to tell Jacobson why he has come.*)

JACOBSON: Gerstein – you?
(*softly*)
I hoped for this sometimes.

GERSTEIN (*has gone back three steps, to shut the door of the hut*):
Good God, Jacobson! You here – I thought
you were in England. Where did they get you?
You had Riccardo's passport.

JACOBSON: On the Brenner.
Apparently the passport photograph,
an old one,
wasn't like me. Still, I stuck to it,
in spite of being tortured
or they'd have killed me then and there.
I stuck to it, that I was the priest.
Understand: I *am* Father Fontana.
I *am* the Father – you understand.
(*During the speech, he has looked round him several times for assurance, but one can see that he has almost identified himself with his role, his only hope. Hoarsely, feverish . . .*)
I have the job of sorting out the luggage

of the ones who've been gassed,
on the outer platform. I quite often find
pieces of jewellery, which I change for bread
with the railway men.
That's what keeps me alive still, that and *hate*.
I want to get out of here,
or I'd have gone to the electric fence long ago.
Now *you* have had me called . . .

GERSTEIN : But it's not *you*, Jacobson.
(*despairingly*)
Don't you see : Riccardo Fontana is in the camp.
It's on *his* account I'm here.
How could I have ever known
that *you* were in Auschwitz ?

JACOBSON (*can't understand*) :
What's that ? The Father – here ?
But he's not Jewish ? How did he . . ?

GERSTEIN : They deported the Jews from Rome,
he came with them of his own accord.
He's been in Auschwitz for a week.
And now they're releasing him.

JACOBSON (*disbelieving – then moved by generosity*) :
Released – from Auschwitz ? Unbelievable !
But . . . I'm glad for his sake.

GERSTEIN : That we should meet here, Jacobson !
I can't bear being so helpless.

JACOBSON (*incapable of hiding his bitterness*) :
No, I'm not a priest, Gerstein –
a priest is worth an ultimatum.

GERSTEIN (*laughs shortly, savagely*) : Ultimatum ? From whom ?
Believe me, I forged
Riccardo's order of release.

JACOBSON : Then forge another order
to get me or that girl there, or
anyone, out of here.

GERSTEIN : Jacobson, you know I can't.
I am only a lieutenant, nothing more.
My life at this moment is in
greater danger than yours – Jacobson !

JACOBSON (*looks away*) :
I'm sorry – you wear the same uniform.

GERSTEIN: How else could I have got here?
This uniform – the fact that I will never be rid of it,
that is my payment on the debt of guilt
which weighs upon us all. Our resistance . . .

JACOBSON: Resistance? – Gerstein, why does this resistance
not even go as far
as to tear up the railway line to Auschwitz?
Where is this resistance of yours?
(*softly, earnestly, despairingly*)
Or are you still – a lone wolf?
How can you all go on living? – knowing
what happens here, day after day, for a year now.
You live, you eat, you procreate children –
and all of you – you know about the camps.
(*He takes Gerstein by the shoulders, tears in his voice.*)
Make an end of it, somehow. Make an end.
(*disconnectedly*)
Why don't the Allies drop arms for us?
Oh, Gerstein, I don't want to accuse you, God knows,
it is you I have to thank that I am still alive . . .
It is just . . . I was numb enough to be able to forget. –
Now you are here, I am conscious once again
that there exists a world outside the camp.
There *is* still something you can do for me.

GERSTEIN: Anything . . .

JACOBSON (*quickly*): Just say I said I was the priest
and then attacked you, when – the real one came.
Shoot me . . .

GERSTEIN: Jacobson!

JACOBSON (*imploring*): Shoot me – Gerstein,
I would have attacked you – that much is believable.
Please, Gerstein – help me. I have not the courage
myself any longer to go to the wire –
it doesn't always kill you straight away.

GERSTEIN: You've survived a whole year,
you must hold out, Jacobson –
another year – at the most another year,
and then the Russians will get you out.

JACOBSON: A year!

GERSTEIN: They've occupied the Ukraine again.

JACOBSON: Gerstein, why don't you do it? – Why not?

(*Gerstein shakes his head, can say nothing.*)
(*turning away*)
Then I will go, so as not . . .
to make it any more dangerous for you and the Father.
GERSTEIN (*helpless, moved, stops him*):
Not like this, Jacobson, don't go away like this.
JACOBSON: Four thousand – five thousand –
some days more than that
are gassed here. Now the only thing that shocks me
is that the world can let it happen.
(*more controlled, objective*)
And here's the cruellest thing of all: one man escapes,
and ten are taken to the cellars, on his account.
It happened once.
They sentenced ten to death by starvation.
We listened to them screaming – for a week.
Father Kolbe was the last, it seems.
That was what stopped me, when there might have been
a chance of getting out, a short while back,
on one of the trucks which took the dead men's shoes
to Breslau.
GERSTEIN: The Father is being released officially,
that's what they think here. No one will have to pay for that
except myself, if it is discovered.
(*Riccardo, speechless and shattered to see Gerstein here, has
appeared behind Jacobson, whom he does not recognize at once.
Riccardo has been irrevocably marked by the work he has been
compelled to do in the crematoria during this last week.*)
Riccardo! –
I have been authorized by the Nuncio to fetch you.
RICCARDO: Gerstein – you should not have come to look
for me any more. Jacobson – you!
JACOBSON: How could you – come here, Father?
I'm still living under your name.
RICCARDO: Jacobson, forgive me, I thought
you had got through, the last time.
JACOBSON: Coming here, voluntarily, unarmed –
who were you trying to help by doing that?
GERSTEIN (*insistently, as Riccardo has obviously not understood*):
Riccardo, you are being released.
RICCARDO: Released?

(*He sits, suddenly all in, on the steps of the guardroom.*)
I can't go on.
I've told myself a hundred times,
it was sheer arrogance that brought me here.
I won't hold out, I simply won't hold out.
(*He cries soundlessly, no one can say a word.*)
for the last week . . .
ten hours a day, I have burned the dead,
and with each human body that I burn,
I burn away a particle of faith.
I am burning God.
Corpses – a conveyor belt of corpses,
an endless belt. History . . .
If I knew that – He was looking on –
(*with revulsion*)
I would have . . . to hate Him.

GERSTEIN (*uncertain. Pulls Riccardo to his feet*):
We none of us understand Him any more, Riccardo,
but now He wants to save you all the same.

RICCARDO (*tired*): How do you know that? And why *me*?
I wasn't speaking of myself . . . the families . . .
(*mumbling, no further relation between his thoughts*)
I am – I would be frightened of salvation
(*points vaguely upwards*)
through Him. – A wild beast that devours its young.

JACOBSON (*stronger than before, decisively*):
Father, speak for us, help us!
Tell the Pope, he *must act* now.

RICCARDO: I won't get near the Pope again – the Pope . . .
(*suddenly*)
What gave you that idea then – to go back to Rome?

GERSTEIN (*feverishly*):
You must survive, Riccardo, *live*, somehow . . .

RICCARDO: Live – ? From there – the crematorium –
there is no going back to life.
(*He points to Jacobson.*)
And him? And – all the rest?
I came here with a purpose, and it must keep me here,
I don't know any more whether it is valid,
I don't know. But if it is not,
then my life is not either . . . Let me go.

JACOBSON: Father, you bring Gerstein into danger
    if you don't go – he has
    only forged the order.

GERSTEIN: You shouldn't have said that.

JACOBSON: So long as he gets out of here – it's urgent!

RICCARDO (*has collapsed*):
    I see – I could have guessed it for myself.
    Gerstein, you were so careful otherwise –
    however brave you were . . .
    (*in despair*)
    how can you be so *mad* as to follow me now?

GERSTEIN (*gloomily*): Because I have you on my conscience.
    I was the one who set you on this path.

RICCARDO (*goes quickly over to him*):
    And what would *I* have on my conscience, if I were not here?
    Do you want me to sidle out of it? – No;
    truly, you are not to blame for my being here.
    Yet I am not to blame either – am I? –
    if, by my staying, something happens to you?
    Do understand: I *may* not go.
    Why do you still lead me into temptation?
    Surely you see I am no longer a match for it.
    (*quietly*)
    I am doing the penance I must do.

GERSTEIN (*agitated*): You made atonement long ago, Riccardo.
    You have come through the fire.

RICCARDO: Gerstein – please: take *him* with you.

JACOBSON: Me?

GERSTEIN: And if he is killed?

JACOBSON (*decided*): Father, I cannot accept that.

RICCARDO: Jacobson, I am not staying for *your* sake.
    It is not a question of me,
    or you.
    Here I represent my Church.
    I may not leave, however much I want to.
    God knows, I want to.
    You have no obligation to me, Jacobson,
    if you don't go, then no one goes.
    (*He speaks with heavy pauses, while Gerstein, to whom it is intolerable to leave both behind, stands there helpless but with gloomy forebodings*)

Put on my soutane once again –
if Gerstein is agreed . . .

JACOBSON: I cannot accept – not from you.
Much less from *him*.
(*He points to Gerstein – both now await his answer. To avoid their noticing his fear of the undertaking, he pushes the decision from him.*)

GERSTEIN: I will say nothing. Decide yourselves.

RICCARDO: You can do everything which I can not.
You can shoot, sabotage –
even so you will not survive.
Gerstein is not going to set you free
so that you can go to ground.

GERSTEIN (*unable to keep silent any longer*):
The practical side – are you, or you,
known personally to any of the camp officials?

JACOBSON: No.

RICCARDO: Only to the Head Doctor.

GERSTEIN (*steps back, horrified*): The Doctor! Hold on now.
If the Doctor knows you, Riccardo,
it makes escape so difficult,
we ought to ask: should we risk it at all?
He lives at the entrance of the camp.
I'm no match for *him*.

RICCARDO (*insistent*): The Doctor – and nobody can *prove*
that you knew me, Gerstein,
or that you knew Jacobson.

GERSTEIN (*with great impatience*):
Yes, that's all right for me, it's the risk I take.
(*He points at Jacobson.*)
What chance though – for him,
if the Doctor finds him with me?
We are only exposing Jacobson to danger.
(*Pause. Both look at Jacobson. He hesitates, then says quietly:*)

JACOBSON: Better to take a risk – and die like that,
than waiting in a line until they count you off,
sooner or later, automatically,
for gassing. Gerstein, they will never learn
from me, I swear, we ever knew each other.

GERSTEIN (*impatient*): It is not a question of me now,
but of you. Decide:

255

either you go back to your work –
for in the station there you might
still survive . . .
then I inform the Commandant
the Father refused to guarantee to
keep silent after his release
and therefore could not be released.
Or: the road to the gates, to the Commandant,
the road which could lead
straight into the Doctor's hands.
What that implies, you know.
The odds are fifty-fifty.

JACOBSON: And then – what happens to you?

GERSTEIN: I'll talk myself out of it – possibly. Probably.
You decide for yourself alone.

JACOBSON (*quick, strong*): Then I will try it.
(*Gerstein from now to the end reacts quickly, unsentimentally and
with the stubborness born of the loss of hope.*)

GERSTEIN: Not here, there in the hut. Good.
Let's try it. Your last word, Riccardo?
There, the cassock's there already.

RICCARDO (*business-like*):
Is my breviary with it? – Leave me that,
then I'll go – Carlotta!
(*Riccardo and Gerstein have gone into the hut. Jacobson, suddenly
afraid, has held back.*)

CARLOTTA (*glad*): Father, you're going free.

GERSTEIN (*urgently to Jacobson*):
Come along, Jacobson, there's not much time.

RICCARDO: I'm staying with you, Carlotta.
Your father is still alive.
I saw him yesterday at roll-call . . .

GERSTEIN (*to the still hesitating Jacobson, irritated*):
Get your clothes off, man, get your clothes off.

CARLOTTA: How did he look? And my mother,
my sister, the children . . .
(*Jacobson now takes off his jacket, and pulls on the soutane over a
filthy torn vest. While Riccardo takes the breviary and the rosary
out of the pocket of the soutane, he tries to hide his face from
Carlotta – he knows the women have already been cremated.*)

GERSTEIN: I'll take your letter with me – is it ready?

RICCARDO (*holding the rosary out to Carlotta*): No. Carlotta, I didn't
see the women.
Your father's doing all right.

CARLOTTA (*takes the scraps of paper from her overall pocket*):
Thank you, I . . . I couldn't write the letter.
Please take – these, so they don't find them on me.

GERSTEIN (*helpless*): The Father is staying with you.

CARLOTTA (*embarrassed, not wanting the rosary, but equally not
wanting to reject Riccardo*):
No, Father, no – keep it yourself.
You're staying?

RICCARDO (*not understanding her refusal, laying the rosary in her
hand, smiling*):
Yes.

GERSTEIN (*to Riccardo, in fear*):
If we meet the Doctor, Riccardo,
you'll see us both again tomorrow – over there.
(*Riccardo gives Gerstein his hand, without a word: Jacobson,
already in the soutane, takes Riccardo by the shoulder.*)

JACOBSON: Thank you.
(*fanatically*)
Survive! We will come back. To avenge you.

RICCARDO (*smiles, with an effort*):
Then you'd better be quick about it . . .
Good-bye. Gerstein, my father must not know
where I am. Tell him
my life has served its purpose. –
The truth you know yourself.
Carlotta!
(*Exit quickly, a tiny gesture betraying his emotion when he is
outside the hut. Gerstein has gone with him to the door, then turns
round. There is a long pause.*)

GERSTEIN (*urgently to Carlotta*):
Just don't fall ill, keep fit for work.
Whatever you do, keep fit for work.
They *can't* kill you all.

JACOBSON: I am ashamed
because I am going and you are staying.

CARLOTTA: I'm glad for you.

JACOBSON: Guard against sadness.
Whoever weeps in this place is lost.

(Carlotta nods dumbly, goes out quickly to get fresh water, but principally to facilitate the departure of the other two. Gerstein gives his instructions with unnatural self-control.

Jacobson has just got on the black stockings over his striped ones, and now changes his wooden sandals for shoes.)

GERSTEIN: We are going now to the Commandant.

Talk as little as possible.

You have been here eight days, understand, eight days.

You will have to sign

a guarantee of silence on the lives of two priests.

Do it without hesitation. Right, come along.

Talk as little as possible.

You were working in the crematoria.

Let's try it.

JACOBSON: Has he been here eight days? – but I've got

(points to his forearm)

a quite different number . . .

GERSTEIN *(gloomily)*:

No one will ask you about that. Are you ready?

(already at the door, steps back)

Over there at the back – the Doctor! Quickly past him.

JACOBSON *(sharp and quiet)*:

He's coming this way – it's finished.

GERSTEIN *(the same)*: Pull yourself together.

(giving an order)

Walk ahead of me, Father.

(They go as casually as possible past the Doctor, who is wearing a forage-cap and standing, his little stick in both hands, with a lanky, helmeted S.S. private, machine gun at the ready. The Doctor is very elegant, from his big, soft gauntlets to his high soft boots and his broad black cloak. The circular saw, very near at hand, accompanies his entrance.)

DOCTOR: In a hurry, Gerstein? Good morning.

GERSTEIN: Heil Hitler, Sturmbannführer – I'm collecting

prisoner Fontana, the priest.

(without pause, in a hopeless attempt to cause a diversion, he says confidentially)

Apart from that, Doctor, there's a girl here . . .

(embarrassed, looks around him)

comes from Rome.

Where is she then? Oh yes, getting more water.

Her fiancé died fighting for Germany.

DOCTOR: Then he won't have to mourn for her.

GERSTEIN: Give the girl a chance, Doctor.

DOCTOR (*laughs*): By all means, if she's so fetching.
  She can work with me in my lab.
  A Roman girl who has survived
  our recent Feast of Tabernacles,
  our last harvest-festival, is a rare bird in the camp.
  But, Gerstein, I got up on purpose
  to say goodbye to the *Father*.
  (*yawns like a barndoor*)
  What a noise you make in the early morning!
  (*looks Jacobson in the face, grinning*)
  In a bit of a hurry, eh? – How touching, how touching;
  since when did the Hebrews belong to the One True Church?

GERSTEIN (*with well-played assurance, roughly*):
  Hebrews? What are you talking about?
  Sturmbannführer Fritsche assured me . . .

DOCTOR (*irritated by this name*):
  Oh, let's not drag in Herr-Dr-Professor-Neuter-Fritscher.
  What's it to do with Fritsche?

GERSTEIN: I have a commission from Obersturmbannführer
  Eichmann.

DOCTOR (*scornful*): So-o-o!

GERSTEIN: To fetch this Jesuit, a diplomat of the Holy See,
  who was brought here by mistake . . .

DOCTOR: Brought here by mistake? – they all were that.
  What do you mean?

GERSTEIN (*unshaken*): . . . back to the Nuncio in Berlin.
  Well, here he is.

DOCTOR: Who? – the Nuncio? Is *that* the Nuncio?
  (*with an elaborate and deep bow to Jacobson*)
  Excellency – is it true that God is sick?
  They say his depressions are on him once more
  like the time when His Church was setting fire to
  the Protestants and Jews in Spain.

GERSTEIN: This is Father Riccardo Fontana.

JACOBSON (*trying to play along*):
  I can believe that God has many worries.

DOCTOR (*playing with his stick, enjoying what he says*):
  Or syphilis, like lots of Saints up there,

259

who lived among whores – and sodomites,
like St Francis . . .
Well, you landed yourself in the shit all right,
Gerstein, you sly old puss – I've seen through *you*
ever since our little trip to Tübingen.
But Christians of your inventive subtlety
amuse me.

GERSTEIN (*angry*):
I forbid you to speak like that, Sturmbannführer.
I demand an explanation.

DOCTOR: I see, you demand, do you? You demand
that I make myself look a bloody fool.
You take me for someone like Adolf Eichmann.
You'll suffer for that, Gerstein.

GERSTEIN: I don't *understand*.

DOCTOR: You understand perfectly; I *know* the Father.

GERSTEIN (*to Jacobson*):
Do you *know* the Sturmbannführer, Father?

DOCTOR (*pushes Jacobson aside with his stick*):
I know the *real* Father, the *real* one.
When he came here eight days ago,
he wanted to convert me on the spot.
A delightful apologist of Christ,
who was going to be my private chaplain
and amuse me
(*points to the glow from the flames*)
as soon as the incense from the ovens
had got into his nose enough
to make him choke on his beliefs.
(*He taps Jacobson on the face with his stick*)
What's so charming about *him*
that makes you want him so much?
Warm, Christian, *brotherly* love?

GERSTEIN: It is very easy, Sturmbannführer,
to make fun of me all the time,
simply because I choose to go to Church.

DOCTOR: Very affecting: a member of the Confessional Church
comes here, to winkle out a priest – and finishes
by smuggling a Jew out of camp.

GERSTEIN (*apparently bitterly amused*): Smuggle? – Ridiculous.
Smuggling a prisoner past Höss in broad daylight?

I'm taking him straight to the Commandant.
What exactly are you hinting at?
Did *I* have the call put out for the prisoner?
If he's not the one they're looking for –
how am I supposed to know?

DOCTOR (*blows on a whistle, laughs nastily*):
How? How are *you* supposed to know?
That's what you're going to tell me.
(*Carlotta comes back with her bucket, and goes on with her work in the hut.*)

GERSTEIN (*interrupts feverishly*):
You're talking as if I'd insisted on bringing
the prisoner to the camp gate myself.
I was going to wait outside.
Just because Fritsche had visitors from Essen,
and for that reason only,
Fritsche, *and* Höss as well, both asked me
to wait for the priest here at the inner platform.
– By the way, there's that girl again –
(*He points at Carlotta; the Doctor blows the whistle again.*)
If you're not satisfied . . .

DOCTOR: Not satisfied? I am having you *arrested*, Gerstein.
You were here together, the three of you,
you cooked this up together.
I wanted to hear first exactly
what sort of bloody fools you think we are in here.
Rome hasn't asked for him at all,
or you would never have swopped him
for that one. Take his belt. He's under arrest!
(*He has spoken the last words to the guard. Gerstein draws his pistol; we can't tell whether he is going to shoot, as the guard knocks it from his hand and kicks it aside. The guard grins, Gerstein gives up his belt slowly. The Doctor turns to another guard who has brought back Riccardo and is standing a little apart. Carlotta, in the hut, senses that something terrible is happening outside. She opens the door and starts to scrub the three steps. Riccardo, trying to grasp the situation, hardly follows the Doctor's chatter.*)
Hallo, Father. Tell me now, were you able
to reconcile Reality and Idea there at the ovens?
This baptism of fire enrols you in

the ranks of the great testes veritatis.
I hope, as my private chaplain, you will
show your appreciation of the fact
that it was I who made it possible
for you to study the Golgotha of Pure Spirit
at the closest possible quarters?
A little shaken, mm? Well, anyone who can
regard World History as a therapeutic . . .
(*He laughs challengingly.*)

RICCARDO (*cool and wounding*):
You can never win, that's what makes you so talkative.
All you can do is triumph – for a while.
What am I doing here?

JACOBSON (*has reached the decision to give himself up, so as to be able at least to save Gerstein. He comes forward.*):
I wish to report that I deceived the Sturmbannführer.
I said I was the priest. Because the priest
didn't come forward when they called,
I went to the guardroom.
He wasn't here . . . he didn't come, so I –

DOCTOR (*after the last sentence, which will tell Riccardo too much, in anger*):
One word, and you will go into the oven
alive. About turn – about turn, I said.
(*Jacobson obeys.*)
Kneel – on your knees! *That's* right!
Now, face in the mud.
(*Jacobson lies on the floor, face down. The Doctor speaks triumphantly to Gerstein as he points to Riccardo.*)
Now, my dear colleague – that one didn't want to go,
or was it that you didn't want him to?
(*ironically*)
That is the one whom the Pope weeps for
all night long
in the Sistine Chapel.

GERSTEIN (*pointing at Riccardo*):
It's the first time I've seen him – how on earth
am I supposed to know which is the real one?
It is not *my* business to examine them.

DOCTOR (*looks at Carlotta*): Let's ask the slut –
You! come here! come along, here.

Oho, Ignatius Loyola,
the *Exercises* – *fire*side reading.
Much read at the stake.
(*With a quick snatch, he has taken Riccardo's breviary from his pocket – with his other hand he grips Carlotta, who has drawn hesitantly nearer.*)

RICCARDO (*speaks to her quickly, then to the Doctor*):
Carlotta, you ? – We were deported together . . .
You still know me, don't you ?

CARLOTTA (*trying to play along*):
Father – I'm glad you're still alive . . .

DOCTOR (*not listening, leafing through the book, his little stick under his arm, says to the girl*):
Come from Rome, with your family ; are you a Catholic ?

CARLOTTA: Yes.

DOCTOR: Where's that bit about the girls now . . .
(*He reads aloud with pleasure, the background and he himself adding point to Loyola's text.*)
The devil on the throne of smoke and fire attracts
like a seducer – I know, aha, here : 'I see with
the eye of imagination the powerful glow of
the flames, and the souls, imprisoned in *burning*
bodies. I smell with the scent of imagination
smoke, sulphur, excrement and
rotting things.'
And the bit about the girls, Father, where's that ?
The sin of fleshly lust, my love of the flesh,
(*laughs*)
the world . . . *there's* something
you can take exception to, Father.
Shall I put you both together ?
(*without pausing, to Carlotta, as he shuts the breviary*)
You've been cleaning here since seven o'clock ?
Were you on time today ?

CARLOTTA (*afraid*): I was on time.

DOCTOR: Your lover is dead, isn't he ?

CARLOTTA: Yes, at Tobruk.

DOCTOR: I see – what was – what was his name ?

CARLOTTA: Marcello . . .

DOCTOR (*quickly*): So you were here on time – !
Came later than the Father, though, didn't you !

CARLOTTA (*confused, dares not answer, stammers*):
I – don't know – I was . . .

RICCARDO (*quietly, points to Jacobson, to help her*):
Was the Father here already when you got here, Carlotta?

DOCTOR (*irritated*): Father, I hardly think that worthy of you.
I saw you wandering round here myself.
(*casually to Carlotta, pointing to Riccardo*)
So, when *did* your soul-mate arrive?

CARLOTTA: The Father – I don't know – I couldn't . . .
(*Although nothing depends on her answer, the Doctor, from a pleasure in tormenting her, forces her to her knees with an iron grip, then almost on to her back. It comes as a surprise. She cries out.*)

DOCTOR: Now – do you know or don't you?

CARLOTTA: I wasn't looking, I only –
scrubbing the floor – I . . .

DOCTOR (*has pulled her up again, with smiling sadism*):
Shall I send you to join your family? Look,
there are the pyres
and there's the fence:
shall I chase you over there – or over there?
(*As Carlotta collapses mentally at the hinted remark about the death of her family – it only needed this news to be added to all the rest – she whispers in a maniac stammer, madness already in her eyes:*)

CARLOTTA: Dead – all dead – dead – all dead – dead . . .
(*She stammers on.*)

DOCTOR (*almost casually*):
There – the choice is yours. Tell me then:
Was he here first – or that one?

CARLOTTA (*looking at him without speaking, her face wildly distorted*):
I don't know, I don't know, I don't know . . .

(*The Doctor has let her go, and Carlotta has already withdrawn a pace or so from him towards the guardroom, while she stares hypnotized at 'the most cunning of beasts' [Canaris, referring to Heydrich], as he is now seen to be. Then she screams, like a woman in labour under drugs, totally uninhibited. It is left to the actress whether she uses words here – perhaps the simplest, the cheapest words can still be spoken.*)

CARLOTTA: No – no – leave me alone – don't – don't . . .

(*Already at her first shriek, which has made even the Doctor pause, she has fled to the hut door with one bound, an action so totally animal, so completely untameable, that it destroys all the efforts made up to now to stylize, to show in the theatre, at one remove, the horrors of the Final Solution which are still close to us.*

Carlotta's screams have changed to a sort of spastic laughter. She snatches off her headscarf, beats about her with it pointlessly, and throws it from her. Her convulsive glance flickers over the men's faces and, the rosary in her hand, she bursts into the guardroom, laughs harshly and savagely into Helga's hand-mirror, then crouches with it in a corner and tries, laughing in short bursts all the time, to tie the rosary round her neck like a necklace. It slips from her hand. The Doctor has pulled himself together, opened his revolver holster mechanically, and mutters:)

DOCTOR: Off her head . . .

(He goes quickly and resolutely into the hut, to do what was always done with deportees who lost their nerve before gassing. He puts down the breviary, picks up the rosary and holds it out to Carlotta. A mad smile crosses her face, for he radiates a 'suggestive sincerity' and her wild eyes come to rest on his. She jumps up, tries to grasp his hand and the rosary, cries out in joy at finding 'him' again, and tries to embrace him.)

CARLOTTA: Marcello! – Marcello!
　　(laughs madly) I was afraid
　　you would never come back, from Africa.
　　It was so long, Marcello, you were away so long.
DOCTOR *(resisting her embrace, with compelling charm)*:
　　Come along – not here.

(She follows without hesitation. He does not touch her, but just extends his arm to her – a graceful, lightly significant invitation to accompany him, while he moves backwards towards the door, without letting her glance stray from his. This all happens very quickly.)

CARLOTTA *(passes him on the top step outside the door: she cries out in fear)*:
　　Marcello! – Marcello!

(Behind her in the door, he pulls out his pistol with a lightning movement and shoots her in the neck. Without looking at the corpse, he puts his pistol up, and at this moment, while the two guards are watching, Riccardo dives for Gerstein's pistol, picks it up, and aims, with the cry . . .)

RICCARDO: Destroy him!

(. . . *at the Doctor, and is shot down by the submachine gun of the guard standing behind him before he can either release the safety catch or fire. Riccardo sinks to his knees, then falls backwards. The guard picks up Gerstein's pistol, and holds it out to the Doctor, shocked and grinning. Gerstein has covered his eyes for a moment with his hand.*)

DOCTOR: Aimed at me? – not seriously.
    Thank you, Scharführer.
    (*bends over Riccardo*)
    Father, in Auschwitz it is almost as hard
    a thing to shoot as it is to pray.
    Pity, I would have liked to spend a week or two
    arguing with you. . . .
    A little nearer God?

RICCARDO (*raises himself, tries to speak, falls back, almost incomprehensibly*):
    In hora mortis meae voca me.

DOCTOR (*stands scornfully*): Amen. Did you really hear Him call –
    there in the crematorium?
    (*to Jacobson, with a kick*)
    Get up – over to the campfire
    (*points to Riccardo*)
    and take that with you – get on, take it with you.
    (*Jacobson rises. Gerstein has bent over Riccardo and opens the coat of the dying man, thereby showing which side he is on. The Doctor pushes without a word between Gerstein and Riccardo. Jacobson, on his knees, his arms under Riccardo's armpits, tries vainly to pull Riccardo up.*)

GERSTEIN: He is not dead. You are a doctor, help him.
    (*shouts*)
    He's still alive!

DOCTOR (*without looking at Gerstein, casually*):
    The fire is a good doctor. It will
    temper the Christian and the Jew.
    (*beckons to guard who saved his life*)
    Take that one to the Commandant.
    Watch out for him –
    I'll be along right away.

GUARD: Very good, Sturmbannführer.
    (*Gerstein, after a last look at his friends, disappears quickly behind*

the hut, to the left, followed by the S.S. man. The other guards have tried, with kicks and blows of their submachine guns, to get Jacobson, who is still half-kneeling, unmanned and stunned with horror, to his feet. Riccardo's head lies in his lap. Very near at hand, we hear the circular saw.)

DOCTOR (*with cutting impatience*): Go on – help the cripple up.
(*points to Carlotta*)
and get *that* cleared away.

GUARD: Very good, Sturmbannführer.

(*Reluctantly he takes Riccardo by the shoulders and Jacobson takes his feet. They go off right. The Doctor goes slowly over to the left of the stage, where Gerstein was led off. Hardly has he got behind the window, when he remembers the* Exercises, *comes back, steps over the dead Carlotta into the hut, riffles through the book, smiles, tucks it under his arm and leaves the stage like a professor after a lecture.*

We hear the imperturbable voice of an announcer reading :)

On the 28th October, 1943, Herr von Weizsäcker, Hitler's Ambassador to the Holy See, wrote to the Foreign Office in Berlin:

(*Here the voice changes, as the glow of the flames dies gradually away, to the gravely modulated organ of a well-brought-up elderly Gentleman of Politics*)

Although investigations show that the Pope has been approached from many quarters, he has not allowed himself to be aroused to any demonstrative utterance against the deportation of the Jews. Although he must reckon with the fact that this attitude will prejudice him from the point of view of our enemies, he has, in this delicate question, done everything not to damage relationships with the German Government. Since further actions against the Jews in Rome are no longer to be carried out, this uncomfortable question, for German-Vatican relations, can be considered to have been resolved.

The *Osservatore Romano* for the 25th October did in fact, carry an official communiqué about the charitable work of the Pope, in which it is stated, in the recognizable style of the Vatican newspaper, i.e. tortuous and obscure, that the Pope extends his fatherly solicitude to all men without distinction of nationality or race. It is highly improbable that objections will be raised to this statement, which only very few people are likely to take as having special reference to the Jewish question.

(*And now the imperturbable announcer returns; the fire is out, the stage is dark, and we can just see the dead girl still on the ramp.*)
In this manner, the gas chambers functioned another whole year. In the summer of 1944, the so-called daily quota of murders reached its apogee. On the 26th November, Himmler gave orders for the crematoria to be blown up. Two months later, the last prisoners in Auschwitz were freed by soldiers of the Russian Army.

Curtain

Historical Sidelights

In so far as it is unusual to burden a play with an historical appendix, I would have liked to avoid doing so in this case. As a stage play the work needs no commentary. Since, however, the events have not been set down as a documentary reportage of historical accuracy, but condensed into a play, the historical figures named in the play and their relatives, who are still alive, have the right to be informed of the sources – often very difficult to come by – which caused the author to see a character or a scene in such and such a light. What is printed here is admittedly only a fragment of the available collection of material, which one day perhaps – should a general interest in it be evoked – will be made full use of within the framework of an independent historical work. It goes without saying that the numerous biographies, diaries, letters and legal procès-verbaux of the time have been studied, and so they have purposely not been enumerated here. The following remarks on controversial happenings and statements, however, should prove that the author of the play has only allowed free play to his imagination when it was necessary to transform the available historical raw material into a form suitable for the stage. The truth has always been respected, but the sediment has been removed.

Anyone who tracks back along the conveyor belt of historical events, loaded with corpses and rubble, or who weighs the contradictory, the smug or the despairing statements of victor or victim, learns at even the most modest attempt to penetrate through the debris and the coincidences of so-called historical fact to the truth, the symbol, that the playwright 'can use no single element of reality as he finds it, that his work in all its aspects must be a work of the Idea, if it is to possess reality as a whole'.

Anyone who ignores Schiller's demand, and does not declare 'open and honourable war upon Naturalism in Art', will have nowadays to give place to any newsreel, if only because it can show 'the raw material of the world' much more drastically and completely than the stage, which only remains true if – as Brecht, the theorist of alienation, was not the first to discover – 'it destroys the illusion which it has itself created.'[1]

[1] *Wallenstein.*

It should be added that the following collection of material, within its – often overlapping – thematic groupings, holds, wherever possible, to the sequence demanded by the course of the play. A more coherent articulation was impracticable, since the same facts often reappear in different scenes – but sometimes in contradiction or even interpreted in diametrical opposition, as the play of the dialogue demands. This is not a work of historical scholarship, nor does it pretend to be. Since neither the Vatican nor the Kremlin permits unrestricted entry to its archives, the historian cannot, in the foreseeable future, interpret these events without leaving some gaps. To tie up the already available facts, intuitively, into an artistic and truthful whole, is the high and seldom attained goal of poetry which, in view of *precisely* such a weight of raw material and all the trouble of its compilation, must not allow itself to be robbed of the specific freedom which alone gives primal *form* to the material.

Kolbe and Gerstein

While many reports have appeared in Germany since 1945 about Provost Lichtenberg[1] and his public recognition of the persecuted, we know almost nothing about the martyrdom of the Pole, Father Maximilian Kolbe. Born in 1894 in the district of Lodz, he became a Franciscan, served before the war as a missionary in Japan and died in August 1941 in the starvation cell at Auschwitz in the following circumstances: one of his fellow prisoners had fled the camp, although such an action was punishable by the sentencing of ten other prisoners to death by starvation. Ten men from the same 'Block' as the escaped man were arbitrarily counted off, among them the prisoner F. Gajowniczek, who had a wife and children. He began to weep and Kolbe stepped forward and asked to be allowed to go to his death in his place. He gave as a reason for his decision the fact that he was no longer fit for work. Although this was clearly a subterfuge, the S.S. must nevertheless have been impressed: the prisoner 16670 was allowed to go to the starvation cell in the place of No. 5659 (who survived the war). The prisoners were locked naked in the completely empty, windowless concrete

---

[1] Since the first production of the play the author has learned that Lichtenberg was not alone in his request to the Nazis. The present Protestant provost of Berlin, Dr Heinrich Grüber, twice asked the Nazis to be allowed to go to the ghetto with the deported Jews. His attempt to enter the camp at Guers, with the assistance of members of the Abwehr, failed and ended with Grüber's arrest.

cell, today a memorial, and were denied even water. A commentator has stated that 'during his hunger strikes Gandhi drank water. The way in which thirst affects human beings can be vouched for by survivors from caravans lost in the desert. . . . The torture of hunger degrades the tortured man into a beast, for human endurance has its limits – beyond which are only despair or sanctity.'[1]

Father Maximilian comforted his dying comrades. The prisoner Borgowiec, whose job it was to clean the death cells, stated that the S.S. men could not endure Kolbe's gaze. On one occasion, when they were dragging out the bodies of the starved, they shouted at him 'Look at the floor, not us.' He was dying too slowly for them, or perhaps his conduct forced the coup de grâce from them: in the end they gave him an injection. One report states that he was the last survivor: another that two other prisoners were still alive.

On 24th May 1948 the inquiry for the canonization of Father Maximilian was initiated at Rome.

From letters on Kurt Gerstein, in the possession of his widow: CHURCH COUNCILLOR O. WEHR, attorney of the Rhineland Evangelical Church for the Saar district, on 24.1.49, from Saarbrücken:

'Kurt Gerstein was known to the undersigned for many years from his youth work in High School Bible groups and his decisive influence, as an evangelical youth leader, on boys at the most formative period of their development. At the time of the Church's struggle against the totalitarian claims of the Nazi state he kept to a clear line. It is personally known to me, that he not only wrote a series of pamphlets addressed to young people in their struggle to preserve their inmost integrity during the Nazi period, but also that as an official in the Mines Office at Saarbrücken he availed himself of every opportunity to distribute the secret encyclicals of the Confessional Church throughout all Germany, until a part of the material, carelessly stored in his office after one such distribution, was used to convict him. All efforts at the time (1936), including those of Minister Schacht, to prevent the arrest of this uniquely qualified official came to nothing. After his release from the concentration camp he surprised me one day with his proposal to enlist in the S.S. On this subject I can give you the following information based on personal conversation with him:

'The final inducement to this decision was the death by gassing, in the hospital at Hadamar, of a relation, the daughter of the late

[1] M. Winowska, *Pater Maximilian Kolbe*, Fribourg, 1952.

Minister Ebeling of the Evangelical Church community of Alt-Saarbrücken. After her interment, he informed me that he had decided to try and discover what was, in fact, behind all the current rumours about this and other criminal actions. My extremely strong misgivings about this plan to enter the camp of the demonic powers he met with a passionate determination. It was not to be doubted that, with the impulsive activity that characterized Kurt Gerstein, he would, with his quite exceptional gifts and capabilities, be able to get where he wanted: into the Reichsführung of the S.S. His success confirms this. From then on he was driven without respite, hither and thither, by ideas and schemes to help and hinder, up to his audacious plans made in the autumn of 1944. He visited me repeatedly on his official journeys and kept me informed about everything, including what he himself went through when seeing the extermination camps in the east, about the satanic, nihilistic cynicism of the murderers and their assistants, great or small, and about the impressions made on him by the despairing victims, which had never since left him. . . .

'A figure like Kurt Gerstein must necessarily appear in twilight, or rather, in the common-sense judgement of ordinary people he must simply seem incredible. The quite uncanny mastery with which he camouflaged his inmost Christian existence under an outward show of conformity, purely for the purpose of helping, makes it ridiculous to apply normal standards. Of his mastery in disguising his own real wishes, I have sufficient examples. A just verdict on this man which really takes into account his inmost character and desires, will resist any moral, political or psychological analysis. From the conversations on spiritual matters for which he sought me out, I have never been in any doubt of the constancy of his inmost character.'

PASTOR MARTIN NIEMÖLLER, President of the Evangelical Established Church, wrote to the Public Prosecutor, Erbs, in Frankfurt on 26th April 1948:

'I knew Gerstein for many years before my arrest in July 1937, from work in Bible groups and in the Confessional Church. He was a somewhat "special saint", but throughout honest and direct. His word was to be relied on, and he stood up for his convictions always and to their final conclusions. I consider him completely trustworthy, and therefore believe it to be quite out of the question that he should ever even have been tempted to abet National Socialism, let alone the crimes committed by it. It is my firm conviction that he was a victim of the consequences of his own actions and of his opposition to National Socialism, taken to its furthest degree, for which he was ready to, and did indeed, lay aside his honour, his family and his life. I do not question one word of his own deposition and am convinced that any doubt cast upon it does him injustice.'

CATHEDRAL CHAPLAIN BUCHHOLZ, who for years looked after the condemned Catholics at Plötzensee before their execution, on the 10th July, 1946:

'I made Herr Gerstein's acquaintance through a former political prisoner at Tegel, an industrialist whose name has unfortunately escaped me . . . and whose release Herr Gerstein was personally involved in, if I am not mistaken, by the purloining of documents. I was invited by this gentleman, in September 1944, to Herr Gerstein's apartment, where I met a group of other men, all of whom had been the victims of political persecution, or had actually been through the Gestapo prisons as political prisoners. My acquaintance assured me that all the men were reliable and that all of them, Herr Gerstein in particular, wished to hear from me further details of what was mostly only known through rumour: the mass executions at Plötzensee. I then, without any concealment, described these fully, including the terrible night in September 1943, when 186 political prisoners were hanged. . . . When he (Gerstein) then . . . gave the names and locations of the death camps, and reported on the "daily activity" of each incinerator and gas chamber . . . this detailed description was so terrible for all of us, who were not totally unaware of these events, that we found it scarcely credible . . . How honest Herr Gerstein was in his description I was able to establish later, in the course of several visits he paid me. It was always a relief and a respite for him on these occasions to be able to speak of these things, without constraint, to a priest. In the same way, it may be taken as a proof of the sincerity of Herr Gerstein's convictions that he not only promised me every possible assistance for my political prisoners, but also brought me cases full of food, cigarettes, etc., which I was able secretly to pass on to them.'

BISHOP DIBELIUS, in 1942, when Gerstein reported to him immediately after his return from the death camps, passed on the information to the Bishop of Uppsala.

The possibility mentioned by Gerstein in the play (Act III, Sc. 2.) of assuring the success of a coup d'état by a false announcement that Hitler had been murdered by the S.S., is based on a plan by one of the conspirators of the 20th July, Graf Stauffenberg. Field-Marshal von Witzleben, however, forbade Stauffenberg even temporarily to announce this.

Gerstein's courage and adroitness, which above all made possible his long, almost suicidal double life in the S.S., make it probable that, in his attempt to report the details about Treblinka to the Nuncio, he was actually able to force his way as far as Orsenigo himself. The urgency of his plea and his cunning determination make it unlikely that he would have let himself be shown the door of the Nuncio's palace by any subordinate priest. But even his widow does not know for sure if he spoke to Orsenigo personally. Whatever the facts, my efforts throughout this play have been to *minimize* many of the events of Hitler's war which are still almost incredible even today, and the number of its victims, because there is no likelihood that in the future, when all the eyewitnesses are dead, the historical truth in its immeasurable horror will still be believed. These efforts have led me to extenuate the shameful ejection from the Nuncio's palace. My intention has been to miti-gate and to reduce happenings down to the scale of the capacity of the human imagination. It is therefore implied that the master of the house at least listened to a man who was obviously in great distress. Soldiers, particularly in an age of general conscription, often meet with conflicts similar to Gerstein's. If Pius XII opened the door to them and granted at least mass audiences to thousands of German and Allied soldiers, then one may not dare to suppose that the Ambassador of the Representative of Christ in Hitler's capital would not only refuse to receive a refugee, in 1942, but would even have had him shown the door. In any case the question is of no interest as far as the play is concerned. Orsenigo stands here simply for the representative of the Curia in Hitler's capital, and, since as Nuncio he had taken on the greatest responsibility, he must now stand in this tragedy for all those clerical dignitaries who – like Bishop (later Cardinal) Count Preysing – were of the opinion that the 'life and deeds' of the commentator of Hitler's race-laws, 'were governed by fundamental Catholic principles'.[1] Against this the

[1] Wilhelm Stuckart and Hans Globke, *Kommentare zur deutschen Rassen-gesetzgebung*, Munich, 1936.

figure of Riccardo stands for all those, mostly nameless, priests who, immediately – and finally with the laying down of their lives – placed the commandment of 'Love thy neighbour' above all considerations of expediency. The exposition of the play would stay unchanged if Gerstein's appearance were, for example, to be transferred to the rooms of Bishop Preysing's legal representative, to whom Gerstein was allowed to report about Treblinka 'with the express plea that the information be passed on to the Holy See'.

From an historical standpoint, moreover, Gerstein could only give the Vatican detailed statements about the murder methods, and the number of victims. The fact that murder-factories existed was already known to the Vatican; the Holy See had numerous sources of information; on an official level, the Polish Government in exile had supplied it with reports, with the greatest zeal and through the most varied channels.

I will never believe that Gerstein committed suicide. Anyone who has concerned himself at all deeply with this man and heard the extraordinary statements made to his widow from Paris, must be convinced that Gerstein was one of the still uncounted Germans and Frenchmen who were murdered without trial in France after the Liberation of 1944. Not many of those who, after the entry of the Americans, ran wild there as resistance fighters against defenceless compatriots and German prisoners, bore the honourable name of resistance fighter with justification: a dark chapter still waiting for its chronicler. On 11th April 1952, the French Minister of Justice stated that since the liberation of France, 10,519 Frenchmen had been executed, only 846 of them after due process of law.[1]

It is also possible, since none of Gerstein's fellow prisoners can apparently remember him today, that he was hanged by fanatical members of the S.S. when they noticed how seriously he took the 'obligation to account to the Allies' that he spoke of in a letter to his father. This letter, first published by Gert H. Theunissen in a radio documentary on Gerstein, was written from Helsinki on 5th March 1944: 'At some moment or other, you will have to stand up for the age you live in, and for what is taking place during it. We would no longer be able to understand each other, nor have anything more of importance to say to each other, if I could not say to you: Do not underestimate this responsibility, nor this obligation to account. It

[1] Gerald Reitlinger, *The Final Solution*, London, 1953.

can arrive sooner than one imagines. I know all about this responsibility. I admit I am eaten up by it. . . .'

In the autumn of the same year he wrote to his father: 'It has certainly fallen to my lot to think out these things, in all their aspects – black and white, good and evil – to their final conclusions, and – please understand this – to suffer them.'

The Concordat

DR RUDOLF PECHEL told me that in German opposition circles the Nuncio was considered a confirmed Fascist and hanger-on of Mussolini. Nevertheless he listened readily when Pechel privately conveyed to him the request of high-ranking officers that he should use his influence to prevent any of the priests particularly sympathetic to the Hitler Government being appointed as chaplains to the Armed Forces.

On one occasion, in November 1939, on hearing of the Gestapo's crimes in Poland from the clergy, from members of the armed forces and from 'protestant academics who came in tears to the Residence, to report upon the atrocities', the Nuncio of his own accord addressed an extremely strong complaint to the Foreign Office and made determined demands for an investigation. Unfortunately he himself removed any official character from his intervention, and emphasized that he was not acting as Nuncio, nor as the senior member of the Diplomatic representatives, but as a private individual. Even at this time Weizsäcker advised, as he was still doing four years later in Rome, against 'interesting oneself in cases of this sort for fear of damaging the very thing one was trying to protect'. The German Government refused the Nuncio in Berlin any rights appertaining to the territories incorporated into Germany during the war, because it wished thereby to blackmail the Vatican into public recognition of the new frontiers. This Rome never did. Because of this Weizsäcker, as late as March 1943, politely returned to the Nuncio the now famous letter of the Secretary of State, Cardinal Maglione, to Ribbentrop – a weighty complaint detailing all the crimes committed against the Church in Poland and demanding their cessation. At that time there were over 1,000 Polish priests in prison in Dachau, and the Vatican knew that many of them had already been murdered. How far the totally pointless wickedness of the Nazis against the Polish people went can be seen from a proclamation forbidding men under twenty-eight and women under twenty-five to marry. If one is looking for a reason for Orsenigo's being persona non grata in the Vatican after 1945, it is hard to find it here.

Orsenigo was probably unable to persuade Pius XII to break off the Concordat with Hitler for the reason that it had been the Secretary of State, Pacelli, not Pope Pius XI, who – like Mussolini among others – had pressed for the speedy conclusion of a Concordat with Hitler's Germany. Reichschancellor Brüning, who must have known more about it than anyone else, said to Count Harry Kessler in Paris in 1935:

'It is not the Pope who is behind the agreement with Hitler, but the Vatican bureaucracy, and its mouthpiece Pacelli. They have in mind an authoritarian state, and an authoritarian church controlled by the Vatican bureaucracy, which can conclude an eternal alliance with one another. For this reason Pacelli and his people are a thorn in the flesh of the Catholic parliamentary parties in the various countries, like the Central party in Germany, and would be dropped without regret. The Pope does not support these ideas.'[1]

Nine years later, as quoted by PROFESSOR FRIEDRICH HEER, the Jesuit Father DELP wrote the following, shortly before he was strangled in Plötzensee, while the Supreme Head of his Church did not move a finger personally, to save him and other Germans in priests' habits from being executed by his partner in the Concordat, Hitler: 'An . . . honest history of religion will have to include bitter chapters on the support given by the Church to the rise of the totalitarian man, collectivism and the dictator-principle.'[2]

Post festum, to nudge the elbows of 'writers of history', Pacelli admitted an honourable motive to the concluding of the Concordat: 'Do you imagine,' he said to a journalist, Morandi, in 1946, 'that I do not know that people have said, and written, that I should not have signed the Concordat with the Third Reich? Yet if Hitler, despite the Concordat, persecuted the Catholic Church so severely, imagine what he would have dared to do without the Concordat. Do you suppose for a moment that his bandits would not have forced their way here, into the Vatican?'

Now in 1934 – when Hitler's S.A. were providing the bandsmen and the organizers at the Exhibition of the Holy Robe in Trier – it hardly seemed probable that he would persecute the Church, nor that he would, nine years later, occupy Rome. (And even when this

[1] Harry Graf Kessler, *Tagebücher 1918–1937*, Frankfurt am Main, 1961.
[2] Friedrich Heer, *Die Deutschen, der Nationalsozialismus und die Gegenwart*, Bielefeld, 1960.

happened Pacelli at no time reckoned on an occupation of the Vatican.) In the year the Concordat was concluded Pius XI was informed of the reign of terror against the Jews in Germany by Dr Edith Stein, a convert, although admittedly he never answered the letter, which was delivered to him personally. Nevertheless Pius XI stated that the Concordat was a platform from which to protest. Little use was made of it for this purpose, as is clear when one looks at the complaints, for the most part extremely lame, which the Nuncio made on purely ecclesiastical matters to Herr von Weizsäcker.

All the same, Pius XI, even in the first audience he gave to VON PAPEN, whom Hitler had sent to Rome for preliminary discussions about the Concordat, had greeted him by saying, how 'pleased' it had made him 'that the German Government now had at its head a man uncompromisingly opposed to Communism and Russian nihilism in all its forms. Indeed, the atmosphere was so cordial that I was able to settle the details of a draft agreement with a speed quite unusual in Vatican affairs . . .'[1] Mussolini, who at that time had no good opinion of Hitler, advised von Papen to proceed with all possible speed: 'The signing of this agreement with the Vatican will establish the credit of your Government abroad for the first time.'[2]

After the war when, as Friedrich Heer wrote in 1960, the situation was so ticklish 'that only a gigantic covering-up operation could save the face of official Christianity in Germany', and when the 'living lie of German Christianity [arose] from the shadows of the ruins of that mighty edifice'[3] – after 1945 the representative of the Holy See in Berlin was, as was foreseen, driven into the desert as a scapegoat. Against all precedent, Pius XII refused Orsenigo the customary obituary in the *Osservatore Romano*, on the Bishop's death far from Rome in the early 'fifties. Even Ernst von Weizsäcker tried to break a lance for the Nuncio in Rome, but without success.

On the attitude of the bishops in 1933 see, *inter alia*, *Hochland* for February, 1961. Referring to the celebration of the opening of the Reichstag in the Garnisonkirche after the elections of 5th March 1933, Herr von Papen writes: 'When we read in Hitler's *Table Talk* today that he conquered the country in the face of the curses of both denominations, and was therefore from fundamental

---

[1] Franz von Papen, *Memoirs*, London, 1952.
[2] Franz von Papen, *ibid.*
[3] Friedrich Heer, *ibid.*

considerations unable to enter the church at Potsdam, this is historically inaccurate. At the time he was certainly aware of the opposition of the Churches, but it was not a question of curses and hatred. He hoped to find a middle way.'

On 14th July 1933 Hitler said at a session of the Reich Cabinet: 'This Concordat, whose contents do not interest me in the least, creates for us an area of confidence which is very useful to us in our uncompromising struggle against international Jewry. . . .'

Had Pacelli been the great diplomat he is today held to be – though Brüning's opinion of him would be much more accurate – he would hardly, after ten years' observation of German internal politics, have fallen into Hitler's trap so quickly. In June 1945 he declared that the Concordat had prevented worse from happening. The frenetic rejoicing of the Catholic bishops in 1933/4, even as they watched at close quarters how murderously Hitler acted towards his opponents at home, proves that this meaning was only applied to the Concordat in 1945, not at the time it was concluded. For what did it prevent, since no threat was ever made to dissolve it in order to protect the Church in Poland or Catholics in Germany from the Gestapo? Giovannetti in *The Vatican and the War*[1] relates how in 1942 even Japan was obstinately fighting for a Concordat with Rome, on the same propagandist grounds which made the Allies, and Roosevelt in person, seek to thwart its conclusion. Hitler himself stated expressly that the Concordat would be expendable *after* victory. Who can then maintain that the Nazis would not have drawn back if Pius had, during the war, threatened them with an interdict? Would they have provoked the antagonism of thirty-five million Germans and the great majority of their satellites as members of a church that was 'an enemy of the State'?

The Vatican and the 'Final Solution'

Whatever reasons persuaded the Pope never at any time in his many speeches to mention, *expressis verbis*, even the deportation of the Jews – it remains incomprehensible that His Holiness should have been unable to bestir himself to make any protest against Hitler at a time when Germany was obviously defeated, but when Auschwitz had yet to reach its highest 'daily quota'. Rome, and therefore the Vatican, was under the protection of the American occupying forces when – in June 1944 – Rudolf Vrba and Alfred Wetzler, two prisoners who had escaped from Auschwitz-Birkenau

[1] Alberto Giovannetti, *Il Vaticano e la guerra, 1939–1940*, Vatican City, 1960.

in April, were able, in the course of a five-hour meeting with the Papal Nuncio in Slovakia, to make an extremely exhaustive report, complete with plans of the camp, the gas chambers and the railway approaches. Details of these atrocities had been published by August in Geneva, and were later being secretly read in Germany by, for instance, the editress Ursula von Kardorff. They were soon supplemented and confirmed from quite another source. On the 24th July 1944 Allied reporters shocked the world with new revelations about the camps. The English *Illustrated London News* and *Sphere* even brought out special issues about Majdanek. The photographs of human remains, of gas chambers, of the camp crematorium with its five ovens, of the card index rooms and the clothes of the gassed women and children, roused Hitler, as Fritz Hesse learned from Hitler's intimate, Hewel, to an 'outburst of rage against the slovenly and cowardly rabble in the Security Service who didn't erase the traces of the two camps in time'.[1] Even these pictures could not rouse the Vatican to protest, although it must have assumed that, of the 380,000 Hungarian Jews deported to Auschwitz between the 15th May and 30th June, many could not yet have been gassed, but must soon take their turn. In fact, as Reitlinger reports, it was not till July 1944 that the 'full capacity of all four crematoria' and of the much more 'practical' open pits was fully exploited to dispose of gassed and shot Hungarians.

But already by 15th May, on the first day of the deportations, the Papal Nuncio, Monsignor Angelo Rotta, 'brought it to the attention' of the Hungarian prime minister 'that the whole world would learn exactly what these deportations signify'. On 25th June, Rotta handed to Horthy a message from the Pope which made an appreciably greater impression on the Regent than the remonstrations of the Hungarian bishops, who 'protested less against the principle of the deportations than against the cruelties that accompanied them. The pastoral letter of Archbishop Cardinal Prince Seredi was a long-winded affair which failed to name the deportations for what they really were. Its publication was delayed and finally withdrawn on 8th July, on an assurance that the Budapest deportation had been countermanded. This and other evidence collected by Eugene Levai suggests that the bishops were only ready to exert their power from the pulpit when deportation threatened the Magyarized Jews, among whom there were many converts. Nor should it be forgotten that the uninhibited collaboration of the

[1] Fritz Hesse, *Das Spiel um Deutschland*, Munich, 1953.

[Hungarian] *gendarmerie* would have been impossible if the Church in Hungary had consistently denounced anti-Semitism in the past.'[1]

This long-delayed message of Pius XII, which was not even addressed to Hitler himself, already had such an effect that the Nuncio was at any rate assured that baptized Jews would no longer be deported. How high the credit of the Pope stood is here proved afresh. For his message, Reitlinger continues, 'was the beginning of a world-wide bombardment of the Regent's conscience'.[2] The deportations from Hungary came to an end before many more than half the Jews had been taken away. Not only was Horthy threatened with reprisals by the American Secretary of State, Cordell Hull, but the King of Sweden and the International Red Cross also offered to assist in the emigration of the Hungarian Jews. On 7th July, Mr Eden protested in the House of Commons against the planned murder of Hungarian Jewry. Even in Himmler's breast, Reitlinger concludes his chapter, the 'protests from the outer world, had rekindled. . . . his most characteristic dream that international charity could be harnessed to the waning German war effort. And to realize that dream there was the Eichmann commando, which, ever since its arrival in Hungary, had been bargaining with Jewish lives.'[3] With what brutality the Hungarian *gendarmerie*, who paved the way for the deportations almost on their own, as Eichmann's commando consisted of only a few men, acted towards their compatriots can be read in the statements of EDITH BRUCK. Her father was among those Jews who, when their families were being brutally ejected, displayed their decorations from the First World War in the unjustified hope that this could save them and their families from being delivered up to the Germans with whom they had once fought shoulder to shoulder.

Referring to the successful protest of the Slovakians against the deportations, Reitlinger poses the question: 'Can one really believe that Hitler was not in a position to suppress this government at his will?' The government, I may say, he could easily have suppressed, but not the Papal Nuncio, who in 1942 literally saved the remaining Jews in Slovakia, after some 52,000 had already been deported, only 284 of whom survived the war's end.

[1] Gerald Reitlinger, *ibid*.
[2] Gerald Reitlinger, *ibid*.
[3] Gerald Reitlinger, *ibid*.

The Vatican, the bishops in Germany and the Nuncios composed the only court of morals for which Hitler, after the unwelcome entry of America into the war, still had any respect. In 1940, after a conversation with Mussolini, he expressly forbade Rosenberg to provoke the Vatican in any way, and in August 1941 he had the euthanasia programme called off on account of the protests from the Church. 'It is probable', Reitlinger says, 'that on no question was Hitler's personal dictatorship more severely challenged than this one on which he acted with quite disgusting cowardice.'[1]

One understands his respect all the more, if one reads the following passage which appeared in November 1937 in *Angriff*, the 'daily organ of the German Worker's Front', and, later, as an introduction to a pamphlet printed in 1938 by the central publishing office of the NSDAP, with a portrait of Secretary of State Pacelli on the title page:

'Why the Vatican is important to us. The Vatican once again! Why exactly? Why make so much fuss about this ridiculous little patch of ground in the capital of the Roman Empire? Several readers of the National-Socialist Press ask these questions. Roosevelt, Ibn Saud, Chamberlain, Dimitroff, Herriot, above all the Duce, they are men of today, on whom depend the politics of the world and of the Reich. But these Roman prelates, these soft-stepping Nuncios and cardinals wreathed in incense – a lot of nonsense!

'This view is based on a false assumption. Chamberlain and Herriot, Roosevelt and Dimitroff are very influential men. Today they have their say in things. Tomorrow – no one will care twopence for them. But the men around the Pope, these silent prelates of the Roman Curia with their bejewelled pectoral crosses, they do not change. They are the same for decades. From time to time they are replaced by others of the same school, and professing the same politics, century after century. They rule nearly 400 million "faithful" throughout the world, they dispose of property throughout the world of an unimaginable extent, they have an influence over the press greater than any of the other Great Powers. . . . We may say, it is more important, for the building of the Community of the German people, to understand this eternal antagonist than any other worldly power. We National Socialists know, better than any, that it is the faith that moves mountains that makes History, not money, not economic laws, not arms alone. That is why we know how to

[1] Gerald Reitlinger, *ibid*.

recognize the significance of a power that has another faith. Lately we learned it afresh during the election struggle for the return of Austria into the Reich. Radio Moscow and Radio Vatican united to sabotage the elections and to pour contumely in the most unworthy fashion on the sensible attitude of the princes of the German Church. In vain! But they still will not admit their game is lost and are again bedevilling German politics from without and within. For this reason be still more on the watch!'

MONSIGNOR GIOVANNETTI, member of the Papal Secretariat of State, confirmed, in 1960 in his book *The Vatican and the War*, on the basis of many examples, 'the importance with which the Holy See was regarded during the war by all sides. In Switzerland in those days one could speak, not without justification, of a real battle between the two blocks of combatants for the conquest of the Vatican: it was a battle for the Pope – a diplomatic struggle for the Vatican's favour.'[1]

ROBERT E. SHERWOOD reports: 'As a measure for coping with the serious Catholic opposition to aid for the Soviet Union, Roosevelt decided to send Myron C. Taylor, his special Ambassador to Pope Pius XII, on another mission to Rome. Even this move raised difficult religious issues, for there were many Protestants, including some important Church leaders, who were deeply alarmed by any signs of collusion between the White House and the Vatican . . . There were some impatient people who thought that the President exaggerated the strength of Catholic sentiment, but it was his way to tread with extreme wariness wherever religious sensibilities were involved; he knew a lot more than his advisers did about these sensibilities.'[2] Harry Hopkins had already, in August 1941, written to the British Minister of Information:

'We are having some difficulty with our public opinion with regard to Russia. The American people don't take aid to Russia easily. The whole Catholic population is opposed to it, all the Nazis, all the Italians, and a lot of people who sincerely believe that Stalin is a great menace to the world. . . . The exhibition of the Russian Army has certainly made all of our military people look a little ill.

[1] Alberto Giovannetti, *ibid*.
[2] *The White House Papers*, Volume I, London.

Anglo-Saxons have a hard time believing that anyone can fight except themselves.'[1]

Hitler knew instinctively better than Roosevelt that the Pope was far from possessing the stature to correspond with his enormous credit in the world. Nevertheless he sent his Secretary of State for Foreign Affairs as Ambassador to the Holy See. And even the arrogant Ribbentrop found it advantageous, at the beginning of November 1943, when a few bombs of unknown origin fell in the Vatican gardens, to telephone Moellhausen, the Consul in Rome, personally to instruct him to persuade the Pope to make a complaint about the bombing. As he knew the Pope personally and also knew that he had not even condemned the deportation of the Jews, he added immediately that the Pope's usual 'vapourings' (*saüselnde Gerede*) would of course, be of no use, and that he must now speak with precision. The former pupil of the Jesuits, Goebbels, who was at least as realistic as Hitler in his estimation of the power of the Vatican, lamented on 9th November 1943 that the *Osservatore Romano* had taken 'such an unfortunately moderate attitude to the whole incident'! 'The Pope obviously does not want, for the time being, wholly to relinquish the idea of acting as mediator between the Reich and the hostile Western Powers.' The falling of a few hostile bombs on the Vatican, Goebbels had written earlier, 'is still a gigantic world sensation. The English have found themselves forced yet again, under pressure of comment in the neutral Press, to deny responsibility and to attempt to blame us'.[2] A few bombs, which injured no one, a gigantic world sensation? Werner Stephan, who was in the Press Section of the Ministry of Propaganda from 1933–45, states that when the Bishop of Münster, Count Galen, was preaching fire and slaughter against the Nazi crimes, Goebbels proposed himself as preacher in Münster, but then did not trust himself enough to go into the cathedral city: 'He would have had to come as executor of a warrant of arrest approved by Hitler against the contentious bishop. That would have been effective at a mass-meeting of Party members and susceptible fellow-travellers. But Goebbels was never able to forget the other side: Galen would have become a martyr, *who could have aroused millions to reckless attack on the totalitarian régime*. The Minister of Propaganda knew only too well the importance of this particular antagonist!'[3] Why,

[1] Robert E. Sherwood, *ibid.*
[2] *The Goebbels Diaries*, London, 1948.
[3] Werner Stephan, *Joseph Goebbels—Dämon einer Dictatur*, Stuttgart, 1949.

one may ask oneself again here, did not the Pope use this power to smooth the way for humanitarian action? Perhaps never before in history have so many human beings paid with their lives for the passivity of a single politician.

'The question of the absence of any threat to excommunicate the instruments of Hitler's extermination policies is a graver one and frankly I am inclined to think that the fact that the victims were Jews was one of the reasons why this threat was never made. Here again, however, neutrality and diplomatic immunity had become an obsession and I do not think this need have happened had there been a better Pope', wrote Gerald Reitlinger to the author.

In 1938 Goebbels warned his advisers at the Ministry against leaving the Church and in a speech to the heads of the propaganda bureaux emphasized that he had had all his own children baptized. Even during the war, he gave his secretary, to whom he wanted to give dictation on Sunday morning, time off to go to church. On Easter Sunday 1943 he entered in his diary: 'The S.D. has requisitioned the so-called Clemenskapelle from the Catholic Church in Berlin. Papen has written me a letter and asked me to restore this chapel to the Catholic Community. I am doing it at once and will call the S.D. to account for how they came to carry out an operation in Berlin which is completely opposed to my instructions.'[1]

Hitler and the most powerful men in his Government, Himmler, Göring and Goebbels, were too crafty to challenge the Vatican during the war by any persecution of the Church in Germany. Extremely disrespectful to the Church in his table-talk, Hitler (like Göring) wrote compliant letters to the protesting bishops, so that the opposition of the clergy might remain, as Friedrich Heer writes, 'within the framework of service to the divinely ordained legitimate authorities, within the framework of service to the Führer and Reichs Chancellor, at whose disposal the broad mass of the believing population were still being placed – for his crusade against Bolshevism – led into battle by ministers of both denominations'.[2]

That Hitler permitted the murder of certain unknown priests apparently did not seriously disturb his relations with the Vatican. On this point, Friedrich Heer again: 'Clergy and laymen, priests and politicians, who dared to think of and practise resistance could

[1] *The Goebbels Diaries.*
[2] Friedrich Heer, *ibid.*

not count on the support of their ecclesiastical leaders either in prison or on the scaffold. The Christian resistance to Hitler bore, therefore, by its very nature, from the beginning, the character of the singular, the out-of-the-ordinary, the unwelcome, the disobedient.'[1]

Only the spiteful, not too intelligent Bormann tended, during the war as well, to issue decrees which must have annoyed even the Vatican. But however much Hitler valued his 'most loyal party member', he called him sharply to heel when it was a case of escapades against the Church. The adviser on ecclesiastical affairs at the Foreign Office stated that Hitler himself had called off anti-ecclesiastical measures three times during the war.

Herr von Papen also reported on it: 'The sermons of the Bishop of Münster, Count Galen, went from hand to hand, and I discovered from Lammers that he had shown them to Hitler. It was therefore not difficult to approach him about this difficult situation. Hitler showed understanding for my explanations and, as had already happened before, pushed all the blame on to the party hotheads. He had, through Bormann, issued a firm edict that this "misconduct" was to be discontinued. He could not afford disturbances of internal peace at this moment.'[2]

This was not bluff, and the decree was carried out. Even HIMMLER, who once boasted to Frau von Weizsäcker, that 'we shall not rest till Christianity has been exterminated'[3] – even Himmler was cunning enough to concentrate his annihilation activities upon social groups whose extermination would not damage the relations of the Hitler State with the Holy See: Jews, Slavs, gypsies, Jehovah's Witnesses, Communists. The Nuncio in Berlin intervened repeatedly with Herr von Weizsäcker on behalf of persecuted Polish priests, sometimes with success. The Polish priests were also considered more dependable. While the Polish priests who opposed the régime were being sent to the concentration camps and on occasions horribly martyred, like Father Kolbe, for instance, GAULEITER FORSTER of Danzig recommended to the Führer that those Poles who were worth 'Germanizing' should not be looked after by priests from the Old Country, but in future by their own Polish priests. 'For under the pressure to which the Polish priests feel themselves to be exposed, they are susceptible to any influence

[1] Friedrich Heer, *ibid.*
[2] Franz von Papen, *ibid.*
[3] Ernst von Weizsäcker, *Memoirs*, London, 1951.

and even inquire at the end of every single week, at the district magistrate's office, what they shall preach about in church. It would be still better, in his opinion, to win the Polish bishop over to a close contact with the Gauleiter, so that through him the required subjects and instructions could be passed on to the priests. In this way it might be possible to assure peace and order through the country during this whole period of transition.'[1] Hitler cautioned against expecting too much from this, since Charlemagne had also attempted, without success, to use the bishops to win the Church over to a 'Germanic' political view.

The Italian Foreign Minister, COUNT CIANO, who said of Himmler, 'He is the only man who really has his finger on the pulse of the German people' – also did not appear to take Himmler's remarks about the Vatican and Pacelli, in 1939, to be bluff: 'Himmler spoke exhaustively about relations with the Church. The new Pope showed sympathy and a modus vivendi was held to be possible. I encouraged him in this direction, by indicating that an agreement between the Reich and the Vatican would also do a great deal for the popularity of the Axis.'[2] In fact, Himmler who, says Reitlinger, could neither tell a lie nor allow free rein to his imagination without making himself ridiculous, may have meant it quite honestly at the time, and perhaps not only out of opportunism. He had his mother buried in 1943 with church rites, allowed S.S. officers to take communion publicly and perhaps only spoke of the extermination of Christianity out of inner weakness and because it was appreciated in certain party circles. When in the winter of 1942 the secret gassing of Poles suffering from tuberculosis was under consideration, Himmler allowed himself to be restrained by the objection that the Church would not keep quiet about it and that 'the planned proceeding will provide excellent propaganda material for our enemies, not only as regards the Italian physicians and scientists, but also as regards all the Italian people, in consequence of their strong Catholic ties'.[3]

At any rate he knew what was unpopular: the extermination of the Jews and the mentally sick – and at first he desired neither the the one nor the other (which was later initiated under his leadership), simply because they were unpopular. He bowed eventually,

---

[1] Henry Picker, *Hitler's table talk 1941–1944*, London, 1953.

[2] Count Ciano, *Diary, 1939-43*, London, 1947.

[3] Alexander Mitscherlich and Fred Mielke, *Doctors of Infamy*, New York, 1949.

not without protest, to Hitler's command, and would doubtless have murdered priests as well had Hitler ordered him to. But he was saying, even after the plot of 20th July 1944 – whose failure (as far as Hitler's person was concerned) he deplored so much that his uneasy conscience towards the Führer would only be relatively appeased by his showing the utmost cruelty towards the conspirators – in 1944 he was still saying to his personal physician, whom he made no attempt to bamboozle: 'We should not have attacked the Church, because she is stronger than us. When I am dead, these priests must pray for my soul as well.'

Himmler has been, in my opinion, best caught by the historian Trevor-Roper, who as Allied Information Officer immediately after the end of war had the opportunity either of questioning the prominent persons later to be sentenced (or released) and their subordinates and secretaries, or of studying their statements at first hand:

'In a civilized world, it is true, such men are seldom tolerated; but if we look back at the cataclysmic periods of society, at periods of revolution and violent social change, his prototype is there. It is the Grand Inquisitor, the mystic in politics, the man who is prepared to sacrifice humanity to an abstract ideal. The Grand Inquisitors of history were not cruel or self-indulgent men. They were often painfully conscientious and austere in their personal lives. They were often scrupulously kind to animals, like the blessed Robert Bellarmine, who refused to disturb the fleas in his clothes. Since they could not hope for theological bliss (he said), it would be uncharitable to deny them that carnal refreshment to which alone they could aspire. But for men who, having opportunities of worshipping aright, chose wrong, no remedy was too drastic. So the faggots were piled and lit, and the misbelievers and their books were burnt, and those gentle old bishops went home to sup on white fish and inexpensive vegetables, to feed their cats and canaries, and to meditate on the Penitential Psalms, while their chaplains sat down in their studies to compose their biographies and explain to posterity the saintly lives, the observances and austerities, the almsgivings and simplicity, of those exemplary pastors, knowing (as Cardinal Newman said) that it is better that all humanity should perish eternally than that one single venial sin should be committed.

'Such a comparison perhaps seems fanciful; but nature is fanciful in designing the human mind, and times of revolution do throw up into positions of eminence men who, in stable periods, remain unobserved in gaols and monasteries. Himmler himself, everyone is agreed, was an utterly insignificant man, common, pedantic, and mean. He was greedy of money and incapable of thought; and yet he could not resist the temptation to speculate, to lose himself in the *O Altitudo*, and entangle himself in the theological minutiae, of the pure Nazi doctrine. Hitler himself, in one sense, was not a Nazi, for the doctrines of Nazism, that great system of teutonic nonsense, were to him only a weapon of politics; "he criticized and ridiculed the ideology of the S.S." (Speer), but to Himmler they were, every iota of them, the pure Aryan truth, which if a man keep not pure and undefiled, he shall without doubt perish everlastingly. With such a narrow pedantry, with such black-letter antiquarianism, did Himmler study the details of this sad rubbish, that many have supposed, but wrongly, that he had been a schoolmaster. He gave Speer the impression of being "half schoolmaster, half crank". During the war, while Goebbels was demanding total mobilization, Himmler was employing thousands of men and millions of marks in the projects of a religious maniac. In one department of his foreign intelligence service, a school of eager researchers studied such important matters as Rosicrucianism and Freemasonry, the symbolism of the suppression of the harp in Ulster, and the occult significance of Gothic pinnacles and top-hats at Eton. The S.S. scientific laboratories laboured infelicitously to isolate pure Aryan blood. An explorer was sent to Tibet to discover traces of a pure German race believed to preserve the ancient Nordic mysteries in those unvisited mountains. Throughout Europe excavators sought for relics of authentic German *Kultur*. When the German Army prepared hastily to evacuate Naples, Himmler's only demand was that it should not omit to carry with it the vast stone tomb of the last Hohenstaufen Emperor. Meanwhile, rich businessmen, if they wished to join his exclusive Circle of Friends, had to buy admission by subscribing perhaps a million marks to the *Ahnenerbe*, a "scientific" institute that made expensive researches into Aryan origins. Even in April 1945, when the whole Reich was tumbling in ruins, Himmler was contemplating the colonization of the Ukraine with a new religious sect recommended by his masseur, and in conversation with Count Bernadotte (having just maintained that he was the only sane man left in Germany), interrupted the discussion of war and peace to digress for an hour on runes. He was particularly interested in runes, the uninterpreted script of the Northmen of the Dark Ages. Studied with the eye of faith, they might, he believed, yield resemblance to Japanese ideograms, and thus prove the Japanese to be Aryans after all. (Speer)

'In such a character no grain of subtlety is discernible. Himmler was an elementary believer. His fanaticism was not the difficult birth of fear and weakness, nor his hesitation the consequence of doubt. Doubt had not yet nibbled at the infantile serenity of his cosmic acceptances.'[1]

Himmler's closest confidant, SCHELLENBERG, with whom he had discussed treason plans since 1942, without ever calling them, even in secret talks alone with Schellenberg, by their proper name, said something one may add here in confirmation: 'Himmler possessed the largest and best library on the Jesuit order and had studied this extensive literature for years deep into the night. Thus the S.S. organization was built by him on the principles of the Jesuit Order. The Constitutions and the Exercises of Ignatius Loyola served as foundations: the highest command was absolute obedience, the execution of every order without contradiction. Himmler himself, as Reichsführer of the S.S., was the general of the order. The structure of the leadership leant on the hierarchical order of the Catholic Church. At Paderborn in Westphalia he had had built a medieval fortress, the so-called Wevelsburg – it was, so to speak, the "S.S. Monastery", whither the general of the order summoned his secret consistory once a year. Here everyone who belonged to the highest ranks of the order had to undergo meditation and exercises in concentration. In the great assembly hall every member had a particular chair with a silver tablet on which his name was engraved. The roots of this mystical inclination of Himmler's may not least of all be traced back partly to his attitude to the Catholic Church, which one may describe as "love-hatred", and partly to his strict upbringing at his father's hands, with its harsh Catholic way of life, from which he escaped into an uncontrollable romantic fantasy. . . .'[2]

How did Hitler stand towards the Vatican during the war? On this point here are a few further sidelights. 'High Church dignitaries in Germany' writes PROFESSOR EUGEN KOGON, 'were never put into concentration camps by the Gestapo. When, on one occasion, a canon of the cathedral Chapter at Olmütz, who happened to be in

---

[1] H. R. Trevor-Roper, *Last Days of Hitler*, London, 1956.
[2] Walter Schellenberg, *Memoirs*, London, 1956.

Buchenwald, was elected Suffragan Bishop of Olmütz, the S.S. released him from the camp immediately.'[1]

The protests of the Bishop of Münster angered Hitler inordinately. He said that after the final victory, Galen would be 'stood up against a wall'. To others he declared with irony that if the Bishop had not managed by the end of war to get himself elected to the Collegium Germanicum in Rome, he would be settling accounts with him down to the last penny – *after* the war. He put a curb on his anger. Apart from his most intimate circles he disguised his aversion to the Church as long as the clergy let him do what he liked politically. Early on he had said to Papen that Rosenberg's *Myth of the Twentieth Century* was not worth the paper it was printed on. He had always simply ridiculed the notion of supplanting the Catholic Church by a new Church of Nazism. He believed the Church would decay of its own accord in a few hundred years. He wanted to accelerate the process, in that he aimed, after the war, to follow the example of the U.S.A. and to give only slender financial support to the Church, which in 1942 was still receiving some 900 million Reichsmarks from the State. The Church would then 'eat out of his hand'. Hitler forbade Heydrich's diabolical plan to send especially gifted Hitler youth leaders to priests' seminaries as apparently devout theologians, in order to break the clergy from within in years to come and inconspicuously to hand them over to the Party. Perhaps he was not sure of being able to keep these young agents permanently on his side.

There are numerous illustrations of how he and GOEBBELS and GÖRING stood during the war years towards the Church. Here is one from the Minister for Propaganda's Diary for 21st March 1942: 'Göring lately sent an extremely sharp letter to Bishop Galen in Münster and Bishop Berning in Osnabrück. He reminded them of their oath of fealty to the State and reprimanded them severely for their treasonable attitude. The answers to this letter happened to arrive while I was there. They are relatively subdued. The bishops are certainly trying to talk themselves out of it and to prove by a lot of technical verbiage that they have kept to their oaths. But this will not be accepted, of course. I suggest to Göring a fresh letter, particularly to Galen, charging him directly with having caused extreme unrest in the Reich by his claim that seriously wounded soldiers are being liquidated and pointing out that his utterances are being used by the English propaganda services against the

[1] Eugen Kogon, *The theory and practice of hell*, London, 1950.

National-Socialist régime. However, on the other hand, it cannot be denied that certain Party measures, above all the Crucifix-edict, have made anti-national propaganda all too easy for the Bishops. Göring complains strongly about it, too. He is quite frank and open towards the Christian creeds. He sees right through them and has no intention of taking them under his wing. On the other hand, he completely agrees with me that it is not possible to wrap up such a difficult and far-reaching problem in wartime. The Führer, too, has expressed this view to him, as he has done over and over to me. In this connection the Führer has declared that if his mother were still alive, she would doubtless be going to church today, and he neither could nor would prevent her from doing so.'[1]

This was at the zenith of Hitler's power, when all Europe apart from England was in his hands. A few months later he said to Himmler, who, relieved by Heydrich's assassination, wanted to proceed more cautiously 'in Church matters as well': 'If full churches will help me to keep the German people quiet, there can be no objection to it from the point of view of the war effort.' Hitler's opportunism went as far as to drag the Oberammergau Passion Play into the service of anti-Semitism. In 1942 he said: 'It is one of the most important tasks to protect the coming generations in Germany from a political destiny like that of 1918–33 and thus to keep the consciousness of the racial danger alive in them. For this reason alone the Oberammergau Passion Play must be preserved at all costs. For scarcely ever has the Jewish peril, exemplified in the ancient Roman world state, been so concretely illustrated as in the interpretation of Pontius Pilate in this passion play: he should appear as a Roman, racially and intellectually so developed that he seems to be a rock in the midst of all the swarm of Near-Eastern vermin. In the recognition of the enormous importance of this passion play for the enlightenment of all future generations, he should be an absolute Christian.'[2]

The figures given by Gerstein in his report,[3] although the author does not doubt their authenticity, have been replaced all through the play with smaller, and therefore more credible numbers which had already reached the Allied Press by this time. On 21st January

[1] *The Goebbels Diaries.*
[2] *Hitler's Table Talk.*
[3] See: Léon Poliakov and Josef Wulf, *Das Dritte Reich und die Juden*, Berlin, 1955 and the *Vierteljahresheften für Zeitgeschichte.*

1943 the representative in Berne of the Congress of World Jewry, Gerhard Riegner, reported that 6,000 Jews were being murdered daily in Poland. This report led to a public protest meeting in Madison Square Gardens in New York. By August 1942, Riegner had sent reports of Hitler's plan for extermination to Washington and had this information confirmed by November in four new, sworn statements to the Secretary of State, Sumner Welles. On 21st July 1942, on the occasion of a demonstration in Madison Square Gardens, Mr Roosevelt had written to Dr Wise: 'The American people not only sympathize with all victims of Nazi crimes, but will hold the perpetrators of these crimes to strict accountability in a day of reckoning which will surely come.' Meanwhile, on 30th September 1942 Hitler publicly repeated his 'promise' to 'exterminate' the Jews in Europe. On 17th December 1942 the Allies solemnly declared that the massacres would be expiated.

Gerstein's description of the gassing in Belzec has been supplemented here by details from the celebrated report of the engineer HERMANN FRIEDRICH GRAEBE, who witnessed, as manager of the Solingen building firm of Joseph Jung, a mass shooting of Jewish families on 5th October 1942 at Sdolbunov in the Ukraine (see Poliakov and Wulf *Das Dritte Reich und die Juden*). Executions like this in Gruben and Steinbrüchen, on the outskirts of Kiev, where 34,000 people were murdered on 28/29 September 1941, could not be kept secret from many members of the armed forces any more than from the local population, from among whom, in the Baltic and the Ukraine, volunteers were often recruited to carry out the man-hunts and the shootings under German guidance. Entries can be found in the diaries of ERNST JÜNGER about the terrible rumours which were reaching him: 6th March 1942, 31st December 1942, 21st April 1943. They were reaching most Europeans . . . in so far as these were strongly interested. On 27th November 1942 THOMAS MANN had also broadcast details over the B.B.C. in one of his impressive monthly eight-minute talks. In the same month a book came out in America which brought together the first twenty-five of Thomas Mann's broadcasts, begun in October 1940. In the talk of November 1941, included in the book, there were already reports of mass-murders of Jews and Poles. In January 1942, Mann reported further that Dutch Jews had been gassed. Details, the number of the victims and the place of the atrocities, Mauthausen, were later provided by the Dutch Government in exile, and once again by Thomas Mann in June

1942, in German, over the radio and in the book mentioned above. It was not yet known that Auschwitz was the centre of the annihilation operations, although the New York *New Popular Press* had already reported (14th July 1941 and 14th March 1942) on the 'torture hell' of Oswiecim (Auschwitz), and a bulletin of the Jewish Telegraph Agency in London of 13th December 1943 spoke of 580,000 Jews murdered there. Six months later (2nd June 1944) this agency estimated the number of Jews killed at Auschwitz up to the middle of 1942 at 800,000. As, however, it was Jews who were concerned, such announcements did not arouse the Christian belligerents on either side to anything like the indignation that they should have done. This was reserved for the daily events of the war. A people at war has enough troubles of its own – this explains a lot. Without question one may completely believe Hitler's promise, given quite publicly, to 'exterminate' the Jews. And there is also no doubt at all that every personality of standing and influence beyond the German frontiers as well as inside Germany itself, knew that the extermination was being carried out, continuously and, so to speak, legally, and that the deportation trains led to annihilation. In October 1943 one could, for example, read in America that 4,000 children, aged between 2 and 14, had been sent, sixty to a truck, from France to the East, separated from their parents and without being told their 'destination'.

On the 22nd June 1943, the Ambassador in Washington of the Polish Government in exile, JAN CIECHANOWSKI, received Lieutenant JAN KARSKI, who had been sent for the second time to London and America as an agent of the anti-communist underground authorities in Poland to give information and eyewitness reports to the appropriate civil and military authorities. Karski was also received by the President and had the opportunity of giving Roosevelt 'a picture of the concentration camps in which mass murders were already the order of the day. He told about Oswiecim (Auschwitz), Majdanek, Dachau, Oranienburg, of the women's camp at Ravensbrück, and gave the President a nerve-shattering description of how he himself, disguised as a policeman, had visited the two camps at Belzec and Treblinka, where Jews were being gassed in railway trucks. "I am convinced, Mr President," he continued, "that the reports on the situation of the Jews do not exaggerate. Our underground authorities are completely convinced that the Germans wish to wipe out the entire Jewish population. Reliable reports from our agents state that up to the day when I left Poland,

1,800,000 Jews had been murdered in Poland alone. . . . The leaders of our underground organizations have instructed me to inform the British and American military authorities that these mass exterminations can only be halted or at least slowed down if retaliatory measures are put in hand immediately, and if, after millions of leaflets have been dropped which clearly explain to the Germans that they will be bombed as a punishment for the annihilation of the Jews, a mass bombardment of German towns is actually carried out." '[1]

In actual fact, Allied bombers had, in the summer of 1943, dropped leaflets over Germany which had told of the extermination of the Jews, and given several details, such as the discovery of the mass graves in Kharkov. Youth leaders, that is 12- to 14-year-olds, were often detailed to pick up and burn the leaflets. Probably Karski's description, among other and appreciably earlier reports, moved the President, through his special envoy Myron C. Taylor and other channels, to beg Pius XII to pronounce ex cathedra against Hitler's crimes. The former Polish Ambassador to Washington (in a letter to the author), in answer to the question whether he had transmitted Karski's report to the Vatican, said that he had not only passed on this information to the apostolic delegate in Washington (now the Secretary of State, Cardinal Cicognani), but also to the American Congress, to the Cardinals, the Bishops and the Universities – and he continued repeatedly to give this information to the people mentioned until he was recalled on 5th July 1945. Even before Karski's arrival, from May 1941 onwards, Ambassador Ciechanowski had done everything within his power to acquaint Washington with what was happening.

When PROFESSOR GOLO MANN[2] maintains that the Allies knew nothing of the gas chambers in Austria and Poland during the war – his father had already made public accusation of gassings in Mauthausen by 1942 – he is continuing, unconsciously of course, the attempts of the English and the Americans to find an excuse for the disregard with which for years they had treated the most reliable information about the mass murders. Their horror and rage when they broke into the camps in 1945 sprang not least of all from the blame they felt attached to themselves. Who can count the Jews who fell victim to the 'Final Solution' (not that this excuses it, of course),

---

[1] Jan Ciechanowski, *Defeat in Victory*, New York, 1947.
[2] See Golo Mann, *Deutsche Geschichte des 19. und 20. Jahrhunderts*, Frankfurt am Main, 1960.

because they were heartlessly and needlessly refused entry to another country? – a tragedy in itself. When in January 1944 a half-Jew told the Berlin journalist Ursula von Kardorff of the 'terrible judgement' that the Allies were to inflict on the Germans at the war's end, she wrote in her diary: 'To be sure, we have piled up terrible guilt upon ourselves, but so have the others, the Americans and the English, who made entry so difficult for the escaping Jews. They have no cause to play the judge, like Pharisees. Bärchen asks: "Where were the others then, when the Jews had to leave us on the night of November 30th, 1938? Who made immigration so hard for them that many of them gave up and then, after war broke out, were delivered up to an inhuman existence?" She told me how she had tried again and again, without success, to find a way for a Jewish friend whose brother was already in America, to emigrate, how she had gone from Consulate to Consulate armed with letters of introduction from diplomats and influential journalists. For hours she stood in a queue in front of the American consulate, three days one after the other, and then an American secretary there said to her, quite astonished, that she could not understand how a German could side with a Jewess, and anyway, wasn't it forbidden?

'I do not know whether we convinced Dr Meier; he is desperate, because his Jewish father starved to death in a camp near Darmstadt. That he hopes we shall be punished, I cannot take amiss. Outside the best are falling, for a victory which I fear – for if Hitler wins, we are lost. And if he does not win?'[1]

In 1955 Professor Mann wrote of the last months of Carl Goerdeler,[2] in the winter of 1944: 'One is ashamed of one's own attitude during these months, ashamed of Germany, of the Allies. . . .' And, about Goerdeler's famous letter to Kluge[3]: 'If

[1] Ursula von Kardorff, *Berliner Aufzeichnungen aus den Jahren 1942 bis 1945*, Munich, 1962.

[2] *Carl Friedrich Goerdeler* (1884–1945), Reich Price Control Commissioner 1931–3; Mayor of Leipzig, resigned in protest against anti-Semitic measures of the Nazi Government; principal civilian leader of the German underground; arrested after plot of July 20, 1944; condemned to death and executed at Plötzensee after protracted torture, February 2, 1945.

[3] *Günther von Kluge* (1882–1944), Field-Marshal; Army Group Commander in Russia and France; in correspondence with resistance circle from November 1942; committed suicide in August 1944 to avoid arrest by the Gestapo.

In July 1943 Goerdeler wrote to Kluge begging the Field-Marshal, in view of the certainty of Allied invasion in the following year, of the inevitable advance of the Red Army into the frontiers of the Reich and of the destruction by bombing of the cities of Germany, to abandon his customary hesitation and join the

the Anglo-Americans had only known then that such letters were being written by important men in Germany. If they had only taken any serious trouble to find out, and drawn any serious conclusions from it.'[1]

In the case of the extermination of the Jews they did not even have to take trouble: they were told over and over again till they did not want to listen any more. Ambassador Ciechanowski writes, about the summer of 1942: 'The incredible details of the extermination system practised by Hitler's gangs were still for the most part unknown to the Americans. But thanks to the system they had perfected of daily contact with the underground organizations, the Polish Government was thoroughly informed of all these happenings. From the information I received, and continually passed on to the American Government and the Press, and spoke of in numerous lectures in American towns, there emerged a clear picture of Hitler's monstrous project of wiping out the Polish Jews, and Jews of other countries who were being deported to Poland. The underground resistance movement urgently demanded that our Government should broadcast these facts to our allies, and above all to the American Government. General Sikorski was busy doing so in London, and I, in Washington, was passing on his requests to the President, the State Department, and the Chiefs of Staff. . . .'[2]

Ciechanowski gives in addition the most macabre description of the desperate search for missing Polish officers – mostly missing without trace – and reports the fact that a quarter of a million Polish Jews had been deported to Siberia. He then tells how he had already tried in 1942 in person to get Roosevelt to institute reprisals and a protest of the Great Powers against the massacres, but in vain. . . . 'In general, at that time, one could not help being struck by a widespread ignorance of the barbarities which the Germans were committing, and by a quite definite friendliness towards the Germans. These became suddenly apparent in many of my relations

---

resistance forces in assassinating Hitler. Further, emboldened by hints from a Swedish source that Himmler had been putting out feelers for peace, he wrote: 'I can also make Herr Goebbels and Herr Himmler your allies if you desire, for even these two men have long realized that with Hitler they are doomed.' See Gerhard Ritter, *Goerdeler und die deutsche Widerstandsbewegung*, Bonn, 1954, and J. W. Wheeler-Bennett, *The Nemesis of Power*, London, 1953, for exhaustive surveys of the July plot. Tr.

[1] Golo Mann, article in *Merkur*, 1955.
[2] Jan Ciechanowski, *ibid*.

with American officials and representatives of public opinion in America . . . and even officials who possessed the means to acquire a thorough knowledge of the facts hesitated to believe that the Germans could be capable . . . of such cruelty.'[1]

Ciechanowski gives three reasons for the fact that the popularity of Germany was appreciably on the increase in America in 1944, a whole year after Karski's visit to the President: 'The more certain the final victory became, the more the innate sportsmanship of the American people asserted itself.' Secondly: 'The elections were approaching. The numerically strong and staunchly organized group of Americans of German origin had a certain influence on the elections.' Thirdly: 'The feeling of friendliness to the Germans increased because the fear of Russia and Communism was growing. The idea that Germany, after being purged of National Socialism, could be used as a convenient barrier against Soviet expansion was gaining more and more supporters.'[2] It is dishonest to close one's eyes to the fact that the Jews as a whole could not hope to receive from any nation, except possibly Denmark, nor from the Vatican nor the Red Cross, the same support that was given to non-Jewish victims of persecution. That is a terrible truth. Herr von Kessel, who spoke in Weizsäcker's favour at Nuremberg, was asked in court: 'As you worked for some considerable time both with the International Red Cross *and* in the Vatican, I would like to ask you for a comprehensive opinion on two questions. Did these two great humanitarian organizations ever make a protest, on grounds of principle, to Hitler against the anti-Jewish measures?'

Answer : No, neither.

Question : Can you tell us definitely whether such a plan was ever under consideration by the Red Cross?

Answer : Yes, a member of the Committee of the International Red Cross met me one day in Geneva and said: 'Something terrible has happened. A woman member of the Committee is demanding that we make an official protest against the persecution of the Jews in Germany. How are we to do it? Switzerland is enclosed by National-Socialist-ruled territory. If we protest, Hitler will revoke the Geneva Convention, and we will have to abandon our entire work, both for the Allied and the German prisoners-of-war, for the occupied territories, the poor and the civil internees. We are in a dreadful position.' A few days later I met the same man again and he said: 'Thank God

[1] Jan Ciechanowski, *ibid*.
[2] Jan Ciechanowski, *ibid*.

it was finally decided after hours of negotiations *not* to protest officially. It is a fearfully difficult decision for all of us, but at least we can go on working.'

Would the Red Cross have marked time quite so cleverly if it had been told, for example, that shot-down Allied bomber pilots, who had dropped incendiaries on civilians in Germany, had been killed like the Jews – as they were in Japan?

On 13th December 1942, GOEBBELS noted: 'The question of the persecution of the Jews in Europe is in great favour with the English and the Americans and is being treated in the grand manner. . . .'[1] On 14/15th December: 'Jewish rabbis in London are organizing a huge protest meeting under the banner "England Awake!". . . . The Jews in London are having a day of mourning because of the cruelty of which we are apparently guilty on their account in Poland. In Sweden and Switzerland feeling towards us has cooled extraordinarily.'[2]

EMANUEL RINGELBLUM, in his chronicle of the Warsaw ghetto, has recorded 26th June 1942 as the 'Great Day' on which for the first time the extermination of the Jews in Poland was made public to all the world: 'This morning the English radio reported on the fate of the Polish Jews. . . . For months we have suffered, because the world has remained deaf and dumb in the face of our unexampled tragedy. We accused public opinion in Poland and the negotiators, who had contact with the Polish government in exile.' So writes the chronicler who was later killed in March 1944, with his family. 'Why did they not publish it to the world, that the Jews in Poland were being wiped out? Did they keep silent on our tragedy, so that their own would not be overshadowed? . . . Today's broadcast drew up the balance sheet: the number of the Jews so far killed was put at a figure of 700,000.'[3]

LÉON POLIAKOV, the historian living in Paris, who translated Ringelblum's narrative into French, likewise claims (in a letter to

[1] *The Goebbels Diaries.*
[2] *Ibid.*
[3] Quoted from *Der Spiegel*, 1960

the author) that 'in June 1942 the information about the destruction of the Jews in Poland was also officially conveyed to the Vatican'.

About the extremely extensive activity of the Vatican's information and reporting services for the benefit of refugees and prisoners-of-war during the years 1939–46, there is an instructive *Aperçu sur l'oeuvre du Bureau d'Informations du Vatican*, issued in 1948 by the Tipografia Poliglotta Vaticana. In books about Pius XII and the Vatican in general one reads that the Holy See is the best-informed institution in the world. Thus BERNARD WALL: 'Priests are situated in places where no secret service agent of any of the great powers has ever been. They meet people of every class of society. As celibates and lacking family responsibilities they can devote themselves whole-heartedly to their work. . . . There are plenty of priests behind the Iron Curtain. There are priests in prisons and concentration camps still, and others who have been liberated only recently. All this information reaches Rome, where it is carefully docketed and filed. . . . Hitler's attack on Russia was no great surprise to the Vatican: it seems as if the Jesuits had received news of the preparations in very good time through the Polish Father Provincial of their order.'[1]

As the Pope's best informant during the war, one may point to the Archbishop of New York, CARDINAL SPELLMAN, who, as American military chaplain, travelled all over the world, stopping off frequently in Rome. HERBERT TICHY wrote in 1949 in his book on the Vatican[2]: 'Probably the Vatican had at the time – not only through Spellman's efforts – astonishingly accurate knowledge of most of the secrets of the warring powers. In February 1943, that is two and a half years before Hiroshima, the Pope made a reference to the atomic bomb in an address to the Papal Academy. "We know," he said, "that a uranium atom, when bombarded with neutrons, divides, setting free two or more further neutrons, which, in their turn, destroy further uranium atoms, and thus produce a wave of energy. One cubic metre of uranium-oxide can move 100,000 tons to a height of 27 kilometres. . . . It is important that the liberation of such unimaginable power should be chemically controlled, in order to prevent the destruction of our planet."

Weizsäcker, in his memoirs, implies that not only Ribbentrop, but Hitler too, had had him sent to the Vatican in order to get rid of

---

[1] Bernard Wall, *Report on the Vatican*, London, 1956.
[2] Herbert Tichy, *Auf einem Hügel der Ewigen Stadt*, Vienna, 1949.

him. After the war that was the most convenient version; not, however, the most credible. Hitler was disturbed about rumours that Mussolini was not going to be able to last much longer. In fairness to Mussolini, Hitler had forbidden a security service to operate in Italy. He hardly trusted his Ambassador to the Quirinal to be able to control the situation diplomatically or to provide the necessary information. From this point of view, it was reassuring for him to send Weizsäcker to Rome as well. But for another reason too: no one who reads how deeply preoccupied Goebbels was by the idea, which he put before Hitler, whether 'something might not be managed' with this Pope from the point of view of peace negotiations, will believe that Weizsäcker was transferred to the Holy See simply to play *boccia*. He himself may, by the end of 1943, have already made up his mind never to negotiate a compromise between Hitler's Germany and the Western Powers, but only to act as a negotiator for a Germany without Hitler. To a confidant in Germany he wrote on 29th December 1943: 'Carl Friedrich is very well. He could, of course, be a lot more active: and I have told him so. But naturally Carl stands in his way, or at any rate in the way of the success of his efforts. What is one to do?' By 'Carl Friedrich' he meant the Pope, by 'Carl' Hitler.

PROFESSOR LEIBER says: 'Herr von Weizsäcker, particularly during the time he held the post of ambassador, was understandably extremely reticent on the subject of what was happening in Germany.'[1]

This ties in with what I was told by one of the few surviving confidants of ADMIRAL CANARIS, who had spoken to the Vatican twice during the war, on, among other things, the extermination of the Jews. In doing so he was exceptional. Most exponents of resistance inside Germany – including Weizsäcker – consciously avoided describing to the world the extent of the crimes committed in the name of Germany, so as not to destroy all readiness to compromise abroad. Indeed, one was in the meantime to learn that the world identified the Germans and the Nazis, but even so, for Germany to remain a power to negotiate with, the fronts would still have to be held after Hitler was gone. It was therefore necessary that no more

---

[1] Article in *Stimmen der Zeit*.

should become known about the atrocities than was already known anyway, if Germany was to remain a power to be regarded as at all worthy to negotiate with.

If the English and Americans are still being reproached today for showing the opposition circles in Germany insufficient co-operation, this takes too little account of the refinement with which Heydrich and Schellenberg, in the late summer of 1939, deceived and damaged the British Secret Service over the 'Venlo Incident': how could the English have any confidence a second time in plans for the downfall of Hitler made by high-ranking German officers?

Weizsäcker's many-faceted, unfathomable character is, from an artistic point of view, one of the most fascinating in contemporary history – it would be irresponsible to treat this man as a secondary character in a play, which is why it is better to leave him out altogether.

He was one of the first to hear, through Canaris, about the mass murder of the Jews: he was also, later, on terms of the most intimate confidence with the Chief of Intelligence, who must certainly be reckoned one of the four or five best-informed Germans of the Hitler era.

TROTT ZU SOLZ said in front of Freisler, when he knew Weizsäcker to be safely in the Vatican, that the Secretary of State had been the leader of the Wilhelmstrasse conspiracy against Hitler. Yet despite these and many other indications of his resistance activities, Weizsäcker often acted quite without mercy: for instance, when the Swedish envoy pleaded with him to be allowed to bring into Sweden Norwegian Jews who were being taken to Auschwitz, Weizsäcker reported to Ribbentrop that he had refused even to discuss the matter. Poliakov and Wulf have printed documents of September and October 1942, according to which Weizsäcker forced the Hungarian ambassador to agree to the 'resettlement' in the east of Hungarian Jews likely to 'cause panic': there is also the fact that Luther, the motive power in the Foreign Office behind the deportation of Jews from the various countries of Europe, always laid plans for the 'steps to be undertaken by us' before Weizsäcker for permission.

Weizsäcker himself wrote that he had, so as to leave no stone unturned, already aroused Ribbentrop to a general protest against such cruelty by the winter of 1941, when he learned of the massacres. 'What came of it, I did not discover. For me the whole Jewish problem was absorbed in the greater general problem: how could we most quickly make peace without Hitler?'[1] To know that the Jews in the east were being massacred en masse: to instigate a protest against it, and, when it remained unanswered, not to take the question up again for two whole years, while he was involved in deportation orders to the east or even forcing foreign embassies to load up their Jewish populations – is this on the face of it understandable?

'To be misunderstood,' says Weizsäcker, haughtily summarizing his activity in Berlin, 'is one of the risks of the diplomatic profession. To anyone who could not understand me automatically, I had nothing further to say.'[2]

'In recommendations after September 1938 I never said otherwise than that Hitler was to be got rid of,' wrote Weizsäcker. But he also said, and not to twelve-year-old Hitler Youth members but to diplomats returned from America, on 20th May 1942, after the fall of Beck, in the Kaisersaal in Frankfurt: 'If you have survived the withering fire of enemy propaganda lies across the Atlantic, and if you have observed how our enemies are waging a war of words, then you will now realize that we in Germany are waging a war of action. Here you will experience no "American way of life": here the good old German way of taking care of things is still paramount. With us there are no discussions in committee. With us it is the "leadership principle". Here you will not find "fireside chats": you will find rather initiative, power of decision, command, aggressiveness and blows against the enemy. . . . For us, only what the Führer orders is valid: his will is our will, his belief in victory our belief in victory.'

Already by September 1941 Ribbentrop had let Weizsäcker know he wanted him transferred to the Holy See. When, a year after the speech quoted above, he presented his credentials in Rome, because the Vatican in his opinion offered 'the best opportunities for influence and at the same time a good look-out post', the Curia had become 'quite uninteresting in general to our leaders'. One has every right to doubt this, as long as the contents of the conversations which Pius XII had with Hitler's Ambassador remain 'after the good custom of the Curia' confidential. At any rate Goebbels did *not* look on the appointment to the Holy See as a sinecure, and Weizsäcker himself said, on his farewell visit to Hitler, that he was going

[1] Ernst von Weizsäcker, *ibid*.
[2] Ernst von Weizsäcker, *ibid*.

to some extent into enemy territory. One can gather from Goebbels's diaries that, at this time in particular, he was far from uninterested in the Vatican. He told Weizsäcker he would not entrust this job with the Holy See even to himself. Weizsäcker replied: 'But *I* would entrust it to you,' 'and our conversation ended in malicious laughter on both sides.'[1] Even the admonitory remarks of the Pope at their first meeting, when Weizsäcker presented his credentials, 'contrary to the usual practice, were never published'. At least Weizsäcker created the impression that there was a great deal more to it than appears on the surface.

The Jesuit father, PROFESSOR LEIBER, a close confidant of the Pope, has written an article in *Stimmen der Zeit* for March 1961 on 'Pius XII and the Jews in Rome'. The occasion of his historical research was the publication of the book of photographs, *Der gelbe Stern*, in which was reproduced Weizsäcker's letter of 28th October 1943 (see the end of the play). Here are one or two amplifications of Professor Leiber's article:

It was in extenuation that Weizsäcker wrote: 'Since further actions against the Jews in Rome are no longer to be carried out.' It is not only Father Leiber who states that the hounding of the Jews 'continued until the withdrawal of the Germans from Rome on 4th June 1944'. Pius XII therefore had not betrayed a momentary weakness, but had for nine months silently looked on while the victims were 'herded to their death from the very shadow of St. Peter's'.

One should examine the strategic situation then obtaining: by 16th October 1943 the Americans had already crossed the Volturno, on 13th October the Badoglio Government had declared war on Hitler. It was not the case that the Vatican still had anything seriously to fear from Hitler. The author was repeatedly told, in the Vatican, that no one then had seriously imagined Hitler would be so stupid as to occupy the Vatican and remove Pius XII to a sort of Avignon-like captivity, whatever rumours to this effect may have fired several harmless souls to think at the time. A suggestion that the Curia should emigrate to South America for the duration of the occupation of Rome was not seriously considered for one minute by the Vatican. Hitler, airing to his closest circle his rage and disappointment at the arrest of Mussolini – so shortly after he had had a meeting with him – did consider for a moment the idea, 'when arresting the responsible men in Rome, not to neglect the Vatican'.

[1] Ernst von Weizsäcker, *ibid*.

It was reported to Headquarters that the Vatican was involved in a fever of diplomatic activity. Himmler, as Schellenberg reports, professed himself 'most strongly opposed to it', as did Goebbels and Ribbentrop. Goebbels writes, 'I do not believe it is necessary to break into the Vatican; on the contrary, I consider such a measure would affect other measures taken by us disastrously throughout the world.'

On the same day Goebbels added to this entry in his diary: 'At all events, everyone, including the Führer, is now entirely agreed that the Vatican must be excepted from any measures taken by us.' Before the Germans occupied Rome in September, the Vatican asked officially, through Weizsäcker, whether its rights would be respected. Hitler sent an affirmative answer to this inquiry. After the entry of the Germans, the Town Commandant, General Stahel, made contact with the Vatican, and mounted sentries who 'were under orders to prevent any infringement of Vatican territory'. It was probably also difficult for refugees to break through this armour round the Vatican without being registered.

RAHN, German Ambassador to the Quirinal, who in his memoirs considerably exaggerates the importance of his efforts to protect the Vatican from Hitler, closes his report to the Führer–HQ on the situation in occupied Rome: ' "I forgot, by the way, to report that I have, through General Stahel, concluded a special little concordat with the Vatican." Bormann, the bitter enemy of the Catholic Church, went up in the air, and Hitler looked at me with surprise. In the manner of a commercial brochure I then reported on the uses of the Vatican for restoring peace and order in Rome, for which our only two available reserve companies would never have been sufficient. For the purpose I had naturally been compelled to undertake that the person of the Pope, the Roman clergy, and the property of the Church were protected whatever happened. "It is a business deal," I concluded, "and the balance is at least as much in our favour as in the Vatican's." I seemed to have struck the right note. Hitler said: "Yes, the gentlemen in Rome understand business deals." '[1]

Most of the Italian Jews, warned in time, had fled to the south, to the American troops. Under the Papal Relief Programme, the League of St Raphael organized the emigration of 1,500 Jews to America, and 4,000 were hidden in monasteries and convents.

Professor Leiber writes that Weizsäcker's letter to the Foreign

[1] Rudolf Rahn, *Ruheloses Leben*, Düsseldorf, 1949.

Office takes on another aspect seen against the backdrop of these measures of assistance. That Herr von Weizsäcker found the deportations 'painful' is painful to read. The satisfaction at the Pope's not protesting appears so clearly in his letter that no one would suspect the sender to be a fighter in the resistance against Hitler. Who in Berlin would have suspected Weizsäcker – who in addition devotes not a line in his memoirs to the deportation of the Jews from Rome – even if he had made play with the 'indignation' of the Pontiff, and created the impression that Pius XII would come out with extreme decisiveness against the butchers? But he did exactly the opposite.

By his ironical allusion to the heartless rubbish in the *Osservatore Romano* he so completely pacified Berlin that the Jews were hunted in Rome for eight more months, whenever the fancy took the Germans to do so. The letter also duly emphasizes the ambassador's diplomatic skill in his handling of the Holy Father. It is all the harder to grasp, therefore, why Weizsäcker sent this letter to Berlin at all, when one reads that ten days earlier, when the arrests began, he had written straight away to the Foreign Office that the Curia was most upset, that the Pope would be forced to abandon his reserve, and that enemy propaganda would incite 'discussion between ourselves and the Curia'. Why did he later find it necessary expressly to remove Berlin's last trace of uneasiness about Pius XII?

It seems only too easy to insinuate that he wanted to show Berlin the importance of his position as Ambassador to the Vatican, since this swing of opinion in the Vatican must of necessity be ascribed to his influence. But is there any other explanation? – since it is assumed that Weizsäcker really did not want the deportations. Already in the autumn of 1941, Canaris had informed him of the mass-murder of the Jews – for which reason he can hardly have had any belief himself in his own version of 'used for labour in Italy itself'. In addition he followed the Allied news bulletins. It was known that it was women and children who had been taken away rather than men. For labour? It is most improbable he did not know that in the order for the arrest of the Jews which S.S.-Führer Kappler had received from Berlin the 'liquidation' of the Jews was mentioned expressly. Moellhausen, consul at the Embassy to the Quirinal, who had been reprimanded for using the word 'liquidate' in an official telegram, told Weizsäcker's closest colleague, the Embassy secretary, von Kessel, about his intervention on behalf of the Jews, and they were both relieved at the thought that the Jews could buy their freedom with ransom money and so would at least 'be physically spared'.

In court at Nuremberg, VON KESSEL, to whom Weizsäcker had certainly spoken on the subject, said: 'If [the Pope] made no protest, then it was because he had, with justification, told himself: if I protest, it will drive Hitler to fury. In this way not only are the Jews not assisted, but one must reckon with the fact that they may then be persecuted all the more. . . .' During the 1943 arrests von Kessel was of a different opinion. Today, in the Vatican, it is said that he was the one certain strong anti-Nazi in the German Embassy. He acted accordingly, along with GERHARD GUMPERT, the Legation secretary in the financial division of the German Embassy to the Quirinal. Gumpert agreed with von Kessel that the Father-General of the Salvatoriani, PANCRAZIUS PFEIFFER, should take a letter to the German Town Commandant, in which 'for the first time since the outbreak of war' a personal statement by the Pope would be threatened. This letter was immediately signed by Bishop Hudal, rector of the German Catholic Church in Rome, without reference to higher authority. Hudal asked 'that the arrests in Rome and the surrounding district should be immediately discontinued: I am afraid, if not, the Pope will publicly protest against them, which will inevitably be used by anti-German propagandists as a weapon against us Germans'. This letter alone – for there is none like it from the pen of an Italian bishop to put beside it – should have been enough to protect Bishop Hudal (now living in complete retirement at Grottaferata) from being calumniated simply because he allowed himself, like almost all the clergy, to be bamboozled by Hitler at the beginning. He also hid Jews in the monastery dell'Anima.

Gumpert quoted from this letter when applying to the Foreign Office to go to Berlin. Weizsäcker, too, referred to it in his letter to Berlin of 17th October 1943. He did not, however, as Gumpert said on his behalf, 'emphatically demand the immediate suspension of the deportations of the Jews'.

There is, as was said before, no polite expression for the fact that ten days later Weizsäcker also sent his pacifying letter to the Foreign Office.

He did in fact 'advise' the Vatican in Hitler's favour. Gumpert reported on it at Nuremberg: 'When I later said good-bye to Weizsäcker, because I had been transferred to an Embassy in Northern Italy, he began to talk about those events again, and said, word for word: "That was a messy business all right." ("Das war wieder eine Schweinerei.") After the reports they had got cold feet in Berlin and suspended the deportations at once. He added: "I can tell you, too, that at the time I spoke very confidentially to Montini (then Under-secretary of State)[1] and informed him, that any utterance of the Pope's would only have the effect of making the deportations all the more thorough. I know the reaction of these people to us. Montini was very understanding, by the way." '

This is a quagmire: Weizsäcker's closest colleague, von Kessel, is trying to force the Vatican out of its reserve. When at least one German Bishop intervenes, Weizsäcker appropriates his request temporarily as his own. He threatens Berlin with a protest statement from the Pope, in which he clearly sees, therefore, a deterrent. At the same time, however, he tells the Pope's closest colleague that an utterance by the Holy Father would only have the effect of 'making the deportations all the more thorough'. And Montini, or the Pope, is only too glad to hear it – although they both know, as every child in Rome knows, that the first Jews have already been herded into the trucks; that the raids will continue one way and another; and that Weizsäcker's words are therefore – to put it mildly – unnecessary.

When the following week-end (25/26th October) the *Osservatore Romano* finally announced that the 'Pope's universal and fatherly work of assistance . . . knows no frontiers', the first 615 Romans had already arrived at Auschwitz the day before, and 468 of them were already in the crematoria.

It is Father Leiber's contention that Pius XII did not protest because he thought 'more comprehensively'. When Professor Leiber reports, for example, that the deportations in Rumania were discontinued after the intervention of the Nuncio there, that only confirms the main thesis of the play: that Hitler, in fact, drew back from the annihilations the moment the high German clergy (in the case of the euthanasia programme) or the Vatican, represented by the Nuncios, intervened to any considerable extent. Hitler then drew back – in every single case. For this reason it does not carry the smallest conviction when Leiber infers that the support of these isolated measures of assistance by a powerful word from the foremost Christian of the world 'would in all probability have doomed (these attempts) to failure'.[2] On the contrary.

In addition one should not, in reading an essay otherwise so objective, fall prey to the impression that the S.S. terrorized the

[1] Now Pope Paul VI.
[2] Article in *Stimmen der Zeit*, March 1961.

clergy. The S.S. knew very well that many monasteries and convents were hiding-places for Jews and other refugees. They even knew that a radio set was being operated from the Lateran by General Bencivenga, and that an American agent had sent wireless messages for a time from the Deutsches Haus on the Campo Santo Teutonico. Despite this obvious misuse of clerical buildings, Kappler took care not to break into extraterritorial properties. Of course, there were exceptions to this rule: PROFESSOR AUGUST BEA, Rector of the Pontifical Bible Institute, complained to Weizsäcker that in October 1943 five S.S. men had looked for a 'formerly Jewish' servant in his Institute.

The worst and, in its consequences, most serious disturbance of Vatican property, however, is to be laid at the door of the Italian fascist militia, under their brutal robber-chief Koch, who was hanged after the war. These Italians were, in fact, responsible for the attack on the Monastery of San Paolo-fuori-le-mure, which Father Leiber ascribes to the German S.S. At all events, in the same month that the foreign Press reported the atrocities in Rome and, perhaps in desperation over their disappointment at the passivity of the Pope, invented the ridiculous idea of the Pope's being, so to speak, held prisoner by the Germans, the Curia published an official communiqué in the *Osservatore Romano*. 'This recognized and acknowledged that our troops had respected the Curia and Vatican City,' wrote Weizsäcker with great satisfaction. 'In this communiqué we promised to maintain a similar attitude in the future.'[1]

Herr von Weizsäcker could not have placed his answer to the world press on the indignation of the Allies about the events in Rome better than in the *Osservatore Romano* in the month of Terror, October 1943.

Weizsäcker stayed in office to avoid worse things befalling: Pius XII was silent, as Leiber says, to avoid worse things befalling – how can one actually say such a thing, when it is impossible to imagine worse than the worst, the most comprehensive manhunt in Western history? Leiber and Giovannetti protest that the Pope was not able to attack in detail the actions and misdeeds of one warring power, since that would have been exploited for propaganda purposes by the others. But about any occurrence that touched him at all nearly, Pius XII made extremely well-aimed and succint comments. For example, he wrote personally to Roosevelt about the bombing of Rome and protested against the destruction of San Lorenzo. He also

[1] Ernst von Weizsäcker, *ibid*.

protested against the exceptionally cowardly and senseless bomb-throwing in the Via Rosella, in which thirty-three German soldiers, most of them South Tyroleans not even voluntarily wearing Hitler's uniform, and ten Italians, including six children, lost their lives. But why did he not then condemn the equally criminal act of vengeance for this attack, namely, the murder of 335 hostages, or the manhunt for the Jews? – But above all: how could a protest against the extermination of the Jews have been considered as a partisan intervention in the events of the war? What had Hitler's measures for the annihilation of an entire race in Europe to do with the Second World War? They happened at that point in time and were made possible by the fact that German arms had subdued the Continent. But did they decide one battle? Are Auschwitz or the gigantic mass-graves of murdered civilians – theatres of war? Both war parties committed ruthless crimes in bombing open cities and allowing prisoners to starve or, in short, murdering them: in these cases, it would have been adequate to react as Pope Benedict XV did during the First World War, namely, as Leiber says, 'to protest against injustice and violence wherever they may occur', even if this should have been done in concrete rather than abstract terms. The 'Final Solution', however, like the euthanasia programme, is not to be treated as the passing transgression of a warring power. No greater spur can be given to a legend in favour of Hitler than to regard his plan to gas an entire race and the crimes connected of necessity with this plan, as being within the framework of the general conduct of the war. And does not the excommunication of active Communists prove that Pius XII could act with decisiveness in the political field when he wished?

When Father Leiber adds the thought that 'Providence entrusted the guidance of the Church during the war years to Pius XII, not Pius XI' precisely because Pacelli, in contrast to his energetic predecessor, was not easy to persuade to any public expression of opinion, one can, as a layman in the affairs of faith, only stand silently astounded at such eccentricities in the ordinances of Creation.

The question still remains of whether it was not a tragedy for Christendom and the victims of Hitler that Pius XI should have died just before war broke out. He was a man.

Several cardinals were at first opposed to his chosen successor: 'Pacelli is a man of peace,' they said, according to CARDINAL TARDINI, 'and the world now needs a Pope of war.' If they had only succeeded. One cannot read without emotion the report of one of the last audiences which the already ailing Pope Pius XI, shortly before his death, gave to Chamberlain and Lord Halifax. *The Times* reported on 11th February 1939: '. . . and then the Pope . . . told them exactly what he thought of reactionary régimes and of the duties of democracies; of racial persecution and of the pressing need of helping refugees . . . He pointed to a diptych containing portraits of Sir Thomas More and Cardinal John Fisher – two Englishmen, he said, who were often in his thoughts, "I often sit here thinking of the English. I am happy to believe . . . that these two Englishmen stood for what is best in the English race; in their courage, their determination, their readiness to fight – to die, if need be – for what they knew to be right. I like to think, indeed, I am sure, that those qualities – the courage and the readiness – live on still among the English. You agree with me?" None spoke, held by the words of the old man . . . the Pope talked on – not lecturing them, rather leading their thoughts to the problems and struggles before them. The problems were many, greater perhaps than other ages had to face. They had a hard task – "But you know better than I do what is in the English race." '

That was a testament, an unmistakeable *avis au lecteur* addressed to Hitler who at that moment was preparing to march into Prague. No one ever heard such direct words from Pius XII, who immediately following Hitler's arrival in the Hradcany Palace, said to Count Ciano that he wished to introduce a somewhat more easy-going policy towards Germany than his predecessor. This is the Pacelli that Chancellor Brüning got to know when he refused to tolerate the intervention of the Nuncio in German domestic affairs: at which Pacelli is said to have begun to weep. One can find no words in all the carefully tortuous speeches of this constantly speech-making pontiff that approach in significance those of the already dying Achille Ratti, at whose demise Mussolini exulted: 'Now that obstinate old man is dead.' For him as for the Nazis, Pacelli was a satisfactory choice.

On the Pope's death in 1958 *L'Arche*, the Jewish newspaper in Paris, published an extraordinarily embittered essay on 'The silences of Pius XII', which differed radically from the usual obituaries and went as far as to express the opinion that one of the reasons for Pius XII's silence had been the medieval anti-Semitism of the Catholic Church. The author, Rabi, based this thesis on the attitude of the French clergy and of the Vatican towards the anti-Jewish laws in

Vichy France: the Church, although it spoke out through the Caritas organization against the physical persecution of the Jews, nevertheless approved the social discrimination against them in the name of Justice. Thomas Aquinas was quoted . . .

In *The Representative*, on the contrary, it has been continually stressed that Pius XII and his clergy had no feelings of anti-Semitism – I wished to keep purely to provable facts – nor shall I quote here from the statement of the Italian banker Angelo Donati, to whom many Jews owed their salvation. This brave man's bitter personal experiences with individual priests during the time of the persecution are cancelled out by the numerous instances of help afforded by other priests. But what Donati reported to the Centre de Documentation Juive Contemporaine (Documents CC XVIII-78) about the official attitude of the diplomats of the Holy See, should be quoted. In the autumn of 1942, Donati had a note referring to the situation of the Jews in Southern France delivered to the Pope through the agency of the Father General of the Capucins, in which he asked for Papal assistance. It was not forthcoming.

In August 1943, the British Ambassador to the Holy See, Sir D'Arcy Osborne, declared to him that in the course of 1942, he had repeatedly requested the Pope to make formal condemnation of the German atrocities. Osborne told Donati that, after the Pope's Christmas message of 1942, which condemned the horrors of war in general terms, Cardinal Maglione, the Secretary of State, had said to him, Osborne, at a reception: 'You see, the Holy Father has taken notice of your Government's recommendations.' Osborne explained that such a comprehensive condemnation, which could equally well have applied to the bombing of German towns, was not exactly what the English Government had been asking for.

This statement is confirmed from various different sources.[1]

While the *Osservatore Romano* was condemning Stalin's agression against Finland in terms ('calculated crime, law of the jungle, most cynical aggression of modern times') whose extreme severity is so different from the non-committal article on the Jewish deportations out of Rome and the imprecise complaints of Pius XII about the war; while Cardinal Maglione was saying to Sumner Welles (early 1940) that Germany had for a long time always drawn the short straw in her diplomatic relations with Stalin, and emphasizing Italy's anxiety that Stalin might make further inroads on the Balkans

[1] See notably *Foreign Relations of the United States, Diplomatic Papers 1942, Volume 3*, Washington, May 1961.

as well, the moment was approaching when, in the face of Hitler's overwhelming victory, even the Vatican temporarily saw in Stalin the lesser of two evils. This is not only the statement of the Papal physician. Maglione also said it to Prince Colonna at Christmas 1941. Mussolini was relieved, indeed overjoyed, at Hitler's defeat outside Moscow. Ciano noted very soon, however: 'Alfieri (Ambassador in Berlin) writes that the failures on the Russian front have already, in their effects, passed the point where they can still be useful to us.'

The Vatican as usual saw things in a considerably more sober light than many of the bishops, or indeed the Turkish Foreign Minister, who cried, as soon as Hitler entered Russia: 'It is not a war – it is a crusade!' The Minister, at the wish of von Papen, was instantly ready to invite the British Prime Minister, via the British Ambassador, to bury their differences in Europe 'to stand together united against the Power whose programme is the destruction of the West'. The attempt misfired. On the following day Churchill told the world: 'The Nazi régime is indistinguishable from the worst features of Communism. . . . It excels all forms of human wickedness in the efficiency of its cruelty and ferocious aggression. . . . We have but one aim and one single irrevocable purpose. We are resolved to destroy Hitler and every vestige of the Nazi régime. . . .'[1]

Herr von Papen, who ignores the question whether the Russians would have marched to the Elbe if Hitler had not attacked them, maintains that the Prime Minister, in this speech, 'introduced the policy that has led to the present condition of Europe' – an opinion which enjoys increasing popularity – and already by 1959 is shared by all who condemn Churchill and Roosevelt for lacking the insight to defend the Christian West, shoulder to shoulder with the architect of Auschwitz.

There is no doubt that Franz von Papen was never the friend, and only seldom the confidant of Hitler, who had already had the Vice-Chancellor's (later Ambassador's) co-workers liquidated before the outbreak of war. The fact that Papen, as a good Catholic, was nevertheless convinced that his nephew, sent by Hitler to the battlefields of Russia, had fallen there 'in the struggle against disbelief and the powers of darkness' shows once more how important it was for Hitler, particularly in this campaign, to have at least the outward appearances of peace with the Vatican. No one had, of course, ever

[1] *The War Speeches of the Rt. Hon. Winston S. Churchill*, Vol. I, London, 1951.

believed Roosevelt when, as Giovannetti puts it, 'he repeatedly told the Pope that he thought it possible that in the future there might be a conversion of Bolshevism to Democracy and a renunciation of the Marxist-Leninist demand for world revolution'.[1]

More to be feared even than the Nazis and the Russians, however, was something that now appeared – the spectre of a new agreement between Hitler and Stalin. It will probably never be possible to find out exactly what was behind the approaches of the two parties – it is likely that for the most part they were simply rumours and attempts at deception. Hitler himself mistrusted most of the proposals. Herr von Papen, who realized early on that Germany could not conquer Russia on her own, sent an emissary from Ankara early in 1942 to the closest colleagues of the Pope, who told him they saw no possibility of persuading the Western Allies to consider peace talks. Papen comments: 'In this phase of the war a compromise between Hitler and the Soviet was, as we know, greatly to be feared. For this reason alone, one was quite against any thought of agreement.'[2]

Already in August 1943 Hassell was noting: 'If Hitler comes to terms with Stalin, the resultant disaster cannot be imagined; it would be different with a decent politically self-respecting Germany'. And Fritz Hesse maintains that it was on hearing the sensational announcement by Schellenberg that Hitler was intending to negotiate with Stalin over the Tenno that Stauffenberg made an immediate decision 'to carry out his original plan for an assassination and putsch . . . and not to wait till . . . the bloodthirsty monster had, by this treacherous gamble with destiny, renewed his strength to keep himself going and drown the earth in German blood'.[3]

It will now never be possible to discover, with any final exactitude, to what steps the Pope allowed himself to be persuaded in order to promote peace between the Third Reich and the West, since, ludicrously enough, it has, since 1945, been considered 'impossible' to confess that there had been ever any idea of considering peace with Hitler – for peace's sake. As if the opposition circles in Germany during the war had ever had the credit abroad that has been – posthumously – ascribed to them.

Up to now it has in general been too unwillingly recognized, for example, that efforts were being made for a cease-fire with the

[1] Alberto Giovannetti, *ibid.*
[2] Franz von Papen, *ibid.*
[3] *The von Hassell Diaries, 1938–44*, London, 1948.

Western powers by the German Secret Service, loyal to Hitler, furthered by Count Ledochowsky, the Polish Jesuit General, who died early in 1943. In the middle of 1942 it is possible that the Weizsäcker circle thought for a moment that, since England was not prepared to make peace with Hitler in any event, the moment had passed.

Nor will one ever be able to discover finally whether the Spanish Foreign Minister, who wrote in February 1943 to the British Ambassador to Madrid 'that England must be convinced, after mature reflection, that in the event of a Soviet victory over Germany, no one would be able to retain Russia within her frontiers'[1] – whether Count Jordana, when in April of the same year he offered the services of Spain as negotiator between the Reich and the West, had been authorized by the Vatican to place such great expectations in the Pope. About this time the Vatican quite definitely declared that it had not the slightest connection with the war aims of the Western powers. . . .

Krupp

The use of foreign forced labour by, among others, the most reputable German industrial concerns became a political issue of the first importance because of the treatment of these labour forces by the firm of Krupp. Although it is a very typical chapter in contemporary history, it is only possible in *The Representative* to mention it in passing.

First of all, one must not ignore the fact that not only were there many large industrial concerns, like Bosch and Reusch, but also many subordinate managers who found it quite possible to keep their humanity. One such was Karl Beckurts, manager of the state-owned Gustloff armament factory in Weimar, who employed countless prisoners from Buchenwald during the war, and who in 1949 was brought to Hamburg by one of these very prisoners, Erik Blumenfeld, now a member of the Christian Democrat party, as director of the North German Coal & Coke Works. Berthold Beitz, in 1953 general manager at Krupps, formerly the obscure administrator of the oilfields at Boryslav in occupied Poland, was able to help persecuted Jews and Poles: in addition, the eagerness with which several works managers held on to their Jewish workers prevented their being deported to the gas chambers.

Would not a reputable heavy industrialist, whom Hitler often

[1] Sir Samuel Hoare, *Ambassador on Special Mission*, London, 1946.

visited, have been able to command respect from subordinates in the Nazi Party? We are here faced with the same problem as with the clergy: the anonymous priest endangered himself if he helped. The German bishops and cardinals, however, were not arrested when they proceeded publicly against Hitler's decrees.

As always, in those days also it was a question of the human characteristics of the individual. It was a question of the extent to which it was still possible for a man to recognize his fellow man, even in a prisoner. Even at Krupps there were people who every now and again would slip a piece of bread to a little Jewish girl in rags and clogs, who had come from Auschwitz to drudge in the rolling-mills. This was forbidden and would have been punished – had anyone from the works informed on them. How was it possible that the head of the firm could have remained ignorant, as he walked through his plant, of the conditions in which his foreign employees had to live and work? How could he remain ignorant of the fact that members of the Krupp Works Police beat the deportees? Even Hitler gave every one of his bodyguard in the war permission 'to bring their personal problems to him' as he walked through his H.Q. Sentimentality! one says today. But if the largest employer in the Greater German Reich and the members of his family had, during the war, allowed a little more of this sort of sentimentality to show through – then perhaps 98 of the 132 children of factory girls from the East would not have died in the camp at Voerde, near Essen, and perhaps the letters to and from the Eastern workers in Essen would not have been intercepted and burnt twice a week.

On the 26th June 1947, ALFRIED KRUPP VON BOHLEN told the Nuremberg Tribunal that he was only aware of one single occasion on which there had been an attempt to maltreat a worker from the East: this took place at the period when Eastern workers were allotted to the Krupp works for the first time. After this the Head Office had officially forbidden any mishandling of foreign workers. In other respects, he, Alfried von Bohlen, had been confident that his colleagues and subordinates would not allow a repetition of such injustice.

When, on 16th December 1942, eighteen Dutch workers who were working in Essen-Bergeborbeck sent a personal letter to Alfried von Bohlen, with an entreaty to improve the meagre rations, he commissioned Max Ihn to remedy the abuse and submit a report to him.

The great difficulties of victualling and housing the foreign workers were often being aired on the Board of Directors of Krupps, of which Alfried von Bohlen was already a member by the outbreak of war and whose meetings he usually attended – from April to December 1943 as chairman, after 1943 as sole proprietor: efforts were continually being made to remedy these difficulties.

But even if one acknowledges the fact that after 1942 Alfried von Bohlen no longer heard about the way members of his Works Police used their rubber truncheons in his factories and camps, nevertheless the disturbing question of responsibility remains unchanged and undiminished – and attaches to more than this one man and this one firm. In his book *Die Krupps*, NORBERT MÜHLEN has raised, very impressively, the questions whether 'moral short-sightedness, cowardice and lack of feeling on the part of a political economist are crimes' and whether in general 'the treatment of human beings under a totalitarian régime can be judged by the criteria of a society which assures every citizen his freedom of conscience and action'.

Thilo von Wilmovsky, brother-in-law and co-worker of Gustav Krupp, and president of the Central European Economic Council, and Ewald Löser, general manager of Krupps, made their decisions with regard to these questions in a most honourable manner: after the revolution of 20th July 1944 they were both unmasked as close confidants of Carl Goerdeler and Ulrich von Hassell. Wilmovsky was sent to a concentration camp. Löser was sentenced to death, but the end of the war saved him from hanging. The Allies sentenced him to seven years imprisonment at the Krupp Trial, although he had voluntarily resigned from the Board of Directors in March 1943. Ulrich von Hassell, who as a member of the governing body of the Central European Economic Council was closely connected with industry, noted in 1943: 'Krupp's general manager, Löser, a clever, clear-sighted man, told me recently that the leading lights, with the servile Krupp-Bohlen and the cold-blooded egotistical Zangen (leader of the Reichsgruppe Industrie) naturally at the head, were both standing behind Hitler, because they believed they would in this way make a good profit and keep their workers in line. Among the proletariat, even the Communist sections of it, the national emergency was much more widely and clearly recognized. It is admittedly very difficult to arrive at a plebiscite of the opinion of the workers, owing to the frustrating and confusing prevalence of informers.'[1] What Löser told the Allies in 1945 about Alfried von Bohlen remains in part unpublished in Paris.

[1] Von Hassel, *ibid.*

In his *Deutsche Geschichte des 19. und 20. Jahrhunderts*, Professor Golo Mann writes on the subject of the last free election in March 1933: 'The Nazis knew to what degree it was possible, given the necessary intelligence and cheek, to use governmental power in an electoral struggle to bewitch one's supporters, subdue the weak, and strike down one's opponents. "It will be easy now to carry on the fight, as we can call on all the resources of the State", the party's Propaganda Minister wrote in his diary: "The radio and the Press are at our disposal, we can stage a masterpiece of propaganda. Of course we are not short of money this time either." Indeed they were not. A circle of industrialists, led by Krupp, had allowed themselves to be talked into placing an election fund of three million marks at the Government's disposal: the new Prussian Minister of the Interior, Hermann Göring, had explained to these gentlemen that since it was the last election for ten, and in all probability for a hundred years, a little generosity would not be misplaced. . . .'

He promised the industrialists neither more nor less than a dictatorship. Why does Norbert Mühlen find the discussions at this Berlin meeting so moderate?

Alfried Krupp von Bohlen was given back his fortune. Something like the half of of his sentence had been remitted. His promise to the Allies to break up his empire and to sell the mining and steel plants at moderate prices was hardly likely to have to be honoured. So far, perhaps, so good. But it was not enough for certain politicians in Bonn. The American president had just dispatched General Lucius Clay, initiator of the Berlin air-lift, to Germany again, so that he could once more take over the defence of West Berlin – nevertheless the politicians in Bonn chartered a special train in November 1961 to visit the firm of Krupp as if it was a National Monument. It was at this man's trial in 1949 that the same General Clay had stated expressly 'The full evidence will offer to History an unparalleled example of how greed and avarice can lead unscrupulous hands to bring misery and destruction upon the world. It is therefore understandable, that in examining the cases that were laid before me, I should have felt no compunction in ratifying the sentences.'[1]

It was a distressing footnote to the suffering of the Krupp slave-workers when Theodore Heuss, the disciple of Naumann, in an official speech made it appear, by his reference to the past, that Krupp had been sentenced only for doing what countless other armament manufacturers had done all over the world. The Ukrainian

[1] Lucius D. Clay, *Decision in Germany*, New York, 1950.

Khrushchev must also have had a short memory, to judge from the toast he drank to the House of Krupp during the course of the 1959 Leipzig Fair, although he must have heard of the experiences of some of his countrymen whom the Gestapo had 'transferred' to the Krupp works in Essen. (See, inter alia, Documents NIK-12 362, Prosecution exhibit 998. Green series, vol. IX, p. 1321).

Der Spiegel wrote on the occasion of the firm's jubilee: 'To be present or not to be present is a political declaration.' Among those members of the Bonn Corps Diplomatique not present were the Russian, French, British and American ambassadors. The Bishop of Essen was, however, present. One would like to know whether any of these ecclesiastical dignitaries in the neighbourhood of Essen during the war ever once managed to get into one of the 'work training-camps' erected by Krupp at the behest of the Gestapo, which were described at Nuremberg by a Catholic priest – one of the shaven-headed slave-labourers interned there.

Part of the documents and the verdict are available in print, in English: *Trials of War Criminals, vol. IX*. Institutes in Göttingen, Nuremberg, Munich and Paris possess the documents, sometimes only in part, in the original language. Here are two documents which were consulted, among others less innocent, for Act I, scene ii, and Act V:

'Memo.   Gbf. 15 Oct. 42.

Ref: Telephone call from Colonel Breyer of OKW (High Command of the Armed Forces), Prisoner-of-war Department, Berlin.

'Colonel Breyer, who wished to speak to Herr von Bülow, asked me to pass on the following message to him:

'The OKW had recently been receiving a considerable number of reports, from its own offices and also anonymously from the German civil population, on the subject of the treatment of prisoners of war by the firm of Krupp (it is said in particular that they are beaten, and further that they are not receiving sufficient food, e.g. the prisoners have not had potatoes for six weeks).

'This state of affairs no longer obtained elsewhere in Germany. The OKW had already asked several times that the prisoners should be given their full rations whatever the circumstances. In addition they should, if they were engaged on heavy work, receive the corresponding rest periods, the same as German workers. Colonel Breyer also gave notice that the conditions at Krupps would be the subject of an investigation, either by the Wehrkreis or by the OKW itself.

He had asked General von der Schulenburg to call on Krupp in connection with this matter: this had unfortunately not yet proved possible.'

But even the Nazi district commanders, according to the statement at Nuremberg of MAX IHN, the co-defendant of Alfried Krupp von Bohlen, had had to intervene by 1942 on behalf of the foreign slave workers. Ihn stated: '. . . on March 31st, 1942, I was a representative member of the Directorate. I came at this time in contact with Herr ALFRIED KRUPP. There were about 1,000 clerical workers under my direct control. In 1943 there were about 15,000 clerical workers in the cast steel works, and about 55,000 manual workers (including foreign labour), so that about 70,000 people were employed in all. The highest number of foreign workers employed was around 22,000. I have quoted this figure from my own knowledge and not from the letter of Herr Kuppke, in which he told me he had, under interrogation by the F.S.S., quoted a figure of 20,000.

'The working hours of the foreign workers were fixed by the management and were my own responsibility. Among those employed were minors, even down to 14-year-olds. Foreign workers arrived for the first time in 1942. In the summer or autumn of 1944 the first concentration-camp prisoners arrived, although Krupps had already demanded, on 22nd September 1942, a figure of 1,100–1,500 concentration-camp prisoners.

'The recruitment of these people, and the correspondence on the subject of the employment of concentration-camp prisoners, were my responsibility. Since I cannot remember from whom the instructions came for the correspondence about the concentration-camp prisoners, I must shoulder the responsibility for it myself. The provision and maintenance of all camps, including special camps and concentration camps equally, was my province. I admit that at first there were a great number of complaints from the foreign workers about the bad food, whereas later complaints came about the rations in isolated cases.

'I knew that steel whips had been issued in the plants (but not in the camps). I had been informed that workers in the plants and camps were being beaten. I reported these circumstances to the Board of Directors and spoke about the incidents, in particular to Herr Janssen, and gave orders that no more beatings were to take place. I admit that ill-treatment had already taken place in Herr Löser's time.

'The 420 concentration-camp prisoners employed at Krupps

were furnished by me following the instructions of the Board of Directors. The application was discussed by the Board in my presence, and most probably in that of Herr Alfried Krupp von Bohlen. As far as I know these prisoners came from Buchenwald. I spoke personally on one occasion at Krupps to the camp commandant of Buchenwald, and he gave me information about the conditions under which we could employ concentration-camp prisoners. On my authority Herr Lehmann drove to Buchenwald to establish the conditions under which we could be assured of the supply. It was unknown to me that twenty-two prisoners from Auschwitz were employed at Krupps.

'The concentration-camp prisoners were accommodated in wooden huts in the Humboldtstrasse. I was informed of what went on in this camp.

'I repeat that I was responsible for questions concerning Labour problems (both German and foreign) during 1942. At that time conditions in the camps were already such that even Gauleiter Schlessman wrote on one occasion that he would intervene in person if they were not changed. Dr Löser certainly spoke to Herr Gustav Krupp von Bohlen on the subject of the conditions then prevailing.

'Workers unfit for work were deported. Dr Hannsen suggested that the 520 Jewesses employed at Krupps should be got rid of, and to Buchenwald, before the occupation. I can only suppose that Herr Alfried Krupp von Bohlen knew of this. When I fell ill, on 22nd February 1945, I assigned to Dr Lehmann the job of sending these people back to Buchenwald.'

Hitler himself, in a discussion with Speer, his Minister of Armament and War Production, on 21/22 March 1942, forbade that the Russian workers should be so scantily provided for and kept behind barbed-wire like prisoners of war. He gave orders that the Russians were to get enough to eat and that Sauckel, Reichs Plenipotentiary for Labour Recruitement, was to see that Backe, the Minister of Food, should make sure the necessary measures were carried out.

Krupp sent his engineers to Auschwitz in July 1943, not in October as indicated in Act V. In a letter written shortly afterwards on 7th September 1943, ALFRIED KRUPP VON BOHLEN UND HALBACH writes:

'. . . I ordered Herr Reiff to take over the preparations in Auschwitz, which he is best placed to do, from Breslau. Herr Reiff has already found occasion, some months ago now, to visit Auschwitz and discuss the necessary questions with the people there. As far as working with our technical office in Breslau is concerned, I can only say that the closest co-operation exists between this office and Auschwitz and will assuredly continue. With best regards and Heil Hitler. . . .'

Weinhold, the engineer, and the thirty foremen and builders from Essen who put up the workshops with the prisoners of Auschwitz were forced to sign a written declaration that they would keep secret everything relating to the camp at Auschwitz. On September 1st – for example – Krupp paid in 23,973 Reichsmarks to the account of the S.S. Garrison Administration at the Reichsbank in Catowice – for prison labour. But already by October 1st, Krupp had again got out of his contract and ceded his workshops to the Union firm, who had had to evacuate their own detonator factory at Kharkhov.

In his biography of Krupp[1] MÜHLEN says:

' "Later," Johannes Schröder, the valued chief of the Central Department (Finance) of the firm, recalled; "Affected by these air raids and the military situation, we (the Directors) realized that Germany had lost the war, and we discussed it in the strictest confidence with each other." Krupp then acted against the law for the first time in the Nazi era, and systematically ignored Nazi directives, even if only in the firm's interests. The Nazi Government had given orders that every industrial concern had to invest its entire fluid assets immediately in new installations for war production. In face of the approaching defeat the Board of Directors of Krupp were more interested in "at least saving something for the post-war period; we wished to lead the firm into the future in some condition of financial stability, which would make its continued existence possible," Schröder reports. Even if Germany was to be destroyed, the House of Krupp must survive. Instead of applying the available assets to the war effort and making a loss, the firm secretly followed a new course, namely that of "keeping their assets as fluid as possible. They exempted themselves from the Government loan, cashed in their war damage claims and collected their debts from the Government".'

Various Details

The location of the bowling-alley scene is invented, but not the

[1] Norbert Mühlen, *The Incredible Krupps*, New York, 1959.

fact that the murderers discussed their atrocities over the table or in the mess as if they were discussing farming. EICHMANN himself, who, in the court-room at Jerusalem played the correct Civil Servant that he was, stated that at the official *Wannsee Conference*, where representatives of the Ministries in Berlin as well as the gentlemen of the S.S. met under Heydrich's chairmanship on 20th January 1942 to decide on the launching of the Final Solution – even here a great deal was drunk: 'Orderlies were continually bringing brandy, and in the end everyone was talking at once – with no holds barred.' The usual barrack-room humour is not likely to have been absent on this occasion either.

ADOLF GALLAND, one of the most famous fighter pilots of the Second World War, has described in his memoirs the way in which it was customary to fasten one's decorations to the collar.

While the Roman Catholic Bishop of Bohemia and Moravia was asking Hitler for permission to ring bells and say a requiem for Heydrich, VLADIMIR PETRIK, a chaplain of the numerically very small Czech orthodox church of St Kyrillus and Methodius, after discussion with the Patriarch of Prague, hid the patriots who had killed the Reichsprotektor in the crypt of his church. Like the Sacristan and the Bishop, he paid for his courage with his life. He sided with the persecuted of his own accord.

The ORDER OF CHRIST, founded by Pope John XXII in 1319, consists of a double gold chain from which hangs a cross ornamented by a crown. Little attention has been paid here to the question of orders: Count Fontana would never have received this order, as it is reserved for heads of state, including such impressive sovereigns as King Victor Emanuel III of Italy, who in 1941 elevated the Pacelli family to princely status at about the time, as it so happens, that the Italian Royal Family was rumoured on the Roman Stock Exchange to have transferred a considerable portion of its fortune abroad through the agency of 'Opera Religiosa', the Vatican's private bank established by Pius XII.

It was not in February 1943, but on 31st October 1942, that Pius XII undertook the 'dedication of the Church and the whole race of Mankind to the Immaculate Heart of Mary'.

CARDINAL TARDINI reports that the Pope, after the death of Cardinal Maglione in 1944, said: 'I don't want people to work with me, I want them to obey me.' It is well known that the Pope did not reappoint anyone to the extremely important key-position of Cardinal Secretary of State right up to his death.

The result of the meeting of Churchill and Roosevelt in CASABLANCA in January 1943 was the demand for the unconditional surrender of Germany.

On the 23rd February, STALIN declared that the Russian armies were having to bear the whole burden of the war alone: somewhat hard, in view of the declaration made a few days before by Mr Stettinius, the American Lease-Lend administrator, that America had already sent 2,900,000 tons of war material to Russia. In the first years of the war Stalin had declined so much as to meet Roosevelt.

November 1942: exchange of telegrams between STALIN and the METROPOLITAN SERGIUS on the occasion of the 25th Anniversary of the Revolution. Goebbels, who recommended a diplomatic handling of the Catholic Church, and also of the Russian Church and civil population, noted around this time in his diary, on 13th December: 'It is, for example, very disagreeable for the Party that the local group leader has to break the news to the bereaved when a son, brother or husband has died a hero's death. Formerly the Church did this. Now the Party has been charged with it, with the result that in little villages people are scared to death whenever the local group leader comes to their home. The local leader is frequently looked upon as a funereal character and in some parts of the country has been nicknamed "Bird of Death" (*Todesvogel*). Before this innovation I gave an insistent warning as I foresaw the consequences. But certain sections in the Party in their short-sightedness and blind hatred of the Church insisted on driving out the devil with Beelzebub. The results now are anything but pleasant.'

LÉON BERARD, the Vichy-French Ambassador to the Holy See, asked for an official comment from the Vatican on the occasion of passing of the Pétain Government's first laws discriminating against Jews in France, in June 1941. He was able, later, to report to Vichy:

'It would be unreasonable in a Christian country to allow Jews to exercise control and thereby to limit the authority of Catholics. From which it follows that it is legitimate to disqualify them from admission to public offices, and equally legitimate only to allow them in restricted numbers (numerus clausus) into the University and the professions. . . .'

The Jewish mistress of the commandant of Auschwitz must have survived the war. After Rudolf Höss had been replaced, she was interrogated by the S.S. Judge Wiebeck. In my search for the procès-verbal of the interrogation, the Institute of Contemporary History in Munich informed me: 'The statement deals with erotica of such a nature that it is treated by us as confidential.'

Epilogue

> So then because thou art lukewarm, and neither cold nor hot,
> I will spue thee out of my mouth.
> REVELATION 3,16.

As this play was going to the printer the German edition appeared of a book on the Vatican[1] by CORRADO PALLENBERG, a German-Italian non-Catholic who was for twelve years a newspaper correspondent in Rome. This not uncritical book achieves a semi-official status from its foreword by the German Ambassador to the Holy See. It must therefore be taken seriously when one reads: '. . . a prophecy, which we can make with some confidence, namely, that Pius XII will be canonized. His character as Pope, his ascetic life, his total devotion to the highest duty . . . his visions and also a number of miracles ascribed to him, these are all factors which contribute to a canonization which will certainly be announced in the not too distant future.'

The author of this play, who numbers among his earliest and therefore most permanent spiritual experiences the reading of Theodor Lessing's *Geschichte als Sinngebung des Sinnlosen* ('History as a way of making sense out of nonsense'), is not surprised by this prophecy. He has also, without indeed much hope of attaining any practical result, set the motto from Kierkegaard's polemic against the beatification of the Danish bishop Mynster, at the beginning of his play. There is no cure for death or myth. When one has learned

[1] *I segreti del Vaticano*, Milan, 1959.

to know Napoleon from his conversations with Caulaincourt and Metternich, and Hitler from his Table Talk – and then one reads what even such an ironic spirit as Heine could write, only a few years after the wilful destruction of the Grande Armée by its Emperor, about a man as pursued by the hatred and curses of his contemporaries as Napoleon, one can hardly avoid the horrifying deduction that the historians will soon be hanging up their pictures of Hitler also, and that the architect of Auschwitz will have the right to repeat Napoleon's words: 'As long as men speak of God, they will speak of me, too.' Hitler was not even as cynical about his soldiers as the 'world spirit on horseback', who is said to have remarked, looking at the 75,000 corpses of Borodino: 'One night in Paris will replace them all.'

It will probably long be remembered of Hitler that he fought at Kiev the biggest battle in history: less well remembered the fact that this battle, fought against the better judgement of his generals, probably ruined his chances of conquering Moscow: and it will not be remembered at all that, immediately after the occupation of Kiev, he had 34,000 people shot on the outskirts of the town.

All of two years after Hitler's death, the former Spanish Foreign Minister, who, despite his admiration for the dictators in Rome and Berlin, had worked so stubbornly to keep his country out of the Second World War that Hitler eventually came to loathe him, wrote about Hitler: 'The time has come to utter this truth as well: beaten and vanquished by disaster, perhaps responsible themselves for great catastrophes (Mussolini was not *by nature* subject to this), they were both great men nevertheless, with great dreams which they wanted to realize, who loved their peoples and wished to serve their greatness. The world of today has a jealous hatred of great men and with a corresponding zeal seeks out the mediocre: so the law of Fatigue ordains. There is no doubt that one day they will turn round and once more admire them.' The first wreaths had not yet withered on the graves of the victims of these two men when these words were being printed.

PIUS XII, a cold sceptic, did not believe in 'History' either, as we know from a conversation he had with ADOLF VON HARNACK. No doubt it was *precisely for this reason*, however, that he soberly calculated that he had a good chance of being canonized if only he himself contributed a little material towards it; which is what happened. It was not only his unpopularity within the Vatican which was responsible for the fact that the sarcasm of the Monsignori of Rome went so far as to impute to him the intention, by beatifying Pius X and immediately instituting canonization proceedings for Pius IX, of establishing precedents with regard to his own elevation.

If only a few of the reasons and sources are named which have led to the Pope being represented as he appears in this play, it is because even now it is impossible for the author to help respecting the Pius Legend. The historical material speaks against the Pope's ever having even seen himself in such a conflict – which would almost have excused him – as in this scene.

Protest or keep silence – this awkward question is answered in Act IV in a manner which almost justifies the Pope. This happens however, from purely artistic considerations: Father Riccardo needs an adversary of stature, and the Pope must be convincing on the stage – independently of whether he was convincing historically or not. The Pope, too, speaks here, as he always did, two completely different languages. At one moment he is the objectively calculating politician in his intimate circle, at the next he speaks 'officially', during the composition of the article for the *Osservatore Romano*. (The article is certainly not by him personally, but he often read galley-proofs and always gave most precise instructions to the newspapers.)

Anyone who listens to the Pope's dictation should not then reproach the author with having lapsed into a revue sketch, or with playing jokes in the doggerel of *Reineke Fuchs*: it is a simple quotation. It is not the author's fault that this garland of paper flowers should here be strewn on the grave of the victims – and with a pretension, a gesture, a pathos whose hypocrisy is all the more frightening since patently none of those present, least of all the Pope himself, *could* have believed that the protest had any practical value. It is impossible that Eugenio Pacelli, the intellectual whose favourite author was Cicero, should have believed that such a rhodomontade was even going to reach Hitler's ears. There is no doubt that Pius XII was one of the most intelligent men of the first half of the century. As Professor Leiber has credibly assured us, he was exceptionally clear-headed, sceptical, realistic, and in addition mistrustful, cold, unsentimental and with a liking for being sarcastic in conversation. Even to a diplomat as hard to impress as the Japanese Foreign Minister, Matsuoka, who, in March 1941, had seen his allies Hitler and Mussolini at the summit of their power, Pius seemed the most important man in Europe. All the more tormenting is the question – if question it still is – whether the

Pope can even have been speaking in good faith at all when he delivered this protest to the world – this and all his other countless, cautiously banal, flowery, imprecise utterances and strings of clichés, which always moralized round and about the general subject of the war, and in which he never once named by name a single politician, a single country – except Poland – nor the actual fact of the deportations carried out over a period of years. In 1942 Mussolini remarked of the Pope's Christmas message – and who could contradict him: 'God's vicar is the Representative upon Earth of the Lord of the Universe. He should never speak and should keep himself in the clouds. This speech is full of platitudes and might just as well be by the priest of Predappio.' (Predappio was the village where Mussolini was born.)

The feature of this scene which will strike any spectator who knows the Pope solely from the newspapers as being the least credible of all, is not invented; even just before his death, filled with a vision of Christ, he still had cheques delivered to him personally. Cardinal Tardini has described it.

Pacelli's flowery loquaciousness in the worst prize-day style – 'As the flowers wait in the earth, beneath the thick blanket of the winter snows. . . .' etc. – is word-for-word quotation: though Pius said 'Poles' not 'Jews'. The author would not have dared to imply that the Pope was trying, with nonsense of this kind, comfortingly to explain away the brutal reality to himself and to that section of humanity persecuted by Hitler's henchmen.

When a few years ago details of the close co-operation of the clergy and heavy industry were published in the Press, *Der Spiegel*, for example, wrote (August 1958): 'In World War II the Society of Jesus earned money from both sides with this raw material (mercury). While the Spanish firm supplied predominantly the Allies and the Russians, the Italian mines provided the German armament factories.'

Catholics have not been alone in waiting in vain for an official denial of this fact. The allegations of the Vatican's being the largest shareholding company in the world have not been disputed by Rome, though it is not the author's intention to suggest that the Pope's silence was due to anything as primitive as an unwillingness to damage financial relations between the Vatican and Germany.

The holding in Hungarian State Railways, to whose acquisition there can be no objection, was bought after the conclusion of the Lateran Agreement (1929).

No doubt it can be held against the author that a disturbance of this nature would never have been possible in the presence of His Holiness. This speaks, however, not against the play, but against the facts of history. The author has no better opinion of Pius XII than is in accordance with the historical facts, nevertheless he pleads in the play the implication that the deportation of the Pope's fellow citizens did actually stir up a similar agitation in both his conscience and his apartments. If anyone wishes to attack the author on this point, he should recall that the character of Riccardo Fontana has no historical prototype: at no time did the Curia attempt to provide anyone to take care of the souls of the victims, although there were so many Catholics among them: no priest accompanied them.

With further reference to the hand-washing scene, the reader must believe that this act had been written some time before the publication in France of the indiscreet memoirs of the Pope's personal physician, Galeazzi-Lisi, in which there is a description of Eugenio Pacelli's excessive mania for hygiene. The idea of Pius XII in this play finding it necessary to wash his hands after he had signed the article occasioned by the deportation of the Jews, suggested itself forcibly to me after reading the speech which the Holy Father made to the College of Cardinals on 2nd June 1945, shortly after the collapse of the Nazi régime. His doctor declares that Pius XII had his hands disinfected after every audience and combated his physical revulsion at the daily contact with pilgrims by an exaggerated passion for hygiene, a picturesque detail to be set beside the fact that Hitler, too, had a compulsion amounting to mania for washing his hands. Unfortunately Hitler's obsession with cleanliness did not go as far as the Pope's, who used to wash his mouth out with a solution of hydrochloric acid, which by upsetting his stomach, caused such violent attacks of hiccups as to hasten his death.

'Psychology leads easily to impiety,' says Thomas Mann. But only a knowledge of the personal characteristics of Pacelli, the introverted mystic, can finally explain his attitude to the deportations. Cardinal Tardini's book,[1] intended as a panegyric, is unintentionally instructive: one can read in it, to take one example among countless others, about the 'considerable timidity with which he received high ecclesiastical dignitaries and priests'. And yet it is in no way the purpose of the play to imply that it was out of fear of

[1] Cardinal Domenico Tardini, *Pio XII*, Vatican City, 1960.

Hitler that he kept silence – as a leading historian has recently maintained.

Moreover this Pope, who had himself made up to appear in an Anglo-Italian film about the Vatican ('Pacelli – das ist die Duse', Annette Kolb said to Reichschancellor Brüning), had far too lively an instinct for effect actually to *fear* displays of force against his own person or against St Peter's. 'Can you imagine how the image of the Church would have grown if that had happened?' one of Pius's chaplains asked me. There is no doubt the Pope must have seen that a protest against Hitler would, as Reinhold Schneider says resignedly, have placed the Church on a footing it had not held since the Middle Ages – he must have realized it, if he had given any thought to the matter whatsoever. If, in this play, his silence has the appearance of a calculated renunciation painfully extracted from him, the historical facts are, alas, not quite so pretty. The Pope cannot have been so deeply disturbed by the yearlong persecution of Europe's defenceless inhabitants. His speeches – of which he bequeathed twenty-two volumes to the world – show what trivialities he was preoccupied with at this time. He was not a 'criminal for raison d'état', but a political neuter, an over-industrious careerist, who often wasted time in irrelevant amusements while, as Bernard Wall writes, a world in torment waited in vain for a word of spiritual leadership from him. This clever, devout Catholic, who went on a pilgrimage to Pius XII, found the Pope personally charming, subtle, witty, not very profound. He said of the Pope: 'He radiated friendly concern for me in a way that made me almost sorry; it seemed so touching and pathetic that I shouldn't be more concerned about the concern.'[1] It was, in fact, as is proved by the frigidity of Pacelli towards his co-workers, purely for show, for ornament – like the *Osservatore Romano* article of 25th October 1943.

Here the question of responsibility is raised again, a question which, if pushed to its logical conclusions, may make the play itself out of date – in an age of political neutrality. When Norbert Mühlen writes, so convincingly, that the largest employer in Europe, master of 55,000 foreign workers, really did not understand what there was for him to be charged with at the Nuremberg trials; when there were, among the millions of unfortunates whom Rudolf Höss caused to be incinerated at Auschwitz, as many men who might well have been suitable for the position of Camp Comman-

[1] Bernard Wall, *ibid.*

dant as there were among their murderers, whose most terrible legacy is the knowledge that even such jobs as were performed in Auschwitz can be carried out without friction by a peaceful, normally constituted, completely interchangeable paterfamilias – if this is the case, then the question of guilt can no longer be discussed on the stage with any hope of arriving at a fair conclusion. There are, admittedly, in our epoch very few of the great dynamic personalities who make history. But how far can the Neutral Man be held guilty? Further – what can one expect of the Neutral Man when General Conscription and such statutes lead him into situations which are easier dealt with by saints than men? A refusal to obey orders? How can anyone demand such a thing from someone who has not, since his confirmation, even felt the need to reflect on the problem of Good and Evil? However, the moment the individual is no longer to be held responsible for anything, either because he has nothing more to decide about, or because he does not grasp the fact that he has an obligation to decide, then an alibi has been created for all guilt: the play is over. For 'without continual freedom of choice, there can be no dramatic conflict'.[1]

[1] Siegfried Melchinger, *Theater der Gegenwart*.